THE LITERATURE OF MEMORY

The Literature of Memory

―――――――――――――――――――――――――――――――――

Modern Writers of the American South

BY RICHARD GRAY

―――――――――――――――――――――――――――――――――

The Johns Hopkins University Press
BALTIMORE AND LONDON

Manufactured in the United States of America
The Johns Hopkins University Press, Baltimore, Maryland 21218
The Johns Hopkins Press Ltd., London
Library of Congress Catalog Card Number 76–18941
ISBN 0–8018–1803–6
Library of Congress Cataloging in Publication data will be
found on the last printed page of this book.

To Joyce

Contents

Preface

My basic aim in writing this book was quite simple and can be described very quickly. I wanted, and have tried, to offer a critical account of the literature of the Southern "renaissance," an account that concentrates on the major writers and that considers these writers principally in terms of their involvement in a common history and a particular—in fact, unique—society. But this aim, however limited and specific it may appear to be, has brought a few problems of definition along with it; and it implies certain broader beliefs, interests, or perhaps sheer prejudices that need, I think, to be stated. As far as problems of definition are concerned, my main one has been something that anybody who writes about the region must face at some time or another; and that is the problem of deciding exactly where the South begins and ends, just what its geographical dimensions are. The eleven states that formed the Confederacy are Southern, certainly. But should the border states be included? Are those states that are part of the "census South"—Delaware, West Virginia, and the District of Columbia—to be considered? And is Oklahoma, in any meaningful way, a part of the South? Obviously, any solution to this problem must be slightly arbitrary, because it will be influenced by the individual's understanding of what it means to be a Southerner, how the region differs in detail from the rest of the United States. What I have done, anyway, is adopt a fairly tentative, shifting line of demarcation: concentrating on the former states of the Confederacy—the eleven, that is, that actually voted for Jefferson Davis in 1861—but bringing in certain border states, particularly Kentucky, Maryland, and Missouri, whenever I felt justified in doing so. This is established practice, a fact which perhaps will make it seem a little less arbitrary or, at least, less idiosyncratic; and, in any case, it reflects quite accurately, I think, the shifting, elusive nature of the actual subject. After all, it is not as if temperament and life style are exactly the same in, say, New Orleans, the Southern Appalachians, and Natchez, Mississippi, and then are radically and mysteriously transformed at some regional boundary. The South must be seen for what it is, a various and contradictory place beneath its apparent (and, of course, sometimes real) unity, the northern limit of which is a zone of land, a gradually altering geography, society, and consciousness, rather than a definite line.

As for broader interests, here I may be pointing out what is obvious enough already—that I have written this book in the belief that literature is closely related to history and, in many cases, to historiography as well, and that I have tried, however tentatively and occasionally, to consider these relationships. While examining the particular achievement of modern Southern writers, in other words, I have depended upon, and begun in a very hesitant way to explore, certain general ideas concerning the kind of knowledge of history that literature gives us; the relationship between this and other forms of historical knowledge; and the possibility of assessing as well as describing any imaginative work in terms that make its social and historical context primary. As I see it, the historical consciousness is not something that is active in poems, novels, and plays only when a given and generally well-known historical event appears in the narrative, but a force or process basic to many a writer's way of thinking, something implicit in his way of understanding and ordering our lives in time. In turn, historiography does not, I believe, exist prior to the imaginative impulse, supplying a body of objective knowledge to which the poet, dramatist, or novelist then gives fictive covering. It is itself a form of knowing, produced out of the dialectic of subject and object, idea and fact, and as such analogous to—although quite definitely not the same as—historical *literature*. Equally, history does not, I think, simply provide a background to imaginative writing, it helps to create it, both its forms and its subjects, and is in a sense created by it—if only because it is through imaginative works, among other things, that we achieve contact with the past, reinterpret it and then use it to understand and shape the present and future. And so, finally, an awareness of what is commonly known as the historical and social context is not merely useful when discussing certain kinds of writing, such as that traditionally described as historical fiction. It is essential, I feel, in order to understand any work properly; in order, that is, to form a judgment of it that is not purely subjective and impressionistic but grows out of and informs ordinary shared experience. All these, the other and more general beliefs behind the book are, as I say, only very tentatively presented here, and only occasionally do I even begin to express and explore them directly. But it would be disingenuous of me not to mention that they *are* here, forming the basis of my approach; just as it would be disingenuous of me to deny that, in adopting this approach in the first place, I owe a great deal to the many critics and historians who have considered the relationship between literature, history, and historiography in infinitely greater depth and with infinitely greater consistency of purpose than I ever could.

There are other debts, of course. I must thank the Commonwealth Fund for a fellowship that enabled me to conduct research in the United States for two years; the many Southern writers and critics who were kind enough to meet me and answer my interminable questions; my friends and colleagues at the University of Essex and elsewhere, especially Herbie Butterfield, Gordon Brotherston, George Dekker, Norman Grabo, Dan Patterson, and Tjebbe Westendorp; my parents, for their help over many years; and, above all, my wife. They must take most of the credit for such value as this book possesses, and none of the blame for what it leaves undone, unproved, or unexplained, or for what readers will decide are its more active vices. I would also like to thank the following for permission to use material that first appeared, in different forms, in their pages: *Journal of American Studies, Dutch Quarterly Review of Anglo-American Letters, Southern Literary Journal, Indian Journal of American Studies, Southwestern American Literature, Canadian Review of American Studies, Southern Review, Appalachian Journal*—and the Cambridge University Press for some material from the notes to my anthology, *American Poetry of the Twentieth Century.*

1. The Social and Historical Context

~~~~~~

The South in Transition

"What history teaches," according to Georg Wilhelm Hegel, "is this
—that people and governments never have learned from history, or
acted on principles deduced from it." Hegel was a man who took active
delight in exposing the tension and contradiction latent in experience.
So probably it will surprise nobody if I say that this epigram generates
its own series of contradictions: paradox acts as a catalyst for thought
here as much as anywhere else in his writing. But if I add to this two
riders—that the paradoxes discovered in this case are of special relevance to the imaginative writer, and to certain writers of the American
South in particular—that, perhaps, is rather more surprising and requires some explanation. Hegel's immediate interest here is a political
one, of course, which is why he refers to "people and governments."
But, as I see it, the literary reference is important too if only because
a work of literature is (inevitably) both a product and reinterpretation
of historical experience; it is at once "of" history and "about" it, and
is therefore as implicated in Hegel's remark as politics, "people and
governments" are. Not only that, what Hegel is saying connects up, I
think (in an uncannily, almost prophetically accurate way), with one
body of literature in particular—the literature, that is, of the Southern
"renaissance," produced by those writers from the eleven states of the
Confederacy and one or two border states (especially Kentucky), who
first appeared in print in the period between the two world wars. For
they have not just been interested in the convolutions of their inheritance, the burdens and legacies the past transmits to the present; they
have, really, been *obsessed* by them. The things they say, and the ways
in which they say them, seem to have been defined with extraordinary
completeness—we could even say circumscribed—by the paradoxes
implicit in what their history has taught them.

Perhaps I should go back to that first sentence for a moment, so as
to explain the precise nature of this connection. History, Hegel seems
to be implying here, teaches people in the sense that it can be and is
used as an intellectual and moral resource—one never-failing means
of suggesting the righteousness of your cause being to identify your
ideas with those of your ancestors. That is why so many Americans
have appealed to the priorities established by the Constitution, and to
the examples set by Washington and Jefferson, when defending their
various opinions. What history also teaches, however, is that the lessons learned in this way owe more to the pupil than they do to the

instructor: investigating the past in the light of our own prejudices or principles, we end up receiving little more from it than what we gave to it in the first place. The man talking about the Constitution may be doing no more than talking about an apotheosized version of his own program for action. Invoking Washington and Jefferson, he may merely be invoking an idealized and historicized version of himself. This is the major paradox, and it generates many others. For no generation, of course, has a monopoly on this tendency to reverence history and at the same time distort it. Every one of them has done the same, with the result that the very material given to this present generation for manipulation and change has already been subjected to a long process of manipulation. We are not, in other words, presented with a simple continuum of events that we can then proceed to rearrange at will, but with a complicated network of events and interpretations, the interpretations being those given to the events by the people who participated in them, and by the several generations who intervened between that time and ours. As a result, the version of history to which we commit ourselves, as individuals and as members of a cultural group, is further complicated by its necessary involvement with other versions of history as well as with the historical facts themselves. The structure of mythology through which we see the event is set in tension with other structures so as to make possible an immense variety of interpretations of any particular historical sequence. William Faulkner, certainly the greatest of all writers from the American South, has one of his characters describe the situation like this:

> . . . you are born at the same time with a lot of other people, all mixed up with them, . . . all trying to make a rug on the same loom only each one wants to weave his own pattern into the rug; and it cant matter, you know that, or the Ones that set up the loom would have arranged things a little better, and yet it must matter because you keep on trying or having to keep on trying. . . .[1]

Faulkner is making a crucial point here about the individual consciousness and the "long parade" of history to which it belongs, and what he says applies with special force to writers from his own native region. The different writers participating in the Southern "renaissance" all drew on the same resources of history for the subject matter of their narratives and poems and, more important, in the formulation of the moral and intellectual frameworks of their writings. Invariably, though, these resources meant different things for each of them—partly because they concentrated on different aspects and interpretations of their history and partly also because they each had different priorities of value, quite separate ideas of what, exactly, the significant in experience was. They were all concerned with the history and the myth of the South, and the mutually effective tension between the two, but in the last analysis the consequences of their concern were quite different for every one of them.

The story of their differences can be left until later, however. What should be mentioned first is the common stock of experience with which they began. For while they did have conflicting ideas of what the meaning of their history and tradition was, the very fact that they were interested in history and tradition at all—and *their* history and tradition in particular—supplied them with a certain common ground marked out for them by their region. Their freedom was limited and, in a sense, given meaning by the specifics of the contemporary situation and by the details of a shared history, which, although it was complex, was nevertheless susceptible to tentative and provisional definition. The two things, the contemporary situation and the interest in a shared history, were in fact linked, since it was precisely the disorienting experience of social change in the present that eventually drove the writers of the Southern "renaissance" to an investigation of their past. During the 1920s, the years when people like William Faulkner, Robert Penn Warren, and Thomas Wolfe were beginning to write and to examine their regional environment, the American South was at last acknowledging the death of its traditional way of life, based on the small farm and the great plantation, and recognizing its absorption into the strange new world of industrialism and advanced capitalism.[2] Of course, it could be argued that the impression of sudden change was an illusory one, in the sense that the South had been altering slowly since the end of the Civil War and had, even before then, had an agricultural economy founded more on the business principles of the marketplace than on the agrarian principles of self-subsistence and production for use rather than profit. What matters, though, is that there was a general *belief* that things were changing; and this belief could at least be defended in terms of specific contemporary events and statistics.

The First World War was a major precipitant here, since it created an enormous demand for manufactured goods that could no longer be satisfied in Europe, because of its almost total participation in the conflict. The United States became a major supplier of material to armies and markets in Europe, and, in turn, those areas of the United States which had up until then escaped full involvement in the Industrial Revolution witnessed a sudden and radical transformation of their economy. Specifically, the emergence of the New South, epitomized by the smokestack and the skyscraper, was drastically accelerated. The old seaport of Norfolk, Virginia, will serve as an example. In 1910 it had a population of less than seventy thousand people, most of whom were devoted to the exporting of agricultural produce and the importing of manufactured goods, but within a few months after the outbreak of the war it was invaded by a hundred thousand newcomers, drawn by the demand for labor at the government naval stations and in the new industrial centers. According to almost contemporary reports, the town became "overnight the centre of government activities involving the expenditure of millions and transforming its outlying districts into hives of industry crowded with navy workers. . . . Business of all kinds . . . expanded beyond facilities to handle it."[3] Norfolk was in some ways a special case, of course, being a seaport, and it could be argued that the impact of the First World War was temporary, being followed by the apparently inevitable postwar recession. The fact remains, though, that what happened to Norfolk happened to other places, large and small, all over the South; and that the brief depression that occurred immediately after the ending of the conflict did not so much stop the process of industrialization as slow it down. The steady exodus to the towns continued in the postwar years, together with the growth of dependence on industry, and both became a subject of conventional and sometimes almost lyrical complaint:

> The good land lay idle beneath the sun. The pale green stripes of growing corn and cotton and sorghum . . . had become solid green mats of weeds and grass. The mules stood idle in their pastures for there were no longer people to work the good land. The plows stood unused at the end of the rows and the weeds grew taller and taller and hid all but the sweat-stained handles from sight . . . the fields became smaller and smaller. Grass grew over the furrows, covering the wheel tracks, and the ditches choked with weeds and filled and overflowed. And the fields lay idle beneath the sun. For the people were moving to town.[4]

To some readers the lyricism might sound suspect, but it could easily be substantiated, with reasons for the exodus not far to seek. Apart from the extrinsic attractions exerted by the high wages and comforts of the town, there was the fact that Southern agriculture was suffering from intrinsic difficulties that made its survival as a viable enterprise pretty dubious.[5] The Southern farmer had always been dependent on cash crops, such as cotton and rice and tobacco, which, while obviously lucrative, rendered him susceptible to the forces of the marketplace. And when, in the first decades of the century, he was faced with competition from farmers in the Western states and North Africa, all of whom were able to produce more cheaply than he could, the extent of his susceptibility became depressingly obvious. The Western farmer could use larger areas to lower the costs of production and could reap the benefits of a soil that was relatively unused, whereas the Southern farmer was confronted with the crippling economic difficulties of the sharecropping system—under which the farmland was divided up into small and uneconomic units—and by the even more urgent problems posed by soil exhaustion. The North African farmer, in turn, could rely on an even cheaper labor force than that available to the Southerner, who was in any case forced to raise the wages or the share of the crop he offered so as to compete with the new privileges available in town. One major result of this is obvious, and is illustrated by the simple statistical fact that within thirty years after the ending of the First World War the number of farms in the region had nearly halved. Another result, although not quite so obvious, was no less crucial. For those people who did remain on the land underwent a drastic personal transformation. The poorer among them, the small farmers and the tenants, were obliged to take additional, nonagricultural work in order to survive—a remedy that might improve their material situation but that also meant that their lives could no longer be said to be circumscribed and defined by their rural environment. If they did not do this, they were faced with the kind of economic and moral degeneration that Arthur Raper and Isa Reid outlined in their book on sharecroppers:

> Take a look at the South and you will see a shiny machine-made tin roof on a sharecropper's cabin, paid for with hand-grown cotton; the poorest people of the region concentrated on the richest land as sharecroppers and wage hands, now being thinned out by the impact of crop control and increased mechanization . . . the piling up of the surplus population in the poor-land areas, which already had the highest birth rates and the lowest per capita wealth of any communities in America; the displacement of rural and urban Negro workers by stranded whites who prefer erstwhile Negro jobs at Negro pay and working conditions to unemployment and relief, . . . the emergence of industry often fashioned after the cotton plantation system, and nearly always occupying a colonial status to the region's wealthier regions. . . . And woven through it all—apathy and fear and indecision.[6]

The wealthier landowner, meanwhile, was required to make similar compromises. He had to realize a profit as much as, or even more than, the poorer farmer did, and the only way he could do this was by introducing the methods of industry into his holdings—streamlining production and marketing methods so as to make them accord with the best principles of business efficiency. The importance of this, in terms of the disorientation it produced in the South's image of itself, was located by the Southern journalist Wilbur J. Cash, who was himself more committed to that image than he cared to admit:

> One obvious thing was that . . . Southerners were passing into the mold of Babbitt—that the passion for money-making, pride in and admiration for acquisitiveness, carelessness as to the means employed to the end, and the spirit of calculation in general were all feverishly increased.[7]

An obvious reply might be, "When was it ever otherwise?" The great plantation owners of the ante-bellum period were hardly uninterested in the accumulation of fortunes; and their enterprises, for all the advice to diversify and live at home, were clearly geared to the marketplace.[8] There was a difference, though, between these men and the ones Cash was talking about, and it was essentially one of vision, of the kinds of meanings men were able and willing to attach to their particular way of life. The great landowners of earlier periods may have been more ambitious entrepreneurs than anything else, but they did commit themselves to an ideal of gentility, of the benevolent and cultivated squire, which could engage with reality at certain points. No matter how much they might conduct certain areas of their life on what they considered to be sound business principles, they could still at the same time enjoy a few of the privileges, and display one or two of the graces, traditionally accruing to the gentleman—and without any consequent sense of the inappropriate. A great planter like William Byrd of Westover, for example, a member of a leading family in colonial Virginia, could claim that he lived "like one of the patriarchs,"[9] and not feel he was distorting the truth too much, simply because there was some recognizable basis for the comparison. His conduct and aims were sufficiently tempered by his pretensions toward gentility to make such an identification possible. Those who successfully occupied a similar economic position in the period following the First World War, however, found the disciplines of their business routines so exacting—or perhaps to describe it more accurately, the rewards offered by the life of the businessman so intrinsically satisfying—that they more or less discarded any other pretensions. In a word, they became "Babbitts" in vision as well as in fact. Limiting their aims to those defined by the terms of economic success, they became indistinguishable to observers from that familiar Southern stereotype of the mercenary entrepreneur, the "Yankee."[10]

The South *was* changing in the 1920s, then. Many people were moving to the towns and to the new industries. Others remained on the land, but found themselves obliged to adopt a life style that identified less and less easily with the traditional Southern notions of the good life. The more successful of these, in turn, had solved the problem by rejecting all principles other than those of progress and profits, but quite a few considered this solution an impossible one and so found themselves in an intolerable situation. For while every aspect of their economic life told them of the complete transformation of the Old South into the New, they still felt the pull toward the old allegiances. Part of them was still committed to values that another part of them felt to be utterly obsolete. There are numerous examples of this in the history of the time—in the attempts to administer the new factories on the old plantation pattern, for instance, or in the continued resistance to the idea of collective action. But perhaps as good an example as any, because it brings together so many of the conflicting forces present in the South in the twenties, is the famous "Monkey Trial," which took place in Dayton, Tennessee, in 1925.[11]

Early in 1925 an obscure Tennessee legislator, John Butler, introduced a bill to prohibit the teaching of evolutionary theories in the state schools. The bill was one index of a growing apprehension about the intellectual implications of the new forces at work in the South and, as such, was passed into law without much difficulty. In the same year a young teacher named Scopes, employed by a high school in Dayton, Tennessee, was asked by the American Civil Liberties Union to defend a test case. He was to teach evolution to his pupils so as to provoke the authorities into enforcing the new law, which would, in turn, enable opponents of that law to test its validity. Scopes was unwilling to do so at first; and then a curious thing happened. A group of civic boosters, men who wanted to put Dayton on the map and attract new investment, came to see Scopes, to persuade him to accept the offer made by the Civil Liberties Union. In effect, they wanted to exploit their community's commitment to its inherited values in order to improve its business status. They wanted to use the principles of the Old South to advance the interests of the New, and so turn the ambiguities of their region to their advantage.

Scopes was persuaded, and the rest is familiar history. A trial was held that soon turned into a showpiece, the two top-of-the-bill attractions being William Jennings Bryan, who acted for the prosecution, and Clarence Darrow, the principal lawyer for the defense. Scopes was found guilty, but the fine imposed on him as a punishment was overruled by the Tennessee Supreme Court on a legal technicality. The constitutionality of the state law was never questioned in the federal courts because the case never went that far, and the story deteriorates thereafter into anticlimax. What matters in the present context, though, is not so much the results the trial produced as its causes. A general anxiety about the way in which the South was progressing created the law, whereas a more specific desire to accelerate that progress occasioned the trial. The ambivalent loyalties of the American South in the 1920s set the scene, and this ambivalence was suitably reflected in the final verdict on Scopes, which found the accused guilty and then refused to punish him. The division could scarcely have been more absolute or, in terms of its implications for those divided, more disturbing, either.

Disturbance and disorientation are not necessarily bad things, however, especially in the field of literature. In a sense, they make possible

that analysis of personal motive, the examination of the premises on
which our own beliefs and those of our society depend, which is surely
one of the characteristic qualities of a good piece of writing. What
happens when a community undergoes a radical transformation such
as the South did in the third decade of this century is that suddenly
the assumptions behind that community are brought into the open, by
being questioned and even altered to fit new requirements. People are
confronted with the fact that the values by which they and their
fellows have lived seem to be strangely inappropriate to their changing circumstances; and consequently they are obliged to investigate
those values to see if any of them can survive the change, to be carried over into the new society. The significance of this was perceived
by one Southern writer, Allen Tate, when he described it as "the perfect literary situation." Admittedly, the remark was made in an essay
on the nineteenth-century poet, Emily Dickinson, and bore specific
reference to New England during her lifetime,[12] but it does not take
too much effort to see that both the remark and the argument Tate
uses to support it are relevant to the state of the American South in
the twenties, and as such deserve special attention here. For what
Tate does in his essay is to define the relationship between a crisis
point in history and a literary "renaissance" in a way that, perhaps,
nobody but a person directly involved in a renaissance of just this kind
could do.

Tate's argument is briefly this. When a society forms one more or
less homogeneous unit, such as New England did in the years of the
"puritan theocracy," there is a general acceptance of the "great idea,"
the system of values, around which that unit is structured. This is good
as far as the customary life of the members of the society is concerned,
because it gives "an heroic proportion" to their every act: their daily
lives demonstrate a dependence on the "great idea" and in return draw
meaning and substance from it. It is not so good, however, for the
creation of a genuinely critical literature, which can only be critical
if its allegiance to the "great idea" is incomplete. As Tate puts it, literature "probes the deficiencies of a tradition," and this is only generally possible when a relatively homogeneous society is breaking up.
Before the process of breaking up has begun in earnest, there will be
a strong tendency to identify with the tradition rather than analyze it,
and test one's self against it; and after it has broken up there will be
no tradition left to analyze. Only at a crisis point in history, when
one definite form of society is disappearing and another is emerging,
can writers as a group employ their inheritance as a "source of ideas"
and metaphors and still be sufficiently detached from their inheritance
to be critical of it. Then only is it possible for the poet or prose writer

of average ability to use his tradition rather than be used by it, and so contribute to a broader literary "renaissance." This condition, in which a real dialectic can be said to exist between a "system of ideas" and an accompanying "sense of the natural world" that that system does not encompass, is one that Tate sees existing in England at the end of the sixteenth century, and just after; in New England, of course, by the middle of the nineteenth century; and, he might have added although he leaves it implicit, in the American South in the period immediately following the First World War.

Tate's argument suffers from the brevity with which it is stated, an inevitable limitation the essay form imposes on him, and this results in a number of questions remaining unanswered. It might be argued, for example, that all ages can be described as ages of transition and that consequently his definitions are not nearly precise enough. A distinction has then to be made, which Tate himself does not bother to make, between those periods—the more frequent ones—when the transformations produced by the historical process occur at what appears to be a regular pace and those few moments when the pace suddenly seems to accelerate, and there is as a result a sense of radical dislocation between the immediate past and the present. In a sense, the twenties in the United States and Europe as a whole were just such a moment, when the old world of bourgeois certainties seemed lost forever: but there can be little doubt that the American South offered an even more acute version of the same, since it was plunged with very little preparation into the twentieth century during this period. Despite qualifications, then, related both to the relative precision of Tate's definitions and the limits of their applicability, his central argument is clear and, seen within the context of that literature to which he himself contributed, quite effective and stimulating. For, as he suggests, the primary result of the metamorphosis of the American South after the First World War was to send its writers back to an analysis of their own history and tradition.

The Region and the History: Two Types of the Ideal

This introduces the problem of the tradition of the Old Confederacy, the precise nature of the resources available to the Southern writer; and here in a sense a comprehensive definition is impossible, because the very concept of tradition involves at its best the idea of growth and development. Idea and event interact so as to produce that continuously evolving system of values which is tradition, and this must be drastically simplified as soon as it is described in abstraction from the historical process. John Peale Bishop, a poet and novelist from West Virginia, puts the matter in this way: "Tradition is all the learning life which men receive from their fathers and which, having tried in their own experience, they consent to pass on to their sons. What remains is, if you will, a technique."[13] This description is useful, and not least because, translated into a literary context, it suggests the kind of preliminary definition that is possible here. A tradition that has been subject to development over several centuries, since the time when the Southern colonies were founded in fact, obviously cannot be treated to definitive analysis. Its nature is too complicated, and its implications too many, for that. But an understanding of the tendencies of its "technique" is feasible, I think, and even necessary. An idea of its character, in other words, can be gathered from an examination of the process whereby that character was achieved in the first place, and then developed. From this, possibly, will come some notion of the "available source of ideas" on which the writers of the Southern "renaissance" drew, and this in turn might provide some of the information necessary for understanding and estimating the relationship of the individual writer to his regional tradition.

The story takes us back to the seventeenth and eighteenth centuries, to the days when Virginia, then Maryland, Carolina, and Georgia were established as colonies.[14] The people who first came to settle these regions were venturing into a strange new land on what seemed the other side of the world from their native England. But what strikes a reader now in looking at their descriptions of this land is not so much a feeling of strangeness as one of familiarity—a sense of *déjà vu* that springs from the fact that the colonizers tended to see the Southern colonies as a place appropriate for the recovery of an older style of life, long since abandoned in the mother country. In effect, the new "Eden" that they saw in Virginia and the other Southern colonies was an idealized version of the historical past rather than a projection of future possibility. To many observers, England at just around the turn of the sixteenth century was a society that, as John Donne put it, was "all in peeces" with "all cohaerence gone."[15] Englishmen had forgotten the old pieties, and, it was argued, could only rediscover them in another country—"a Virgin Countrey" like that across the Atlantic, which had apparently been "preserved by Nature out of a desire to show mankinde fallen into the Old Age of Creation, what a brow of fertility and beauty she was adorned with when the world was vigorous and youthfull."[16] The "Promised Land" situated in the American South seemed to be not only in front of the colonizers, but behind them as part of their lost inheritance as well.

Promised the land might be, but there was some disagreement about the nature of its promise. Both the colonizers and their backers fell to quarreling among themselves, even if only indirectly, as soon as they tried to describe the nature of the pieties to be reasserted; and this was perhaps predictable, since they had several and quite contradictory ideas of exactly where the strength of England lay before its decline. In detail, these ideas were almost as numerous as the commentators, but ultimately their versions of a lost Eden fell into one or other of two categories. The more popular one, among the earlier colonizers at least, centered upon the figure of the small independent farmer—the "true labouring husbandman" or "yeoman" who relied on nobody but himself, working "under his fig-tree . . . gathering and reaping the fruites of their [sic] labours with much joy and comfort." The general impression was that this figure had been banished from the fields of England, the victim of economic change; and from this several commentators drew what seemed to them the obvious conclusion that the "Plantations" across the Atlantic, of which "God himselfe" seemed to be "the founder and favourer," offered him a providential refuge. In the New World, so the argument ran, the yeoman could have as much ground as he could farm, and in these circumstances would quickly recover his ancient virtues—his pride and independence, his love of freedom, his generosity, and his hospitality. Several commentators were so carried away by the prospects that they transformed what they had seen or just heard about into a pastoral dream, peopled by idyllically happy farmers:

> Those to whom she [Virginia] vouchsafes the honour of her Embraces, when by the blessings of God upon their labours sated with the beauty of the Cornefield, they shall retire into their Groves, checkered with Vines, Olives, Mirtles, from thence dilate themselves into their Walkes . . . paved with Oranges and Lemmons, whence surfeited with variety, they incline to repose in their Gardens upon nothing lesse perfumed than Roses and Gilly-flowers. When they shall see their numerous Heards wanton with the luxury of their pasture, confesse a narrownesse in their Barnes to receive their Corne. . . .[17]

The picture was an attractive one, but perhaps the visionary nature of this attractiveness betrayed a certain unease. For the ideal of the simple and independent farmer was not the only one crying for attention among those interested in colonizing the American South. At least as important a concept in shaping the ideas and lifestyles of the early English colonizers was that which had the feudal aristocrat or squire for its dramatic projection. In this case, too, the New World was seen as an appropriate context in which to recapture a system of values already lost to the Old. The landed gentry, it was claimed, had disappeared from England, to be replaced by the nouveau-riche businessman and the absentee landlord, who were sometimes one and the same person. With them had gone the virtues of a benevolent patriarchy.

> Hospitality, which was once a relique of Gentry, . . . hath lost her title, merely through discontinuance; and great houses, which were at first founded to relieve the poor, and such needful passengers as travelled by them, are now of no use but only as waymarks to direct them.[18]

The gentleman was dead in England, that was the opinion, and the only place to resurrect him was across the Atlantic—an idea that many of the early colonizers took so much to heart that they set about a wholesale imitation of what they conceived to be the proper life style of a squire. One example of this out of many is offered by William Fitzhugh, a Virginian planter of the seventeenth century.[19] Fitzhugh, a first-generation immigrant, was in fact the son of a Bedford draper, and had no substantial claim to the title of gentleman at all. Nevertheless, after he had been successful in his struggle with "fortune's adverse hand" and could live on his plantation, as he put it, "contentedly and well," he immediately set about acquiring a coat of arms and purchasing silverware on which it could be engraved; eventually he even trained one of his slaves to be a "singular good engraver." As a further index of his new pretensions, he imported a "calash" from London, a vehicle monstrously unsuited to the poor roads of the Old Dominion. His indigent sister, whom he hardly knew, was made a beneficiary of this self-transformation, too. She was summoned from London to Virginia, arrangements having first been made that she be "genteley and well clothed" with "a maid to wait on her." For as her brother explained with perfect frankness, a suitably imposing appearance when she first set foot in the colony would attach to their family "credit and reputation, without which its uncomfortable living."

The example of William Fitzhugh is crucial, because it suggests how much more the idea of the gentleman, or for that matter the idea of the husbandman, was than an unapplied and inapplicable abstraction. The two ideas were *used,* engaging with the historical circumstances of the American South so as to produce enormously complicated situations. Many immigrants, for instance, did try to realize the life of the simple husbandman in the Southern colonies, and to a certain extent succeeded until general economic conditions started to work against them.[20] That is to say, they managed more or less to conduct their affairs in accordance with the precept of self-reliance until well on into the seventeenth century. Then, the deterioration of much of the land and the growing demand for tobacco abroad encouraged the development of larger holdings based on the principles of commercial rather than subsistence farming; and this spelled doom to the small, independent freeholder for the time being. In turn, those who developed these larger holdings did attempt to assume the role of feudal aristocrat—this despite the fact that most of them were, like Fitzhugh, "men of low circumstances"[21] who in any case were obliged to run their plantations as business enterprises, manufactories of tobacco, rather than landed estates. As a contemporary historian, Hugh Jones, observed, "the Habits, Life, Customs, Computation etc., of the Virginian" might be "much the same as about London," but these habits consorted ill with the wilderness of the surroundings and the onerous nature of business and financial activities in the colony.[22]

The involvement of the two ideas was not simply with the historical reality, of course, but with each other, since the people who celebrated the possibilities of the South and tried to live their lives according to these possibilities could not be neatly divided into two separate categories, the one defined by the principles of the good husbandman and the other by the customary graces of the fine gentleman. The categories tended to mix so as to produce very different types of belief. Men might agree, that is, that they were describing the South and its unique way of life, and their descriptions might be seen to stem ultimately from two distinct systems of value, but in the event their personal formulations of just what "Southern-ness" was were almost innumerable in their variations. At this point, the story becomes complicated—so complicated, in fact, that generalizations no longer seem feasible. And in the face of this, perhaps only one alternative remains —to concentrate on a few crucial moments in the subsequent history of the Old South so as to suggest something of the nature and scope of the variations that did occur. The tradition on which the writers of the Southern "renaissance" drew was, as I have said, a product of the engagement of idea with idea, as well as of idea with history; and perhaps as good a means of understanding this process as any is to look at a few works and statements that illustrate the tensions produced by these engagements.

Two Gentlemen of the Revolution: William Wirt and John Taylor

When the American people accomplished a revolution, almost against their will, at the end of the eighteenth century, they had the Southern colonies to thank more than any other area for the success of the enterprise. For the South provided the most important military leader, George Washington, as well as the man who became the intellectual spokesman of the revolutionary movement, Thomas Jefferson. It was a major battleground for most of the war, and its leading statesmen were among those who were most committed to the doctrines of the Enlightenment. The principles of Reason, Truth, and Justice, and the concept of human equality, were in fact part of the intellectual climate of the South at the time. There was no simple cause and effect sequence involved in this, of course. Rather, the ideas of the Enlightenment helped precipitate the Revolution—and the success of the military venture, in turn, encouraged the further dissemination of those ideas. One result of this interaction was crucial: stimulated by the warlike and various nature of the age, the more articulate Southerners turned their attention to their society and to the assumptions implicit in its structure, so as to analyze it in terms of the criteria of "natural rights." Their purpose went beyond analysis, ultimately, to the discovery of some being who embodied the best possibilities of a good society, *the* good society that might complete the Revolution; and, when their investigations were completed, most of them agreed with Thomas Jefferson about the ideal human type. He was the simple husbandman, the man celebrated by Jefferson himself in a famous passage in *Notes on Virginia:*

> Those who labor in the earth are the chosen people of God, if ever he had a chosen people, whose breasts he has made his peculiar deposit for substantial and genuine virtue. . . . Corruption of morals . . . is the mark set on those, who not looking . . . to their own soil and industry, as does the husbandman, for their subsistence, depend for it on the casualties and caprice of customers . . . generally speaking, the proportion which the aggregate of the other classes of citizens bears in any state to that of its husbandmen, is the proportion of its unsound to its healthy parts.[23]

Jefferson wrote at a time of special optimism, however, when the possibilities for the future in the South seemed enormous. Within a few years of the publication of *Notes on Virginia,* his hopes came to seem almost naïve—and for a number of reasons.[24] In the first place, the hopes rested on the chances of seizing the land from the great tobacco entrepreneurs, the descendants of people like William Fitzhugh, and those chances grew slimmer with every year they remained unaccomplished. More important than this, though, was the fact that the great entrepreneurs were themselves suffering economic difficulties at this time, consequent upon the exhaustion of the land and the loss of preferential treatment in the English market. Accompanying this, and related to it, was a growing sense among many Southerners that a new society was emerging in parts of the country very different from the one anticipated by Jefferson, and hostile to farmer and planter alike. This was a society that seemed to be founded on the factory rather than the farm, the dweller in the slum rather than the tiller of the soil, and it seemed to confirm some of their worst fears about the tendencies of the new Republic. The result of this complication, as far as these Southerners' attitudes toward themselves and their region were concerned, was highly significant. Instead of proposing a specific type of agrarianism for the South founded on the life of the simple farmer, and criticizing the great planter by comparison, they grew reluctant to criticize any version of the rural life they professed to find in their embattled region, in case it should weaken their attack on the life style of the town. In effect, they adopted a strategy of more or less fruitful confusion.

One writer who adopted the strategy with no great deliberateness was William Wirt. Wirt, who was for many years the Attorney General of the United States and once even a presidential candidate, had close connections with many of the leading Virginian politicians of his day. So it was not particularly surprising, given his enthusiastic interest in writing and history that is, that in 1817 he should have published a biography of one of them: the famous revolutionary orator, Patrick Henry. What was surprising was the enormous popularity the book enjoyed. It became a standard work, perpetuating Wirt's versions of Henry's speeches for many generations to come. And what was more surprising still was the fanciful nature of the biographical material: it read in fact, and still reads, like a piece of fiction. With his very first description of the young protagonist, "obscure, unknown, and almost unpitied, digging in a small spot of . . . earth for bread," Wirt established Henry as a representative and almost epic hero—a man whose every quality made him identifiable with "the body of the yeomanry." In every respect, Henry was elevated by his biographer to the status of a familiar ideal—the good farmer, who supplied a corrective warning to a generation that seemed in danger of succumbing to the false glamour of the city. The very environment that Wirt created for this minor historical myth seemed to glow with significance. For Henry, a man of "primeval simplicity," was presented as an integral part of his natural surroundings—the index of an historical development as inevitable, apparently, as the growth of his own crops.[25]

Taken in isolation, the portrait of Patrick Henry might lead the reader to suppose that Wirt was wholly committed to the Jeffersonian idea, but he would be wrong if he did so. The reason for this was quite simple. The principal target of Wirt's animadversions was, as it turned out, the corruption of his contemporaries—a corruption that he associated with the emergence of the town as an emblem of the national and regional life. And in order to hit this target he was willing to employ more than one weapon. That became clear enough when he turned to the description of Virginian society as a whole during the time of Henry's youth. With feelings of obvious sympathy for his subject, Wirt described the Old Dominion as a "centre of emulation, taste and elegance, of which we can form no conception by the appearance of the present day." It was, he averred, the home of an essentially feudal culture, and as the products of this culture the landowners of colonial Virginia could be remembered as aristocrats in the best sense of the word. That is to say, Wirt's *fictional* planters were all that the *real* planters on whom they were modeled had tried, but mostly failed, to be. A brief sketch that Wirt gave of one of them, Richard Henry Lee, illustrates the transformation:

> . . . Richard Henry Lee was the Cicero of the House [of Burgesses]. His face itself was on the Roman model; his nose Caesarean; the port and carriage of his head, leaning persuasively and gracefully forward; and the whole courteous, noble and fine.[26]

Certainly, Lee and his kind were shown succumbing to the new political force represented by Patrick Henry, and to that extent Wirt endorsed the Jeffersonian program. But a complicating note of nostalgia had entered into the endorsement, a product of the writer's misgivings about his own optimism. To put the matter at its simplest, Wirt committed himself to the idea of the good farmer and then hedged his bet by refusing to discard the idea of the gentleman planter.

This same process of hesitancy producing ambivalence occurs with a difference in the work of another distinguished Southerner of this period, the political theorist John Taylor of Caroline. Taylor, an important figure in the history of the Southern mind who has only just recently been rediscovered by historians,[27] was one of the first American historical commentators to propose the existence of a close relationship between the economic and political structure of the country. Taylor's arguments were elaborate and often quite complex, but what matters here is those specific parts of them which discuss the indispensability of agriculture.[28] For, good Southern agrarian that he was, Taylor rivaled Jefferson before him in his insistence that the farmer provided the only secure foundation for a republic. In fact, he took many of his arguments from Jefferson, insisting as he did that the rural way of life encouraged the development of exactly those qualities, such as industry, honesty, and thrift, which were necessary to the maintenance of good government. There was a difference between them, however, and it stemmed from the fact that the virtues that Jefferson attributed to the plain farmer were those which John Taylor tended to associate with agriculture in general. That is to say, he would argue at length that the agrarian way of life was "the best architect of the complete man,"[29] and that landowning was the best possible stimulant for good citizenship—but then leave it vague as to whether the land owned should be small or large in extent, and whether the "complete man" he talked about was a husbandman or a planter.

This ambiguity, which apparently was quite deliberate, was encouraged by the curiously two-faced nature of the criteria Taylor used throughout his argument. At one moment he would invoke the Jeffersonian value of "natural rights," arrived at by a process of logic. At the next, however, he seemed to reject the doctrines of the Enlightenment altogether and appeal to the test of experience, a test that had inevitably conservative implications. The diversity of his procedures would not have mattered so much were it not for the fact that they could not help but affect the nature of his conclusions. For the theory of "natural rights" led him toward one interpretation of the good life, seen in terms of the equality of all well-meaning men, while the ideas of "moderation" and caution implicit in the concern with experience led him to quite another. In this case, things as they had been, as represented by the great planters who had dominated the colonial South for such a long time, were adopted as a standard of evolution; and the reader was presented with a philosophical equivalent of that nostalgia so noticeable in the work of William Wirt.[30] Taylor appears to have been aware of this uncertainty, however, in a way that Wirt was not. At least, much of his language was devoted to minimizing the contradictions he had created, and diverting attention to his critique of industrial capitalism. And what this meant in the long run was the development of a rhetoric that was to become an integral part of the Southern argument and tradition.

Taylor's principal rhetorical device was simple. The industrial way of life was associated with the mechanical and destructive qualities of experience, agrarianism with the "natural" or the genuinely "human." The associations were pervasive, appearing almost every time he described one or the other society, and occasionally were developed to such an extreme that they assumed an almost surrealistic quality. At such moments, industrialism was transformed into an "engine of power and oppression," an "artillery" or "battery" dedicated to ending life rather than sustaining it.[31] Naturally, this kind of associative technique did receive some support from the argument; there was, for example, a sense in which it could be said to illustrate all that Taylor described as the exploitative aspect of capitalism. But the support was a pretty weak one, and what was obviously more important to Taylor was the spellbinding power of his associations, which dissipated uncertainties and defied opponents by throwing them on the defensive. It was a power that many subsequent Southern writers were to recognize, and to imitate in passages like the following.

The primitive and patriarchal, which may also be called the sacred and natural, society . . . has been almost everywhere superseded by the modern, artificial, money-power system, in which man—his thews and sinews,

his hopes and affections . . . are all subject to the dominion of capital—
a monster without a heart—cold, stern, arithmetical . . . working up human life with engines and retailing it by weight and measure.[32]

The verbal ploys used here are characteristic of those who learned
their lesson from Taylor, either directly or by proxy. Certain normally
morally neutral words, such as "primitive," "natural," "solid," and "traditional," acquired connotations of positive value; whereas others, like
"modern," "arithmetical," "ideal," and "artificial," were shaped into
terms of abuse.[33] The effect of this device, and ones like it, is perhaps
self-evident. It made the kind of agrarianism the writer was defending
appear unimportant, since what mattered, evidently, was a "naturalness" vaguely registered in all rural life styles and an "organic" structure associated with all agrarian-based societies. Elaborate rhetorical
gestures were enough, it was assumed, to present a convincing alternative to the new industrialism; and it seemed pedantic, after that, to
ask who was "natural," what was "organic," or exactly what these
words were meant to signify.

Taylor did not create the rhetoric of agrarianism, by any means.
There had been many writers before him who had made the same
verbal associations, and abandoned definitions of the rural society they
celebrated in favor of the pastoral orthodoxies. Quite a few of these
writers, too, had identified the object of their celebrations with the
South. Despite all this, he does seem to have been the first Southerner
to exploit the rhetoric systematically: his predecessors, by comparison,
only resorted to it on occasion and at random. The systematization
probably had a lot to do with the fact that it had a specific purpose
for Taylor, enabling him as it did to draw attention away from his
unwillingness to define his case: he was apparently aware that he was
uncertain about whose side he was on, and the rhetoric served to compensate for this uncertainy. Anyway, whatever its causes, it helped
make him an even more crucial than William Wirt in the development of the Southern tradition. The Revolution and its immediate aftermath had added a further series of tensions to the continuing dialogue between idea and historical process in the South, and
many of these tensions Taylor had consciously reflected in his work,
allowing it to dictate, among other things, that language of calculated
imprecision which was to become the staple idiom of many a subsequent Southern writer. After him, there were different crises for the
South, of course, requiring different sets of defenses: but the defenses
were usually ones built with his help, although he himself would tend
to go unacknowledged.

The Old South and "Aristocratic Democracy": John Calhoun and John Pendleton Kennedy

In a sense, it seems almost superfluous to talk about specific difficulties occurring in the South in the years after Taylor and his contemporaries had left the stage, because by then the region as a whole seemed to be existing in a state of permanent crisis. This was partly due to the fact that, within four decades from the founding of the Republic, the Southern states had been reduced to the position of a conscious and embattled minority in an aggressive and growing nation. In every sphere of activity, it appeared, the interests of the region differed radically from those of the North and, in some instances, from those of the West as well.[34] For example, the South was by now firmly committed to commercial farming of cotton and tobacco, whereas its Northern neighbor had become primarily an industrial center. This meant that they had opinions that were precisely the opposite of each other on such questions as the founding of a national bank, strong in its ability to create and fund debts, and the imposition of a high tariff. The North wanted protection and strong economic controls, the South wanted as much freedom as possible—and the situation might simply have been one of stalemate, were it not for the fact that the North was slowly assuming a position of strength from which it could enforce its opinions. For during these years its towns and factories were encouraging a rapid increase of population, which in turn entitled it to a greater proportion of representation in the central government. The irony was that at the same time this was happening, the South was failing to encourage a rapid population growth precisely because of its commitment to large-scale farming founded on slavery. As a result, its voice in the government was diminishing in strength at just the moment when it needed to be as strong as possible. Not for the first time, the South seemed to be caught in a dilemma of its own making.

The sense of accumulating differences went beyond the economic, of course, largely because as the Northeast moved into the industrial age the orthodoxies of its old theocracy were being replaced by the liberalisms of the nineteenth century. The priest was supplanted by the reformer and, as more than one Southerner observed with contempt, Northern society was gradually infested with "Bloomers and Women's Rights men and strong-minded women, and Mormons and anti-renters, . . . Millerites, and Spiritual Rappers and Shakers, and Widow Wakehamites, . . . and Grahamites."[35] There was a touch of hysteria to the criticism, traceable ultimately to the fact that the South, after all, was directly affected by this reforming zeal. For, carefully avoided though the subject normally was when Southerners were blasting the Northern "isms," the most important reform movement to which New England gave birth during this period was abolitionism. In 1831, William Lloyd Garrison began publishing *The Liberator*, an event that heralded the emergence of a concerted Northern effort to end American Negro slavery—and, added to everything else that was happening in state and nation at the time, this served to confirm the regional sense of persecution in the most dramatic manner possible. As far as anyone from below the Mason-Dixon line could see, battle had been joined with the Yankee, and there was a greater necessity than ever for defending the South and celebrating its best possibilities.

One man who clearly felt that this was the case, and whose life as a result became almost identified with the cause of the South, was the statesman John Caldwell Calhoun. Calhoun was in turn a Congressman, a Secretary of War, a Vice-President, and a Senator, but more important than any single office that he held was his unofficial post as spokesman for his entire region. The post became his in 1828 when he prepared the "South Carolina Exposition," which asserted that any state was justified in seceding from the Union if it considered the laws passed by the national government to be unconstitutional. The assertion bore specific reference to his own home state of South Carolina, and its opposition to the 1828 tariff, but it possessed obvious relevance for the entire South because of its minority position in the legislature. This was at least one way of asserting minority rights, and, recognizing this, Calhoun subsequently developed the flat statements of the "exposition" into an elaborate system of political theory, founded on his own interpretation of the American Constitution.[36] The theory belonged, of course, to the states' rights school of thought, vesting ultimate power in the local authorities, but in this context the precise nature of Calhoun's argument is less significant than his idea of what this argument defended. The initial purpose of his theorizing, and its ultimate one as well, was to preserve the South from the encroachments of outsiders—to keep it in its pristine condition and intact. The moment Calhoun tried to say just what that condition was, however, a familiar ambivalence set in, which could only be encompassed by terms of paradox, such as "aristocratic democracy."

Calhoun, in fact, praised all the possibilities he discovered in his region, and praised them as if they were achieved facts. The result was an inevitable loss of consistency. A man of ambiguous background himself, he could describe the "large, educated planter" and the poor farmer with equal enthusiasm and then go beyond this to declare that they both offered a paradigm of the South.[37] Sometimes the contradictions implicit in his position did seem to occur to him. His solution was then to insist on the idea of a "Greek" or "white" democracy, which managed to combine the better features of both the aristocratic and the more equalitarian states. "I fearlessly assert," he would say, "that the existing relation between the two races in the South . . . forms the most solid and durable foundation on which to rear free and stable political institutions";[38] and he would follow this up by arguing that all *white* men, at least, could be regarded as equals because they belonged to a privileged caste. So, by a series of neat tricks of logic, Calhoun tried to apotheosize the farmer and the planter simultaneously and identify them both with his region. The argument was usually presented with great persuasiveness, but it tended to ignore the fact that the interests of the two were—as the history of the region had proved—not all that reconcilable. And in any case it seemed strangely at odds with statements like the following.

> Men are not born free. While infants they are incapable of freedom . . . and . . . they grow to all the freedom of which the condition in which they were born permits by growing to be men. Nor is it less false that they are born "equal."[39]

Occasionally, the idea of the husbandman or that of the gentleman did monopolize Calhoun's response to a specific controversy. The good farmer, for instance, was clearly in his mind in all his speeches on the division of public lands. Then, his rhetoric was all at the service of those "poor, but honest and independent"[40] people who, he felt, would benefit especially from the gift of a hundred or more acres of soil. In turn, the identification of the gentleman planter as the backbone of Southern society was implicit in most of his discussions of the peculiar institution of slavery. The feudal community "with the master at its head" was transformed in such cases into the chief "blessing of this state of things"[41] below the Potomac. But in general, and despite the rationalizations, the two ideas were almost inextricably confused—with the result that Calhoun could write two letters to the same man in the space of a few months, praising first the patriarchal planter of "property and information" as an epitome of the good life, and then describing the plain farmer in almost exactly the same terms. That Calhoun should have prided himself on the ability to "banish the perplexity and doubt by which ordinary minds are overwhelmed and confused"[42] suggests how little aware he could sometimes make himself be of the inconsistencies inherent in his approach.

The problem of potential inconsistency was given one solution by someone contemporary with Calhoun who stands at the fountainhead of Southern literature, the writer and critic John Pendleton Kennedy.[43] Perhaps it would be appropriate, though, to describe Kennedy as a *littérateur* more than anything else, as his chief talent seems to have been for analyzing the more important literary tendencies of his day, and then exploiting them. This is illustrated in one way by his relationship with Edgar Allan Poe. Kennedy discovered Poe in 1833, when he awarded the then unknown writer first prize in a short story competition for his "MS Found in a Bottle." Thereafter, he acted as an unofficial patron, unearthing a post for Poe as editor of the *Southern Literary Messenger,* supplying him with a series of informal "loans," and in general offering exactly the kind of financial and moral encouragement that the young writer so desperately needed. Motives are hard to read over such a long distance in time, but, as far as one can see, all this was prompted by intelligent selflessness. Kennedy seems, in fact, to have been a sort of early Southern counterpart of somebody like Ford Madox Ford—a person for whom writers were a race apart, to be helped and cherished, and for whom the perpetuation of literature as such was a matter of principle unhampered by any considerations of personal gain. The analogy with Ford carries over into the creative side of Kennedy's life as well. For both were, at their best, superb technicians, "inventors" in the sense given to that word by Ezra Pound[44]: men, that is, who did not produce works of the first rank themselves but who nevertheless mapped out areas of imaginative possibility that writers succeeding them—who *were* as it happened of the first rank—could employ for their own purposes. The various books that Kennedy wrote during his lifetime were clearly the products of solid industry rather than inspiration. What matters here, though, is not so much their intrinsic limitations as the fact that two of them at least represent the first significant articulation in imaginative literature of the divergent ideas shaping the Southern tradition. As such, they make their creator a crucial figure—perhaps *the* crucial figure—in the history of ante-bellum writing in the region.

The way in which Kennedy dealt with the two heroes of agrarian thought, and so with the problem of possible self-contradiction, was straightforward enough: the two were separated from each other, and then presented as different alternatives in different books. This simultaneous commitment to the plain farmer and the fine planter was unusual if only because of its deliberateness, but the reasons for it are not that obscure. For different as the two characters might be, they were yet alike for Kennedy in one crucial respect—namely, in their stern fidelity to principle. Both, in other words, were possessed of just that independence and integrity which Kennedy felt had been drained from the national life, to remain only in the South in isolated areas. Quite simply, Kennedy's initial impulse was one of reaction against a society that had been "rubbed down," as he saw it, to one "uniform" level by a creeping standardization of behavior.[45] His principal aim was to supply an incisive criticism of this, rather than to develop a consistent positive argument, and to further this aim he felt entitled to formulate more than one alternative to the dull new world around him. In *Swallow Barn*,[46] for example, published in 1832, the alternative offered was the familiar one of the "feudal" experience. The book, which was modeled on the episodic fiction of Washington Irving, consequently stands at the beginning of that tradition of plantation fiction which *is* "Southern literature" for most readers.[47] There at the center of the action was a prototype of the "Virginian gentleman," Frank Meriwether, a patriarch whose "kind" supervision of his community was matched only by its "affectionate reverence" for him. The very "model of a landed gentleman," he was presented as the owner of an estate, Swallow Barn, in every way worthy of him—"a lordly domain" where "wassails" and "jousts" were apparently regular occurrences and the "manners of large cities" were happily ignored.[48] The other inhabitants of Swallow Barn helped to flesh out this portrait of a nicely articulated community, and in describing them Kennedy presented the reader with a gallery of characters that were to become standard in subsequent Southern writing. Lucretia Meriwether, for example, Frank's wife, and Bel Tracey, the daughter of a neighbor, offered illustrations of the woman's place in this world, with Mrs. Meriwether epitomizing the domestic virtues of good housekeeper and mother and Bel, the object of courtly devotions among the young "cavaliers" of the county, locating the more chivalric side of plantation life. The "cavaliers," in turn, were best represented by Frank's son Ned Meriwether, nicknamed "Ned Hazard" by his companions. From this vantage point in time he sounds, as Kennedy described him, like nothing so much as a preliminary sketch for Faulkner's Bayard Sartoris I, or Henry Sutpen.

> He is now about thirty-three, with a tolerably good person, a little under six feet, and may be seen generally . . . in an olive frock, black stock and yellow waistcoat, with a German forage-cap . . . rather conceitedly drawn over his dark, laughing eye. This head-gear gives a picturesque effect to his person, and suits well with his weather-beaten cheek, as it communicates a certain reckless expression that agrees with his character. The same trait is heightened by the half swagger with which he strikes his boot with his riding-whip.[49]

This was about the only context in which a whip appeared in the book; the slaves, it seemed, enjoyed a "mild and beneficent guardianship, adapted to the actual state of their intellectual feebleness,"[50] that precluded violence of any kind. Slavery became in effect not so much a business as a charitable institution, part of the patriarchal dream that Kennedy spent so much of his time elaborating.

Swallow Barn was not just the projection of a dream, however, and the reason it was not was Kennedy's oblique recognition of the reality. The recognition was not sustained, certainly, but it was nevertheless *there* to limit and qualify the approval; an undercurrent of satire ran intermittently through the book, as a means of suggesting the possibility of a division between the ideal and the fact. It was present, for example, in the portrait of a minor character, Singleton Oglethorpe Swansdown, through whom Kennedy delivered a trenchant critique of Southern romanticism. Swansdown's very name suggested his function as a type of the effete poetaster, and this suggestion was confirmed by his practice of wooing several different women simultaneously, using always the same "multitude of pretty sayings"[51] to do so. He was conceived of as being as much a part of the South as the Meriwethers. In fact, he was integrally related to them; his pride was only a slightly distorted version of their pride and his affectation of gentility, the romantic silliness of his every act, offered an effective parody of their pretensions toward the "aristocratical." In case the reader should miss the point, Kennedy even permitted himself an occasional satirical comment on the major characters themselves. Thus Frank Meriwether was not entirely forgiven for the autocratic control he tried to exert over the opinions held by his neighbors, which were considered "wholesome" only if they echoed his own; while his belief that "the magistracy of Virginia is the staunchest pillar supporting the fabric of the Constitution"[52] was clearly held up for ridicule. The qualifying note sounded here was significant, and not least because it betrayed the difficulties that Kennedy encountered in trying to identify the dream of a feudal kingdom with the available reality. That he wanted some kind of an identification was obvious, but his own critical intelligence tended to prevent him from quite making it.

That is to say, Kennedy's intelligence prevented him from making a present connection. The situation altered drastically when he directed the attention of the reader to the historical background of his narrative—to the past in general and colonial Virginia in particular. Then the dream of "feudal munificence"[53] was allowed to range unhampered by any perception of a limiting reality: the planters of earlier centuries were described as demonstrating the kind of finished aristocracy of style that had never really been theirs, except as an ambition. This radical alteration of tone, which occurred every time Kennedy referred to the past, was illustrated by the difference between the presentation of Frank Meriwether and that of John Smith, the navigator and writer whose life was so closely interwoven with the history of colonial Virginia. For all the praise showered on him, Meriwether emerged from *Swallow Barn* as "an easy and cultivated country-gentleman" whose larger pretensions were described with some reserve. Smith, on the other hand, was presented as an accomplished exponent of all those graces to which Meriwether could only aspire; in every sense, he was "a True Knight of the Old Dominion."[54] It was the difference in time that accounted for this, of course: idealization was so much easier from a distance. And, as if to confirm the point, there was the evidence offered by Kennedy's changing opinion, over the years, of the civilization represented by Swallow Barn. For, some two decades after the publication of the book, he was asked to write a preface to a second edition. He obliged with an essay in which Meriwether and his world were as much identified with the past, if only the recent past, as John Smith had been. In the event, the essay became an elegy for a vanished civilization.

> *Swallow Barn* exhibits a picture of country life as it existed in the first quarter of the present century. Between that period and the present day, time and what is called "progress" have made many innovations therein. The Old Dominion is losing somewhat of . . . the mellow, bland and sunny luxuriance of her old society—its good fellowship, its hearty and constitutional "companionableness" . . . that overflowing hospitality which knew no ebb.[55]

There is a profound nostalgia here, quite excluding the satirical touch that created a Singleton Oglethorpe Swansdown.

"The past presents a mellow landscape to my vision," Kennedy said in another one of his essays, "rich with the hues of distance. . . . The present is a foreground less inviting, with . . . sharp lines and garish colors wanting harmony."[56] That was to become a recurrent impulse in Southern writing. Discontent with the present would encourage an investigation of the past; and this, as in Kennedy's case, might lead to a mythologization of that past, in which its possibilities were accepted as accomplishments. *Swallow Barn* offered one demonstration of the process, and Kennedy's second book, *Horse-Shoe Robinson*, was to offer another. Only in this case the mythologizing process attached the South, not to the dream of the feudal planter, but to that of the simple husbandman. The time of the narrative was significant. It was set during the American Revolution, and so complete was the association of the titular character with this event that he seemed to be a paradigm not only of the "lusty yeoman" but of the entire rebel forces as well.

> Nature had carved out, in his person, an athlete whom the sculptors might have studied to improve the Hercules. Every lineament of his body indicated strength. His stature was above six feet; his limbs sinewy and remarkable for their symmetry. . . . With all these advantages of person, there was a radiant, broad, good nature upon his face; and the glance of a large, clear, blue eye told of . . . shrewd, homely wisdom.[57]

Kennedy allowed no doubts to remain as to the origins of this man "as big as a horse." Robinson was, as his creator never tired of repeating, a "ploughman" or "Kentucky farmer"—a man whose principal trade might be that of a blacksmith but who combined this with the cultivation of a "little farm on the Waxhaw settlement," so as to make himself quite independent of his fellows.[58]

Independence was, in fact, the determining force in the character of Horse-Shoe Robinson, the quality that acted as a catalyst for all the others. It was responsible, among other things, for what Kennedy called his "acute insight," acquired without benefit of formal education, and for his profound dislike of the manipulations practiced by financiers. "Squaring up and smoothing off," as he said, "and bringing out this or that shilling to a penny" did not "come natural" to him.[59] Beyond this, it contributed to Kennedy's perception of his protagonist as a type of the "chosen people of God," as those people had been defined by Thomas Jefferson. And just in case the reader should miss the point, by taking him as an isolated phenomenon, Horse-Shoe was surrounded by characters who reflected different facets of his own personality. For all his epic stature, he was consequently seen as a person who articulated and combined virtues occurring, with a difference, in the rest of the community. In a way, just as Horse-Shoe Robinson represented the revolutionary army, so the revolutionary army represented him, its ranks being filled with the kind of "bold, enterprising, and hardy characters"[60] who could suggest a diminished version of himself. So the Revolution was transformed into an ideological struggle, waged by the insurgents on behalf of a specific type of agrarianism. What the American army appeared to mean for Kennedy was the Southern army, which meant in turn an army of yeomen fighting for all the principles traditionally associated with their type.

These principles conflicted, of course, with the ones established in *Swallow Barn*—and yet not entirely. As Kennedy perceived, there was a common denominator in the sense that both Frank Meriwether and Horse-Shoe Robinson could be described as "indwellers upon the land . . . altar and fire-side defending men."[61] And no matter how fragile this common denominator might turn out to be when examined in detail, there was still the saving fact that the gentleman and the "ploughman" offered different but equally viable means of criticizing a society characterized by its blandness—a society that Kennedy labeled "Jacksonian"[62] after the President of the time, but for which later writers from the region preferred the epithet of "Yankee." This was one means by which Kennedy avoided the difficulties in which Calhoun embroiled himself—by firmly distinguishing between the two ideas at the root of the dilemma, and then placing them in separate fictive worlds. Another ploy that complemented this was to reject any temptation to identify one idea or the other with the contemporary South, where the sense of contradictory facts would be painfully inhibiting, and then to locate the Great Good Places of the regional imagination in the more congenial setting of the past. The result was a significant one for subsequent Southern writers. It was especially significant for those who could adopt the prototypes evolved by Kennedy but then use them as part of a personal criticism of life—and by so using them manage to go beyond them.

The New South and the Old Problems: Ellen Glasgow

We have almost returned to the era that witnessed the explosion of literary talent known as the Southern "renaissance"—almost, but not quite. For the aftermath of the Civil War managed to develop the problems and possibilities of the Southern tradition still further, and so complicated the "source of available ideas" on which the writers of that "renaissance" could draw.[63] One development can be stated quickly: as many people saw it, the idea of the feudal plantation could now be elaborated unhampered by any sense of contingency—the recalcitrant nature of actual circumstances—because that idea could be firmly located in the past. The "aristocratical" life of the gentleman, that is, could be celebrated as a phenomenon of the ante bellum era that had been swept away by the Union Army. For the evident rift between past and present the war stood conveniently as both symbol and explanation, while the decline of local conditions could be invoked as a means of reinforcing the general sense of loss. The memory of defeat in arms after a genuinely heroic resistance, the sense of enduring deprivation, and the general drabness of life in the years of the Reconstruction: all these specific factors, as well, tended to heighten the loyalty felt by many writers to the days "before the war." And those days, suitably apotheosized, could supply a comforting illustration of all that the South had fought for and had taken from it. In the event, nostalgia was exaggerated into a positive obsession with the past of the kind indicated by the following. It is taken from one of the many plantation romances of the era, and, with a superb sense of the inappropriate, it places the elegy for days gone by in the mouth of an emancipated slave.

> Dem wuz good ole times, marster—de bes' Sam ever see! . . . Nigger didn' had nothin't all to do—jes' had to ten' to de feedin' an' cleanin' de hosses an' doin' what de marster tell 'em to do, an' when dey wuz sick . . . de same doctor came to see 'em what 'ten de white folks . . . Dyar warn' no trouble nor nothin'.[64]

More interesting than this full-blown romanticism, though, because
they engaged more directly with the social and economic realities of the
postwar South, were those writings which demonstrated the existence
of possibility as well as loss in the world they described. In a way,
the possibility was related to the loss. For if the good times on the
old plantation were a thing of the past, it was argued, then perhaps
they could be replaced by something approximating more closely to
the Jeffersonian dream. The "rise of the small farmer" might just become the "most notable circumstance of a period"[65] characterized by
social and economic upheaval. The poet and essayist Sidney Lanier
was one person to commit himself to this possibility. Consulting the
census reports for 1880, and reading a lot more into them than was
warranted, Lanier announced the imminent emergence of the husbandman as the founder of a new community in the South, and then
went on to elaborate his prophecy.

> . . . small farming means . . . meat and bread for which there are no notes
> in the bank; pigs fed with home-made corn—yarn spun, stockings knit,
> butter made and sold (instead of bought): eggs, chickens, products of
> natural growth, and grass at nothing a ton.[66]

On the basis of a little evidence, and a great deal of speculation, the
conclusion seemed to be that Horse-Shoe Robinson had been born
again.

One writer who certainly began by believing in the new departure
sketched out by Lanier, and whose work provided a kind of bridge
between the hopefulness of the Reconstruction era and the years of
the Southern "renaissance," was the Virginian novelist Ellen Glasgow.[67]
Glasgow's convictions underwent several changes during the course of
her life, and they were always qualified by her commitment as a
writer to the presentation of diverse human forms, but her initial
stance at least, the point from which all explorations started, was a
simple one and understandable. It was to accept, quite happily, the
premise that the old feudal order was in the last stages of decay, as
a fact and an idea, and that the "plain man" of the land was "building
the structure . . . of the future" that would replace it. That done, Glasgow then went on to develop two fictional strategies which she hoped
would enable her to investigate the implications of her premise, and
dramatize them. One strategy invited comedy, a satirical inventory of
the weaknesses of the "aristocratical" person—the aim being, in effect,
to show how "stationary and antiquated"[68] he was, and how imperative
it was to replace him. The other, by contrast, was more in the heroic
line. It required the writer to concentrate her attention on the poorer
white and the qualities, latent in his character, that appeared to guar-
antee his eventual success—and this as a prelude to the presentation

of his actual success story. Necessarily, the result of using two such different strategies was to create two different types of novel; Glasgow herself liked to refer to them as "novels of history" or "of the town" on the one hand, and "novels of the country" on the other. But despite all their differences, the same optimism usually managed to shine through them both and betray their common authorship; satire and heroic tale were equally shaped by the conviction that the small farm was about to secure the state.

Just what that meant as far as the state was concerned was something Glasgow implied in her portrait of the farmer characters, all of whom tended to be variations on certain themes. They belonged, so the author argued to a tradition going back to the colonial years, which had given them stern lessons in self-reliance and the capacity to endure. The life of the husbandman was defined by its rigor, and this had bred a common resilience in all men of his type; a "vein of iron" running so deep that his "secret self" "could not yield, could not bend, could not be broken,"[69] even under enormous pressure. He would stand fast in a decaying environment, and perhaps use it to his advantage. In some ways, of course, this was no more than a rehearsal of conventional notions about the resilience of country folk—as faded as the pastoral dream, if rather different in its assumptions. But in the best of her heroic novels, Glasgow managed to go beyond the accepted and encompass an almost mystical belief in the efficacy of direct contact with the earth. The religious motive and the utilitarian were then combined in such a way as to strengthen them both. Here is an example of what I mean from one of her best novels, *Barren Ground*. It bears comparison with the more uninhibited moments in Jefferson's *Notes on Virginia*.

> The storm and the hag-ridden dreams of the night were over, and the land which had forgotten was waiting to take her back to its heart. Endurance. Fortitude. The spirit of the land was flowing into her, and her own spirit, strengthened and refreshed, was flowing out again toward life. This was the permanent self, she knew. This was what remained to her after the years had taken their bloom.[70]

The point about this passage, I think, is that Dorinda Oakley, the heroine of the novel and the person who achieves the particular recognition described here, is not simply any woman experiencing a moment of transcendent contact with nature, but a farmer's daughter rediscovering her proper vocation. Her perception is of the good life as a special mode of behavior, with its own blessings and sanctions attached to it, and it is upon this that her resurrection of the spirit depends.

This association of a program for political and social action with what can only be described as the vision of a new moral order received its complement in Glasgow's comedies of manners. And here, too, the success of the enterprise depended on her ability to personalize the action; in other words, to make the specific movement of the narrative—in this case the charting of a decline rather than a resurrection—seem dramatically inevitable and individually relevant rather than the result of some preconceived design. *The Romantic Comedians* was perhaps the best of her novels describing the collapse of the old patriarchal order. In it the fate of the central character, Judge Gamaliel Bland of Richmond, Virginia, emerged as the only possible one if the demands of dramatic justice were to be met. The novel unfolded the Judge's unfortunate marriage to a woman half his age, whom, in accordance with the dictates of the chivalric code, he had idealized completely and quite inaccurately into a creature of fragile innocence. Cuckolded, and then abandoned, his rewards were those of the innocent hypocrite; and for both the innocence and the hypocrisy Ellen Glasgow blamed the society that had fostered him. The social point was more or less explicit in the Judge's subsequent meditations on his wife's infidelity.

> If only women had been satisfied to remain protected! . . . If only they had been satisfied to wait in patience, not to seek after happiness! For it seemed to him . . . that there could be nothing nobler than the beauty of long waiting and wifely tolerance . . . surely it was not too much to insist that the true feminine character had never flowered more perfectly than in the sheltered garden of Southern tradition.[71]

There is a nice balance in this passage between personal misunderstanding and the social mechanisms that have created it, a balance characteristic of its author at her best. And through it all shines the perception that the ironic conflicts contained in an attitude like the Judge's were as responsible for the collapse of an entire class as were the more obvious factors of invasion and economic ruin.

That does not mean to say Glasgow was not interested in such factors; of course she was. She had to be, actually, because of her belief that the personal and social dramas of the South were inseparable. The private face was related to the public place in nearly all of her fiction; and this required her to devote at least some attention to the activities of the meeting house and marketplace. A few of her books even went beyond this, openly concerning themselves with political themes, and in such cases the larger implications of Glasgow's message were stated with a clarity and insistence that approached the polemical. Her story, *The Voice of the People*, for instance, read (as its title suggests) like a program for action. Its hero, Nicholas Burr, was a "po' white" of uncertain origins whom Glasgow described rising to the position of state governor, thanks to sheer effort and the vigor of his character. One reason offered for the ease with which he attained this eminence was the dormancy and apathy of the ruling class, so hypnotized by its "dream of the past," apparently, as to be unaware of the changes taking place around it. But even if it had been aware of them, the author argued, the consequences would have been the same, the "mental thinness, emotional dryness," and "intrinsic weakness" of the "old feudal order" being such that it could offer little more than a token opposition in any circumstances.[72] To call this situation one of conflict would be to overdramatize it. Like a morality play, *The Voice of the People* presented a battle, between a gallery of fools and a protagonist graced with all the advantages of a culture hero, which was over before it had begun. The reader hardly had to read to the end to know that the triumph of the plain man would be complete.

The triumph was a peculiar one, however, because it was fictional in the most limited and limiting sense possible—a product of wish fulfillment rather than engagement with historical fact. That was why Glasgow's contemporaries only had to look around them to discover forces calculated to deny her dream, and make prophecies like those in *The Voice of the People* seem ridiculous. The New South, as we have seen, was to be nothing like the society Ellen Glasgow anticipated. It was not, as it turned out, a place populated by happy farmers, but another witness to the industrial age, with a financial and technological structure to rival any of its neighbors'. The very fact that the industrialized North had defeated the rural South in the Civil War had tended to ensure this, and yet Glasgow would not acknowledge it. Seeing something of what was happening around her, she nevertheless failed to see the whole; and occasionally she seemed quite willful in her refusal to do so. Certainly, her blindness in this connection should not be exaggerated. Even in her earlier novels she betrayed some awareness of the possibility that things might not develop as she had expected. It was implicit, among other things, in her portraits of the businessmen occupying the periphery in some of the novels: a certain Cyrus Treadwell, for instance, one of the minor figures in *Virginia*, who was said to be so controlled by the "shibboleth" of success as to "resemble a machine" deprived even of the "ordinary animal capacity for pleasure."[73] But, unnerving as the thoughts aroused by such characters might be, they scarcely affected the prophetic core of the narrative. For anything more than a few symptoms of apprehension, the isolated warning flag, the reader had to wait for Ellen Glasgow's last book, *In This Our Life*, which was published several years after the others.

The event was worth waiting for, since what the novel represented was a complete volte-face—a reversal of all the predictions Glasgow

had previously made. The reasons for this change were obvious
enough, perhaps: by the time that Glasgow came to write *In This Our
Life* the New South, and the recognition of its character contained in
the literature of the "renaissance," were both established facts. The
course of a new society had been charted and could no longer be ignored. But that did not make the change any the less surprising, in some
of its ramifications at least, or any the less significant either. The book
was a testimony to hope betrayed, and its personal basis was only
nominally concealed by the use of a male surrogate for the author,
called Asa Timberlake. Asa, a gentleman of the old school, was not so
much a protagonist as a central consciousness, observing and commenting on the activities of the characters placed around him. And
most of his comments were reserved for the members of his own family—the younger members, that is, through whom Glasgow projected
her vision of contemporary life. Needless to say, they were nearly all
in the negative. His children and grandchildren, as Asa saw it, were
eccentrics, deviations from the traditional norms who demonstrated
by their deviation the "general breaking-up in the pattern of life" to
which they belonged. They had lost touch with the controls normally
placed on human behavior, with inherited codes and systems of belief;
and they had nothing with which to fill in the gap that was left except
their own random impulses. "Responsibility and integrity" had disappeared, as facts and standards of judgment, and all that remained to
distinguish one man from another was "the superiority . . . a very wide
margin of vested interests . . . [could] confer"—in other words, the
cash nexus. An interesting corollary of this situation, according to Glasgow, was that in a way Asa's young relatives had ceased to exist at all.
Lacking any code other than the fiscal, they lacked whole and func-
tioning personalities; and lacking this, they lacked reality. Like the
"unreal, unsubstantial"[74] houses in which they lived, they offered nothing more than a series of appearances, empty gestures, and meaningless façades.

The verdict was a damning one, a diatribe without qualification, and
what made it all the more so was the standpoint from which it was
delivered. Asa, like his creator, was an old person living in a strange
new world, which he hardly understood and certainly did not like.
It was natural, then, that he should turn to his memories for relief—
and as a means of confirming the deficiencies of his contemporaries.
This was the basic strategy of the book—to judge times present in
terms of a comparison with times gone by, and so use the heroic impulse as a means of satire. The past was mythologized rather than the
future, and then accepted as a yardstick, something to which existing
circumstances could be compared and found wanting. There could be

no doubt about this, that Asa and Ellen Glasgow were criticizing the New South with reference to the Old. Nor could there be much doubt that the particular form the Old South assumed in the novel tended to identify it with the aristocratic idea. It was, to use some of the words favored by Asa, a society characterized by its "elegance, grace, dignity and beauty,"[75] a perfect feudal type. Asa's own father was taken as its paradigm, a man as accomplished as Kennedy's Frank Meriwether and as gracious as Wirt's portrait of Richard Henry Lee. This passage, describing his relationship with his employees, will serve to illustrate.

> In the old days his father had known the name and face of every man he employed. One and all, he and his men belonged to a single social unit, which . . . was held together by some vital bond of human relation. . . . There had been injustice . . . but one had dealt with flesh and blood, not with a list of printed names.[76]

The contrast proposed here is between a social structure that supposedly expresses the personal values of "family feeling" and romantic love, and one that reduces all motives to the economic—the "human" and "vital" on one hand, and on the other the mechanical. Perhaps that sounds familiar. It should, since it represents an only slightly modified version of the conflict described in the work of John Taylor of Caroline; and that in itself may suggest how Glasgow had altered in her attitude toward the "old feudal order."

The situation was steeped in irony, like something from one of her own comic novels. Ellen Glasgow, the self-appointed advocate of the plain man, had ended her creative life with a novel that celebrated the virtues of the old patriarchy. Turning her back on her own arguments, she had endorsed the cultural myth from which she had once revolted and the tradition she had dismissed as anachronistic. It was a strange course, but in its very strangeness something of a representative one as well. For, after all, weren't her own alterations paralleled throughout the entire South? And didn't the change in her opinions repeat the drastic transformations of attitude that followed the Revolution? Just after the Civil War, and as we have seen just after the Revolution too, there was a feeling in the region that the plain farmer was about to seize the day. The feeling was not universal, to be sure, but it was very widespread; and it was encouraged in both periods by the recognition that certain sections of the plantation community, if not all of it, had fallen into serious difficulties. The old order seemed to be changing, making way for the new, and this necessarily stimulated the growth of utopian visions. Things did not work out as expected, however, either in John Taylor's time or Ellen Glasgow's. Hopes for the future were disappointed, as far, at least, as they involved the resurrection of subsistence farming, and it was only natural for some people to seek relief from their disappointment in a comforting dream of the past. The dominant tendency, it seemed, was toward a different kind of progressivism from the one anticipated, in which progress was identified with industrialization; and in this situation the agrarian might well feel justified in becoming a reactionary. Certainly, Ellen Glasgow felt justified. Moving across from one side of the regional tradition to the other she declared, "I was a radical when everyone else . . . was conservative, and now I am a conservative when other people appear to be radical."[77] The remark located the change that had taken place in her thinking accurately enough, but it did so with a touch of bravado that tended to distort other things. For whatever Glasgow might have liked to think, she was no more of a special case in her old age than she had been in her youth. *In This Our Life*, as we have seen, was a book written at the crossroads, a witness to the sense of disorientation suffered by its author. As such it belonged to the New South, the age of paradox and upheaval, in exactly the same way that a book like *The Voice of the People* had belonged to the optimism of an earlier period. Perhaps it would be simplistic to assume a straight equation between Ellen Glasgow in her last years and the writers, a generation younger than her, who participated in the Southern "renaissance." Quite apart from anything else, they were in closer touch with the problems of the new society than she could ever be. Still, it remains true that the dilemma with which she was eventually confronted compared with their dilemma; and that her interest in the resources of her past, or the uses of nostalgia, offered only a slightly less sophisticated version of their own.

By the time she came to write her last novel, then, Ellen Glasgow had experienced the transition from Old South to New, and translated that experience into fiction in ways that make her as much a representative of the twenties as of the immediate post-Civil War era. Through her we have returned to the moment from which we began, the decade when the Southern "renaissance" came into being; but we have returned, I hope, with a clearer perception of that moment, its nature and advantages. Among other things, we can now see perhaps that the 1920s were not that unique. There had been other crises in the history of the region, crises that had encouraged an investigation into the uses of the past quite similar to the one conducted by William Faulkner and his contemporaries. Of course, the investigation could assume a number of different forms, varying from full-blown nostalgia to a clinical detachment. The investigator might, for example, just want to emphasize the separation of the past from the present and so exacerbate the sense of loss; or he might try to discover the sources of present discontent *in* the past—a more difficult task, admittedly, but a more valuable one. Whatever he did, though, his preoccupation with history and the "source of available ideas" that it offered would be a constant, the polestar of his journey. And whatever he said, the plain farmer and fine planter would remain the men at the center of his message, the points around which the energies of his traditionalism seemed to gather. As a result, when the writers of the renaissance did begin to explore their own "postage stamp of native soil,"[78] they found that that soil was already steeped in legend, and that the strategies of exploration they could use had been anticipated by earlier Southerners. Their traditionalism, they discovered, and the terms in which that traditionalism could be expressed, had been prepared for them even if only in a rudimentary way by a line of predecessors stretching back to colonial times.

At this point it might be asked why, if this was the case, and there were such close similarities between the twenties and other moments of stress in Southern history, there had been no literature of major importance in the region before. After all, "Southern renaissance" is a pretty inaccurate term if it is meant to imply the recovery of something previously achieved. The nineteenth-century South offers few writers to compare with the New England pantheon of Emerson, Hawthorne, Longfellow, Dickinson, and Thoreau, and nothing like the rich life of the mind to be found in such places as Boston, Cambridge, or New Haven. Sometimes it seems that all it does have to offer has been described by one minor belletrist of the period, in a couplet that has become famous for its ghastly sense of the appropriate:

> Alas for the South! Her books have grown fewer—
> She never was much given to literature.[79]

For years the region was very much as H. L. Mencken once described it: a "Sahara of the Bozart" or cultural desert, where talented writers were as thin on the ground as registered Republicans. Why was this so, if the factors that encouraged the appearance of a genuinely regional literature in the 1920s were present at earlier moments in Southern history as well? Why, in short, did people like Mencken seem to be so right? In a way, if we ask the question at enough length it will begin to answer itself because the assumptions behind it will become clearer—and, I think, much more arguable. The main assumption seems to be that literature can be explained entirely in terms of historical circumstance, and its emergence or absence ascribed to laws of causality that are strict and systematically applicable. There are certain conditions, it is implied, for the existence of a major body of writing; and given the appearance of these conditions then a major body of writing must appear soon afterward. Put in this way the assumption is clearly an absurd one, which we might counter simply by saying, "Things aren't like that." Historical circumstances, we could reply, do not determine the state of literature, its presence, or its character when it is present; they merely provide a context, of positive and negative possibilities. They do not, in other words, ensure that a movement like the Southern "renaissance" *will* occur but only offer an occasion on which it *might*. This is the simplest answer we could make, and it is not a completely misleading one, either. Apart from anything else, it does remind us that the writer is more than an automaton reacting semiconsciously to events, something worth doing at a time when some literary historians have tried to reduce him to just that; and it does imply, too, that the writer's relationship with history is two way. He uses history as much as history uses him. Still, it can be misleading if we interpret it too simply, by ignoring the question of degree. For there can, surely, be different degrees of possibility. Several different periods in the history of a region may favor the emergence of a literature, admittedly: but this does not mean that the conditions they offer are equally favorable. Indeed, it would be surprising if they were. And given this we can say that, while the twenties did not differ in *kind* from other moments of crisis in the South, they did differ as far as the *extent* of the crisis was concerned.

This, I think, we have to say. There had been moments of change before in the South, or of suspected change, but they had never been quite so radical or universal as they were in the 1920s. During that period, the region was experiencing a transformation so drastic that it put into question its every way of looking at itself. The scale of the transformation was unprecedented, and what complicated the situation even more, deepening the general neurosis, was the fact that similar events were taking place across the Union. No place seemed to be secure, to offer a relative peace, because no place from the Atlantic coast to the Pacific was untouched by the mechanisms of change. This leads us to another comparison—and this time not with an earlier society or societies, but with a contemporary one. For in the twenties, as most of us know, the entire United States apart from the South was evolving through the last stages of industrialization, and completing that progress toward the urban and industrial idea that in some cases, New England's for instance, had begun over a century earlier. At that moment in time, the number of people living in towns and cities began to outnumber the rural population. It was the era of Babbitt and the managerial revolution, the "Jazz Age" with its search for a code of behavior more appropriate to the new styles of living; and how people

reacted to it generally raises some interesting points about the differ-
ences between the South and the rest of the nation, or between
Southerners and their neighbors. Here is how the historian Lawrence
Levine describes the reaction, in a recent essay on the period:

> The central paradox of American history . . . has been a belief in progress
> coupled with a dread of change; an urge towards the inevitable future
> combined with a longing for the irretrievable past; a deeply ingrained be-
> lief in America's unfolding destiny and a haunting conviction that the na-
> tion was in a state of decline. This duality has been marked throughout
> most of America's history but seldom has it been more central than during
> the decade after the First World War.[80]

As Levine sees it, there were two distinct impulses operating in the
United States during the twenties: the progressive impulse, which
had already committed the nation to mobility and change, and a
nostalgic impulse symptomatic of certain doubts it had about the
consequences of this commitment. They had been present at other
times in American history as well, but, he insists, never quite so obviously as then—when a major alteration in the social fabric was
virtually complete. For once, what Emerson had called the Party of
Hope and the Party of Memory seemed to be exercising an equally
powerful influence.

Levine's argument is a convincing one, I think, and easy to prove
as long as it is confined to the North, the Midwest, or the West. But
when the South is brought into the picture things become more
difficult—not because the argument is in any way wrong but because
its emphases then tend to be misleading. For below the Mason-Dixon
line people experienced more changes in ten years than some of their
neighbors had known in fifty. Everything was vastly accelerated there,
and this had the effect of making the sense of disorientation that much
more acute. On top of that, it made the recognition of steady progress
toward a specified goal—the articulation, in other words, of what
Levine calls "the progressive impulse"—a peculiarly difficult thing for
Southerners to manage. They had had little preparation for thinking
about progress along accepted national lines; certainly the sluggishness
of previous economic development in their region had not prepared
them for it. So while the future might be as attractive for them as it
was for other Americans, they also tended to find it much more bewildering and frightening than anyone else did. At the same time their
relationship to the past was more complicated than their neighbors'
was—partly because they were nearer to the past, or at least seemed
to be, but also on account of the unique complexion of their memories. There were areas of darkness in Southern history that were not to
be found elsewhere, at their most obvious in the story of slavery, and

these qualified Southern nostalgia with feelings of guilt and terror. Looking backward or looking forward, it scarcely mattered: the Southerner's emotions were just as painful and ambivalent in either case. And the net result of this was to translate what Levine calls "the paradox of American history" into an acute form of schizophrenia. The South, it was clear, was caught between two intolerable alternatives to an extent that other sections of the country could not really begin to appreciate. An earlier inhabitant of the region, Edgar Allan Poe, had described the state well in one of his poems.

> A voice from out the future cries
> "On, On!"—but o'er the Past
> (Dim gulf!) my spirit hovering lies
> Mute, motionless, aghast![81]

It is the intensity of Poe's tone, bordering on hysteria, I want to emphasize here, because it was precisely this kind of intensity that helped to distinguish the Southerner in the 1920s from his contemporaries. Division affected his being so deeply that it made him a special case in his time, even if not a unique one.

In not one but in two ways, then, the South presented its case with a difference in the years immediately following the First World War. It was experiencing a crisis that was similar in kind to other crises in its history and yet quite different in degree, the scope and nature of its implications. And although the outward and visible signs of this, the changes occurring in the regional landscape, invited comparison with the general mobility of the nation at the time, events were so much more accelerated and traumatic in the South that they seemed to be without parallel—and, in terms of the responses that they provoked, almost *were* without parallel. The effect of this was to make the setting at once typical and special. With a certain amount of hindsight we can say that the region in the 1920s posed ideal opportunities for the emergence of a new movement in literature—better, even, than those offered by the rest of the country during the same period. To be more exact, it supplied the perfect setting for a literature concerned mainly with the uses of history, and the network of entangling alliances that history creates. Writers could benefit from the given situation by making detailed comparisons between the old structures and the new that were replacing them, so as to arrive at specific value judgments and for the more general purpose of analyzing social change. They could study the individual with reference to the transformations taking place in his environment; and then from this study articulate a relationship between the two, the possible ways in which they shaped and affected each other. There was a past available to be mythologized and a mythology, a system of inherited argument and metaphor, ready to be used as a means of understanding and evaluating the present. It is difficult to summarize a complex situation in a few words, and especially a situation as complex as this. But perhaps we can explain the importance of the Southern context to the Southern writer, without deviating too far from the truth, by saying that one major factor was a time of unprecedented change, another the dialogue between idea and event that constituted the regional tradition; and that the body of literature now known as the Southern "renaissance" was to offer the reader a series of engagements between these two forces—demonstrations of what men can learn from history if they try hard enough.

2. The Nashville Agrarians

~~~~~~

I'll Take My Stand *and the Language of Southern Literature*

Perhaps no group of Southern writers has been more conscious of a commitment to its region, the close ties binding it to its history and changing social structure, than the group of poets, novelists, and essayists who were centered at one time in Nashville, Tennessee, and became known (for a while) as the Agrarians. Other writers, and most notably William Faulkner, may have surpassed the individual achievement of people like John Crowe Ransom, Robert Penn Warren, and Allen Tate, but Ransom, Warren, Tate, and their colleagues have had the advantage of being far more deliberately aware of their historical circumstances, and the relationship between those circumstances and their mythologizing tendencies, than any of their contemporaries. As a result their work offers the most coherent demonstration possible of the impulses that helped generate the "renaissance" of regional literature during the period between the two World Wars —and an illustration, also, of the kinds of forms and interests that that "renaissance" fostered. In a sense their fiction, verse, and essays, taken collectively, could be said to constitute what Ezra Pound once christened a "Paideuma"[1]—a center of cultural reference, that is, containing "the gristly roots of ideas that are in action" and as such available for general development. And for this reason, if for no other, any account of the modern literature of the South must begin with them.

The story of how the Nashville Agrarians came to be aware of their involvement in their region has been told often enough and at some length; but it is worth retelling.[2] The story begins in 1915, when a small group of writers, students, and *littérateurs*, most of whom were associated with Vanderbilt University, began to meet once or twice every week for discussions on philosophy and literature. Scattered by the war, they reassembled in the autumn of 1919, and, although the nominal head was a local eccentric named Sidney Mttron Hirsch, it soon became clear that the group depended for its intellectual strength on John Crowe Ransom, then a teacher at Vanderbilt, and three students: Donald Davidson, Robert Penn Warren, and Allen Tate. Eventually, in 1922, the group began publishing *The Fugitive*, a small poetry magazine, the title of which referred, among other things, to the self-conscious cosmopolitanism of the contributors and their opposition to the idea of a regional literature as such. "The Fugitives flee from nothing faster," Ransom declared in the first issue, "than from the high-caste Brahmins of the Old South."[3] Donald Davidson went even further. For when the editor of *Poetry*, Harriet Monroe, appealed to American writers for a "strongly localized indigenous art," he replied by ridiculing the very concept of a Southern literature. The Southern tradition, he asserted, could be "called a tradition only when looked at through the haze of a generous imagination."[4] It was mediocre and would appeal to none but mediocrities.

Statements like this read ironically now, because it did not take long for Davidson and other Fugitives to change their tune and become preoccupied with the very regionalism they had begun by repudiating. A number of events conspired to bring about this change of opinion. One of these, the pressures created by accelerated social development, has been mentioned already. But at least as significant as this larger development was a personal experience shared by a few of the more distinguished members of the group. By the end of 1925, *The Fugitive* had ceased publication, and several of its former contributors and editors were leaving the South, either for New York or for Europe. The effects of this move were crucial. Passing from a fairly homogeneous and static community, which they had accepted without thinking, to a society with far more dynamic notions of the human, people like Tate and Warren became witnesses to the vaster change. They experienced in their own lives a version of the metamorphosis from old into new that was taking place all around them; and they reacted to it, perhaps predictably, by discovering how attached they really were to the old. The South, once these ex-Fugitives were separated from it, was translated into what Louis D. Rubin has called a "faraway country"[5]—an alternative, apotheosized by distance, to the urban complexes of New York, Paris, and London.

This alteration took place over a number of years, of course, but things came to a head in the late twenties with the Scopes trial. As soon as the trial began, the benighted South became the butt of every American satirist from Mencken downward, and the Tennessee anti-evolution law was cited as a conclusive instance of regional backwardness. Extremes of reaction tend to breed their own extremes of counter-reaction, so it was not surprising that many Southerners, who would not otherwise have dreamed of doing so, leaped to the defense of their region and the law. Some of the ex-Fugitives in particular professed to see in the case a valuable paradigm of Southern rootedness, attachment to the pedagogical and metaphysical implications of a traditional culture. But in their case at least this was not simply a political act, a way of getting back at the satirists. On the contrary, what they did was to think out their situation in response to the new challenge, and establish clearly in their own minds the nature of their loyalties. Then and only then, when they were sure that they held many of the beliefs being ridiculed, did they move into the debate. John Crowe Ransom began work on a book called *God Without Thunder,* which was to use religious myth to counter the deification of science. Donald Davidson, once again going a step further than Ransom in explicitness, published a series of articles in defense of fundamentalism; and Allen Tate, declaring that he had "attacked the South for the last time,"[6] began a lifelong search for spiritual roots that was to lead eventually to the composition of his "Ode to the Confederate Dead." Gradually, as Ransom and Tate and Davidson recognized the similarity of their new concerns, they began to draw together again and to attract other allies, some of them from among their former acquaintances at Vanderbilt. The result was the formation in 1926 or 1927[7] of a loose but mutually profitable association of individuals who shared, and to some extent still do share, concerns that are distinctively Southern. As one commentator has described it, in charting the transformation of the Fugitive group into the Agrarian, "the Fugitives, who had begun in flight from the South, stood finally at the very center of the new historical focus in Southern literature."[8]

Just what this change meant was demonstrated to the reading public a few years later, in 1930, when twelve of the Agrarians collaborated in writing a manifesto, *I'll Take My Stand,*[9] which took as its thesis the enormous superiority of the Southern and rural mode of life to the one practiced in the cities of the North. The twelve contributors were: Ransom, Davidson, Tate, and Warren; four other creative writers, Andrew Nelson Lytle, John Gould Fletcher, John Donald Wade, and Stark Young; a historian, Frank Owsley; a psychologist, Lyle Lanier; a journalist, Henry Kline; and a political scientist, Herman Nixon. Given the differences in their disciplines, their approaches were necessarily dissimilar, and they chose different aspects of Southern history and society to describe. But they were drawn together by a common hatred of contemporary society in all its aspects—its economy geared to production for profit, its restless pursuit of change and assumption of limitless power over nature, even its social and moral philosophies of liberalism, relativism, and the centralization of power. And their sense of a shared commitment was confirmed by their positive beliefs —and in particular by their conviction that the best kind of society is one "in which agriculture is the leading vocation, whether for wealth, for pleasure, or for prestige."[10]

It is this, in fact, the evaluation of the new industrial state in terms of the old agricultural society—and more specifically in terms of rural images supplied by the Old Confederacy—which makes the symposium a Southern as well as an agrarian one. And the advantages to be reaped from this rich accumulation of metaphor are perhaps obvious:

the writers can then benefit from a sense of arguing for something concrete and demonstrably possible instead of just against a given set of facts. They can anchor their argument, as it were, in time and space. But there is a less obvious *dis*advantage accruing to any use in discursive argument of an alternative, such as the Southern one, which is compounded equally of history and myth: which is the disadvantage of never quite knowing if one is dealing with a poetic metaphor, a system of purely imaginative reference, or going beyond this to make substantial economic proposals. Did the old Southern society, or rather societies, that the Agrarians describe really exist or did they not? Are they still feasible or aren't they? At times the answer is a more or less qualified yes and at others it appears to be an unqualified no.[11] This is one radical contradiction existing within individual essays and the symposium as a whole, and it is by no means the only one. There are several others, stemming from disagreement about, or uncertainty as to, the exact nature of the agrarian alternative being offered, which, taken together, might well have proved fatal to the entire argument. In the event, they do not, and the fact that they do not is really attributable to one thing—the skill with which the twelve contributors to the symposium deploy the traditional rhetoric of their region, first marshaled into a system of verbal defense by apologists like John Taylor of Caroline. What the Agrarians do, effectively, is use their language to minimize the divisions between metaphor and fact and so encourage a belief in the *possible* existence of all that is being celebrated. The world or worlds described as characteristically Southern in *I'll Take My Stand*, the implication is, might have existed, ought to have existed, and, with the help of a willing suspension of disbelief induced by the rhetoric, do seem to exist while the reader reads the book.

Before examining this rhetoric, however, it might be useful to look briefly at the substance of the Agrarians' argument, if only because that argument acts as a gloss to so many novels and poems of the "renaissance." It explains what other Southern books tend merely to invoke or commemorate. And what it explains first of all is the major premise of every essay—that the true and significant in experience can be learned only from the "teachings of history." History, so the argument goes, communicates to us a "humble sense of man's precarious position in the universe" and reminds us that "evil is the common lot of the race." Man, it seems, is radically limited, and he learns this by examining his past. This is a difficult, a virtually impossible, lesson to learn in an advanced industrial society because it has no contact with that past. It has lost touch with the concrete processes of history, and reveals this by dealing with problems "in an abstract

fashion"—without relating them, that is, to personal or racial experience. The rural community presents quite a different case. There the
constant struggle with the environment, in which the victories are
invariably partial, encourages a salutary recognition of human limits,
which in turn fosters a dependence on what has been proved to be
possible by previous experience and "traditional background." And
this tendency to accept the teachings of history is reinforced by what
is called the "organic"[12] development characteristic of agricultural societies. They evolve gradually, at an almost infinitesimal pace, and
the result is that a radical break with the past never occurs. Its store
of experience is always there for use.

The idea of the human, and of the perfect social structure, that
grows out of this commitment to historical experience is presented in
some detail in the various essays. The human being, it is argued, is a
complex creature requiring the kind of "imaginatively balanced life"
that is only available to him in a rural society. He is at once an individual, a member of a particular community, and a member of the
human race, and he requires consideration on each of these levels.
His work activities, for example, must not only answer his material
needs but provide the basis for proper moral conduct as well—a dual
requirement that only agricultural labor, with its customary and various duties, appears to fulfill. That conduct must itself draw its strength
from an ethical system that appeals to the emotional side of man, as
well as his intellect, to do which it has to be founded on the local and
familial, the injunctions of the blood rather than those of abstract
law; and again the rural community, with its traditional codes of value
and behavior, seems to be the only one to fit the bill. Even in the area
of religious belief, apparently, it offers the one form of life that satisfies the demands of the "whole man"[13] by generating a mode of worship, thoroughly integrated with the routines of weekday life, which
depends on ritual as much as doctrine, faith as well as reason.

This commitment to the concept of an interdependent organism reappears in the Agrarians' discussion of the various other social structures available to man, and defines the scope of their critique of industrialism. The new industrial state is dismissed essentially because
it represents total dislocation and encourages a radical dissociation of
the personality: men in towns and cities, it is argued, become functions
rather than men. Their education, for instance, with its disconnected
curriculum and "top-heavy" classes, tends to produce specialists rather
than "men of the world" with "a balanced character"; and their subsequent involvement in a "jungle of speculation" in which periods of
"stimulation and depression" follow one another in an "aimless flux"
only takes this process a stage further. Coinciding with this is a col-

lapse of the moral sensibility, brought about by its division into "contradictory halves." On the one hand, the doctrine of progress promotes the conviction that man's power over nature is complete: but on the other a suspicion that he is "still unable to control the elements" is hard to suppress whatever the effort. These conflicting beliefs encourage the growth of quite irreconcilable systems of value and end by reducing the psyche to bewildered impotence. Man in industrial society, as the Agrarians see it, is emasculated, a half man in a half society; and if he has any religion at all that is a "half-religion," too, which ignores mysticism in favor of the partial truths of "naturalism and practicality."[14]

What I have said so far about *I'll Take My Stand,* or rather the paraphrase I have tried to make of its argument, might give the impression that it is a temperate socioeconomic analysis, an account of contemporary problems that is controversial only in its tendencies and not in its tone. That, of course, is not so; and the reason it is not brings us back to the rhetoric, the use of language in the symposium to conceal discrepancies and turn a defensive posture into a positively aggressive one. The case presented for the rural life by the Agrarians is inseparable, finally, from the words in which it is put, because it is the words that make the case effective and memorable—occupying a sort of unique hinterland between fact and fiction. Let me take as an example of what I mean the basic rhetorical device of most of the essays. This is simple and, within the context of the regional tradition, familiar as well. But it is nonetheless striking for that. It involves a series of broad contrasts between a South characterized as mature and "seasoned," an old society and a society good because it is old, and a North which is dismissed as "immature" or "primitive."[15] As far as historical authenticity or logic are concerned, the contrast is a pretty dubious one. Usually, though, the reader cannot help being moved by it, conditioned even—and this if only because it is assumed more than asserted, as part of the hidden structure of the argument. It is there as a force in the language, creating certain kinds of vocabulary and metaphor, rather than as a point to be considered and contested. We may guess at its presence from the recurrent association of the South with the idea of antiquity, the civilizations of Egypt, Greece, and Rome, and from a pervasive tendency to invest this idea with notions of moral significance. Alternatively, we may suspect that it is responsible for the reversal of the normal connotations of certain words— the kind of reversal, for example, that enables one writer to dismiss "progress" as "a comparatively modern idea," using "modern" as if it were a term of abuse, or another to juxtapose "industrial" and "cultural" as though they were antonyms.[16] But such guesses and suspicions are not normally enough to provoke our full recognition of what is happening—the types of arguments that are being assumed—and failing this the language will have its intended effect on us. We will have been made that much more sympathetic toward the standpoint from which the defense of the South is made, and the attack on the North launched.

It is, anyway, on the assumptions made at this level of the language that the portraits of the two regions depend; including the more detailed and deliberately composed portraits that occur at irregular intervals throughout the symposium. Accepting them, we are more likely to accept the Agrarians' description of the North as a barbaric place, lacking any knowledge of the "amenities of life." The Northern states can be, and are, equated with visions of dark Satanic mills, and these in turn with a form of existence so rudimentary as to approach the infantile—in which all men are reduced to "boys" or "adolescents" and all life to a "jungle" of conflicting impulses. In a significant reversal of the usual associations, the urban community can even be defined as savage, and its concern with "simplifying, standardising, and equalising"[17] ascribed to an atavistic dislike of the different. As befits a savage state, its members are then said to wage unrelenting war on nature, each other, and on the various societies located around them. They lead a life that is portrayed by the Agrarians in almost Hobbesian terms, as nasty, brutish, and short. For the Agrarians, though, if not for Hobbes, such a life is not at all normal; and the sense that it is not provokes another series of regional contrasts, which stem from the "old"-"new" comparison but are rather different in some of their connotations. This is the series that identifies the South with an organic and spontaneous style of existence, and the North with artifice. Thanks to it, the agricultural community can be said to have "roots . . . fixed . . . somewhere . . . between the rocks and in the shade of the trees"[18] and to grow naturally with the help of an earth presented as a kind of lover. The state of perpetual conflict identified with the town and factory seems miraculously to disappear, as does the sense of estrangement from nature that is its necessary result; and man and his environment are presented in a relationship so harmonious as to make them describable in exactly the same terms of "grace" and "bounty," "magnanimity" and "tranquillity." It is a nice turn given to the rhetoric, and an important one, by means of which the association of the South with antiquity, and the sanctions of men, leads the essayists to connect it also with the fresh and vital—and so with the benevolence of nature.

Of course, this emphasis on the natural can lead the Agrarians to present the Old South occasionally as if it were a version of the pastoral—a temptation to which they were not the first or the last to succumb. This it does in the case of Frank Owsley, whose portrait of the Southern farm seems to derive more from literature—and idyllic celebrations of the shepherd's life—than from experience. We can almost hear the echoes of Gray and Wordsworth in a passage like the following.

> Each word, name, sound, had grown from the soil and had behind it sweet memory, stirring adventure, and ofttimes stark tragedy. . . . The houses were homes, where families lived . . . working together, . . . when death came, they were buried in their own lonely peaceful graveyards, to await doomsday together.[19]

Owsley is simply relying on received concepts and images here, to supply the sort of positive energies to his description which he is unable to generate himself. Memory is doing all the work for him, his own memory and the reader's, filling in the gaps and supplying the associations at which the words merely gesture. And this happens all too often in the symposium, an illustration of what Southern rhetoric can do at its worst: we are almost returned in such cases to the evasive tactics of the magnolia-blossom school of writers or the feeble epigones of Thomas Jefferson. Fortunately, though, it does not occur all the time. There are a few passages in *I'll Take My Stand* in which the uses of the rural life are realized with more immediacy, a few landscapes that are individually understood and authentically rendered. Andrew Nelson Lytle's account of the rituals of a small farm is a good example of these.

> Before dawn the rooster and the farmer feel the tremendous silence, chilling and filling the gap between night and day. He gets up, makes the fires, and rings the rising bell. He could arouse the family with his voice, but it has been the custom to ring the bell; so every morning it sounds out, taking its place among the other bells in the neighborhood. . . . One or two of the girls set out with their milk-pails to the barn, where the cows have been kept overnight. There is a very elaborate process to go through with in milking. First, the cow must be fed to occupy her attention; next, the milker kneels or sits on a bucket and washes the bag. . . . After the bag is clean, the milking begins. There is always a variation to this ritual. When the calf is young, the cow holds back her milk for it; so the calf is allowed to suck a little first, some from each teat, loosening the milk with uniformity, and then is pulled off. . . . This done, the milking begins. The left hand holds the pail, while the right does the work, or it may be the reverse. The hand hits the bag tenderly, grabs the teat, and then closes the fingers about it, not altogether but in echelon.[20]

In a way this description has its own literary ancestry, too: the reader can hardly help noticing the parallels with the milking scenes in *Tess*

of the D'Urbervilles, for instance, which demonstrate a similar concern
with the minute particulars of an activity raised to the level of ceremony. But here the associations merely add to an experience that is
directly apprehended: the meaning grows out of the dramatic action,
and its impact is in direct proportion to the force with which that
action is described. In Owsley's case, as we have seen, the writer relies
on previous literature to apprehend his subject for him, and communicate its meanings. Owsley, we could say, allows himself to be
used by his tradition, because he is limited to its conventional idiom;
whereas Lytle makes a genuine attempt to *use* it.

Having once established the South as a "natural" society, and the
North as its "unnatural" enemy, the Agrarians then develop this contrast in a number of different ways. Or perhaps it would be more accurate to say that one series of metaphors generates another in a
process that often seems to be never ending. The "old"-"new" contrast
leads to the "natural"-"unnatural" contrast, and this in turn explains
a perpetual tendency to associate the rural life with health and the
industrial life with disease; or to insist that the Old South realized a
harmony and balance quite beyond the scope of the New. New South
and industrialized North alike are characterized by flux and blur—a
radical instability accepted as the only principle governing the forms
of life. It is on the basis of assumptions such as these that the Agrarians can then renew the familiar Southern attack on the "isms" of the
North, which, they argue, produce only "internal dissension" and
eventually revolution.[21] Disorder, they follow their ancestors in pro-
claiming, is the inevitable product of the industrial order. There is
a curious paradox here, in the description of the psychic and political
consequences of urban life, which recalls the contradictions inherent in the stereotype of the Yankee. Like the Yankee, the man whom
the Agrarians describe as being committed to the life style of the
town is condemned for what are apparently two quite different things
—his materialism and his idealism. At once a "robot" pursuing specifically materialist ends and a theorist who tries to impose doctrin-
naire programs on the "complexities of life,"[22] he demonstrates that
peculiar combination of avarice and abstraction that William Faulkner
was to dramatize in the character of Flem Snopes. The comparisons
with the Yankee and Snopes possibly explain the nature of the paradox. For all three—the Yankee of Southern legend, the hero-villain of
Faulkner's trilogy, and the *bête noire* of the Agrarian symposium—
are conceived of as *representative* failures, as figures increate with
myth who are intended to map out for us the spiritual geography of
their surroundings. Their personalities are split, certainly, but that
does not make them eccentrics; still less does it make them unaccept-

able. And this is because they have been split by the disintegrative nature of their environment, the city (or in Flem's case, the urban idea), which is presented both as a "juggernaut," a "mass-production factory" churning out products rather than people, and as a kind of dreamland, something unreal and intangible. The ultimate irony, implicit in all these portraits, is that a society that prides itself on its realism, its deliberate attachment to the facts of life, and that sacrifices so much in the name of these facts, turns out to be founded on an illusion. It represents a failure to recognize what the true and significant in experience is; and the "abstract . . . pale creatures"[23] who commit themselves to it, deprived as they are therefore of any sense of completeness, demonstrate just how much it has failed.

Completeness, the notion of human wholeness: this in itself suggests that the naturalness celebrated by the Agrarians is the naturalness of the humanist rather than the primitivist. If it were otherwise, the "old," or traditional, and the "natural" could hardly be equated. Because it is so, a natural society, it is assumed, is one in which the complex demands of each individual are satisfied as far as is humanly possible.[24] And not only assumed: the initial premise, that "the only reality . . . worth considering is that of human beings which associate together" is stated quite clearly—and matched with the conclusion that the "capitalistic system . . . does not offer a satisfying substitute in human values"[25] for the essentially humane order of agrarianism. So the idea of the organic engages with the idea of the whole man; and this enables nearly all the contributors to the symposium to bring a further set of rhetorical counters into play. We need only return to the passage quoted from Owsley for a moment to see what they are. "The houses were homes, where families lived . . . working together": that establishes the general tendency, a series of references associating the Old South with the values of home, hearth, and family.[26] The whole man is the humane man, and the humane man is, as he was in the work of John Pendleton Kennedy, an altar- and fireside-defending man. He is the center and paradigm of an organic social group. That much is clear. But what is not at all clear, making Owsley's large rhetorical gestures peculiarly appropriate in this context, is the exact complexion of such a group—and, consequently, the sort of life style to which Southern humanism leads. It is easy enough to agree that the Old South encouraged the domestic virtues, a loyalty to roots and an affection for the past, and to claim that "the greatest, most luminous defence of any point of view is its noble embodiment in persons"[27] such as the good family man. It is not so easy, however, to decide just what this domesticity involves, or to include references to the family man that come together in a single and homogenous portrait. The doubleness of the regional tradition sees to that. Kennedy himself found it a difficult task, and divided his attention equally between farm and plantation; so did people as different as John Calhoun and Ellen Glasgow. It is hardly surprising, then, that the twelve Agrarians should experience even greater difficulties, and end by drawing a picture of the old Southern home that is notable chiefly for its ambivalence.

One familiar version of the old home is to be found in Donald Davidson's contribution to the symposium, "A Mirror for Artists." His essay, as its title implies, is principally concerned with assessing different societies in terms of the opportunities they make available to the creative intelligence: the artist is in this sense a "mirror" to his age, while his contemporaries in turn supply him with a "mirror" for his own plight. The subject necessarily involves Davidson, though, in an analysis of larger social differences, and it is at this point that his acceptance of an essentially aristocratic notion of the Old South is revealed. For him the complete man, whether artist or otherwise, is the "compleat gentleman" of the Elizabethan manuals of behavior. He accepts the notion of gentility as his lodestar, and it is this acceptance that dictates his terms of reference: his continual appeal, for instance, to what he calls "classical" society—a term he associates equally, and rather confusingly, with the reigns of Elizabeth and the early Hanoverians, the cultures of ancient Greece and Rome. At a more fundamental level, it also explains the kind of persona he adopts for the course of the essay. For in order to demonstrate his argument he becomes, to all intents and purposes, the very gentleman with a "genuine taste for oratory" that he is celebrating. The style is adapted to fit the assumed character with results that are illustrated well, I think, by the following, which is taken from the conclusion to the essay.

> The artist should not forget that in these times he is called on to play the part both of a person and of an artist. Of the two, that of the person is more immediately important. As an artist he will do his best to flee the infection of our times, to stand for decentralization in the arts, to resist with every atom of his strength the false gospels of art as a luxury. . . . But he cannot wage this fight by remaining on his perch as an artist. He must be a person first of all . . . less of an artist . . . in that general direction his duty lies.[28]

There is a feeling of almost Johnsonian certainty here, a product of the elaborate inversions and grandiloquent antitheses into which the prose is wrought. With just the right amount of incantatory force the writer moves toward a conclusion, the justice of which, he assumes, will be accepted by all sensible men. The staple idiom of the essay may be common to all the contributions to *I'll Take My Stand;* indeed,

the references to disease in this passage, and the plea for decentraliza-
tion, suggest that it is. But Davidson has rung his own changes on it,
and in the process expressed a personal version of the rural theme.
Ultimately, it is possible to say, the order he is talking about is *there*
in the movement of his sentences—where security and stylishness
have found their appropriate form.

Something similar could be said of the essay written for the symposium by Andrew Nelson Lytle—with the qualification, the radical
qualification, that the man at the center here is a farmer rather than a
gentleman planter. The reader is being reintroduced to the Jeffersonian norms in this essay, and the metaphors Lytle chooses for his introduction are drawn from the sights and sounds of the countryside
rather than the library. The very title he chooses for his contribution,
"The Hind Tit," illustrates his strategy. It refers, Lytle tells us, to the
runt pig, the feeblest member of the litter, who is "squeezed and
tricked out of the best places at the side" of the sow and "forced to
take the little hind tit for nourishment."[29] A folk metaphor for any
exploited person or group, it becomes his favorite way of defining the
place of the countryman in the changing social structure of the South:
but at least as important as this is its function in establishing the tone,
a sense of belonging to the soil and the rural community that is vital
to our conception of his persona. It has the same purpose, in fact, as
the closing words of the essay—which are its equal for deliberate
earthiness. Lytle is calling on all farmers to stick to the life they know,
and the reason he gives for this advice, simple enough though it is, is
a calculated attempt to identify himself with them.

> As for those countrymen who have not gone so deeply in the money econ-
> omy, let them hold to their agrarian fragments and bind them together,
> for reconstructed fragments are better than a strange newness which does
> not belong. It is our own, and if we have to spit in the water-bucket to
> keep it our own, we had better do it.[30]

The passage has a sting in its tail, establishing the writer's allegiances.
His life, the implication is, is the same as the farmer's life; his words,
their words. Even his enemies turn out to be their enemies. For the
people Lytle chooses to criticize, and so locate the virtues of his
country folk, are quite different from the ones chosen by Davidson.
In Davidson's essay the epitome of urban life is the big businessman,
whose interest in art is strictly financial and who judges artists as he
does everybody else, by the amount of money they make. Lytle, however, has other interests to defend, which can only be defined in opposition to other characters. The people he picks out for attack, as the
enemies of the old sanctions, are the idle and effeminate—those who
do not work at all rather than those who work only in a certain way.

The effete poetaster or dilettante replaces the businessman as satirical butt, because he offers a far more effective contrast to the robust virtues of the poor farmer. He has the kind of lethargy and corrupt sophistication that can place Lytle's rustics in an appropriately flattering light. If he sounds, as a result, as much like Davidson's *hero* as his villain, this is because he has some of the qualities that Davidson positively admires: leisureliness, for example, and a taste for the amenities of life. Virtues in "A Mirror for Artists," they have now undergone a sea change. The populist context of "The Hind Tit" has transformed them into vices; and that in itself is a measure of the distance between the two essays.

The division of interest that emerges when we compare "A Mirror for Artists" with "The Hind Tit" tends to run through the whole symposium. John Crowe Ransom, for example, likes to dwell on the "eighteenth-century social arts" of the Old South, its elaborate manners and models of courtesy; whereas Robert Penn Warren describes *his* South in terms of the "garden and . . . cotton patch," and a life whose every aspect is "rooted in the soil."[31] As a result they hardly seem to be talking about the same place. Other contributors cannot even confine themselves to the same place for the course of their essay. Thus Owsley spends some of his time praising the "yeomanry," who "reeked of the soil, of the plow and spade," and the rest of it in descriptions of the "fine balls and parties" held by the genteel planter. Admittedly, he tries to relate the two figures in a single image of the Good Life—a life that, he says, is "leisurely and unhurried." But this, vague as it is, seems to be a pretty flimsy basis for any close identification; and in any case it is contradicted by the portrait he draws elsewhere of the poor farmer—as a man wrestling "with virgin soil and forests," his "hands . . . rough with guiding the plow."[32] It is difficult to see how anyone can combine the labors of a Hercules with the leisureliness of a Horace, and this difficulty makes Owsley's argument an unconvincing one, more of a rationalization than a defense. The only thing that can be said in its favor is that it does at least represent an attempt to reconcile a basic contradiction of the book; in most other cases this contradiction is ignored completely, or acknowledged only to be dismissed.

So there are two contradictions at the heart of *I'll Take My Stand*, contradictions that have remained a problem for the Agrarians and other writers in the South ever since. One owes its existence to the doubleness of the regional tradition, the debate that started nearly three centuries ago between advocates of farm and plantation. And the other, which I mentioned earlier, is the direct result of an inability on the contributors' part—or perhaps a positive unwillingness—to distinguish between idea and fact. At one moment the reader will be told that it is a metaphor he is being offered, a system of values that existed as no more than one possibility among several others during ante-bellum times. The farm or the plantation, in other words, is described as an imaginative *idea*. But at the next he is told quite the opposite, that the Golden Age and the civilization of the Old South were one and the same thing. The past can sometimes present a mellow landscape to the Agrarians, with every discomforting feature blurred by distance; and when it does they seem tempted to equate history with its mythical dimension, the idea of old times with the things those old times really achieved. Necessarily this creates fresh confusions, gaps and inconsistent arguments designed to fill in those gaps, and they have a lot to do with the typicality of the Agrarian argument as well. They are as much of a reason for its status as a representative case, in fact, as its more positive energies are.

That *I'll Take My Stand* does have more positive energies, though, is something we should never lose sight of, amid all the talk about its contradictoriness and confusion. Indeed, a case might even be made for seeing the confusion and the energy as inseparable. For the book is above all a lively source work—a "Paideuma," to use Pound's word again, bristling with ideas—and it is this precisely because it covers so much of the regional tradition, warts, inconsistencies, and all, opening up more possibilities than it can conveniently pursue. Its unevenness is a part of its achievement, as an "open" work so suggestive in what it says that often all other Southern writers seem to do is extend it by providing a commentary on its text. And not only in what it says. How it says it is just as suggestive, in the sense that its uses of language supply an exemplary strategy, a series of correlatives for the regional debate. Language, the Agrarians show—that is, *the inherited rhetoric at the disposal of every Southern writer*—can be employed in one of two ways: to conceal meaning, by glossing over weaknesses in the argument, or to enact it and so provide a sort of verbal equivalent for the life style the writer is honoring. It can blur things or alternatively it can explore and dramatize them. We have seen something of both techniques already, how they work in the various essays, and there is no need to spend much more time on them now. Before leaving the subject, though, there is one aspect of the Agrarians' use of language that I would like to reemphasize, because it is so much a part of their representativeness. I am referring to the way in which they use words occasionally to establish what is of equal significance in otherwise conflicting ideals—what is shared by them. There is, after all, an area of common ground where the notions of good farmer and fine planter meet. It is painfully vague and undemarcated, but it is still there, in the commitment both demonstrate to the natural in the sense of the genuinely humane, the demands and responsibilities of the mature, independent, yet socially oriented "whole man." And it is this common ground that the language discovers. It locates this one area of genuine consensus in the essays even while it creates the impression, and the largely false impression at that, that there are many more besides, or that the area is much more clearly defined than it is. This may not sound like much: but only, I think, until we realize what it means. What it means is that for once the Agrarians use words, the common idiom of their region, to earn agreement rather than just assume it or pretend to it. Arriving at this idea, of a complete personality that realizes itself in the developing rituals of the group, they find something they can all defend without qualification—a minimal belief, as it were, on which they and other writers in the South can all take their stand.

New Assessments: The Agrarianism of the Agrarians

Agreement is one thing, and identification another. The Agrarians may certainly have agreed that their stand was a humanist one, but they could still disagree about the priorities established by this humanism, and consequently about the nature of a genuinely humane society. Within the context of a shared commitment to their region, there remained differences that no amount of verbal or argumentative skill could settle. The differences become particularly obvious when we leave *I'll Take My Stand* to look at the work of individual members of the group, how they conceived of agrarianism both before the symposium was published and after. Indeed, the interest of their work lies partly in this, that it is so various; the variousness serving to remind us, even if nothing else did, that the relationship between a writer and his inheritance is a reciprocal one, occasioning activity and change on both sides. For while it is the South that provides the tradition, it is the Southern writer who transforms that tradition into a new system of reference for his work—and, in the process, forces it to live and grow. It relies on him for survival, just as much as he relies on it for stimulus—a "source of available ideas" and inspiration. In a sense it also relies on him for coherence, since one result of the richness of the Southern tradition is that it always tends toward the self-contradictory; the conflicting implications of farm and plantation are alone enough to ensure that. As an ideology to be transmitted or a consistent system of belief it hardly exists at all, beyond the broad reference to the humane; and really it depends on the convictions and ability of the individual writer for such unity as it may possess. It can

be coherent, rather than suggestive, only at the level of personal interpretation.

Four of the Agrarians stand out from the rest because of the interest
their interpretations offer in this respect. Two of them, John Crowe
Ransom and Donald Davidson, are chiefly poets; and two, Allen Tate
and Robert Penn Warren, have written both fiction and verse. Their
achievements are not commensurate, of course, and they are not precisely because they are trying to do something more than just transmit
their inheritance and describe their environment. They are struggling
to formulate values as well, to discover an authentic relationship between themselves and their circumstances in the South—and to do this
by reshaping those circumstances and integrating them into their own
"structures of feeling" (to use a phrase coined by Raymond Williams)
and belief. This raises an interesting question. John Crowe Ransom
is clearly superior as a poet to, say, Donald Davidson. Has this superiority anything at all to do with the ways in which the two writers
deal with their given circumstances? Do the differences to be found
in their uses of their social and historical context account, or help to
account, for the differences in the sheer quality of their work? If the
answer is yes, then obviously to discuss these and other writers with
reference to their Southern-ness becomes an evaluative task as well
as a descriptive one; placing a writer in his tradition means assessing
and defining him at one and the same time. But to find out whether
it is yes or not, and whether if it is yes that "yes" carries any qualifications with it, we shall have to look at what Davidson, Ransom, and
the others wrote in some more detail. We shall have to go back, as
we should, to the particular text.

The Compleat Gentleman: John Crowe Ransom

There are several reasons for looking at the work of John Crowe
Ransom first among the Agrarians. One reason is simply that he is an
extraordinarily fine poet whose reputation among modern American
writers has remained secure for the last thirty or forty years: his verse
has not been the victim of those rapid alterations of critical opinion
that have characterized criticism of Allen Tate, for example.[33] Another
is that he was always a kind of father figure to writers like Tate,
Davidson, and Warren—first as a teacher at Vanderbilt and subsequently as editor of the *Kenyon Review,* a journal dedicated chiefly
to the propagation of the New Criticism. And Ransom, not one to
neglect a role that implied obligation as well as honor, returned the
compliment by demonstrating an almost paternal interest in the
careers of his colleagues—colleagues who were, in fact, only slightly
younger than himself. They may soon have dissociated themselves

from his ideas and methods, but that never prevented him from maintaining a certain benevolent interest in their work. His appreciation of Allen Tate, written in honor of Tate's sixtieth birthday, is characteristic of this and besides leads us into the heart of his own attitude toward experience. For in this essay Ransom offers the reader a detailed examination of the *character* of his subject, as much as of his literary achievement. He makes us see what he thinks of Tate not only as a poet and novelist but also as a man, and what he thinks of him is defined in principle in the opening sentence: "The poet, the thinker, the whole man—Allen Tate's personality is greatly distinguished in our time."[34] "The whole man": that is essentially how Ransom presents Tate, and all whom he admires. No praise could be warmer from a person for whom the ideal of human completeness remained a source of continual inspiration—such inspiration, in fact, that it would not be too much to say Ransom's entire work depends on a comparison between this ideal and the sense of fragmentation he associated with more recent events.

Ransom's conception of the whole man does not involve any simplification of experience. On the contrary, its complex and specific nature is constantly emphasized. This is the result, largely, of his belief in the dual nature of the human personality, its indebtedness to both the reason and the sensibility. The reason, as Ransom sees it, man employs in his attempts to understand experience ,to discover and use the universal patterns latent in the "world's body." The sensibility on the other hand simply enables him to enjoy experience, the fine qualities of particulars, including all those that cannot be absorbed into any pattern formulated by the rational element.[35] So far what Ransom has to say may sound thoroughly commonplace, a hardly individualized version of a generally held idea. What distinguishes his argument, though, is that he manages to relate this conventional distinction to his comparative analysis of agrarian and industrial societies, and to do so in detail. The thesis that nearly all of his writing sets out to prove, in one way or another, is that only in a traditional and rural society—the kind of society that is epitomized for Ransom by the antebellum South—can the human being achieve the completeness that comes from exercising the sensibility and the reason with equal ease. With the rise of science and industrialism, the thesis continues, these two elements have become dissociated. Science and industry demand control of nature, and in pursuance of this man has had to exploit his reason and deny his sensibility. The image of the whole man, consequently, has been replaced by a concept of personality that emphasises its "appetitive and economic"[36] functions at the expense of everything else.

In the course of his career Ransom has managed to apply the implications of this change to his analysis of several kinds of human activity, including the broad activities of work and leisure. Labor in a traditional society, for example, is described in essay after essay as performing "one of the happy functions of human life." This, so the argument goes, is because agriculture is the major form of employment in that society; and agriculture satisfies not just the reason of man, by supplying him with the requisite "material product," but his sensibility as well. Both the "infinite variety of nature" that precludes routinized work and the leisurely pace at which agricultural duties are usually conducted tend to make farming a "rich, free and delicate aesthetic experience." The contrast offered by the industrial state, where the "whole duty of man . . . is . . . to increase . . . production" and nothing else, is made patently clear; and the contrast is sustained even when tools are downed. For like most of the Agrarians, Ransom insists that the cultural forms characteristic of any particular system are integrally related to the forms of its economic life, and so the "right attitude to nature" that rural labor is said to promote is extended into a definition of its artwork as well. The arts in a traditional community satisfy the two sides of human nature just as its agrarian experience does, in the sense that they demonstrate "the power of the material world to receive a rational structure and still maintain its particularity."[37] Belonging essentially to what is called a "classical" mode of imitation, they manage to reflect both the constant and the contingent elements in life; whereas the artistic forms generated by an urban society cannot help but betray a bias in favor of one element or the other.

An inevitable consequence of Ransom's commitment to the idea of a unity of personality is that his discussion of one function of the consciousness tends to fade imperceptibly into a discussion of its other functions, so his essays on aesthetics are often transformed into essays on ethics about halfway through. And this particular tendency is reinforced by Ransom's own insistence that the only satisfactory system of morality—the kind of system, essentially, that is characteristic of a rural environment—is one that appeals to the aesthetic sense as much as the conscience. The beautiful and the good then become inseparable. His argument is an elaborate one here, requiring an illustration; and in this case his own favorite illustration, drawn from sexual relationships, is as good a one as any. As Ransom sees it, the sexual relationship in a traditional society is defined by the ceremony of courtship, and the slow and circuitous pursuit of the desired one partly in the name of self-discipline, as a demonstration of the belief that effects the ritualization of the desire. The ceremony is devised that man is not the slave of his senses but their master, who can pace them as he will. But that is not the sole reason for its existence. It satisfies not only the conscience but the sensibility too, with an "infinite variety of innocent experience" that a more precipitate relationship would make impossible. In other words, the traditional man commits himself to the principle of courtship so as to train the instincts *and* so as to enjoy the subtler forms of pleasure it makes available to him —the detached contemplation of the object of desire, for instance, and the carefully discriminated and graded series of excitements that precede the final union. It is an enormously sophisticated interpretation of the scope of emotional experience, and beside it the prescriptive code of a more utilitarian society, where the "moral-beautiful compound"[38] is supplanted by a simple moral imperative, seems a poor thing and a crude one.

Ransom is ingenious enough to extend the imputation of crudity to his analysis of the spiritual differences obtaining between agrarian and urban communities, this despite the fact that it was the charge of religious backwardness and crudity, leveled at the time of the Scopes trial, that initially stimulated his interest in his region. Indeed, there is a touch of characteristic bravado in the way Ransom insists that the very fundamentalism for which the South was mocked is a mark of its achievement. His argument is not a difficult one to grasp, although it is possibly more difficult to swallow. It depends on a rather pragmatic approach to religion, which insists that those varieties of belief are good which promote a "working definition of the relation of man to nature." The more thorough the definition is, apparently, the better the religion until one arrives at that variety which manages to hold in equilibrium two diverse interpretations of the human role—one of which depicts nature as "usable and intelligible," the other of which insists that it is "mysterious and contingent." God, according to this form of belief, can be understood, but only partly. He can be obeyed, and yet still remain mysterious and unpredictable. The ideas are, of course, contradictory. Ransom insists, though, that they can be reconciled in experience because they both grow naturally out of the practice of agriculture, in which the human being combines a certain understanding and control of nature with a sense of his "proper limitations . . . and . . . precarious position." This represents the most valuable mode of worship. At the other end of the scale is the contemporary mode, which reduces the deity to a "Big Scientist," a figure devised by the reason for its satisfaction alone. Situated "behind the scenes . . . making the cosmic engine run" this fragmentary or "Demi-God"[39] is an apt revelation, according to Ransom, of the consciousness that created Him.

That consciousness is, of course, the subject of the majority of Ransom's poems, which describe the dissociations for which a society ex-

pressing itself in "a series of isolated perfections" is responsible. There
are, for example, the lovers in "Eclogue," the failure of whose relationship is directly ascribed to the fact that they are "one part love/
And nine parts bitter thought."[40] Their lack of inner integrity, the
suggestion is, has prevented them from enjoying a complete relationship. And there are the lonely protagonists of so many of the poems,
like "Miriam Tazewell," whose alienation stems from an inability to
relate the complexities of their interior being to the abbreviated definitions of identity available in the world around them. In these and
similar cases an alternative system of value—in which wholeness and
consequently an integration of the inner and outer worlds does seem
possible—is not made explicit, as it is in the essays. But it is nevertheless there, in the idioms of the verse. This is because poetry at its
best, according to Ransom, should devote equal stylistic attention to
what he calls "structure" and "texture." By "structure," Ransom explains, he means the totality of the poem, the "logical object or universal" that appeals to the reason; and by "texture" is meant "the tissue
of irrelevance" and particularity that caters more to the demands of
the sensibility. "A beautiful poem," according to these criteria, "is one
that proceeds to the completion of a logical structure, but not without
attention to the local particularity of its components."[41] Obviously,
Ransom would consider it arrogant to claim that he achieves this
beauty in his verse, but it is clear enough that he aims for it. Almost
from the beginning of his poetic career, he has tried to articulate a
form which involves the simultaneous evocation of contradictory responses, catching the complex and yet unified reaction of the complete man to experience. And where the attempt has been successful,
as it has been in many of his poems, the result has been a type of
discourse that demonstrates its positives in its methods of expression.
Manner, in such cases, offers a definitive comment on matter.

Ransom's poem "Dead Boy"[42] is a good example of this. Its occasion
is a simple one, the death of a "little cousin" of the narrator. With the
help of radical alterations of diction, metaphor, and metrical effect,
though, Ransom suggests a response to this occasion that is far from
simple. Here, by way of illustration, are the first three stanzas.

> The little cousin is dead, by foul subtraction,
> A green bough from Virginia's aged tree,
> And none of the county kin like the transaction,
> Nor some of the world of outer dark, like me.
>
> A boy not beautiful, nor good, nor clever,
> A black cloud full of storms too hot for keeping.
> A sword beneath his mother's heart—yet never
> Woman bewept her babe as this is weeping.

A pig with a pasty face, so I had said,
Squealing for cookies, kinned by poor pretense
With a noble house. But the little man quite dead,
I see the forbears' antique lineaments.

The feelings aroused by this portrait are, I think, quite labyrinthine. The orotund and Latinate diction of the first three lines, and the elevated image in the second, suggest one reaction to the death, which is to distance it with the help of ceremonious language and gesture. But this is hastily qualified by phrases like "outer dark" and "black cloud full of storms" which echo the King James version of the Bible and consequently help to place the event in a larger, religious context —where it is seen as part of a universal process. And it is flatly contradicted by such lines as the ninth, in which the staccato rhythm combines with a dismissive image and harsh alliterative effects to suggest the intrusion of a more realistic assessment. The interplay of conflicting reactions continues throughout the poem, archaisms jostling with a more colloquial idiom, and the mellifluous cadences of one line being denied in the eruptive movement of the next; and eventually the reader might infer that he is being offered the reactions of quite separate people to the one event. If he did so, though, he would almost certainly be wrong. For the different attitudes toward the experience described in "Dead Boy" are not meant, I think, to belong to several men. On the contrary, they belong to one man, a complete personality who is capable of a true assessment of the case—which is to say a complex and sophisticated one, a series of weights and balances. He can love the boy and yet admit his frailty; abhor his death but recognize that his world was doomed in any case; realize the "poor pretense" involved in the talk of ancestors and funeral rites while at the same time understanding the value of the beliefs—in tradition and ritual—so illustrated. The style of the poem, in other words, dramatizes the subtle personality of its narrator, and that personality defines for us in turn the nature of Ransom's positives.

Not that it is always left, as in "Dead Boy," for the style to perform this function in Ransom's verse: just occasionally he is more explicit. This is the case with one of the few poems where he is directly concerned with the Southern tradition, "Antique Harvesters."[43] It is perhaps Ransom's most famous piece, and the fame is, I believe, quite justified. For in it he locates the meaning of his regional experience. He indicates, that is to say, the context of inherited belief on which his own work depends, and establishes the imaginative significance of his region for him—as a place where unity of consciousness is still possible and even likely. The South, in the poem, represents both a resource and a myth; and the poem itself consequently belongs at the

center of his life's work. The fact that this is so—that "Antique Harvesters" has a centrality that none of Ransom's other poems possesses
—is more or less suggested in the opening lines, which have the density and gravity of ideas brooded over for a very long time.

> Tawny are the leaves turned but they still hold,
> And it is harvest; what shall this land produce?
> A meager hill of kernels, a runnel of juice;
> Declension looks from our land, it is old.
> Therefore let us assemble, dry, grey, spare,
> And mild as yellow air.
>
> "I hear the croak of a raven's funeral wing."
> The young men would be joying in the song
> Of passionate birds; their memories are not long . . .

The poem is set on the banks of the Mississippi during the autumn, a
season that as in the Keats ode reminds man of his mortality but also
allows him to see that mortality as part of a general cycle of growth
and decay. It is too a time of pause, offering him an opportunity to
consider his harvest, material and spiritual. One thing gained from
the land is suggested by the opening description of the old men, and
that is endurance, the mildness of those who are as "dry" and "spare"
as the earth they love. Another is suggested by the reference to the
raven with its "sable" wings—an intimation of death and human limits,
the humility acquired in any engagement with the soil. And, as if this
were not enough, the third stanza of the poem introduces something
else yielded by the land. For, as the old men talk and the descendants
of long generations labor in the field, the sense of a usable past and a
traditional life style becomes unavoidable.

> We pluck the spindling ears and gather the corn.
> One spot has special yield? "On this spot stood
> Heroes and drenched it with their only blood."
> And talk meets talk, as echoes from the horn
> Of the hunter . . .

The comparison between the conversation of the old men and "echoes
from the horn" prepares beautifully for the appearance of a new element in the scene:

> Here come the hunters, keepers of a rite;
> The horn, the hounds, the lank mares coursing by
> Straddled with archetypes of chivalry;
> And the fox, lovely ritualist, in flight . . .

With the appearance of the hunters, a new feeling of ritual begins
to enrich Ransom's portrait. Certainly, the more romantic associations

this feeling dictates are tempered by the mundane detail, but the feeling is still present, and powerful enough to be carried over into the
subsequent description of the harvesters. For when the poet returns
after a while to these laborers in the field, they are addressed as if
they were participants in a rite as well. Their activities, as described
in the concluding stanza of the poem, seem to be as decorous and significant as the ceremonial of the chase that interrupted them—the
only difference being that in this case the activities are directed toward
the honoring of "our lady" the earth rather than a simple fox.

> True, it is said of our Lady, she ageth.
> But see, if you peep shrewdly, she hath not stooped;
> Take no thought of her servitors that have drooped,
> For we are nothing; and if one talk of death—
> Why, the ribs of the earth subsist frail as a breath
> If but God wearieth.

The ending is a thoroughly appropriate one, a convincing demonstration of the scope of Ransom's dualism. It affirms the dignity of the
antique harvesters, the sense of decorum and heroism with which their
commitment to the land is accepted; and yet it does so without rejecting the original recognition of the facts in the case of the farm laborer,
or in the case of any man destined to work and then die. Nothing
of that firm grasp on the actual demonstrated by the opening of the
poem has been lost, but a great deal has been added to it and gained.

This gain is registered among other things in the staple idiom of
the verse, which offers a characteristic reflection in word and manner
of the contraries of thought on which the argument depends. The very
title, "Antique Harvesters," gives a clue to this, referring as it does both
to the concepts of tradition and ritual and to a particular event in the
farming year. And throughout the following discourse equal weight
is given to these two terms of reference: elevated and romantic metaphors, such as the description of the fox as a "lovely ritualist," are
drastically qualified by the "dry, grey, spare" setting in which they
appear, and the occasional use of an elegant or archaic word is braced
by a sustained commitment to the colloquial. The result, as in a couplet like

> The horse, the hounds, the lank mares coursing by
> Straddled with archetypes of chivalry,

is an interplay of contradictory terms so complex that it almost defies
analysis. And of course, that it should defy *immediate* analysis at least
is part of Ransom's intention, since what he wishes to do essentially is
to express the possible coexistence of these terms rather than their
separateness. Agriculture, the premise is, brings the ceremonious and

the mundane levels of experience together by transforming ordinary life into significant ritual. Its activities, and the moral and religious practices it encourages, supply the basis for that sense of tradition and even chivalry that surrounds all those who participate in them. This is the *donnée* of "Antique Harvesters," making it—to the extent that Ransom succeeds—not so much a portrait from life as a minor historical myth, in which the notion of unity of consciousness is proposed and then firmly attached to the Southern and agrarian idea.

This reading of the rural life, which identifies it at once with the decorous stance and the commonplace gesture, helps to resolve what would otherwise be a puzzling ambivalence in Ransom's agrarian argument—the argument we find developed in his essays. When he is arguing along strictly economic lines, he seems to offer an idea of agrarianism which approximates to the one suggested by the mundane or "low" set of terms in "Antique Harvesters." He insists on the importance of subsistence farming, and even proposes government aid in the form of bounties and free land for those willing to be their own producers and consumers, carpenters and builders.[44] But, when other considerations to do with the quality of life are introduced, he tends to present a more aristocratic image, related to the "high" set of terms used in the poem. Emphasis is then placed on the belief that an agricultural society is a traditional one, promoting quite sophisticated codes of expression and behavior.[45] Coming across these arguments consecutively, the reader might think that Ransom was a man who did not know his own mind, quite ready to praise the same mode of existence for possessing disparate virtues. The fact is, though, that Ransom did know his own mind and that the self-contradiction is more apparent than real. "Antique Harvesters" demonstrates this more decisively than anything else, because it brings together qualities that Ransom discovered in the agrarian experience and elsewhere tended to deal with separately; its basis in hard work, that is, and the ritualized forms of conduct to which it leads, the onerous details of agricultural labor and the sense of ceremony that this labor fosters. As usual with a writer who delighted in turning his opponents' accusations back upon themselves, the argument is a sophisticated and very deliberate one, but no amount of sophistication can disguise one thing—the fact that its roots are in the Southern inheritance. For what Ransom does essentially in his work is to draw on the idea of the good farmer *and* that of the fine planter and then devise an imaginative alternative composed of elements from both. His version of the complete man represents a resolution of traditional conflicts—an idea of the good life which depends on his region for much of its content, but on him for its coherence.

The Burden of History: Robert Penn Warren

Ransom's case is not a unique one, of course; in different ways the other major writers involved in the Agrarian movement have tried to vary their regional inheritance, and so betrayed a similar interest in the relationship between history and idea. Even Robert Penn Warren, whose work appears to be less engaged with the mind of the South than the work of his colleagues, is, as it turns out, firmly committed to notions of experience and explorations of identity that establish him as a Southern writer. Admittedly, he has written few pieces as obviously attached to the region as, say, Ransom's "Happy Farmers"; even his contribution to *I'll Take My Stand* is more concerned with the Negro than with agrarianism. But, if some of the more superficial aspects of regionalism are missing from his work, that may be all to the good, and it certainly does not prevent a commitment to the *principles* on which the regional traditions are founded. Warren has always been a "philosophical" writer, a man who likes to use literature as a means of exploring ideas. So it is perhaps not surprising that it should be the broader ideology of his inheritance that interests him, rather than anything else, and helps to shape his critical and creative material. His backgrounds in Kentucky and Tennessee have supplied him with a framework for his writing, and to some extent with the idioms in which he writes as well; but all this has been done below the surface, as it were, or before Warren has started to put pen to paper. Consequently, although his debt to those backgrounds is at least as great as Ransom's, if not greater, it is much more difficult to locate.

Some of the more specific reasons for this difficulty are indicated, I think, by the conceptual framework of his fiction and verse; where the difficulty has to do with the transformation Warren works upon old material. Drawing on both Calhoun's arguments in favor of the status quo, and Jefferson's pleas for change, he devises a new structure of values, a new synthesis, which recognizably depends on the traditional arguments and yet turns out to be quite different from them. Like Calhoun, Warren demonstrates a profound belief in the imperfections of this imperfect world. "Man," as one of his characters puts it, "is conceived in sin and born in corruption and he passeth from the stink of the didie to the stench of the shroud." And, although the melodramatic ring of this identifies it as an overstatement, there is no doubt that similar, if less extreme, feelings have prompted Warren to place emphasis time and again on the importance of the "historical sense"— the faculty in man, that is, that instills in him a healthy awareness of the "massiveness of experience" and the consequent limitations circumscribing his own capacity for action. Already, the argument is beginning to sound like a familiarly conservative one in which scepticism, or some notion of original sin, is used to deny the ideal of progress. Before it can go that far, however, Warren counters this premise with another: that the alternatives represented by the actual and the possible are not absolutes, because man lives "somewhere in the dialectical process" between the two. He may be "of the brute creation by origin," Warren admits, but he also demonstrates a potential that would place him only "a little lower than the angels." So, while it might be sentimental to imagine that change is possible without pain, it would be equally sentimental and unrealistic for that reason to abjure change. Fulfillment depends on understanding—of one's self and of the landscapes that serve to locate that self—and this, the conclusion is, depends on a crucial recognition: that man, as a separate person and as a part of a larger social organism, has to create values that "grow out of the act of living" and that "even as they grow . . . modify living."[46] The controlling idea becomes one of a continuous process, in which historical event and moral principle operate a kind of complicated interchange, with immensely profitable results for those actively involved.

This idea is a fairly sophisticated one, requiring constant and quite subtle discriminations when it is exercised—and it is, constantly, in Warren's creative work. In practice, which means in his fiction and verse, he has to combine an extraordinary moral rigor with an appreciation of the difficulties of judgment: issues must not be simplified, even though his major purpose is to understand and evaluate them. He might have tried to make things easier for himself, for instance, by resting on the similarity between the illustrations of moral failure that populate his writings and the traditional stereotypes of the Yankee. Certainly, there is a connection between them. Yankees, according to Southern legend, fall victim either to materialism or idealism, or perhaps to both, and so do most of the people Warren criticizes. A failure of principle—an unwillingness to engage principle with event or event with principle—occurs in either case; and nothing would have been easier than for Warren to use this as an excuse for reproducing the old stereotypes. He does not, though. In effect, his own principles will not allow him to do it. What he does instead is to adopt the stereotypes, those of the crass businessman and the starry-eyed philanthropist, and then change them by substituting acceptable complications for polemical simplicities. An atmosphere of familiarity consequently surrounds his defeated characters, but it is qualified by the fact that each is placed back in history—as a personal situation.

In the case of the idealist, the first stage in this metamorphic process, from type into personality, is the distinction Warren insists on making between those who believe that "the world must redeem the idea," and try to dramatize their large ambitions in experience, and the characters who withdraw completely from the "contamination . . . implicit in the human condition" so as to keep their ideals intact. This is a radical distinction, but for Warren it is only a preliminary one: within the two categories so established, each idealist is presented as a complex being, whose idealism supplies a catalyzing agent for his other qualities. As a result, the second category can include a character like Lucy Burnham in *Night Rider,* who tries to compensate for the shabbiness of her life by devoting herself to the past, a past that gets "ever and ever more magnificent and fantastic"[47] as she grows older. And it can also embrace somebody like Amantha Starr, the heroine of *Band of Angels,* who is driven by motives that are more positive than Lucy's (if equally dubious) to construct a neat and quite unauthenticated picture of the world out of moral abstractions. When characters like these realize that the particulars of experience do not confirm their ideas, they may retreat still further—into cynicism, as Duckfoot Blake does in *At Heaven's Gate,* or, like Dorothy Murdoch in the same novel, into the mechanical solutions offered by alcohol and drugs. Whatever the forms of their escapism, though, they remain thoroughly attached to the exigencies of the case—a part of a specific history.

Warren's revised version of materialism, and the various forms the materialistic attitude may assume, is just as personal. Naturally, there are characters in Warren's fiction who recall the Flem Snopes prototype; he could hardly be called an agrarian if there were not. Bogan Murdoch, for example, a major figure in *At Heaven's Gate,* is actually drawn after a finance-capitalist of the day; and into his portrait Warren pours all the venom that Southern writers have traditionally reserved for his kind. He is a liar and a fraud, totally amoral, and as such the reader infers he is a frightening indication of the course of the new society. Even Murdoch, though, is regarded as more than just an epiphenomenon of his times, a sociological type. There is a sense of corruption attached to him that extends far beyond his lust for gain; and what it extends to, I think, is indicated by the other materialists in the book—or, perhaps even more clearly, by the character called "Gran' Boz" in *World Enough and Time.* "Gran Boz," a pirate living in the swamps of Louisiana, is also based on an historical character. This is how Warren introduces him:

La Grand Bosse—known on the river as Old Big Hump or Gran Boz— . . . had been spewed up out of the swamps and jungles of Louisiana, or out of some fetid alley of New Orleans—out of that dark and savage swill of bloods—a sort of monstrous bubble that rose to the surface of the pot, or a sort of great brute of the depth that swagged up from the blind,

primal mud to reach the light and wallow in the stagnant flood, festooned
with algae and the bright slime, with his scaled, armored, horny back
just awash, like a log.[48]

What the figure of the "Gran' Boz" suggests here is that the materialistic impulse, the sort that exists at the opposite extreme from idealism,
is not just a matter of acquisitiveness—the traditional Southern idea of
capitalism in action. It encompasses the notion of original sin as well,
and any person who embraces that sin by rejecting possibility. The
businessman may be described as such a character—certainly Bogan
Murdoch is—but only if he conducts his business in such a way as to
demonstrate no interest in value. His life style, in other words, can be
seen as a symptom of evil but never as its cause. Its sources lie too
deep for any environmental explanation to satisfy. Here, as in his treatment of the idealist, what Warren has done is to develop the premises
of agrarianism a little further than most other Southerners—to extend
and explore the implications of the common argument until its specifically regional elements seem to disappear.

A similar transformation of the inherited program occurs in Warren's
presentation of the Good Life. Of course, his sense of how life should
be is indebted to the agrarian tradition of the South, just as much as
Ransom's is or Davidson's, but again the debt is owed with a difference. That is why a character does not have to be attracted to the
land to act as a positive reference in Warren's work, only to exhibit
the kind of humility and self-knowledge that the land, *among other
things,* may teach to a man. Aaron Blaustein, for instance, whose commentary offers the reader one means of judging the narrative in *Wilderness,* is described as a rich New Yorker; Dr. Burnham, a "good man"
in *World Enough and Time,* is a scholar; and "Izzie" Goldfarb, his
counterpart in *Flood,* is a small-town tailor. Even when a character
does enjoy this attachment, when he is a landholder of some kind, his
economic status can vary so much that a specialized interpretation becomes impossible. Willie Proudfit, an important moral touchstone in
Night Rider, is a poor white whose life is monopolized by labor. He
has nothing except the language of the Bible with which to express
his new-found understanding of himself. "The Lord's give me more . . .
than a man kin ask," as he puts it, "but it looks lak He holds just one
thing back from a man, so a man kin know . . . He's the Lord."[49] He is
a primitive, quite different from the Calhoun family, an essentially
bourgeois group who perform a similar evaluative function in *At
Heaven's Gate,* or Captain Todd, "a gentleman of the old school" who
complements Willie Proudfit as a representative of principle in Warren's first book. They may all happen to be farmers, indeed their position as farmers may help them toward some understanding of them-

selves. But there is never any suggestion that their moral achievement is *dependent* on their economic status, still less that there is a particular status that spells success. And, just in case the reader should still miss the point, there is one example of the good man in *World Enough and Time*, a Colonel Fort, who seems to collapse farmer and planter into one. "He *was* the son of old Kaintuck," Warren says, ". . . *was* the sober squire, *was* the gentleman of honor." An almost Protean being, he serves as a neat reminder that Warren's use of the agrarian prototype should never be taken too literally, since his commitment is to the principles behind the Southern argument rather than to the systems, ambiguously composed of fact and metaphor, with which those principles have usually been associated in his region.

Another way of describing Warren's strategy here is this: in nearly all of his work, the rural metaphor is used in such a way as to wear its identity as metaphor upon its face. It is seen quite categorically as a projection of something larger, as an emblem of certain values that the country life may encourage but cannot be said to monopolize. Here is an example of what I mean, from the opening pages of *World Enough and Time*. It describes the region in which the protagonist of the novel, Jeremiah Beaumont, was born.

> Beyond, south and west, were the farms just snatched from the wilderness, with the black stumps from the slashing and burning still visible before the corn got high, and the shadow of the forest still stunting the corn along the edge of the field. . . . The people had come here to stay. . . . They would possess the wild land, but the wild land possessed them too. . . . The dirk . . . and the Bible might lie side by side on the table, or Plato and the duelling pistols on the mantel shelf. . . .[50]

This is the Great Good Place of the narrative, the type of homestead that Beaumont deserts for a strange new world, which eventually destroys him. As such it is the equivalent of the idyllic rural setting in "Antique Harvesters," or the farms and plantations that are celebrated in *I'll Take My Stand;* but it is so *only* on the level of metaphor. For what is important about this description, I think, is the perspective Warren chooses for his description. He does not dwell on the routine life of the farms, or the minute particularities of their appearance. Quite the contrary, all that he is interested in is their halfway position between the forest and the town—or rather the possible use of that position as a term of reference. The clearing as he presents it exists in a condition of equilibrium, between the primitive energy of the wilderness on the one hand and the structures of civilization on the other. It is a border country between two worlds. The main result of this is that Warren can then take it as a paradigmatic case. It becomes an emblem of the dialectic between raw experience and formed principle at which all people, according to the author, should aim. Obviously, this has nothing to do with the economics of rural existence; Warren has simply abstracted elements he has found there and made them express some larger theme. But it has everything to do with his habitual strategy of transforming a process of argument into a metaphor—the use of farm and plantation, in other words, to represent the Good Life rather than circumscribe it.

Other Agrarians use this strategy too, of course, but with them it is complicated by an interest in the political aspects of agrarianism. They tend to think of the good farmer and fine planter as real possibilities, maybe the only possibilities if the South is to be saved from ruin, and so qualify their status as metaphors even while they exploit it. With Warren this rarely occurs, if ever, because he is not really interested in the agrarian notion as such, only in the principles implicit in agrarianism—in them, that is, and in the application of them to all types and varieties of experience. How an individual transfigures his environment, and himself in relation to it, is much more important to him than the exact location of the environment that is discussed. Fulfillment is shown to be possible in the small town and city, as well as on the farm and plantation, and given this new freedom of context it is possible for Warren to exploit both ploughman and gentleman as projections of value—not only possible, perhaps, but necessary so as to indicate that the values which are being projected involve a recon ciliation of elements from the two sides of the Southern tradition. In the process an enormous expansion of reference occurs. The moral and metaphorical structure of the work is still dictated by the agrarian idea, but that idea is interpreted in such a way as to encourage new departures—into areas of experience other than the rural—rather than inhibit them. His regionalism is there as a guiding principle in his work—and it is there, it turns out, even when he is talking about another country, or another race.

Not that Warren does necessarily go outside of the South for his subject, even though he has made it easy for himself to do so. Often, there is no real need because it is in the South that he can find many of his most abiding concerns, dramatized in the story of its past. The backward glance over his own region is so frequent in his work, in fact, that it is obviously more than an accident. It is, besides, evidence of his interest in history—as a fact and as an energy shaping the conditions in which the consciousness must operate. This brings us to another side of Warren's traditionalism, a second point where his own concerns and those of his region tend to meet. With extraordinary consistency, he has drawn on episodes from the legends of his family or locality for the sources of his narratives. The story of the tobacco wars, for example, is the basis of *Night Rider,* while the incidents described in *World Enough and Time* have their origin in an actual murder committed in Kentucky a hundred years ago. In using these episodes, though, Warren has not been content merely to record what happened, or to spin a few cobwebs of historical romance; what he does instead is transform the remembered events into an inquiry, a dramatic examination of what he once called "the historical sense." Certainly, an interest in the embryonic detail of the past still remains; it is registered among other things in the persona of historian or bibliographer, delving among the records of the past, that he seems to have borrowed from Hawthorne and Melville. But like his models Warren reaches out beyond an interest in detail, the particulars of the remembered scenes, to attempt an analysis of the entire relationship between man and history as it can be discovered from those scenes. His final concern, characteristically enough, is with the *notion* of history rather than any series of historical events. The importance of this can scarcely be exaggerated, since what it means is that Warren has not been content just to use the Southern tradition. More than once, he has actually placed himself at its center, by committing his work to an analysis of its seminal idea.

Perhaps I can explain better what I mean by this by referring to an example—and here one of the best examples possible is offered by *All the King's Men,* the novel, first published in 1946, with which the name of Robert Penn Warren is usually associated. The association must have become a tiresome one for Warren by now because of its very frequency, but it is still, I think, well warranted. Occasionally, a case has been made for the superiority of one of his other novels, and there have been one or two attempts to locate the center of his work in the poetry.[51] But these have been scattered, infrequent, and in the event unconvincing. Warren is a writer whose bias is toward the kind of specificity and social density that is the special preserve of fiction; and *All the King's Men* represents his major achievement in the genre. In a sense, it is his most characteristic production as well, so that any assessment of him as a historical writer has ultimately to focus upon it.

As soon as anyone tries for this assessment, though, he becomes aware of the peculiarly frustrating nature of nearly all previous discussions of the book. Ambivalence is its chief characterisic; for two schools of criticism have been at work on *All the King's Men* since its publication, and they have virtually divided the field between them. The lion's share has gone to a formalist school, which generally places the novel in some vast ahistorical context so as to pay com-

pliment to Warren's handling of the techniques of fiction—the use of
image and symbol, for instance, or the presentation of narrative point
of view. In such cases, the critic assumes that the book is written in
a kind of code that it is his task to crack. When he does crack it, or
some part of it, he seems so pleased with his success that the value
or validity of the message so communicated hardly engages his interest. To be more exact, the uses to which history and specific social
circumstances are put in *All the King's Men,* and the larger meanings
Warren extracts from this, are rarely brought into question. The
writer is accepted on the basis of his more obviously symbolic intentions, without reference to some of the rather dubious means by
which those intentions are fulfilled, and the result is frequently commentary like the following.

> The symbolic fable of the book embodies the world of fact in Willie
> Stark ("stark" fact) and the world of idea . . . in Adam (innocence of
> the world of fact) Stanton, while the Eves of the piece, Anne Stanton and
> Sadie Burke, are the agents by which knowledge of evil is transmitted to
> Jack Burden (who must finally bear the full burden of knowledge, as he is
> regenerated.)[52]

The point about such commentary is that it isolates *All the King's
Men* from those powers of history which supply the spine of its narrative and the center of its interests and, in doing so, it inevitably
impoverishes the meaning of the book. Supposing what is said here to
be true, the reader would surely be justified in asking why so much
praise has been showered on Warren; and for what reason Warren
should have felt himself impelled to adopt a set of given historical
circumstances only to alter them.

This is precisely what other commentators on *All the King's Men*
do ask, of course—those constituting the second major stream of criticism on the novel.[53] Their questions assume many forms, and are
presented with different degrees of vehemence, but all have as their
purpose a rebuttal of Warren's reading of history—and more particularly the history of the Louisiana demagogue Huey Long, on whom
the protagonist of the story, Willie Stark, is based. By what right,
they ask, has Robert Penn Warren transformed Huey Long into
Willie Stark? The transformation required an alteration of many of
the accepted facts, and even the suppression of some of the more un-
savory aspects of Long's career, and how can this ever be defended?
Their very phrasing of the questions suggests their bias, for most
of them are firmly convinced that Warren is guilty of irresponsibility
or, worse still, of the imaginative equivalent of bad faith. There is an
irony to be found here. Most of these commentators see themselves

as offering a reply to the formalist school of criticism on *All the King's Men*, raising historical issues that that school prefers to ignore; and yet if to reply can be said to involve the idea of engaging directly with the other side, of achieving some kind of exchange with it, then what they do does not really constitute replying at all. The most that such commentators do is to point out the discrepancies between the facts and the fiction. The possibility of a justification for these discrepancies is hardly raised, because, whereas in the case of the formalists the writer is assumed to be isolated from the processes of history, he is here seen to be so immersed in them as to make his proper status that of their recording instrument. The ideal of the poet without any responsibility to history is replaced by the ideal of the scientific historian who has no responsibilities other than this one. The two ideals can hardly engage, being no more than mirror opposites of one another. And the irony is compounded by the fact that this curious state of affairs is ultimately an example of that "terrible division" between philosophical ideal and historical reality that *All the King's Men*, like much of Warren's work, exists to demonstrate—the division implicit, that is, in the contrast between Willie Stark, the political realist, and Adam Stanton, the naïve man of ideas. This in itself suggests that a minimally acceptable interpretation of the book has to bring the two schools of criticism together, to see what made Warren change history in the way he did and whether his motives, as defined by the structure and purpose of the book, are an adequate justification for these changes. If nothing else, it might indicate to what extent the writer has succeeded in implementing his own recommendations, by squaring his inner needs and beliefs with the "awful responsibility of Time"[54] imposed on him by the outer world of event.

Perhaps one way of understanding what Warren has done in *All the King's Men*, as a preparation for assessing his achievement, is to concentrate in the first place on his raw material—that is, the historical facts with which he was presented in the story of Huey Long.[55] Like most stories, Long's is in detail a complicated one, but its main outlines are clear enough. He was born to a poor family in the poorer part of Louisiana, so it was only by virtue of enormous industry that he managed to find time to study for a law degree and then, armed with this, to carve out a political career for himself. That his industry was enormous is demonstrated by the fact that, despite all his initial disadvantages, he first took political office at the minimum age of twenty-one. And it was just eleven years later, in 1928, that he was elected governor of the state. Once in power, it began to seem unlikely that he could ever be removed. He gradually assumed control of the state legislature, using a mixture of bribery and blackmail, and then so redesigned the political structure of Louisiana as to make almost every public official answerable to himself. According to local legend, even the ratcatchers had to prove themselves loyal Huey Long men if they wanted to stay in office! Regardless of whether this legend was true or not, it certainly was true that Long managed to place the state militia and the highway patrol at his disposal, and so transform Louisiana into a miniature police state. Elections were rigged, the newspapers were carefully watched and punished with heavy taxes if they proved hostile, and it began to seem that to oppose Huey Long openly in Louisiana was to invite self-destruction.

That is not the whole story, though: if it were, Huey Long would be no more than one in a long line of Southern demagogues, although perhaps more powerful than most. But the fact is that Long did not just want power as an end in itself. He wanted to use power to implement the kind of schemes that had been his ever since he had been able to think about his situation, and the situation of people like him. He wanted to help the poor farmers who continued to support him no matter how dictatorial his scheme of government appeared to be. Toward this end, a vast highway system was completed for the state, creating new opportunities for those, usually the poorer classes, trapped until then in the interior. New hospitals and welfare institutions were opened up, and, most important of all, universal education was transformed from a theory into a fact when Long made the state rather than the individual responsible for the purchase of school textbooks. The same embryonic socialism characterized his national ambitions. By 1934 he had decided to run for President, and as a preparation for his candidacy he formulated a "Share Our Wealth" program for income redistribution that makes the New Deal look positively conservative. It provided, among other things, for the liquidation of all personal fortunes over three million dollars, generous minimum wages for every American worker white *and* black, a national pension scheme, and, in general, close governmental supervision of the economy. Of course, Long's motives in formulating this scheme were practical as well as idealistic: he wanted to appeal to the mass of workingmen in the nation just as he had appealed to the poor folk of Louisiana. The scheme cannot be dismissed as simply as that, however, since other Southern demagogues have proved that there are easier ways of appealing to the popular vote. In the circumstances, to accuse Huey Long of wholesale opportunism would surely be as wrong as to see him as an idealistic man of the people. He was both, and as such perhaps best defined in terms of the paradox one essentially unsympathetic commentator favored when he described Long as "a moral idiot of genius."[56]

That is surely the point about Long: that, among those who know or have examined him closely, even those least sympathetic to his cause have tended to call his story tragic rather than iniquitous.[57] It is the story of a man born into a specific set of historical circumstances that demonstrated to his dissatisfaction that the times were out of joint. In every sense they denied the demands of his innermost being, what Warren habitually calls "the idea." The alternatives in these circumstances seemed fairly clear to him. We can perhaps define them by drawing on an earlier distinction between the several types of failure examined in Warren's work to say that, as Long saw it, he could choose either to be an "idealist" or a "materialist." That is, he could either retreat into himself, and the kind of self-protective narcissism that rejects the world after acknowledging its irremediable iniquity; or he could commit himself to the desperate maneuvers and partial fulfillments imposed on him by events. Long apparently chose the second course. He tried to use corrupt means, in this case the means made available by the political machinery of his state, to achieve his aims; and in the process he could not help corrupting both those aims and himself.

What was true of Huey Long is also true of Willie Stark, no matter how much Warren may alter or condense specific details to make his point. Stark's story is also a tragic one, as tragic and as poignant as, say, that of Brecht's Mother Courage. For Willie Stark and Mother Courage are both placed in situations that demand the worst of them, if they are to survive, even though they may recognize and sometimes wish for the best. In this context, scene 3 of *Mother Courage and Her Children,* in which the protagonist denies her son, a German soldier, so as to avoid the confiscation of her property by the Swedish army, is comparable to the moment in *All the King's Men* when Willie Stark ruefully accepts the resignation of Hugh Miller, his attorney general. Miller, a man of genuine principle, resigns because Stark refuses to prosecute one of his underlings for attempting to divert state funds into his own pocket. Stark *will* punish the man privately, but to commit himself to any public form of punishment would be, as he realizes, to invite political death. His enemies, the people removed from power after he was elected, have already caught the scent of corruption and are eagerly looking for some evidence to use as a means of pulling the Stark empire down. Willie Stark recognizes what he is doing: he is protecting the unprincipled and denying principle in order to survive. The fact that he wants to stay in power in order to implement his principles only adds a further dimension to the irony—and Stark acknowledges as much when he says to Miller, just before he goes, "You're leaving me all alone with the sons-of-bitches. Mine and the other fellow's."[58] The scene epitomizes the novel, or at least Willie

Stark's part of it. Stark tries to use the powers offered by his given circumstances to realize an idea, but he eventually becomes so involved in the mired complexities of the power game that the idea is forgotten or, worse still, prostituted. And part of the tragedy lies in the fact that Willie Stark senses what is happening to him even while it is happening.

What Robert Penn Warren has done in the case of Willie Stark, then, as far as his relationship to his historical prototype is concerned, is to take the authenticated facts and reproduce them so as to emphasize their tragic pattern. Certain particulars, such as the nature of the powers assumed by Huey Long in Louisiana and the number and the scope of the reforms implemented by him, may be changed, but the paradox that informed the character and life of "the Boss" is not. Perhaps this can be clarified a little more by pointing to one specific example of Warren's treatment of his raw material; and, as in other tragedies, an example more striking than most is supplied by the death of the protagonist. Warren ascribes the death of Willie Stark, with a fine sense of poetic justice, to Dr. Adam Stanton; and he accounts for it by suggesting that Adam believed he had been given the directorship of the Willie Stark Hospital in return for favors received by the governor from Anne Stanton, Adam's sister. In fact, Huey Long was shot by a Dr. Weiss, who resented the attempts made by the state political machine to deprive his father-in-law, Judge Pavy, of office; and who was even more resentful of remarks made by the governor to the effect that there was black blood in the Pavy family. The differences here between fact and fiction appear to be radical, but they are only apparently so. Long, as one authority on the subject has explained, "fell victim . . . to the Southern tradition of personal honor and personal violence"[59] when he was killed. His death was occasioned by a characteristic failure to remember the sensibilities of others, and more especially by his apparent inability to remember just how sensitive Southerners can be about the racial taboo, which prohibits any overt acknowledgment of miscegenation.[60] The death of Willie Stark is caused by a similar and equally characteristic failure that involves him, although indirectly, in a violation of the *sexual* taboo.[61] Stark takes Anne Stanton, a woman from an old Louisiana family, as his mistress, and in the course of their relationship gives her financial help with her orphanages and appoints Adam director of the state hospital. What he does is not done as a simple means of paying Anne for her services; he is rarely as crass as that. But there can be no doubt that his generosity toward her is related to his affection for her, and that this affection in turn encourages him to make overtures to Adam Stanton. The offense against the Stanton pride, the smear of prostitution, is implied

in the situation, and Adam, with his acute sensitivity, merely makes
the offense explicit. Perhaps it is unnecessary to spell out the details,
though. The point is that the deaths of Huey Long and Willie Stark
are comparable, in terms of their connection both with previous
mistakes and with a general insensitivity to the narcissistic pride of
the idealist. In specifics the two stories may differ, but the tragic pattern of blindness occasioning destruction is the same in either case.[62]

To talk about *All the King's Men* only in terms of Willie Stark, however, is to talk about one half of the novel. His story is no more or less
important than the story of Jack Burden, the narrator, whose situation
throughout most of the narrative is quite the reverse of the protagonist's. Burden, as he himself acknowledges, is an "Idealist" who has
retreated from responsibilities into that kind of dismissive cynicism
which is perhaps the special prerogative of the disillusioned naif. His
characteristic stance, and the reasons for it, are neatly suggested in a
passage like the following.

> . . . I'd be lying there in the hole in the middle of my bed where the
> springs had given down with the weight of wayfaring humanity, . . .
> watching the cigarette smoke flow up . . . against the ceiling . . . like the
> pale uncertain spirit rising up out of your mouth on the last exhalation, as
> the Egyptians figured it, to leave the horizontal tenement of clay in its
> ill-fitting pants and vest.[63]

What is interesting about such a passage, I think, is its violent yoking
together of heterogeneous ideas, corporeal and spiritual, so as to
emphasize their heterogeneity. As Burden sees it, the world can only
become flesh by adopting an outfit so ludicrous that it loses all its
original character and value; and in these circumstances the best the
idealist can do is to stand on the sidelines, mocking the world and its
squalor. When this in turn becomes intolerable, and the mask of cynicism begins to slip, there is still what Burden calls "the Great Sleep,"
that retreat into vacuous nonbeing that is always available to the man
of ideas when the world is too much with him.

Jack Burden falls into "the Great Sleep" several times during the
course of the narrative, and the first time is perhaps one of the most
significant. This occurs after his abortive attempt at being a historian.
Many years ago, Jack explains, he tried to write a dissertation about
Cass Mastern, an ancestor who spent most of his life in Kentucky. The
facts were compiled over a period of several years and the final draft
almost completed—and then something happened. Perhaps the later
Jack Burden, the man who emerges out of the story of Willie Stark,
can describe it best himself.

. . . Jack Burden could not put down the facts . . . because he did not know Cass Mastern. . . . Cass Mastern lived for a few years and in that time he learned that the world is all of one piece. He learned that the world is like an enormous spider web and if you touch it, however lightly, at any point, the vibration ripples to the remotest perimeter and the drowsy spider feels the tingle and . . . springs out to fling the gossamer coils about you. . . .

But how could Jack Burden, being what he was, know that? . . . to him the world then was simply an accumulation of items, odds and ends of things . . . one thing had nothing to do, in the end, with anything else.[64]

What seems to have happened, in effect, was that Burden suddenly found that the dispersed facts in the case of Cass Mastern were assuming shape and significance. The growing coherence of his "items," and the discovery that that coherence was precipitating, were both inviting him to recognize his involvement in history. It was not just that he was being asked to see that he was as implicated in his times and circumstances as Cass Mastern had been in his. This was a part of the offered vision but not all of it. He was also being asked to acknowledge the existence of a direct relationship with Cass Mastern, founded on mutual dependence.

That the dependence is mutual is the important point. It is perhaps not difficult to see that, in the context of the interpretation of history that Cass Mastern offers to Jack Burden, the past can be said to shape the present; it is not difficult to see this, and there would probably be few who would disagree with it. What is at once more difficult and more interesting is something that Robert Penn Warren—and eventually Jack Burden—takes to be a corollary of this: that, in a sense, the present can be said to shape the past. The meaning of an event, in other words, is not principally in the event itself but in its complicated relationship with events before and after it. One moment in time interacts with other moments in time. So a pattern is created that is greater than the sum of its parts and that gives an added dimension to each of those parts. This is what Jack Burden cannot see when he is placing "odds and ends" of the past side by side and supposing that, as a result, he is learning the truth about historical experience. He is not learning the truth; and he is not simply because he does not realize that what is brought to the past, in terms of the present experience, is at least as important as the separate moment of the past itself.

Such an interpretation of history, which proposes the existence of a dialectical relationship between past and present, is relevant to more of *All the King's Men* than just the story of Jack Burden and Cass Mastern, of course. For it has enormous bearing on the entire structure

and meaning of the novel as well. To begin with, it gives the reader
a clearer idea of the positive tendencies of the narrative, which demonstrate the familiar Warren balance between idealism and materialism—that equal commitment to actuality and possibility, the fact and
the dream, which I have described as the initial premise in all of his
work. History, from this standpoint, is neither the set of given and unalterable conditions that Willie Stark takes it to be nor the raw material for the idealistic impulse that Jack Burden would have liked it
to be at one time. It is, in a way, both—a product of the continuing
interchange between the human consciousness and circumstances past
and present. To fail to recognize this is to fall victim to what Burden
eventually refers to as "the terrible division of [the] age," to emphasize one term of the dialectic, that is, at the expense of the other. And
that the narrator *has* recognized this as a result of the experiences he
is now narrating contributes a lot to the extraordinary richness of the
book. For having learned the truth about historical experience, Jack
Burden can discover the meaning of his own story as well as that of
Cass Mastern. In *All the King's Men* he is at once describing the sequence of events that led him to know that "the world is all of one
piece" and, by reformulating his past in the light of his present rec-
ognitions, offering the reader a practical demonstration of his knowledge.

Jack Burden is only the narrator of the book, though. The real teller
of the tale is Robert Penn Warren, and this brings us back to the original issue of the relationship between the real Huey Long and the
fictional Willie Stark, and the possible point of that relationship. It
is surely right to say that, in recasting the story of the legendary "Boss"
of Lousiana, Warren is merely doing on a large scale what his narrator does on a slightly smaller one. His revision of history repeats the
narrative procedure on another level. For what Warren does is to take
the given story, the facts in the case of Huey Long, and set it in the
kind of dialectical relationship with an idea that creates a new shape
and meaning from both. He does not distort the story, at least in terms
of its essential pattern. What he does instead is to place it in such a
context as will demonstrate its direct and effective relationship with
our own experience. The present is changed by the past, in the sense
that Warren has found in a specific set of historical circumstances a
means of analyzing his own predicament and, as he sees it, the predicament of his "age" as well. And what is more to the point, perhaps, the
past has been changed by the present since it is only now, in the
writing of *All the King's Men,* that the meaning and emphases of the
story that Warren recounts have become clear. The "odds and ends"
of historical memory have been woven into a pattern that makes them

"all of one piece" with each other and with the lives of those remembering. Structure in this context becomes a necessary projection of meaning, with the relationship between the writer and the raw material of his tale offering perhaps the most incisive demonstration possible of those uses of history with which the narrative is concerned. In a way it is a nicely ironic point, which Jack Burden in one of his more sardonic moods might have appreciated, that the reshaping of fact into fiction that so many critics have questioned in *All the King's Men* is really a part of its meaning and formal achievement.

I have spent some time discussing Robert Penn Warren, and *All the King's Men* in particular, but that is because I think of him as a writer who is usually underestimated—in part, perhaps, because of the very scope and volume of his work. It is difficult to encompass the achievement of a man who is one of the founders of an international school of criticism, an eminent teacher, and a commentator on national affairs, as well as being a poet, novelist, and a poetic dramatist of major reputation. Nor is the task made any the easier by the fact that this range is accompanied by an extraordinary depth in various fields. Indeed, as his uses of agrarianism will bear witness, it is the very extent of his commitment to specifics—to the principles, that is, of any particular subject—which makes the variety of his interests possible. His habitual strategy encourages an interdisciplinary approach, because it is concerned with individual disciplines as different expressions of man's continuing involvement in history. Quite apart from this, a book like *All the King's Men* demands close examination in its own right, as a kind of paradigm of the Southern case. For the reinterpretation of the past that it demonstrates, and even argues for, is a founding principle of the Southern "renaissance"; a *donnée* or given circumstance, as it were, that every Southern author has had either to deal with or confront. That is why its problems, deriving from the interaction between event and dream, or history and myth, are ones we shall find characteristic of Southern writing—a common element binding together pieces like "Antique Harvesters" and Donald Davidson's "The Tall Men," William Faulkner's *Absalom, Absalom!*, and *The Confessions of Nat Turner* by William Styron. Perhaps this may sound strange, at first, that a specific series of problems should assume such centrality in works otherwise quite different from one another; but it is a strangeness that, I think, can be easily explained. The traditions of the South emerged, after all, out of the consciousness of a relationship between past and present, a mutually effective relationship for good or ill. So it is only natural that writers in the South should regard the direct analysis of this relationship as one of the most valuable means of engaging with their tradition. In such cases, of which

All the King's Men offers us an example, the idea of history provides not just a context of assumption for a Southern book, but the main object of its concerns as well.

The Idea of a Tradition: Allen Tate

History is central to the concerns of a third member of the Agrarian group to acquire a major literary reputation during his lifetime, Allen Tate. In Tate's case, though, it is history seen, not as a sequence of living events, but as a code of behavior and belief that those events have handed down to us, their inheritors. His idea of history, that is to say, is perhaps more accurately perceived as an idea of tradition, with tradition being defined as "that quality of life that we have got from our immediate past."[65] It is a far more static version of experience than the one the reader encounters in the work of Robert Penn Warren, static in the sense that it presupposes certain absolute standards to which the good society, if it is to be a good society, must conform. Of course, the way in which any group demonstrates a commitment to such standards may vary somewhat according to the specifics of its time and place; but the commitment, as Tate sees it, will remain essentially the same and so prevent the variations from being anything more than superficial. History as an absolute process is replaced, in effect, by history as a complete and relatively unchanging framework of value. Traditions, once established, alter very little. There is a touch of the dogmatist about Tate, as anybody who has read his literary essays will agree, and it has come as no surprise to many that in recent years he has exchanged the absolutes of historical tradition for the absolutes of religious orthodoxy. Indeed, there have been some readers who have argued that the acceptance of religion, as an indispensable confirmation of value, has always been implicit in his writing.

Be that as it may, orthodoxy of one kind or another has always been a major interest, and for much of Tate's career the orthodoxy to which he has subscribed is that of the traditional society. What is a traditional society, according to Tate? The answer seems to contain an uncharacteristic element of flexibility, when he describes it as "any community of men who pass to the next generation, under a definite conception of human nature, a code of conduct." But, as usual, this initially open-sounding statement is then limited by a rider. No society can do this, Tate insists, that is not primarily an "agricultural order." This is because land is that form of property alone, the possession of which always involves "not only ownership but control; not only rights but duties; not only material welfare but moral standards." Like all property it supplies the basis for wealth, of individuals and of nations. But unlike most it also fosters the "historical sense of obligation" fundamental to all moral values, that link with the past and its sanctions which other forms of ownership tend to discourage. And on top of this, working in the fields educates men into the "experience of evil," the sense of human limitation and dependence on powers beyond man's control that is the essence of religious belief. So land, the argument concludes, must be regarded as the one effective means of creating and perpetuating "moral unity"—the only method by which the traditional man can make his living and the traditional society transmit its heritage. By an elaborate process of logic, the writer returns us to a familiar idyll.

> . . . the traditional community is made up of men who are never quite making their living and who never quite cease to make it: they are making their living all the time and affirming their code all the time. In societies dominated by the moral and religious view, the life of men and their livelihood approximate a unity in which to speak of one is to speak of the other.[66]

When this new version of the pastoral disappears, Tate conceives of only two alternatives being possible, and even these are really just two parts of a single process of decline, a way of confirming, as it were, the value of all that has been lost. The immediate alternative is called "the antitraditional society" and actually represents the destructive process, all the forces combining to dissolve the old pieties. As such, it is identified with the period "from the beginning of the Industrial Revolution to the Great War"—from the time of the triumph of industrialism in England, that is, to its triumph in the American South. Out of it emerges the "untraditional society," the point of vantage from which Tate himself is writing. In this context, man is deprived of moral unity because the structures of his environment are founded on finance-capitalism, "a system of money references that the moral will cannot control." Property and the sense of moral responsibility are separated from one another, and the result is a general fragmentation of experience: the personality is reduced to a series of separate functions, bearing no apparent relationship to each other. Tate manages to retain a tone of dry abstraction even when describing this in his essays, but it cannot disguise the fact that the vision is an apocalyptic one, creating a landscape of nightmare that serves as an appropriate contrast to his portraits of the rural life.

> . . . in ages which suffer the decay of manners, religion, morals, codes, our indestructible vitality demands expression in violence and chaos . . .
> . . . illiberal specializations . . . have . . . proliferated into the modern world: specializations in which means are divorced from ends, action from sensibility, matter from mind, society from the individual, religion

from moral agency, love from lust, poetry from thought, communion from
experience, and mankind in the community from men in the crowd. There
is literally no end to this list of dissociations because there is no end, yet
in sight, to the fragmenting of the western mind.[67]

The contrast between the rural and the mechanical is a conventional
one, of course, as is the idea of a tradition that this contrast can be
used to celebrate; but what makes it unconventional in Tate's case is
the rigorous intellectual framework within which everything is put.
The reader knows precisely what Tate means by "tradition" because
it is defined in the course of the argument. He can say exactly what
Tate's celebration of agrarianism involves since the moral and intellectual implications of that agrarianism are worked out rather than
simply asserted: logic is recruited in support of metaphor. There is a
vital tension in most of Tate's better essays, between a precisely articulated dogma and an almost melodramatically conceived drama, and
this tension extends from the individual essay to define, on another
level, the relationship of his critical work as a whole to his creative
writing. For in the fiction and verse that Tate has written over the
course of his long career, there is always a feeling that the ideological
framework created by the criticism has defined the limits of the imaginative discourse, and even at times restricted them. The thought precedes the work in the fullest and best way possible—a fact that is
demonstrated clearly enough, I think, in Tate's two major creative
achievements. One is his "Ode to the Confederate Dead"; the other,
called *The Fathers,* his single long piece of fiction.

With both of these works, Tate's basic strategy is disconcertingly
simple: it is to accept the legendary version of the Old South, presenting it as a fulfillment of the feudal ideal, and then use this as a
projection of his argument in favor of traditionalism. The ante-bellum
plantation, in other words, is transmuted into a paradigm of the good
—for which read "traditional"—society. As usual, Tate is quite conscious of what he is doing, and has even constructed an argument
that, by implication at least, defends it. For elsewhere, in his critical
and historical essays, he has shown himself to be thoroughly aware
of the deficiencies inherent in the *actual* society of the ante-bellum
South, and has even ascribed its eventual failure and collapse to those
deficiencies. He has insisted, for instance, that its evangelicalism was
anomalous, an inappropriate form of worship that failed to supply
the metaphysical substructure that every traditional society requires.
As he has put it, the Old Confederacy was "a feudal society without
a feudal religion" and to that extent was fatally incomplete. And this
was only one aspect of its incompleteness: there were others, Tate
insists, that made the reality quite different from the dream. But (and

this is the crux of the situation) Tate then goes on to say that this hardly matters, since the proper function of history is to demonstrate, not "the scientific ideal of . . . truth-in-itself" but rather a "cultural truth which might win the allegiance of the people."[68] In keeping with Tate's rather static version of experience as a whole, history is seen as a kind of resource, a repository of dramatized value. In the case of a traditional society, it represents a distillation of the best possibilities, the ideals, of the group—as, say, the Homeric vision of the past does, or the narratives of Herodotus. And in the case of the untraditional society, its purpose is to dramatize those principles which the group has betrayed, to supply a consciously mythologized version of the alternative to the present disorder.

This idea of history has radical dangers, of course, implying as it does an almost Stalinist notion of the past as raw material, to be shaped according to the prejudices of the present. But these are dangers that any idea of history that goes beyond the commonplace acceptance of a linear sequence must encounter; and in any case they are ones that, I think, Tate manages to avoid in practice. He does this, quite simply, by using myth as an extension of fact rather than a denial of it, and by making his recomposition of history a deliberate and explicit one. That is to say, his purpose in describing the plantation South in the way he does is not to present a complete distortion of the historical past, but to articulate what *might* have happened if its best energies had been realized. As Tate never tires of pointing out, the Old South was comparatively near to the feudal prototype; and all he does in his imaginative work, consequently, is to develop this proximity into identity so as to supply his readers with a corrective legend—an argument in narrative and metaphor for the principles his own generation has betrayed. It is a sophisticated strategy, but an unconcealed one, so that readers are never in doubt of what is happening.

Not only is it unconcealed: in Tate's best work, this engagement of the present with the past is even emphasized, and this primarily by means of the device of the narrator. In the "Ode to the Confederate Dead," for example, the conflict between the "active faith" of previous generations and the fragmentation of the present one is presented in terms of a series of memories. The narrator, a man who characterizes the contemporary failure, stands by the monuments raised to those killed fighting for the South during the Civil War; and as he describes their lives, or rather what he imagines their lives to have been, the description is transformed into a celebration. The persons described are metamorphosed into an heroic alternative to the plight of the person describing. That is the drama of the poem, accounting for the extraordinary poignancy of lines like the following.

> Turn your eyes to the immoderate past,
> Turn to the inscrutable infantry rising
> Demons out of the earth—they will not last.
> Stonewall, Stonewall, and the sunken fields of hemp,
> Shiloh, Antietam, Malvern Hill, Bull Run.
> Lost in that orient of the thick-and-fast
> You will curse the setting sun.
>
> Cursing only the leaves crying
> Like an old man in a storm
> You hear the shout, the crazy hemlocks point
> With troubled fingers to the silence which
> Smothers you, a mummy, in time.[69]

The point, as I see it, is that here and elsewhere in the poem Tate actually dramatizes the mythologizing process, just as William Faulkner does, for a different purpose, in *Absalom, Absalom!* The reader shares with an identifiable narrator the experience of creating an idea, a complex of possibilities, out of a historical fact, an idea that may be implicit in that fact but which is in no sense encompassed by it. In a traditional situation, of course, this process would be a symptom of confidence, the will to isolate the best of the present in a special vision of the past. But author, reader, and narrator are all placed firmly in an untraditional context here; so in this case it is symptomatic of an acknowledged need more than anything else. The sense of loss that is attached to the narrator, in other words, occasions that development of an heroic alternative—or, to use Tate's own phrase, "an imperative of reference"—which is the actual subject of the narrative.

This is also true, with some additional complications, of *The Fathers,* a book that, despite the fact that it was published first in the thirties, has only just been accepted as one of the more welcome results of the Southern "renaissance." Some commentators have gone even further, claiming that it is Tate's most important creative work as well. Certainly, it is his most characteristic, being a distillation of his principal concerns and a kind of inventory of the metaphors that are elsewhere dispersed throughout his writing. Central to the tale is its teller, Lacey Buchan. Buchan, now an old man, is recalling the years of his childhood and youth in old Virginia before the Civil War; and as in "Ode to the Confederate Dead" this dramatic context of memory is important and emphasized. As Buchan puts it:

> In my feelings of that time there is a new element—my feelings now about that time: there is not an old man living who can recover the emotions of the past; he can only bring back the objects around which, secretly, the emotions have ordered themselves in memory, and that memory is not what happened in the year 1860 but is rather a few symbols, . . .

symbols that will preserve only so much of the old life as they may, in their own mysterious history, consent to bear.[70]

The reader is once again witnessing the construction of a myth, created out of a sense of loss. The only difference is that in this case the sense is not just communal but personal, too: Buchan is close enough to the events and people remembered to feel that the radical disjunction between past and present he is describing is a part of his own history, as well as that of his culture.

This is a crucial addition to the narrative. In a sense, *The Fathers* is about the disintegration of ante-bellum society during the Civil War. But that is accompanied and indeed largely represented by the disintegration of the Buchan family, brought about by the intrusion of alien elements into the group. This has two important consequences. In the first place, it contributes an extra poignancy, a further touch of anguish, to the process of remembering. Lacey is talking about people whom, as he says, he "knew and loved," now "scattered into the new life of the modern age where they cannot even find themselves," and this supplies an especially urgent motive for his reshaping of the past. And in the second it enables Tate to demonstrate his idea of "moral unity" in the actual structure of the fiction—the way in which, in a traditional society, the public and private levels of experience are integrated. It is not simply that the personal history of the Buchan family is taken to be representative of the larger history of the South, although it is partly that. It is also that these two histories, as Buchan describes them, are so thoroughly interrelated as to be inseparable: they do not just represent each other, they affect each other as well. The Buchans as a group, for instance, are torn apart by a crisis peculiar to themselves *and* by the war with the North—which divides their loyalties and is eventually responsible for the destruction of their estate. The "time of crisis" in their story concerns both their "domestic trials" *and* the beginning of hostilities at Fort Sumter. At one point in the novel, when he is describing what he takes to be the extraordinary completeness of life in the South before the Civil War, Buchan declares:

> Our domestic manners and satisfactions were as impersonal as the United States Navy, and the belief widely held today, that men may live apart from the political order, that indeed the only humane and honorable satisfactions must be gained in spite of the public order, would have astonished most men of that time as a remote fantasy, impossible of realization.[71]

The remark is not fortuitous. For it is precisely this interdependence of the domestic and the political which Tate is trying to suggest in his telling of the tale.

The tale itself has two major characters: Major Buchan, who is Lacey's father, and George Posey. The Major is the embodiment of all the values Lacey associates with life before the Civil War, a man who is governed by the forms of his society because his thoughts and feelings have found perfect expression in them. He, in turn, invariably considers the individual quality of any other man whom he meets to be intimately bound up with his social function. The forms in which the Major has been bred are quite complicated: that is their merit, that they are subtle and indeed flexible enough to cater to any event. But at basis they are characterized by extraordinary generosity, of spirit and conduct—a self-restraint and consideration for others that another great believer in forms, Jane Austen, once described as "delicacy." The funeral scene at the beginning of the book offers a good illustration of what I mean by this. The Major has lost his wife (that is who the funeral is for) and he is, certainly, crushed by his loss. The ceremony of the funeral, however, not only helps him to bear it but even gives him the strength he needs to look after the people around him—to treat the guests with the appropriate courtesy, and to make sure that none of the more intimate members of the family, including his wife's own body slave, is excluded from the proceedings. Why is this so? Because, as Tate has explained elsewhere, a traditional society of the kind the Major is taken to represent is one in which the recognition of human limits, and so of mortality, is primary. Death is accepted as "the completion of life,"[72] and that acceptance discovers its formal expression in the ritual of the funeral, which at once reminds its participants of an inevitability and supplies them with a stylized catharsis —a transference of grief. In taking part in the funeral, consequently— indeed, in assuming the role of its organizer—Major Buchan is finding an appropriate form for his own personal grief, *the* appropriate form as far as his society is concerned. He is not in any sense evading his own feelings, although to more jaundiced modern eyes it might appear that he is doing so; on the contrary, what he is doing, as Tate sees it, is to encounter those feelings and do full justice to them. Ceremony, the implication is, offers the Major the only possible means he has of understanding and controlling the more extreme pressures to which he is subject, and of doing this without denying their power. With its help, the amorphous energies of his inner life are projected into the outer, to be given shape and the release that would not otherwise be theirs.

The difference between this stance toward reality and the one attributed to the character of George Posey is radical. Posey, whose own origins lie in the city of Georgetown, marries *into* the Buchan family but he is never *of* it. In a way, he does not belong to the context of the Old South at all because, as an agent and emblem of the antitraditional, he is all that is representative of its destruction. His responses to life are not shaped by any code, and this leaves him curiously unprotected from what Lacey Buchan calls "the abyss"—by which he means, I think, the disruptive energies circulating in and around the isolated self that only such a code can control. Doomed to receive "the shock of the world at the end of his nerves,"[73] Posey's behavior is an unnerving mixture of timidity, as he shrinks from any encounter with this abyss, and hysteria, which occurs when the suppressed energies become too much for him and he must find release in violence. At the funeral, for instance, he shows himself quite incapable of dealing with an extreme situation, since he does not possess the tools of manner and belief that would enable him to do so. All he can do is try to appease his incipient terror by making brutal and offhand references to the physical aspects of death, the rotting corpse and the waiting grave, and, when this fails to escape from the pressures of the event, by riding away.

Posey is, of course, far too complicated and dynamic a character to be immediately identifiable with any stereotype, but there is a sense in which his own failure to realize traditional standards invites a comparison with the familiar figure of the "Yankee." A telling symptom of the disintegrative state of his personality, that is to say, is his tendency to fluctuate between those twin characteristics of idealism and materialism that the Southerner loved, and still loves, to associate with his Northern neighbor. Certainly, Posey has noble ideals of human behavior, but he never quite manages to engage them with reality. His relationship with his wife, Susan Buchan, for example, is fatally affected by what Tate calls his "too personal" attitude toward her. As Lacey Buchan puts it:

> There is no doubt that he loved Susan too much; by that I mean he was too personal, and with his exacerbated nerves he was constantly receiving impressions out of the chasm that yawns beneath lovers; therefore he must have had a secret brutality for her when they were alone.[74]

Posey's love is "too personal" because in a curious way it is too abstract; unlike Major Buchan, he can never objectify his feelings in terms of the society in which he lives. He has no ritual to supply him with catharsis and satisfaction, and so he has recourse to the kind of random violence, the incoherent gestures toward establishing a contact, which succeed only in driving Susan insane. His very idealism about human relationships prevents him from establishing any, with his wife or anyone else, and the irony is that he then has to fall back upon money for his sense of the real; the cash nexus, it turns out, must supply him with the security and certainty he so desperately needs. By the end of the novel he has run his course, more than once, between extremities, and it surely reflects credit on his creator to say that here, at least, these extremities seem to be parts of a credible pattern of human behavior. A paradox in logic, perhaps, Posey's eventual commitment both to absolute ideas and to the statistics of the account book comes across to the reader as the product of personal necessity—belonging to a single, if disastrous, way of life.

It goes without saying, perhaps, that because Posey's life style is so disastrous, so much the result of a fatal series of errors, the moral conflict between him and Major Buchan is a pretty unequal one. We know from the start which character we are supposed to admire, and why, and consequently there can be none of that tension to be found in more conventional novels, where one half-truth does battle with another. But, even though this kind of tension is necessarily missing from *The Fathers*, there is another kind possible, peculiar to elegies, which depends upon our seeing that the moral tendencies of the narrative and its strictly historical direction are at cross-purposes, and this Tate uses extensively. That is why Major Buchan seems so helpless: because the more he behaves as he must—by which I mean, of course, as a traditional person must—the weaker he appears to be. The novel is founded on the premise that traditionalism has disappeared, lost with the passing of time; so any one of its characters who demonstrates traditional virtues, in the way that the Major does, must immediately define himself as a man swimming against the tide. And anyone, in turn, who acts in an untraditional way must appear to have the forces of history behind him; his vices, in these circumstances, become his strength. The tournament scene in Part I of the book illustrates this, for in it Posey rides to a success that virtually depends on a failure of responsibility. In order to win the tournament—and he wants desperately to win—he has to purchase a good new mare, in order to do which he is quite willing to sell his Negro half-brother to the highest bidder. He has few scruples about this because, unlike Major Buchan, his relationship to his slaves, even when there are also blood ties between them, is defined entirely by what Tate elsewhere calls "a system of money references that the moral will cannot control." He simply excuses himself to the Negro by saying, "You're liquid capital, and I've got to have money."[75] He gets the money he wants, he wins; and the reader cannot help feeling, as Tate intends him to, that any victory so won is more than in the tournament—with reasons behind it that have to do with more than the selling out of just one man.

The implications of this tournament scene are multiplied by the presence of several other characters who help us to locate George

Posey a little more precisely. John Langton, for instance, a neighbor
of the Buchans, offers a useful balance to them in that he seems to
represent the worst possibilities of his society just as they do its best.
Described by Lacey as "a bold and insolent man who deemed himself
an aristocrat beyond any consideration for other people," Langton
seems to have assumed all the privileges available to his caste without accepting any of the accompanying duties. He acts without any
sense of responsibility to others, his every refinement of behavior being
merely a symptom of his self-concern—like a man bowing to himself
in a mirror. For all that, though, he comes across to the reader as just
plain silly rather than dangerous or perverse, a person whose more
violent emotions can usually find an outlet, and a relatively harmless
outlet at that, in the rituals available to him. Ceremonies, like those of
the hunt and the duel, make his a radically limited kind of corruption
—limited, especially, when compared to George Posey, whose every
passion is left to feed on itself until it assumes frightening proportions.
Beside Posey, Langton may not be a particularly admirable figure—in
the way, say, that Major Buchan is—but he does at least seem to be
an acceptable one; and made so, we suspect, by a society that has
found in its traditions a name for his evil as well as a name for love.

The traditional society, then, takes account of an extraordinary
range of feelings, externalizing them, fulfilling them, and in the process
making it possible for those who would normally be at their mercy
to exercise some degree of control over them: that, more or less, is
the message carried to us when Tate brings together John Langton
and Major Buchan as the two poles of the local group. It is a message
we have already heard, perhaps, in "Ode to the Confederate Dead";
and just in case we should still miss it, not noticing Langton's relevance as a complement to the Buchan family, it is sounded again in
Tate's presentation of the minor characters. The tournament scene,
in fact, is one of the few occasions on which they are permitted to
speak for themselves (most of the time Tate keeps our attention concentrated, in a very Jamesian way, on a limited group of protagonists),
and the result is, I think, quite significant. For what they do here,
effectively, is perform the function of chorus to the major action of
victory and defeat—not, admittedly, by saying that much about it but
simply by being on hand to act in a normal fashion. Throughout the
various contests, whether as participants or as the spectators, they
behave with a grace and flexibility that reflects real credit on the code
to which they subscribe, the accepted forms that have given their
every step a certain shapeliness. And this, Tate seems to be saying, is
the ultimate achievement of traditionalism: that quite apart from
breeding the exceptional man, the Major Buchans of each generation,

it enables a group of otherwise ordinary people to move easily between the "jargon . . . of paddock and kennel" and the chivalry of
the field. Country humor and the manners of the polite, the smell of
Bourbon or squabbles over political affairs and the elaborate ceremonial that attends the crowning of the "Queen of Love and Beauty,"
the first lady of the tournament: vast and quite diverse areas of experience remain open to these people that are closed to George Posey
and his kind—and thanks simply, we infer, to the fact that theirs is a
traditional, which is to say a landowning, society. A relatively straightforward "means of living" and a formal "way of life"[76] are both parts
of their inherited environment and as such define the scope, the very
considerable scope, of the life style available to them.

It is difficult to talk about *The Fathers,* or indeed any creative work
by Allen Tate, without giving the impression that it is excessively abstract, more disposed toward the communication of an idea than the
articulation of an experience. This is unfortunate, since, although
Tate is concerned with literature as a form of knowledge, it is knowledge that, as he puts it, is "complete" and "of the mythical order"—
that is, it is knowledge realized in a series of living contacts rather
than otherwise. One reason for this is fairly clear. Tate not only has
certain absolute ideas about the nature of a traditional society, he has
absolute ideas about the nature of traditional art as well. Quite
apart from the way in which it treats history, the material of a given
experience, there is the question of the forms most appropriate to it,
and of special interest to Tate in this respect is the case of the traditional *writer.* The traditional writer, Tate argues, identifies himself as such by trying—even in an untraditional environment—to recover in his methods of expression some measure of that wholeness
that is a characteristic feature of the good society. This he does with
the help of what is called "the symbolic imagination"—the faculty
in man which "conducts an action through analogy, of the human to
the divine, . . . of the low to the high, of time to eternity." It is the
business of the traditional writer, Tate goes on,

> . . . to return to the order of the temporal sequence—to action. His
> purpose is to show men experiencing whatever they may be capable of,
> with as much meaning as he may be able to see in it; but the action
> comes first.[77]

The last phrase is crucial. As Tate sees it, the traditional writer must
describe ideas *in action,* and action as a complex unity. In doing this,
he must resort neither to overparticularity nor to large and unsub-
stantiated abstractions: the aim must be knowledge as experience or
the result will be failure.

It does not take an unusual amount of ingenuity, I believe, to see that this kind of knowledge is exactly the kind Tate is after in his verse and fiction. In works like "Ode to the Confederate Dead" and *The Fathers*, absolutely everything is dramatized; there is a genuine attempt to realize the concept of traditionalism in the mode of communication as well as in the matter communicated. That is why there is so much emphasis on the act of seeing, the visualization of the idea.

> Seeing, seeing only the leaves
> Flying, plunge and expire
>
> Turn your eyes to the immoderate past . . .

I see figures on the lawn that morning at Pleasant Hill, I hear voices . . .[78]

Within this context every perceived object assumes significance, each element of knowledge is concretized. The graveyard, for example, appears to circumscribe the action of both the ode and the novel—not just as a setting, although of course it is that, but as an outward and visible sign of the dominant mood of elegy. That is not all, either. For the further details of the two graveyard scenes contain within them intimations of death and life: the "cracked paint" on the walls of the morning room in *The Fathers* is set off against the "first shoots of April green" in the garden. The "mulberry bush"[79] in the Confederate graveyard offers a contrary suggestion to the leaves falling around the headstones. Out of these details emerge more complex assessments of the situations in which they appear. The counterpointed themes, obviously, are those of decay and recovery; and they point to a larger ambivalence of attitude, which juxtaposes the decline of the way of life celebrated with the vitality of the tradition it represents—the death of an order with continuing possibilities for its revival. This ambivalence, as it turns out, is basic to both *The Fathers* and the "Ode"; and the reader is obliged to acknowledge its tangibility, its felt value, precisely because he has not just been told about it. It has been dramatized for him there in the imagined scenes.

This use of images that beget fresh images, and so carry the argument almost secretly to its conclusion, is vital to the success of Tate's work; and as evidence of his dramatizing tendency it applies to far more, I think, than just his rendering of scene. Quite apart from this, there is its relevance to his treatment of character where what is noticeable, perhaps above all, is his scrupulous avoidance of conventional methods of analysis in favor of more figurative ones; character becomes less a matter of psychology and more a question of the kind of significant external details that the author picks out for emphasis. Take George Posey, for example. His is a complex, personal case—as complex, say, as any we are likely to find in more conventional, psychoanalytical fiction—but it is not presented to us in conventional terms. On the contrary, what Tate chiefly relies on to explain Posey to us is a series of associated metaphors. Whenever he appears, a cluster of images almost invariably appears with him, dramatic images that are justified by their context, and these tell us all we really need to know about the way he lives and the things he stands for. Horseback riding, for instance: George Posey's life seems to be bound up in horseback riding, because as Tate sees it this activity is a significant symptom of his restlessness—and, on a more figurative level, a measure of certain more subterranean aspects of his personality as well. He rides away from the funeral of Mrs. Buchan when he can no longer tolerate the thought of death; as a gunrunner during the Civil War he rides back and forth across the Union lines; and, of course, at the tournament he appears on horseback, the only man present wearing a mask and using a vicious curb bit. Eventually, just in case the reader should have missed the significance of all this, he has it more or less explained to him by Lacey Buchan.

> . . . I thought of him always boldly riding somewhere, and because I couldn't see where, I suppose I thought of a precipice. . . . He [Posey] had great energy and imagination and . . . he had to keep moving; but where? I always come back to the horseman riding off over the precipice . . . that is what he gave . . . —mystery and imagination, the heightened vitality possessed by a man who knew no bounds.[80]

The explanation is helpful, but hardly necessary. For the association of the horse with animal vitality, its journey with a flight into chaos, and George Posey himself with the febrile and isolated heroes of Edgar Allan Poe—all this has been achieved, essentially, in the actual portraits of Posey out riding, and the connections established between these portraits and the larger metaphorical structure of the book. The character has already been defined for us by imaginative reference, the meanings attached to his physical situation, and any further explanation or direct psychoanalysis we may be offered comes very close to being superfluous.

Up until now the methods of characterization I have described may not sound all that unusual; they are not very far removed, after all, from a fairly commonplace use of metaphor to convey meaning. The dramatization of the inner life goes much further than this, however, when Tate's subject is the civilization of the Old South, because in such cases the inner landscapes of his characters are not just represented by the outer ones, they are actually expressed by them. The people he portrays consequently assume the kind of status that we tend to associate with more primitive literatures, where all the drama occurs at the level of the spoken word and completed action. Why is this the case? Why do Tate's plantation types present themselves to us in this way? Tate himself has offered us an explanation, I think, in his biography of the Confederate general "Stonewall" Jackson, which he wrote early on in his career. It is quite simply that, as he sees it, this was the way things were in the Old South—or, rather, this was the way things might have been at the best of times. Ideally, the South saw itself as a homogeneous unit, a society with common aims and patterns of belief. Its own best image of itself was as a group so closely knit and perfectly integrated that there was no need for anybody to maintain secrecy over anything; "the man as he appeared in public," consequently, "was the man, his public appearance was his moral life."[81] So when a man like Major Buchan experiences some new mood or emotion he does not have to hoard it up in a separate corner of his being to which we, in turn, must repair if we wish to know all about it. On the contrary, it is acted out for us, in the open, in one of his casual movements—casual and yet, because of its meaning, somehow ceremonial as well—and we merely have to witness that movement in order to know his mood. There is a perfect illustration of what I mean right at the end of *The Fathers*, when Major Buchan can no longer evade the fact that he is a defeated man, with a plantation irremediably ruined by the fortunes of civil war. He has to acknowledge a climactic change, which in turn has to be registered for the reader, and all this is done in a characteristic manner. In the middle of the day, when he should still be working on the plantation, the Major changes from his field clothes into the formal suit he normally reserves for the times when he has nothing to do. It is a simple act but an effective, almost ceremonial, one; and in a way the whole of the man and the culture to which he belongs is contained in it.

The whole of the man and culture, that is, as they are conceived of within the consciously mythological framework of Tate's writing: in the end, the emphasis has to be upon this, his strategy of using history as a moral reference rather than a process—and a reference that calls attention to itself on every page. The dangers implicit in this approach are, I suppose, fairly obvious. Tate puts himself, as a result, in equal peril of turning literature into dogma, should his message tend to restrict the medium of plantation legend too severely, or of lapsing into the kind of easy nostalgia that a book like *Gone With the Wind* typifies, if the message becomes submerged in its glamorous setting. To preach, or to lose oneself in daydreams: both are possible temptations, but in the end Tate does not succumb to either of them. He is saved and what, I think, is responsible for saving him can be stated very quickly: it is his awareness, the astonishing degree of self-consciousness in his performance, which enables him to transform romance into idea, and idea into action. He is, it is clear, aware of *what* he is doing: he is trying to confirm the value of traditionalism. And he is aware also of *how*, precisely, this should be done—by accepting the notion of traditionalism in life as a source of imaginative assessment, a suitable catalyst for his plantation material, and then using the notion of traditionalism in art as a guide to the way in which this assessment should be delivered. Not content to stop there, Tate even seems to be aware of his awareness, the special qualities of his intelligence that have encouraged him to find something of permanent applicability in his own past. For once, when he was asked to comment on the phenomenon of Southern literature, he replied with an essay that makes a distinction between those who have used their regional inheritance with success and those who have not. Predictably enough, perhaps, the distinction is couched in terms of a contrast between the "provincial" or conventional writer and the traditionalist. By the traditionalist here, Tate goes on to explain, he means

> . . . the writer who takes the South as he knows it today or can find out about it in the past, and who sees it as a region with some special characteristics, but otherwise offering as an imaginative subject the plight of human beings as it has been and doubtless will continue to be, here and in other parts of the world.[82]

The description is a good one, offered with a characteristic air of authority—and it would surely not be to convict Allen Tate of undue arrogance to suggest that he might have been thinking of himself when he offered it.

The Failure of Traditionalism: Donald Davidson

The distinction that Allen Tate has made between the traditional writer and the provincial one brings us to the fourth member of the Agrarian group to achieve fame outside of his own region, the poet and critic Donald Davidson; and it brings us to him because with Davidson it is precisely this matter of quality, the measure of creative achievement, which becomes important. He is, the reader senses, inferior as a writer to Ransom, Warren, and Tate—but why? After all, he drew on the same resources of history and local tradition and even claimed to use these resources for similarly mythic or at least emblematic purposes. Why, then, do we feel obliged to bring an evaluative method to bear when comparing his work with something like, say, Ransom's "Antique Harvesters," a method that will help us to define the superiority of the latter? Even more important, do the reasons for this superiority have anything at all to do with the different uses to which history is put in the work of the two poets? In other words, is it possible to claim that Davidson was wrong in supposing that the way in which he used his Southern inheritance was identifiable with the procedures of Ransom, or with those of Warren and Tate; and that once this is recognized the most important step has been taken toward explaining why, quite simply, he is not as good a writer as they are— why his assessment of experience is less vivid and memorable than theirs? Obviously, these are questions which have to do with more than the differences between Davidson and his three more eminent colleagues; by inference they are relevant to the distinction to be drawn when other people from the Agrarian group are involved along with these four. And beyond this they open up the entire problem of evaluating, as well as describing, a writer in terms of his engagement with his historical and social environment. That is to say, once we start explaining why Donald Davidson is inferior to Ransom, Warren, and Tate within the context of their various commitments to their region, we are tending by implication to establish a scale of measurement that evaluates a writer according to the way in which he deals with history—history as manifested in his own experience and that of his locale. Such a scale, it need hardly be added, could be applied to far more than just the literature of the Southern "renaissance."

To return specifically to Davidson for a moment: a comparison between him and at least one of the Agrarians, John Crowe Ransom, is made all the more imperative—and easier—because in his earliest verse, collected in *An Outland Piper*, a definite attempt is made to imitate the tone and ironies of the older poet. The assumption of Ransom's mask, however, does not conceal the differences between the two writers—it merely emphasizes them. The irony is notable only for its uneasiness and ultimate inappropriateness. A short poem called "Dryad,"[83] which describes the seduction of a shopgirl by a small-town gigolo, offers a good example of what I mean. As the discrepancy between the subject and the title suggests, Davidson's initial intention seems to have been to achieve a mock-heroic effect by contrasting the event described and the mode of description, and so to prick the bubble of sentimental pretense. Traces of this intention remain in the opening lines, which associate the young rake with a satyr and the object of his blandishments, "mured at her gingham counter," with a lady imprisoned in her castle. But these soon disappear, along with most of the irony, under the pressure of the poet's emerging sympathy for the girl. Gradually the focus of the action is changed, the detached stance giving way to the involved, until everything seems to be presented through *her* eyes. And with this accomplished it becomes evident that such power as the poem possesses derives from the evocation of her "wasting soul," hungering for the kind of romantic release that she associates temporarily with her lover. In effect, "Dryad" becomes more a defense of the romantic attitude than a criticism of it, a celebration of the impulse to transform "dead finite into infinite"[84] no matter how unjustified that impulse may prove to be. And in the process the poet's scorn is transferred from the romantic alien to those "reasoners" who would deny her romanticism and criticize the alienation.

With the other poems in *An Outland Piper*, too, the tone only becomes consistent when Davidson drops all pretensions toward the dualism of Ransom and concentrates his energies on a critique of the "reasoner," or a celebration of the romantic. And, insofar as this involves an examination of the modes of power and success in contemporary life, the results are all to the good. It makes possible, for instance, a series of effective if not especially subtle satires on such paradigmatic figures as the progressive clergyman, "who sanctifieth Booster's clubs"; or the shop assistant who, by jingling "furtive fingers through the till/ Dropping delicious coins with snap and grin,"[85] demonstrates that the only thing separating him from his employers is an inability to translate greed into action. To the extent that this movement away from the influence of Ransom drives Davidson into a form of escapism, however, it represents a radical simplification of attitude and tone. The poet as "outland piper" is in fact translated into another version of the shopgirl in "Dryad." He is different, certainly, in the sense that there is a heightened degree of awareness implicit in his revulsion from his environment, but like the girl he also seeks comfort in a dreamland, some place where his problems and difficulties seem wondrously to disappear.

This less fortunate consequence of Davidson's disgust with what he has called "the spiritual disorder of modern life" is not obvious in *An Outland Piper*, because at the time when it was published he had not yet found an appropriate location for his dreamland. By the time his next collection of verse appeared, however, he had discovered or rather invented one in history—the history, that is, of his family and region. The title poem, "The Tall Men," indicates the change. It is a long poem, with eight sections linked loosely together, and it more or less illustrates the themes that were to preoccupy Davidson for the rest of his life—as well as his characteristic methods of presenting them. The connecting link between the sections is a dramatized narrator, a representative man whose life the reader shares for the course of one day—from the moment when he is "Flung up from sleep against the breakfast table/Like numb and helpless driftwood"[86] to the hour when he lies half asleep, trying to devise possible means of escape from his situation. During the course of this day the poem ranges back and forth in historical time, although the place is nearly always Nashville, Tennessee, and as a result of this procedure we are supplied with a means of assessing the evidence. The present, in sum, is judged in terms of a past articulated in dream, in memory—or more simply by means of a series of comparisons between places in Tennessee then and now.

Some parts of the poem demonstrate a capacity that Davidson has always had for launching enormously powerful philippics against the "mechanical age." A passage like the following, for instance, effectively dehumanizes the narrator by presenting him as a series of dissociated elements whose functions have been usurped by the machine.

> The modern brain, guarded not only by bone,
> Afferent nerves, withering hair, and skin,
> Requires the aid of mystical apparatus
> (Weights, levers, motor, steel rods, black boy)
> And pyramiding dollars nicely invested
> To float in boredom up to the cool fifth floor . . .
> Assisted to the chair (Grand Rapids) by
> Two slippers (from St. Louis) bites cigar
> (Perhaps Havana) strikes a match (Bellefonte)
> Unwrinkles trousers (Massachusetts) leafs
> The "New York Times" . . .[87]

This passage is related to others in which the association of the present with the fragmented and inhuman, with all that John Taylor of Caroline identified as "the engine of power and oppression," is vigorously reaffirmed. The result is to establish a network of metaphor that gives some kind of support to Davidson's rhetoric, the direct attacks on contemporary civilization that climax in an apocalyptic vision of its destruction by fire.

> The city's burning up? Why good! Then let her burn! . . .
> Citizens awake! Fire is upon you . . .
> Rush out into the night, take nothing with you,
> Only your naked selves, your sound hearts.
> Fly from the wrath of fire to the hills
> Where water is and the slow peace of time . . .[88]

As the reference to the "sound hearts" of the citizens in this passage indicates, Davidson unlike Warren does not believe in original sin, an idea that would make the urban scene at worst a participant in the process of moral deterioration rather than its cause. On the contrary, he tends to locate the root of man's trouble in his environment, without specifying how that environment came into being in the first place,

and so to conclude that a change of scene will bring about an immediate and radical alteration of character. This is determinism of the
simplest kind, and its implications for Davidson's formulation of a
positive life style, the ways in which it leads him to describe alternatives to the urban experience, are hinted at in the last two lines of
the passage. Flight is counseled, in fact—flight into a Great Good Place,
still regarded as possible, which is not so much defined as conceived
of as a series of antimonies to the present discontent.

This brings us to the function of Southern history in the poem: it is
there to supply a notion of the Great Good Place to which flight is to be
made. As such, it has very little to do either with the facts of the case or
with the kind of mythologizing process we have noted in the work of
Ransom, Warren, and Tate—the process, that is, whereby an idea of the
region is shaped into a consciously articulated framework of value, to be
then tested against the pressures of experience. The Old South, Davidson insists, was quite simply everything that contemporary society is not.
The narrator is described as aimless and lost in a "vague, inconceivable
world." So the men of old Tennessee are praised for their certainty, the
sense of moral direction as well as physical that led them to find sanctuary in the land around Nashville. The city is dismissed as a place
where "even the seasons wither"; and so the vanished civilization is
associated with the "new soil" from which it benefited, its people with
the "young cold" and "ravenous spring" on which they depended. The
spiritual landscape is transformed along with the physical, from the
intimations of death contained in such lines as

> Only the blind stone roots of the dull street
> And the steel thews of houses flourish here.
> Skulls hurry past, . . .[89]

to the notions of vitality attached to pioneers of former times and
their "teeming wives." In the event, ante-bellum society emerges from
"The Tall Men," as it does from nearly all of Davidson's subsequent
poems, as another version of that familiar dream of the determinist
when the world devised by his philosophy is too much with him—a
place, essentially, where all is possibility, where the limitations of his
own world disappear and no wish is frustrated by circumstance.

One result of this way of dealing with Southern history deserves to
be mentioned above all others; and that is Davidson's persistent refusal
to discriminate between the two regional versions of the agrarian idea.
The good farmer and the fine planter are endorsed with equal enthusiasm, and with little attempt made to reconcile their conflicting tendencies, because both offer an antithesis to what he has described as "the
new barbarism of science and technology."[90] This leads to extraordi-

nary confusion for the reader who wants a definite idea of what the poem is celebrating. At one moment he is offered passages that sound like poeticized versions of *Notes on Virginia,* where the center of gravity is clearly with those who till the earth.

> . . . A boy's hands thrust
> Insistent swords of corn-leaves from his face,
> . . . The field
> Waits where the mower clicks its teeth . . .
> . . . Here are the teams.
> Wagons rattle and halt. The haft of a pitchfork
> Presses hickory into a youngish palm.[91]

But the impression created here is soon canceled out in other scenes, redolent with glamour, which bring the entire tradition of plantation romance to mind.

> . . . old tremulous histories
> Of slender hands, proud smiling lips and halls
> Peopled with fragile beauty . . .
> . . . tall pillars of a house
> Lording a shadowy park . . .
> . . . Here is the stair
> Where Lady Miranda walked with futile lips
> Gallantly firm . . .
>
> . . . Here are
> In a glass case, pistols that killed a man
> For honor's sake. Here music was and here
> The ghosts of gentlemen who died for honor.[92]

Davy Crockett is placed side by side with a planter described as "the finest gentleman/That ever lived"; and a settler named McCrory, "who drove the Indians from his cabin," claims equal attention with one John Sevier, who invokes the "chivalry of an ancient name" when called upon, as a ghost, to speak out of history. At one point in the poem Davidson refers to these characters and others like them as representatives of "the motley splendor of the past";[93] and lost amid the maze of contrary speculations that they inspire the reader may well be tempted to agree, while placing additional emphasis upon the word "motley."

There is nothing wrong with placing different types and varieties of people within the context of the regional past, of course. On the contrary, it could be described as the most sensible strategy to adopt, since there is every evidence that such variety did actually exist then. What is surely mistaken, though, is to insist as Davidson does that each person he presents is *typical*—without recognizing, apparently, that the notion of typicality involves an implicit acceptance of the principle of consistency. That is to say, to claim in the way Davidson does that any particular figure from the past whom he chooses to apotheosize is characteristic of that past is to translate its several tendencies into accomplishments; and, whereas tendencies certainly can conflict, accomplishment is dependent upon choice, a commitment to a specific goal and framework of value. We can say that the Old South demonstrated a number of different possibilities, aristocratic and democratic, without being inconsistent. We can mythologize it into a version of the Good Life, using one or the other series of possibilities as our point of departure, again without creating any impression of internal inconsistency. We can even, as Ransom and Warren do, establish principles that enable us to reconcile the different series—or at least elements in both—and shape them into a thoroughly credible alternative. But we cannot, with any expectation of coherence and success, disregard all the latent contradictions by simply developing both series into separate indices of the regional achievement. And this, essentially, is the procedure of "The Tall Men."

It is the procedure of most of Davidson's work in prose and verse, following the publication of "The Tall Men," as well. His essays, for example, are ripe with a confusion that recalls some of the worst excesses of John Caldwell Calhoun. One piece will elaborate upon "the graciousness and repose of the old Southern tradition" in which, as Davidson sees it, "the . . . feeling of white responsibility" was answered by "black loyalty and devotion," and every level of the community was "conservative and stable." Another will set up the counter-tradition of a fundamentally dynamic society, peopled by "thorough-going Jeffersonians" and governed by a "natural aristocracy of virtue and talent" that varied with each generation, or even with each year. Once or twice Davidson does indicate some awareness of the difficulties in which he is embroiling himself—as, for example, when he says that "in the Old South, aristocracy and democracy . . . fused and rendered each other mutual support."[94] But like Calhoun he never provides any convincing support for such claims, which consequently serve to weaken his argument still further rather than reinforce it. If any importance is ascribed to them at all it must, in view of the lack of evidence, be for the way in which they betray Davidson's own uneasiness about his case and not for the resolution that they so conspicuously fail to offer. All Davidson does at such moments, in effect, is to demonstrate that to protest too much invariably invites suspicion.

A similar type of special pleading is implicit in Davidson's use of the inherited rhetoric—the rhetoric, that is, devised by Southerners of the previous century in defense of their region. Davidson is by no means alone among the Agrarians in exploiting this rhetoric. In different ways, as we have seen, it supplies the staple idiom of *I'll Take My Stand* and much of the individual work of Ransom, Warren, and Tate as well. But he is exceptional, although not unique, among this group in that he exploits it far more directly and deliberately, which is to say more aggressively, than most of them do. At his best, and this is usually in the poetry, the result is an elaborate network of metaphor reinforcing the identification of the city with the inhuman, and urban man with "aimless motors" rotating in a vast system of machinery. "The Tall Men" supplies many examples of this, and to a large extent, as I have suggested, the success of its assault on the "machine age" depends upon them. At his worst, however, and this is quite often in the prose, Davidson returns the inherited rhetoric to its original function of hiding the gaps and deficiencies in the argument. It is there, in other words, not to add weight to a situation already apprehended but to mask a failure of apprehension. There are many possible examples of this, and one out of the many occurs when Davidson chooses to argue against change, the alterations taking place in the regional landscape. What he does then is not to attempt any persuasion of his reader that depends upon placing the argument within a context of established principle, or taking a larger historical view. Instead, bearing in mind that the bulk of those he wishes to convince are Southerners, Davidson's strategy is to adopt that familiar and well-tried tool of the Southern orator, the racial issue. Change, it is asserted, the kind of change that is implicit in the loss of the old life styles, really means "the . . . elevation of the Negro" and "the degradation of the whites." Urbanization, in turn, signifies an invasion by "immigrant masses." Under the spell cast by Davidson's manipulation of the word, all that is lost is transformed into a nostalgic dream of purity and gentle folkways, while all that is found to replace it resembles the nightmares of some racial paranoiac. This brief passage, describing the eruption of the machine age in the hills, supplies an illustration of what I mean.

> The mountain boy could get a college education, but the system that built him a school also took out of his mouth the mountain ballad . . . and . . . gave him a "mammy song" devised in Tin Pan Alley by the urbanized descendant of a Russian Jew.[95]

In such cases, where language is being used to conceal the lack of a coherent framework of value rather than—as it is in the case of Ransom, say, or Tate—to articulate one, the uses of Southern rhetoric are shown in their least favorable light.

Just a few years after the publication of *I'll Take My Stand,* Donald Davidson was asked by the editor of the *American Review* to write a history of the Agrarian group, its inception and its purposes. He responded with a short and informal essay in which he paid only the most perfunctory attention to the facts in the case of the Agrarians. Events were brushed aside and attention concentrated instead upon motives—the common motives that, in Davidson's opinion, led such different people to contribute to the symposium. One motive was stressed above all others, and Davidson returned to it again and again during the course of his account. As he described it, it involved a peculiar combination of fear, revulsion, and what Henry James once called "the imagination of disaster." Davidson was characteristically emphatic about this: uppermost in the minds of every Agrarian, he insisted,

> . . . was a feeling of intense disgust with the spiritual disorder of modern life—its destruction of human integrity and its lack of purpose; and with this, we had a decided sense of impending fatality. We wanted a life which through its own conditions . . . would engender naturally . . . order, leisure, character, stability. . . . What history told us of the South . . . drove us straight to . . . its tradition. . . . Even in its seeming decline it contrasted sharply with the mode of life that we feared and disliked.[96]

The process that Davidson describes is a plausible one: disgust with the present, it appears, precipitated a turning in upon the past. The revulsion with the machine age occasioned an attachment to a time when factories were still the exception rather than the rule. Plausible though it is, however, it is, I think, inadequate to the extent that it defines *I'll Take My Stand* and its consequences in terms of negatives. Looking at this passage with a certain amount of hindsight we can say that its fatal flaw, and the flaw of the essay from which it is taken, is the stress it places on the defensiveness of the Agrarian response. It begins and ends by talking about fear, the radically unfavorable reaction of the Agrarians to "the spiritual disorder of modern life," and the positive alternative offered by the uses of history enters only by the way into the discussion—as a kind of reverse image, so to speak, which depends on the object being imaged for its existence. There is little sense in Davidson's description of the past being employed as a resource, a series of ideas and values continually interacting with the present, rather than just a retreat; and because there is not it can hardly be accepted as a satisfactory account of the motives leading writers such as Ransom, Warren, and Tate to investigate their region, or of their creative procedures during the course of this investigation. For works like "Antique Harvesters," *All the King's Men, The Fathers,* and "Ode to the Confederate Dead" reflect an attempt to involve the past *with* the present—not the acceptance of historical dislocation implied here.

But while Davidson's account of Agrarianism cannot be accepted as a satisfactory account of the major Agrarian writers, it does supply us with a means of understanding the minor ones. Apart from anything else, it helps explain the nature of Davidson's own work, in the sense that it clarifies his motives for writing in the way he did as well as the variable quality of his achievement. For what is most effective in his prose and poetry is precisely the feeling of disgust with the "machine age" that he discusses at such length in the essay. It is this, after all, which leads him to adopt his familiar role of prophet denouncing the aimlessness of his contemporaries. And what is perhaps least effective is the version of Southern history he formulates as an alternative system of value, which neither reflects a sense of engagement between the past and the present nor offers us a suitable framework of reference. In the event, it is little more than a piece of rhetoric, using "rhetoric" in the Yeatsian sense of will doing the work of the imagination. With all the will power and determination at his disposal, Davidson seizes upon a received image of the past, which has the vagueness and inconsistencies of received images generally, and then uses it as a stick with which to beat his own generation. It is neither freshly seen nor fully discovered; in a way, it is not *seen* at all because its function is to provoke no more than a stock response. Like the dream of the Arthurian Kingdom in some Victorian poetry, the dream of the Old South articulated in Davidson's writing is there to invite large feelings of loss and nostalgia—and that is about all it is there for.[97]

To generalize from specific examples is dangerous—partly because the examples may turn out to be unrepresentative, but even more because the generalization may introduce a certain vagueness and room for misunderstanding that the very specificity of the specific example tended to prevent. This is especially true if the discussion of literature is involved, where the experience of the individual case that is the poem or fiction or play supplies us with a proof that no amount of talking around it and abstracting from it can ever quite match. With all due allowance made for this, though, we might begin to draw some broader conclusions from the differences of quality we have found between Davidson on the one hand and Ransom, Warren, and Tate on the other. In fact, the conclusions are already there to be drawn from what has been said about Davidson and his writing. He is clearly not as good as the other three writers; he is less interesting and memorable than they are. And perhaps this inferiority has something to do with the criteria that inevitably present themselves when we compare his work to theirs, to offer a considered basis of judgment—the criteria, that is, of coherence and inclusiveness. For when we set people like Ransom and Warren beside Davidson they seem strong in exactly those places where he is weak, because they engage with their history while he cannot. They are able, in other words, to absorb some (and maybe most) of the several energies latent in their regional tradition and then to redefine those energies in terms of their own lives and the life of their generation. Within the compass of their work the dialectic between idea and event—the dialectic that *is* their history—is developed into a new version of experience, and a version of experience that is also seen as a part of the continuing historical process. If we are willing to simplify for a moment, we can say that the criteria by which they establish their superiority as traditionalist writers are three in number and relate to three types of ability—separable in critical exegesis if not in the act of creation. These are:

1. The ability to *realize* the inheritance of the past, personal and communal, in the sense of being able to understand the different tendencies that went to make it up.
2. The ability to arrange some kind of mutually effective relationship between this inheritance and a present that is equally conceived of in both private and public terms.
3. Finally the ability to produce out of this relationship, the interaction between past and present, a coherent and yet inclusive framework of assessment that is itself capable of altering as it comes into contact with new varieties of experience.

These seem to offer some genuine standards of assessment, means by which traditionalism becomes an evaluative concept as well as a descriptive one.

Judged by these standards all achievements must be regarded as partial, of course. No writer can hope to satisfy them completely, if only because to do so would imply a capacity for living at once (and completely) inside and outside of the historical continuum, so as to be able to participate in it fully and analyze it with perfect detachment—something that is beyond the scope of any one man. But that does not exclude the possibility of a *relative* scale. The writer is then assessed according to what is possible, and the possible defined in terms of what other writers participating in the same tradition have achieved. It goes without saying, perhaps, that the reference to the absolute is still there, to supply the context within which the criticism is being made: we still have some notion of the broader social and historical landscape that is independent of our experience of particular texts. But for the purposes of a detailed analysis and judgment the strategy must be a comparative one. As William Faulkner once put it, all writers are involved, whether they know it or not, in a quest that must fail. So in a sense the question to be asked about each of them is not whether he has succeeded or no, but how he has coped with the inevitability of failure—what portion of the past, if any, he has managed to recover for the present. This, anyway, has been the question asked about Davidson and the other Agrarians. How have they dealt with the conditions of their time, given that those conditions will yield only a little of their significance to one writer? What is the relative value of the meanings they discover in their history?[98] It is a question that will reappear again, in different forms, as we look at other writers of the "renaissance"—people who have been involved, just as the Agrarians have, in painful, undodgeable encounters with their region.

3. The Good Farmer: Some Variations on a Historical Theme

~~~~~~

Womanchild in a Promised Land: Elizabeth Madox Roberts

Contrary to popular legend, which tends to describe Southern literature in terms of magnolia-blossom romance, there have been two distinct ideas or ideals engaged with the regional experience ever since the region has existed as a separate entity. The notion, articulated most convincingly in *Notes on Virginia,* of the good farmer tilling his own forty acres of land has continually interacted with the more notorious idea of the aristocratic planter to produce that curious mixture of contradictory beliefs known popularly as "the mind of the South." The major crises in the regional history have had their part to play too, by encouraging a transformation of either or both of these ideas under the pressure of experience—and the result has been a rich store of mythologized history, or historicized mythology, for the writer to adapt to his own purposes. This is to repeat what has been said already. Nevertheless it is worth repeating because we are now approaching a number of Southern writers who have not in any sense tried to encompass the totality of the regional experience, but have instead concentrated quite deliberately upon what they consider to be its more interesting and vital elements. In other words, they seem to have recognized that two different worlds of agrarianism exist, or have existed, in the area below the Mason-Dixon line; and rather than try to reconcile them, as, say, John Crowe Ransom and Robert Penn Warren do, they have opted to explore just one of those worlds. This might seem to suggest that they resemble Allen Tate, who, as we have seen, focuses his attention upon the plantation legend to the exclusion of everything else. Any resemblance that does exist is only superficial, however. For, to begin with, the writers we are concerned with here are more interested in the farmer than they are in the planter—that is one difference. And, far more important, their interest is not just that of the mythologizer, the man who looks at history for the structure of metaphors and concepts it may supply, but that of the reporter as well, the person who commits himself to a close study of the relevant *facts.* That is to say, their work bears direct witness to the tension between rural myth, how the agrarian life should be, and rural reality, how the agrarian life nowadays is; and it is from this tension, and the ways in which these writers try to deal with it, that the various strengths and weaknesses of their work derive.

Perhaps this distinction can be made clearer if we look first of all at a writer who has actually moved between the roles of mythologizer and reporter, and who has tried various methods—some successful, some not—for coping with the problems that have arisen along the way. I mean by this Elizabeth Madox Roberts, a novelist from Kentucky who, although she achieved a considerable reputation during her lifetime, is presently suffering the kind of critical neglect that often occurs immediately following a writer's death.[1] The neglect is, I think, unjustified if only because her work, when taken as a whole, witnesses an interesting attempt to come to terms with the idea of her environment and the facts that seem to contradict it—an attempt that might be uneven, and clumsy at times, but which nevertheless betrays a fuller understanding of the issues involved than that demonstrated by some of her more famous contemporaries. The closest she comes to being a mythologizer who, unlike Tate, simply repeats a received image of the Good Life, is in a relatively early novel, *The Great Meadow*, which unhappily is also among her best known. Ostensibly concerned with the settlement of Kentucky in the early nineteenth century, the story in effect acts as a kind of moral exemplum; and in it Roberts does no more than accept a hopelessly ideal notion of the past and then reproduce it without either the intellectual justification or the dramatic emphasis on the myth-making process that are the saving graces of *The Fathers*. Possibility, what the pioneers should have been according to Jefferson and his disciples, is accepted in the book as fact, the result being a sort of populist version of *Gone With the Wind*—a highly romanticized portrait of the past that seems hardly aware of its own romanticism. This is a typical passage, describing the society that the heroes and heroines of *The Great Meadow* are supposed to be building.

> They marched forward, taking a new world for themselves, possessing themselves of it by the power of their courage, their order, and their endurance. . . . Fields turned up by the plow . . . sheep . . . turned in on the hillside to . . . glean a fine rich eatage for themselves . . . stone walls . . . setting bounds to the land, making contentment and limitations for the mind to ease itself upon . . . this man's farm beside that man's, all contained now . . . and shared, and one sinks into the security and lies down to rest himself. Through the farms run lanes . . . ways to meet a neighbor at his own house. . . . Children meeting together to walk down the road to a school-house or a church.[2]

What is objectionable about such a description, I think, is its failure to include the harsher details of wilderness life, or to acknowledge that it is a legendary version of that life which is being portrayed here rather than a factual one. There is no recognition, in other words, of the tension obtaining between the ideal, or the desired, and the real and that ultimately is what is wrong with the book.

Fortunately, this does not represent the entire scope of Roberts's achievement. For in at least one of her novels the conflict between rural myth and rural reality is clearly recognized; one aspect of the historical inheritance of agrarianism *is* tested against present experience, to discover its possible relevance and adaptability. The novel I have in mind is *The Time of Man,* which is primarily concerned with this conflict as it occurs within the experience of its major character, Ellen Chesser. Ellen is born to a tenant family, whose life of wandering and "a-walken" from one small patch of hired land to another is described with devastating accuracy. Nothing is spared or excluded from the report. The cabins she lives in are uniformly unkempt and ramshackle, the land she helps to cultivate is barren, and the various labors she has to perform have little intrinsically to do with the pastoral dreams of some of the Agrarians.

> . . . the near way of the clods, as she knew them, were a strength to destroy her strength . . . the heaviness of the clods pulled at her arms and the field seemed to reach very far before it stopped at the pool by the quarry. . . . She felt the weight of the grass as she tore it away, and now and then a blow so sharp that it made her flanks ache was needed to turn the soil.[3]

Matters do not improve when Ellen marries. She is confronted with the same problems as ever, of having to cultivate other people's land and being forced to move on from year to year; and, indeed, her recognition of the bleakness of her lot only increases the older she grows. As Ellen ruminates after what seems like an eternity of wandering,

> It mattered much less . . . now what country she lived in, here or there, or whether there was a tree in the yard or a spring or a well, . . . a stove for heat or a fireplace. A year on Robinson's place, a year on McKnight's, it was all one.[4]

Nothing could be further removed from the enthusiastic maunderings of *The Great Meadow* or, in strictly journalistic terms, more convincing, either.

That, however, is only half of the story. *The Time of Man* is much more than an accurate account of the conditions of rural life in the contemporary South, and the reason why this is so is that a perpetual tension is maintained in the narrative between this journalistic level, which informs us of what is, and those other levels, which remind us of what might be. Elizabeth Roberts's strategy for achieving this is quite simple: it is to make the reader share in the consciousness of the central character, her dreams of "some better country,"[5] where the independent life would be possible and the Jeffersonian ideal recovered. The strategy recalls that of Allen Tate in *The Fathers* and "Ode to the Confederate Dead"; with the important difference that, whereas Tate assumes a mythologizing process that is successfully accomplished, Roberts dramatizes the process itself—the continuing, never quite completed and never quite defeated, attempts made by her heroine to create a dream of possibility out of the ruins of the actual. In effect, the reader is constantly being reminded—in a way he is not in *The Fathers*—of the conflict, the active conflict, taking place between agrarian myth and the recalcitrant material on which that myth must operate if it is ever to be realized. The legend is defined as legend, something existing clearly apart from and in a sense "above" reality; and at the same time it is celebrated for its power, as a motivating force that can change things given the proper opportunity. Not only that—as a force that *does*, in fact, change things. For if there is one point that emerges unambiguously from the novel it is that—in her own way—Ellen Chesser can manage to use her idea of the Good Life to improve her status. Somehow, with the help of her beliefs, she does succeed in transforming her condition—or, at the very least, in modifying it drastically.

This is a crucial point. Elizabeth Roberts is fond of quoting the English philosopher Bishop Berkeley to the effect that "all those bodies that compose the mighty frame of the world have not any substance without a mind." And, though it would be wrong to credit her with a faith quite as idealistic as this, there can be little doubt, I think, that she attributes considerable power to the human consciousness—as much power, in fact, as she ascribes to external circumstances in the creation of the real. Consequently, the Jeffersonian dream with which she credits Ellen Chesser—the dream, that is, of a context in which each moment of the agricultural routine becomes meaningful—is there not simply as a mode of contrast but as a technique of renewal. The raw material of Ellen's life is drab, there can be no doubt of that, but even at its drabbest Ellen manages to give it meaning, to endow it and enrich it with a certain quality of ritual.

> She would take the turkey bread in her hand and go, bonnetless, up the gentle hill across the pasture in the light of sundown, calling the hens as she went. She was keenly aware of the ceremony and aware of her figure rising out of the fluttering birds, of all moving together about her. She would hear the mules crunching their fodder as she went past the first barn, and she would hear the swish of the falling hay, the thud of a mule hoof on a board, a man's voice ordering or whistling a tune.[6]

What Elizabeth Roberts is doing here, I believe, is to demonstrate, through the perceptions and activity of her heroine, the capacity of an ideal for survival. "Buffeted about by the fates and the weather" though she is, Ellen Chesser can retain hope of a "promised land" where she and her kind really do possess some dignity; and, even more important, she can still *use* that hope to alleviate her circumstances, informing them with a significance they would not otherwise have. This does not mean that the squalid experiences of the tenant farmer are denied or properly redeemed—far from it. But it does mean these experiences are made to engage with some higher notion of the rural life—that the *possibility* of redemption is at least entertained. *The Time of Man,* in other words, bears witness to a continuing tension between event and inherited idea, between the ordinary, dull Southern farm world and the belief that those who till the earth are really "the chosen people of God." And this tension, as it releases itself in the daily routines of the heroine, is, I think, the secret of the book's vitality.

Tension of this kind, however, was something that Roberts apparently found it difficult to maintain. Even *The Time of Man* has its lapses, when the idealism of the heroine seems to be more the product of despair than of any genuinely positive energies; and elsewhere in her work Roberts's chief interest seems to lie in discovering escape routes rather than in creating a possible agency of change. This is especially true of her later novels. Unlike *The Great Meadow* they are mostly set in the present. The difference of location is purely nominal, though, because like that book they represent a more or less complete withdrawal into a dream world. A significant index of this, I think, is the pattern of retreat or flight that occurs so frequently in them. Jocelle Drake, for example, the heroine of *He Sent Forth a Raven,* and Dena James, in *Black Is My Truelove's Hair,*[7] both respond to the cruel exigencies of their situations, the conflict between all that they want and the little they can have, by fleeing into a pastoral kingdom inhabited by characters "new with the beginning of the earth, beyond the reach of truism." They do not engage with the contradictions implicit in their lives, in the way that Ellen Chesser does: they simply acknowledge those contradictions as a preliminary to evading them. And so, also, does their creator when she tries to elaborate on the Good Life which her protagonists discover as a result of their flight. It is still a rural one, supposedly, but it is more or less defined by the motives of wish fulfillment that have brought it into being. Set *in* the twentieth century it is in no sense *of* it; indeed, with its picturesque characters and quaint folkways, it does not seem to belong to history at all. Here, by way of illustration, is a description of a ring dance performed by the members of one such community.

It was a hello and whoo-pee, and a great wonder to see who would be out here in the pasture in the moonlight, it as bright as day, . . . the din of the gathering tinkled and clattered . . . all the bright girls were pleased with the new beauty the moon had brought to their clothing; and they made their skirts dart and flutter in and out of the bright glow, to feel themselves a part of the flashing color and to know that they were lovely. The throng, set in a circle, made a great wheel that turned about a little thorn bush and sang a game song:

"Here we go round the mulberry bush
On a cold and frosty morning . . ."[8]

The best that can be said about this type of writing, I think, is that Elizabeth Roberts may be aware of the fanciful nature of all she is describing. In other words, perhaps this scene, and others like it, are *conscious* fictions. Even to suggest this, though, seems a little abstract and academic, since what really matters is that, seen in any light whatsoever, the world Roberts offers us here is clearly a fake one, representing an evasion of the conflicts that give life, and a genuine relevance, to *The Time of Man.*

Conflict, in fact, is the last thing we can expect to come across in these later narratives because the real and dream worlds, where they *are* both represented, tend to occupy separate parts of the book. First we are offered a brief summary of the drab environment of the present-day South. Then that is dismissed, and Roberts devotes her attention and ours to a full recovery of the pastoral idyll. There is no significant connection made between the two kingdoms, the everyday South that the journalist sees and the Promised Land that the dreamer imagines, and the author almost seems to be insisting that there cannot be. We can, she seems to be saying, live in either the one or the other: either in a place that may not be altered by even the most vigorous act of will, or in a place where the will may operate in conditions of almost absolute freedom. We can accept the determinations of this world, the sense of habitual frustration to which our circumstances reduce us, or we can escape into another dimension altogether—somewhere that is an enlarged projection of our own desires. But we cannot, ever, do both. Roberts seems now to deny the possibility of change, because she has denied the availability, or even the value, of the agency of change—that dialectical engagement between will and event, legend and history, which is so crucial to the life of Ellen Chesser. It goes without saying, perhaps, that this is to split the writer's function as reporter and her function as mythologizer apart completely—and in the process to perform a radical disservice to both.

The Comedy of Frustration: Erskine Caldwell

The twin functions of mythologizer and reporter are also demonstrated, with a difference, by somebody who enjoys the rather dubious distinction of being among the most consistently popular of all Southern writers—Erskine Caldwell. With Caldwell, though, the journalistic aim assumes new dimensions because he is (as he has confessed) not so much interested in verisimilitude as in special pleading—the kind of report that tends to emphasize certain chosen aspects of its subject. He has a number of observations, important observations as he sees it, to make about the South and he makes them to the exclusion of almost everything else. The result is something that is perhaps closer to the art of the caricaturist than to the comparatively objective account of the reporter; particular aspects of the described situation are continually being exaggerated in the interests of theme. What is Caldwell's theme? Stated simply, it is one of degeneracy—the reduction of the human being to the lowest possible levels of his experience. In appearance, at least, his rural characters bear no resemblance to the Jeffersonian yeoman whatsoever. Grotesques responding only to a basic physical urge, they represent an abstraction not merely from the human to the animal but from the complete animal to a single instinct.

> Ellie May got down from the pine stump and sat on the ground. She moved closer and closer to Lov, sliding herself over the hard white sand. . . . "Ellie May's acting like your old hound used to when she got the itch," Dude said to Jeeter. "Look at her scrape her bottom on the sand. That old hound used to make the same kind of sound Ellie May's making too. It sounds just like a little pig squealing, don't it?"[9]

The change of perspective, when we compare this description of Ellie May in *Tobacco Road* with the portrait of Ellen Chesser in *The Time of Man*, is a radical one. Ellie and Ellen are two different kinds of people, illustrating quite contrary notions of the rural life as it exists today; and this is registered among other things in the fact that whereas Roberts takes us inside the consciousness of her heroine, to share the wealth of her inner life as well as the poverty of her condition, Caldwell insists upon keeping his readers at a distance—on presenting his character entirely in terms of externals and, in the process, dehumanizing her.

The procedure is a habitual one with Caldwell. Nearly all of his country folk (the title seems a much more appropriate one than "farmer") operate between the poles of greed and sexual desire, and such comedy as his novels possess is generally the result of the violence that either or both of these instincts tend to provoke. In fact, the comic note is at its wildest in his fiction when the two instincts actually clash, throwing the victim of the subsequent cross fire into confusion. The description of Ellie May quoted above, for instance, is part of a much longer sequence in which Ellie's father, Jeeter Lester, actually uses Ellie to distract his son-in-law Lov while he steals a bag of turnips from him. To summarize the complicated interplay of hunger and lust that follows is hardly to do justice to the Grand Guignol effects of the situation. As soon as Jeeter does grab the bag of turnips Lov turns to recover it, but he is immediately pulled to the ground by his would-be seducer. Jeeter makes off into the woods with his capture, and meanwhile his son, his wife Ada, and his grandmother all keep beating Lov down, whenever he tries to rise up in pursuit, until Ellie May can crawl on top of him. With a mixture of excitement and desperation, Lov then resigns himself to his fate, while Dude, the son, goes off to find his father before all the turnips are eaten, and Ada and her mother-in-law sit whimpering over their inability to participate in either the eating session or the rutting. The scene is, as I have said, a long one and throughout it is presented as a spectacle, something to be watched with detached amazement. That perhaps is why Caldwell places three Negro passers-by at the gate to the Lester farm, to witness the occasion and register appropriate reactions to it: we share with them, as it were, the role of a self-conscious audience. And that also is why he permits even the participants in the action an occasional note of commentary, as if they too were able to stand back from what they were doing and so become their own spectators. Jeeter, for instance, pauses midway in his flight to expatiate on the possible quality of the turnips, and on the relationship between this and his own social condition.

> "Has these turnips got them damn-blasted green-gutted worms in them, Lov?" Jeeter said. "By God and by Jesus, if they're wormy, I don't know what I'm going to do about it. I been so sick of eating wormy turnips, I declare I almost lost my religion. It's a shame for God to let them damn-blasted green-gutted worms bore into turnips. Us poor people always gets the worse end of all deals, it looks like to me."[10]

Here, as when Dude supplies us with a system of deliberate comparisons for Ellie May's behavior, the character seems to be emphasizing the illustrative quality of his own actions—their representative status as part of a series of "Georgia scenes."

The phrase "Georgia scenes" is not chosen at random. For it points to one aspect of his Southern inheritance on which Caldwell leans heavily; an aspect that is symptomatic of the radical differences obtaining between him and such other celebrants of the Southern farmer as Ellen Glasgow and Elizabeth Madox Roberts. More than a hundred years ago, in 1835 to be precise, a lawyer and academic called Augustus Baldwin Longstreet published a book with the imposing title of *Georgia Scenes: Characters, Incidents, etc., in the First Half-Century of the Republic.* To the extent that it *was* imposing, though, the title was a misleading one, since a major purpose of the book was comedy. In a series of sketches that varied in approach from the purely descriptive to the dramatic, Longstreet presented his readers with illustrations of life in the remoter parts of the state. The sketches were linked by the appearance in nearly all of them of a narrator bearing a suspicious resemblance to the author himself—a kindly, generous but rather pompous and patronizing man who tended to treat his subjects, as if they were specimens of some alien form of life, with a mixture of curiosity and amusement. A healthy distance was maintained from characters who were presented not so much as individuals as in terms of their common behavioral patterns; and the combined effect of the detachment, the condescension, and the generalizing tendency was to create an effect of caricature. Here is a typical passage, where the narrator is describing the aftermath of a fight.

> I looked and saw that Bob had entirely lost his left ear, and a large piece from his left cheek. His right eye was a little discoloured, and the blood flowed profusely from his wounds.
>
> Bill presented a hideous spectacle. About a third of his nose, at the lower extremity, was bit off, and his face so swelled and bruised that it was difficult to discover in it anything of the human visage . . .
>
> . . . Durham and Stallings [the fighters] kept their beds for several weeks, and did not meet again for two months. When they met, Billy stepped up to Bob and offered his hand, saying, "Bobby you've *licked* me a fair fight; but you wouldn't have done it if I hadn't been in the wrong—I oughtn't have treated your wife as I did; and I felt so through the whole fight; and it sort o' cowed me." "Well Billy," said Bob, "let's be friends. Once in the fight, when you had my finger in your mouth, . . . I was going to halloo; but I thought of Betsy, and knew the house would be too hot for me if I got whipped when fighting for her, after always whipping when I fought for myself. . . ."
>
> . . . thanks to the Christian religion, to schools, colleges, and benevolent associations, such scenes of barbarism and cruelty as that which I have been just describing are now of rare occurrence, though they may still be occasionally met with in some of the new counties.[11]

In the preface to his book, Longstreet claimed proudly that he was filling in "a chasm in history that has always been overlooked"; and this passage illustrates well, I think, how he reconciled such a claim with the exigencies of comedy. The tone of the description is humorous but the writer clearly hopes that, by means of his humor, he will demonstrate something significant about the backwoods character as well —its simplicity and its capacity for violence. That is to say, the simplification and exaggeration that create the comic note are there because they enable Longstreet to locate what is different about the boy and emphasize it at the expense of any qualities he may share, in a Wordsworthian sense, with the rest of humanity.

This is not the place to go into Longstreet's further motives for emphasizing the specific qualities of the Georgia folk that he did. The virtual impossibility of resolving the problem, anyway, is indicated by the fact that the critical field is about equally divided between those who argue that Longstreet admired his subjects for their "free and active simplicity" and those who say that, as a gentleman and a Whig, he loathed and feared them for the threat they offered to his own life style![12] What does matter, though, and needs to be mentioned here is that, whatever his ulterior motives, Longstreet offered his readers a portrait of the poor farmer that was characterized by three things: detachment, a claim to historical accuracy, and a tendency toward comic exaggeration. These were the strategies that gave *Georgia Scenes* much of its drive and contemporary appeal; and these were the ones also that were variously adopted by the writers following Longstreet, who are now referred to generally as the "Southwestern humorists"— "Southwestern" because nearly all of them were interested in the younger states to the interior (such as Alabama, Mississippi, and Tennessee). Of course, their approach was never uniform. Apart from anything else there was a tendency in later years to reduce the status of the dramatized narrator, or do away with him altogether; the story was then told impersonally or given to the rural character himself to tell. But the qualities I have mentioned continued to supply a point of departure, a common basis, as it were, upon which the individual writer could improvise. And one result of this is that in the work that certainly represents the culmination of Southwestern humor, *The Adventures of Huckleberry Finn*, we can find the same combination of historical and comic intention recurring. The portrait that Mark Twain develops in his book, of old times on the Mississippi, is presented via a technique of violent exaggeration that makes it simultaneously elegiac and critical, a humorous masterpiece and a piece of social history; and that exaggeration is itself symptomatic of a detachment that enables us to place all the characters—*including* Huckleberry Finn himself—even while we may sympathize with them.[13]

Time (and the sheer complexity of the subject) may prevent us from examining Southwestern humor in any great detail. But as a way of indicating some of its further implications, and in particular its relevance for Erskine Caldwell, I would like to look briefly at a writer who stands somewhere in between Longstreet and Twain in terms of achievement and chronology; and that is George Washington Harris. The choice is not meant to be an obscurantist one since, apart from the fact that Harris did exercise enormous personal influence on Caldwell (and William Faulkner as well), there can be no doubt that he represents an important moment in the history of American humor— a time when, in opposition to the dominant climate of prissiness and gentility, it could still be pungent, incisive, and above all broad. Just how broad it could be is indicated by the controlling belief Harris attributes to his major character, Sut Lovingood—that "Man was made a-pupus jus' to eat, drink, an' for stayin' awake in the yearly part of the nites."[14] A native of rural Tennessee, Sut is in effect another example of the creature who tended to become an obsession with the humorists—the primitive or natural man, who stands on the periphery of conventional society and yet can still offer significant comments on it. His life, circumscribed by the animal functions, is a continual drag on our own pretensions, about the nature of our personalities and the efficacy or security of the social system we have organized for ourselves. At one point in his narrative, Sut Lovingwood admits that he has "nara a soul, nuffin but a whisky proof gizzard"; and Harris's habitual strategy, of making us share Sut's life and experience the connection between what he is and how he lives, leads us to suspect that in similar conditions we might be forced to say exactly the same.

It will be clear already that Harris's intentions and techniques are rather different from Longstreet's. For while both share the claim to historical accuracy, and the device of comic exaggeration, they differ in the sense that the placing of their subject (the way they invite us to look on rural folk as a demonstration) is based upon almost contrary premises. Longstreet, as I have suggested, offers us the portrait of a world quite different from our own, which may provoke amusement, perhaps even the occasional tremor of apprehension, but nothing more than that. Harris, by contrast, presents us with a kind of test case that paradoxically derives its impact, the sense of its relevance to our own lives, from the distance it establishes between the literate reader and the illiterate protagonist. Suppose, Harris seems to be saying, we had been brought up in surroundings similar to those of Sut Lovingood: would we be that different from him? Would we not, perhaps, speak the same language and live upon the same level of comic but grotesque animalism? And if this is the case, does it not tend to undermine our pretensions—the belief in our dignity as God-given, rather than acquired as a matter of special privilege? Sut Lovingood is detached from us, certainly—the use of an almost impenetrable dialect sees to that—but he is detached from us only in the way that a mirror image

of ourselves is. We watch him and, in doing so, witness a curious aping
and a criticism of our own behavior.[15]

The criticism is made all the more effective because of Harris's capacity for reminding us, in the middle of Sut's various scrapes, that
his protagonist does possess traces of what we are pleased to call virtue, waiting for the appropriate conditions to bring them into life.
There is his extraordinary pride and independence of judgment, for
instance, which prompts him to consider himself "the very best society" and to punish those who he feels have insulted him in any way.
More telling still is the ability Harris endows him with for sensing
who his enemies are, regardless of whether they have slighted him
personally or not. They are, he realizes, the preachers and the pedagogues, the politic and educated leaders of society who are there not
simply to supply a butt for Sut's fooling, although they certainly do
that, but to remind us of the kind of people—*people like ourselves*—
who are indirectly responsible for his condition. For their privileges,
we must realize, have been bought at his expense; they, and we, are
the beneficiaries of a system from which he is excluded and by which
he is deprived. The mirror is being held up to the readers *as a group,*
in other words, as well as to the reader as an individual. We see in
Sut Lovingood a reflection of possibilities existing in ourselves—*and*
we are forced to acknowledge our complicity in the creation of circumstances that, in Sut's case, have translated possibility into fact.
And just in case we should continue to miss the point, denying Sut
a germ of sensitivity even after all this, there are occasions in the narrative when more energetic hints of his potential are allowed to appear. Instead of a cursory reference to some dormant virtue, we may
then be confronted with a passage of extraordinary lyrical beauty—
not denying the comic framework but actually growing out of it—that
serves as the most incisive reminder possible of those aspects of Sut
Lovingood's character that remain mostly unexercised. Here, by way
of illustration, is what is deservedly the most famous moment in all of
Sut Lovingood's yarns, set characteristically enough at a mealtime.

> Wirt's wife got yearly supper, a rale suckit-rider's supper, whar the 'oman
> 'ove the hous' wer a rich b'lever. Thar wer chickens cut up, an' fried in
> butter, brown, white, flakey, light, hot biskit, made wif cream, scrambil'd
> aigs, yaller butter, fried ham, in slices es big es yure han, pickil'd beets, an'
> cowcumbers, roas'in ears, shaved down and fried, sweet taters, baked, a
> stack ove buckwheat cakes. . . . I gets doing hongry every time I see Wirt's
> wife, ur evan her side-saddil, ur her frocks a-hangin on the closeline. Es
> we sot down, the las' glimmers ove the sun crep thru the histed winder,
> an' flutter'd on the white tabil-cloth and play'd a silver shine on her smoof
> black har, es she sot at the head ove the tabil, a-pourin out the coffee,

wif her sleeves push'd tight back on her white roun' arm, her full throb-
bin neck wer bar to the swell ove her shoulders, an' the steam ove the
coffee made a movin vail afore her face, es she slowly brush'd hit away
wif her lef han', a-smilin an' a flashin her talkin eyes lovingly at her
hansum husbun.[16]

The occasion being described here is mundane enough, admittedly,
but what matters about it is not so much the occasion itself as all
that Harris allows his protagonist to make out of it. Sut, we are forced
to recognize, has a sensitivity—a capacity for recognizing the beauty
and value of a particular experience—which will emerge at the least
available opportunity; although all too often it is left to waste un-
cultivated. The waste is articulated in the rest of the narrative, in
the scenes of comic violence and degeneracy that illustrate the actual
conditions of his existence; and placed in this context it becomes unar-
guable, I think, that Harris even more than Longstreet has used his
humor to reinforce a serious social and historical point. If we are
willing to simplify for a moment, we can say that the comedy in *Sut
Lovingood* defines the given situation, the occasional moments of
lyricism and commentary imply the possibilities that have been more
or less frustrated, and that the activity taking place between these
two poles helps to locate the core meaning of the sketches.

Nearly half a century separates the creator of Sut Lovingood from
the creator of Jeeter Lester, but perhaps this gap in time may serve
only to emphasize the relevant connections between the two writers.
The difference of historical situation may, after all, help to isolate what
is similar in their purposes and techniques and so concentrate our
attention upon it. Be that as it may, it is patently clear, I think, once
we look at him in this light that Caldwell owes a profound debt to
the Southwestern humorists, and to George Washington Harris in particular—a debt that is betrayed among other things by their common
dependence on a broad and grotesque type of comedy. The specific
borrowings from Harris are at their most obvious in *Georgia Boy*,
published in 1943, in which the boy of the title recounts the antics
of his "old man," and in the process draws us the portrait of a delight-
ful and impoverished scapegrace not unlike Sut Lovingood himself.[17]
But these are less interesting, I believe, than the kind of understanding of Harris and his methods that can be inferred from Caldwell's
more important fiction—by which I mean from *Tobacco Road, God's
Little Acre*, and perhaps *Tragic Ground* as well.[18] In such cases it is
not merely the surface structure of Southwestern humor that is recovered but the relationship obtaining between that structure and the
ulterior purposes of the writer. Comic these books may be, but the

comedy is all the sharper, the wit all the more pungent and the characters that much more striking, because (just as in *Sut Lovingood*) everything is unambiguously attached to an underlying and genuinely serious series of intentions.

Exactly how these intentions manifest themselves is (again as in *Sut Lovingood*) as much a matter of context as anything else, the total situation in which the humorous moments are played out. The comedy is still a comedy of waste, of human potential denied and frustrated, and that fact is communicated to the reader in part by Caldwell's barren landscapes—whether it be the decayed rural landscape where his farmers are described living in reluctant exile or the urban scene, to which they may retreat occasionally in pursuit of an illusory alternative. The description in *God's Little Acre*, of mill towns populated by farmers looking for some way of making a living, is typical of what I mean.

> Up and down the valley lay the company towns and the ivy-walled cotton mills . . . the men stood on the hot streets looking at each other while they spat their lungs into the deep yellow dust. . . . In the rear of the houses . . . tight-lipped women sitting at kitchen windows with their backs to the cold cooking-stoves. In the streets in front of the houses . . . the bloody-lipped men spitting their lungs into the yellow dust. . . . The grass and weeds melted in the sun, and the dust that blew down from the . . . uplands settled on the ground and on the buildings like powdered paint.[19]

Even from this comparatively brief passage it is clear, I think, that Caldwell sees the hopelessness of the rural landscape penetrating the town, to make it unavailable as a resource for impoverished farmers. A common dust (similar, perhaps, to the dust that floats in the wake of the Great Gatsby) settles over city and adjacent countryside alike, so creating a pervasive sense of fruitlessness. And this is the stage on which the Lesters, the Waldens in *God's Little Acre* and all their kind must act out their comedies of frustration; or, to be more accurate, this is the environment that prescribes their frustrated lives.

That it *is* a comedy of frustration we are concerned with here, a series of appropriate responses to a thwarting environment, is witnessed by the habitual activity of Caldwell's characters. For the gestures that make them comic have nothing at all to do with intrinsic evil, however violent and grotesque they may appear to be. On the contrary, Jeeter Lester and Ty Ty Walden (in *God's Little Acre*) are exactly like Sut Lovingood in that they are presented as the *victims* of evil, whose strange behavior demonstrates the response of the innocent to circumstances he cannot control.[20] The whole trouble with Caldwell's characters, as with Harris's, is that they have no relevant connection with the emergent social structure, and so are at best anomalies in that structure and at worst encumbrances to it. And Caldwell, unlike Harris, makes sure that the reader is aware of this by explaining, very early on in most of his novels, how people like the Lester family and the Waldens have become the way they are. Both the Lesters and the Waldens were, we learn, once well-to-do land-owners. But they fell upon hard times—partly as a result of natural fluctuations in the cotton and tobacco markets, and partly thanks to the machinations of the financiers, the bankers, and the Wall Street brokers. In the event, they—like so many of their class, Caldwell reminds us—lost their land and had to resort to cropping on shares, a ruinous system whereby they placed themselves heavily in debt to the landowner, and the landowner in turn remained solvent by borrowing at a high rate of interest from the merchant banks. This was bad enough, perhaps, but (Caldwell goes on) matters have since become worse because the sharecropping system has itself collapsed; and land now has to be cultivated in very large units or—as in most cases —not at all. In effect, big business has assumed *direct* control of farming, rather than working through the power of its credit, and in doing so has created a new, large-scale agricultural system in which the Jeeter Lesters and Ty Ty Waldens of this world have no place. Jeeter, Ty Ty, and their kind have been turned into anachronisms, an irrelevant nuisance to the present owners of the land; and the most they can hope for, really, is that they will be left alone on the farms they occupy, to eke a meager existence out of them.[21]

This, more or less, is the starting point for nearly all of Caldwell's fiction, and certainly the basis of his finest novels. The farmer, he argues, has been "robbed of his livelihood by the downfall of the old systems of agriculture,"[22] and this in turn has led to the physical deterioration we now see and to his moral collapse. Treated like an animal he has become an animal; excluded from the human community in an economic sense he has degenerated into a kind of moral leper as well, whose humanity is more a matter of biology than of character. The argument is an utterly deterministic one, of course. But, then, so also is the argument implicit in most stories of the old Southwest. More to the point, the determinism is not, I think, objectionable because it can be seen as part of a total strategy of caricature. Life is simplified and character is distorted in Caldwell's fiction, it may be true, but this is done in a conscious and valuable way—so as to isolate certain specific aspects of the author's given experience and, in isolating them, to explain them.

Given this self-conscious determinism of approach, and the tendencies toward caricature and generalization that accompany it, it becomes less surprising, I think, that Caldwell should impose the status of a demonstration on every aspect of his characters' behavior; the reader is, after all, being summoned to witness what is likely to happen when a certain type of social and historical situation exists. There is a profoundly illustrative quality, for instance, not just about particular scenes in *Tobacco Road* but about its major source of comedy. This is Jeeter Lester's belief that one year, next year perhaps, he will be able to plant a tobacco crop. Under the influence of this belief, he is forever burning the ground in preparation for the planting until eventually, at the end of the novel, he sets fire to his own house, killing himself and his wife in the process. The belief is an idiosyncratic one, certainly, leading to situations that range from the ludicrous to the macabre, but not so idiosyncratic that it cannot act as a gauge of Jeeter's innocence, and the desperate nature of a situation that imposes such desperate remedies on its victims. Similarly, Ty Ty Walden's habitual activity of digging up his land in search of gold, absurd though it may appear to be, is founded on the supremely illogical and revealing logic of the helpless naïf. He cannot live on what he gets *out* of the land, Ty Ty reasons, so why not try to live on what he finds in it? There is perhaps a hint of blasphemy in his behavior too, of the kind familiar to readers of *Go Down, Moses*—the idea that rooting about in the land for gold, oil, or whatever represents a despoliation, an act of rape that is the very opposite of the enrichment offered to the soil by the agricultural activity.[23] But whether this is part of Caldwell's intention or not, there can be little doubt, I think, that he does intend Ty Ty's behavior, like Jeeter's, to achieve the apparently paradoxical feat of being representative by virtue of its idiosyncrasy. Its illustrative quality, that is—as an indication of rural decline and the despair to which this decline leads—is made to depend for its impact on the comic absurdity of the illustration.

The humor is not left in isolation, though, to carry the entire freight of meaning of the book unaided. As in *Sut Lovingood*, the dominant strain of comedy is punctuated by an occasional lyric note that reminds us of what might have been in more favorable circumstances—of how people like Jeeter Lester and Ty Ty Walden could have developed given the proper opportunity. The few times that Jeeter is allowed to express his "inherited love of the land" offer us some beautiful instances of this.

> "I think more of the land than I do of staying in a durn cotton-mill. You can't smell no sedge fire up there, and when it comes time for planting, you feel sick inside but you don't know what's ailing you. . . . But when a man stays on the land, he don't get to feeling like that this time of the year, because he's right there to smell the smoke of burning broom-sedge and to feel the wind fresh off the plowed fields going down inside of his

body . . . out here on the land a man feels better than ever he did. The Spring-time ain't going to let you fool it by hiding away inside a durn cotton mill. It knows you got to stay on the land to feel good."[24]

This passage deserves comparison with Sut Lovingood's hymn to the Good Life, which I quoted earlier, and not just because it helps us to recognize and to accept the latent dignity of the speaker. It does this, of course, but what it does as well is contribute a new dimension of feeling to the narrative, a sense of pathos that depends upon seeing that, within the limits established by the comedy, the desires expressed here are destined to remain unconsummated. Jeeter Lester will *never* really live up to the ideal of the farming experience he is describing, nor will Sut Lovingood ever be able to develop his sensibilities and sensitivity to the full; and that, as their creators see it, is a cause for our honest sympathy as much as our amusement—or, rather, something to give depth and direction to our laughter.

It is only a step beyond this strategy of contrast between the comic episode and the lyric moment to that of placing active commentary in the mouths of the characters—commentary, that is, that does not simply imply a criticism of the given situation but insists upon it. Needless to say, Caldwell frequently takes this step. His characters suddenly pause, as Jeeter does when he is stealing the bag of turnips, and turn upon their own grotesque attitudes in order to explain them. And not only the attitudes but the context of victimization in which they occur as well, for Caldwell differs from Harris in the sense that he makes his characters articulate their own sufferings, so that we are never left in any doubt as to where to place the blame. Thus, when Ty Ty Walden describes the iniquities of the speculative system to his daughter-in-law, and in particular the depredations of the cotton broker, he seems as much as anything else to be offering an explanation of himself to the reader—supplying the kind of direct analysis of the dramatic situation, and its origins, that is normally assigned to a chorus rather than the protagonist.

> "You know what a cotton broker is, don't you? Do you know why they're called cotton brokers? . . . Because they keep the farmers broke all the time. They lend a little money, and then they take the whole damn crop. Or else they suck the blood out of a man by running the price up and down forcing him to sell. That's why they call them cotton brokers."[25]

Statements like this may offer a special problem to some readers. After all, it might be argued, can they be reconciled with the deterministic premises of the rest of the narrative, which require the characters to behave like automatons? Ty Ty betrays a clear understanding of his situation here, as much understanding, in fact, as would be necessary for him to exercise some measure of control over it; and how does this jibe with an action that elsewhere tends to reduce him to the status of a Pavlovian dog?

The problem is only an apparent one, though (at least, in the case of Caldwell's major fiction it is), because it is based on the assumption that the writer is aiming at verisimilitude. And the plain fact, as we have seen, is that he is not. Like Harris, Longstreet, and all the other humorists, Caldwell has complicated the function of reporter by adding to it that of the caricaturist, a creator of the grotesque. On top of that, he has forced on the reader an attitude of radical detachment. Statements such as the one Ty Ty makes about cotton brokers, or Jeeter's comment on the turnips, are part of the pattern of demonstration I mentioned earlier, in which the characters as well as the audience seem to be made aware of the illustrative quality of the action. As a resource this attitude of detachment is, of course, just as much of an inheritance from Southwestern humor as the strategy of caricature is. But Caldwell develops it much further than any previous humorist ever did—so much further, in fact, that perhaps to explain and justify it we need to draw a comparison from a very different field of literature. I mean by this, the program for an "epic" theater formulated more than forty years ago by the German dramatist Bertolt Brecht. For the distance placed between reader and character in Caldwell's best fiction is, I think, significantly related—both in its purposes and its effects—to Brecht's core idea of *Vermfremdung,* or audience alienation.[26] The idea, stated simply, is this: that in an "epic" play the audience, instead of being invited to involve themselves in the action, should be forced to adopt an attitude of clinical detachment toward it. Consequently, what happens on stage will be witnessed as an explicable social phenomenon with its own definite causes and room for subsequent maneuver. The sense of an experience participated in is forfeited, according to this theory, but what (ideally) is gained in its stead is a new certainty—the knowledge that comes from having located the dramatic action firmly in its historical time and social place. The events the writer describes become part of an explicable series—their origins understood, the problems they pose carefully defined, and solutions to these problems offered, ready and waiting, for the audience to act upon. This is very much the notion of playwright—or novelist or poet—as scientific historian, and committed scientific historian at that. And, regardless of whether or not Brecht entirely adhered to his theories when it came to the actual writing of plays, there can be little doubt, I think, that it encouraged him to develop certain specific literary devices. Among these was the device of permitting someone to comment on events of which he was

elsewhere shown to be the victim. Time and again in Brechtian theater, a character will slip into the role of surrogate spectator, to emphasize moments in the drama—or links in the series—that other
spectators may have missed. No one worries about this when it occurs
in *Mother Courage* or *The Caucasian Chalk Circle* because it is part
of the denial of surface realism that is integral to the action—as well
as something that helps to place that action within a context of possible remedies. No one should worry about it when it occurs in *Tobacco Road* or *God's Little Acre* either, and for precisely the same
reasons.[27]

The sense of problem solving—the feeling that we are being asked
to look at the action in very much the same spirit as a scientist looks
at an experiment—is in fact as pronounced in books like *Tobacco
Road* as it could be in any "epic" play—more pronounced, even, since
Caldwell likes to add his own comments to those he puts in the mouths
of his characters. Asides from the author occasionally supplement
asides from his creations, so as to make the didactic intention of the
story perfectly clear. This, admittedly, has some use simply because
it helps to settle any doubts that may be left in the reader's mind—
both about what Caldwell is trying to do, and what he is trying to say.
But, on the whole, I think it is a mistake. At such moments, it is very
difficult for him not to sound like a schoolmaster talking to an excep-
tionally dull pupil.

> Jeeter could never think of the loss of his land and goods as anything but
> a man-made calamity . . . he believed steadfastly that his position had
> been brought about by other people. He did not blame Captain John
> [his landlord] to the same extent that he blamed others. . . . Captain John
> had always treated him fairly. . . . But the end soon came. There was no
> longer any profit in raising cotton under the Captain's antiquated system,
> and he abandoned the farm and moved to Augusta. . . . An intelligent use
> of his land, stocks, and implements would have enabled Jeeter, and scores
> of others who had become dependent on Captain John, to raise crops to
> be sold at a profit.[28]

Caldwell never tires of offering direct advice like this; and as any
reader of *Tobacco Road* or *God's Little Acre* will testify, the specific
proposals he makes are pretty various—ranging as they do from pleas
for more government aid to the occasional invocation of the principle
of self-help, and taking in agricultural schools, crop rotation, and land
recovery along the way. The variety of his proposals, however, should
not prevent us from seeing that everything he says stems ultimately
from one core belief, a single premise. This is how Caldwell states
that premise in one of his books.

> Until the agricultural worker commands his own farm, either as an individual or as a member of a state-allotted farm group, the Southern tenant farmer will continue to be bound hand and foot in economic slavery.[29]

Caldwell, as I think this brief passage indicates, is finally a traditional writer. His characters are traditional; his humor is traditional (although, certainly, it is broader and wilder than the Southwestern humorists' ever was); above all, the social and political program implicit in his work is traditional. For what that program boils down to is a belief in the pieties of the small farm. The dream of a chosen people tilling their own fields in perfect freedom: that is the dream Caldwell expresses here—and that also is the dream which dictates nearly all of his problem solving. No matter how little we may realize it while we are enjoying some of the surface details of his comedy, Caldwell—in every one of his finest stories—is trying to draw us back steadily into the world of Jeffersonian myth.

Once we realize this—that the ideal of the good farmer hovers as an admonitory image at the back of Caldwell's best novels and tales —then, I think, the principal reason for the almost apocalyptic violence of his work becomes clear. All the events that occur in books like *Tobacco Road* and *God's Little Acre* are wild and grotesque, ultimately, because they represent for their creator such a radical departure from the Jeffersonian norm. Jeeter Lester and Ty Ty Walden are not the noble farmers of regional legend and the fact that they are not, the fact that they stand for *a dream or an ideal betrayed*, is, I believe, meant to be the real measure of their absurdity. No blame attaches to Jeeter or Ty Ty for their plight, far from it, but that only makes it the more difficult to bear—the more difficult for them to bear, that is, for their author to bear and, most important of all, for us to bear as well. For it would be putting matters in their right perspective, I think, to say that Caldwell insists on the difference between Jefferson's tillers of the earth and his own Georgia crackers, and then imposes full responsibility for this difference upon a corrupt social machine, precisely so as to arouse *our* anger and encourage *our* demands for change. He is not the only humorist to do this, of course; George Washington Harris, as we have seen, tried to do something similar. But he *is*, as far as I know, the only one to supplement this by talking about the brave new world that may emerge when the machine is reprogramed—to make tentative moves, in other words, toward turning from the dream betrayed to the dream fulfilled.

This, anyway, is what I take Caldwell to be doing when (as in the passage I quoted above) he refers to the mistakes made by Captain John and his class; he is beginning to talk about an alternative environment. And elsewhere, in some of the stories that he wrote after *Tobacco Road* and *God's Little Acre*, these beginnings are carried through to a detailed portrait of that alternative. Caldwell then shows us the reorganization of farm management and the restructuring of rural society actually taking place, and being succeeded in turn by a revival of spirit among his characters. Obviously, the intended effect of these stories is one of uplift; the author wants us to experience a sense of release because the oppressive circumstances, and with them the claustrophobic atmosphere, of the earlier narratives have been dissolved. Their actual effect is a lot less exhilarating than that, however, and the reasons for this take us right back to the virtues of that earlier work: we can define why Caldwell succeeded in *Tobacco Road* and *God's Little Acre* by understanding why he is failing now. For what Caldwell does as a preliminary to drawing his portrait of a better life is to take his rural folk out of the grotesque, comic world of the Lesters and the Waldens—which is a necessary step, certainly, but one that deprives him of his previous excuses for the simplifications and determinism of his argument. The one-sided portrait can no longer be defended as part of a satirical strategy. And having done this he does not really know what to do with his people, because he does not have any other satisfactory approach available to him—one which would make them meaningful and at the same time vivid and believable too. His characters have lost the power of a Jeeter Lester— the power, that is, deriving from the deliberately isolating and exaggerating tendencies of the comic method—without acquiring any of the more complicated interest, or more sophisticated contact with their time and place, that the participants in a more strictly "realistic" fiction should possess. To adopt E. M. Forster's useful terms for a moment, they have no imaginative life of their own either as "flat" characters or as "round" ones. They are merely mouthpieces for utopian attitudes, as two-dimensional and as unprepossessing as some of the less successful heroes of Elizabeth Madox Roberts or Ellen Glasgow are. In *A House in the Uplands*, for instance, a novel published in 1946, the protagonist—who is, of course, a simple farmer—talks to his aristocratic fiancée in this way. It tells us a lot, I think, about the strained, self-consciously heroic posture of much of Caldwell's later work.

> "I'm just as good as you or anybody else who lives up . . . in the big house, and you know it. If I lived in one of those rotting old houses and loafed all the time and borrowed money to live on you'd marry me . . . quick. . . . I'm going to amount to something in life and I can give you a lot more than any other man will ever give you, and money won't be the only thing either."[30]

This is pure melodrama, horribly appropriate to a story that is only a slightly regionalized version of the Horatio Alger dream, and it represents a sad decline from the comic inventiveness of *Tobacco Road*. Admittedly, it is based on the same values as *Tobacco Road* is. The difference, however, and it is a crucial difference, is that what constitutes a background to comedy in the earlier narrative has now been carried into the foreground. The values, previously implied, have been allowed to occupy center stage; and—unfortunately for Caldwell —they have not benefited in the process either from an involvement in credible experience, or from contact with the sort of vivifying literary medium that the comic tradition of the old Southwest represents.

What has occurred in the later fiction is really very simple; and one useful way of summarizing it, within the context of Caldwell's total achievement, might go something like this. In stories like *Tobacco Road* or *God's Little Acre*, Caldwell's success depends largely upon two factors. These are his acquaintanceship with, and his use of, the methods of comic journalism that had been perfected by the humorists of the old Southwest, and his commitment to a dream of the rural landscape that he had also learned from his region. The factors are not just coincidental, of course. On the contrary, they complement and enhance each other here just as they do in the stories of George Washington Harris—with the dream giving power and coherence to the journalism, and the journalism in turn appropriating some sense of urgency and possibility for the dream. As in all the best Southern literature, in fact, idea and event are made to interact so as to produce a thoroughly traditional reading of the environment—a reading, that is to say, that depends on the earlier history of that environment without being circumscribed by it. But in later novels like *A House in the Uplands* this interaction more or less ceases. The idea remains unenlivened by any contact with experience; or, on those occasions when Caldwell does return to journalism—a comic account of things as they are—that journalism does not seem to have an ulterior motive any more. It no longer radiates the kind of significance that would come from its being placed within the framework of a controlling idea. Idea *or* event, dream *or* journalistic report: the two things exist separately, even if they both occur within the covers of one book. And what we are left with, consequently, is either heroic posturing of the sort I have just illustrated or a descent into episodes of comic violence and degeneracy that have no purpose beyond themselves, that are, in a word, sensationalistic. We are not being asked to register the gap between fact and potential any longer; only to indulge in daydreaming about what might happen in the best of all possible worlds, or to enjoy the cheaper thrills offered by a random and meaningless enumeration of some of the more sordid facts of life. The strategy of detachment is, in sum, replaced by one of vicarious excitement. This is a sad end for somebody like Caldwell, who started off so well; but even if it does nothing else it supplements Elizabeth Madox Roberts's story, I think, by telling us a little more about what happens when the functions of reporter and mythologizer are separated for a writer—and history is then translated by him into a refuge for some dormant principle or, alternatively, into a series of disconnected happenings.

What Time Collects: Thomas Wolfe

The two writers we have looked at so far in this chapter both suffered a decline during the course of their writing lives. They started off well enough, and even achieved some resolution of the difficulties facing them as regional authors; and then, for reasons I have tried to explain, things began to go wrong for them—and the answers they had achieved, the syntheses they had arrived at, no longer seemed available. The third writer I want to discuss in this chapter, however, went in precisely the opposite direction to this. He started off haltingly, with no clear idea of what to do with his Southern inheritance and ended up, toward the close of his life, with something approaching a solution. The writer I am talking about is Thomas Wolfe; and the homeplace he had to come to terms with was the mountain country of North Carolina, since he was born and grew up in Asheville in the Southern Appalachians. At first sight this might seem to suggest another difference, and an important one, between him and somebody like, say, Erskine Caldwell, as the mountains have always had their own special culture—their own songs, their own tales, and their own eccentric ways of looking at the world. Once we look at the basic pattern or dynamic of this culture, though, and more particularly at what was happening to it during Wolfe's lifetime, then, I think, many of these apparent differences disappear or, at least, begin to seem fairly superficial. At basis, I believe, the social and historical forces with which Wolfe had to engage, by the mere fact of being a "man of the hills,"[31] were very similar to those confronting a writer like Caldwell; and many of the differences that did exist between these forces involved, in reality, a distinction in *degree* rather than a distinction of *kind*. They stemmed from the fact that the problems facing the mountain people, and mountain culture, in the early years of this century were not so much unique ones as extreme instances of a common Southern dilemma.

In a sense, this has always been the story of the Southern mountains: they are like the South, only more so. If we look, for example, at the beginnings of this story we can find some sort of heightened typicality in the mountain people's acute isolation—they tended to go one better than all their neighbors from Dixie, even in their simple ability to cut themselves off from the rest of the world. Like other Southerners, the mountain folk were isolated from the dominant historical tendencies of the nineteenth century; their society, once established (in the early days of the Republic), seemed more or less immune to the industrial revolution and to urban drift. They seemed to carry that isolation much further than any other Southerners did, however, so that even the few symptoms of change that did appear in other parts of the region—such as improved methods of transport and communication—hardly impinged upon them at all. For over a hundred years they lived in a vacuum, unaffected by events taking place elsewhere, like some outpost of empire that had been colonized once upon a time and then simply forgotten. People living in the last decades of the century sang the same ballads their ancestors had sung, about Bonnie Prince Charlie and the heroes of the American Revolution, and used the same primitive methods of farming and bartering to gain their daily bread. The inaccessibility of the highlands had something to do with this curious state of affairs, of course, but the sheer indifference of the "outlanders" (as mountain folk liked to call their neighbors) also had its part to play. The highlands were relatively barren ground, and there was just no interest in them for most people while the lands to the West were still to be opened up. So they remained an unexplored territory inhabited by a race who, apparently out of weakness or stubbornness or both, preferred what they found there to the more fertile and much more hotly contested soil of other regions.[32]

Then, in the last decade of the century, the "outlanders" slowly began to take notice. The West had been conquered, the possibility of coal mining and timber farming in the highlands was being discussed, and, as weathercocks of the changing attitude, a number of travelers and anthropologists made the long trek into the Appalachians, to bring back reports of the people and way of life they found there. For some of these travelers it was almost like rediscovering the past. Here, they claimed, were the good old days of rural simplicity perfectly preserved, in a setting that might have been devised by Thomas Jefferson: the Southern highlanders were "our contemporary ancestors," demonstrating virtues—immemorially attached to the tillers of the soil—that the rest of the nation seemed to have lost. The reports began to vie with each other in enthusiasm, and as they did so they prepared the way for a sort of minor industry in idyllic portraits of mountain life— some purporting to be fact, others confessing to being fiction, but all of them characterized by a profound need to locate a Great Good Place of the regional imagination in this newly discovered territory. By the time Thomas Wolfe was old enough to take notice, the legend of the mountain man was at its height. Here is one out of many possible examples of the sort of description it encouraged; it by no means represents an extreme.

> . . . the Highlander is the true American, and the type of American usually seized upon as representative of all Highlanders is the early pioneer type. The pioneer is, indeed, still to be recognized in many of his mountain descendants—tall, lean, clear-eyed, self-reliant, never taken by surprise, and of great endurance.
>
> . . . We have, then, in the Southern Highlander an American, a rural dweller of the agricultural class, and a mountaineer who is still more or less of a pioneer. His dominant trait is independence raised to the nth power.[33]

The important thing to remember about this kind of portrait, I think, is that for all its popularity it involved a distortion of the actual circumstances—which is to say, a simplification of them. Admittedly, the highlander did preserve very many facets of an older way of life, ranging from the songs he sang and the ring dances he enjoyed to some more sinister beliefs which helped locate him "just a step and a jump from the Middle Ages"; and these supplied some basis for a comparison between him and the heroes of agrarian myth. But to accept this comparison without qualification was, I think, a mistake because it was in effect to ignore the radical difficulties of mountain existence that went along with its pleasures—the problems and deprivation that tended to drive the highlander quite beyond the Jeffersonian pale. The mountain man had, after all, been *forced* into the mountains in the first place. Like the backwoodsman discovered by Longstreet and the humorists, he had been deprived of the rich tillage of the seaboard and delta country, and the land to which he had retreated was in many ways a last resort—something he could hold onto because nobody else wanted it. This was hardly the ideal location for a rediscovery of the "chosen people of God," at least as Jefferson and his disciples had liked to define those people. In a way, with its barren acres and the root attitude of defensiveness shown by its inhabitants, it was more a paradigm of rural poverty—an example of the kinds of hardships that result from an inequitable distribution of the land—than it was a subject ripe for mythologizing. And anybody who did not take this aspect of mountain life into account inevitably lay himself open to the charge of daydreaming.

The charge only became the more applicable, and forceful, as time passed and the mythologizing process got well under way. For a special irony was added to the situation by the fact that the very people

who discovered their "contemporary ancestors" in the hills were, as
I have said, the harbingers of change: they represented the first stages
in an invasion that was to end by destroying such few claims as the
mountaineer ever had to identification with the good farmer of legend.
The "outlander" came in to observe the "old, common, native" customs,
and, by the mere act of coming in, tore down the barriers that had
helped to preserve those customs. The highlander's contact with the
outside world, which had been abandoned for over a century, was
renewed—and the vacuum in which the old dispensation had been
preserved was suddenly punctured. A breach had been made, and into
it poured every kind of feasible business investment. Mines and factories were opened up, cities were built and a tourist industry established in places like Wolfe's own hometown of Asheville; people could
then come in their thousands to look at the communities they were
helping to destroy. These changes in the highland landscape led in
turn to others with implications that were even more radical, having
to do with ways of life rather than means of living. For the mountain
man was no longer defined by his rural environment, Jeffersonian or
otherwise, and this could not help but affect his entire experience
world, his behavior outside of his work. As the Appalachian historian,
Thomas Ford, has put it,

> . . . the growth and improvement of public education . . . rural electrifica-
> tion . . . mass communication . . . improved roads . . . all contributed to
> the weakening of traditional values. . . . It was a period of novel ex-
> perience, new opportunities, and unprecedented prosperity and after it
> was all over there would be no complete return to the old ways.[34]

The period Ford is referring to here is the early twentieth century—
precisely the time when the Jeffersonian equation was being insisted on
more than ever before. A familiar paradox, I think, lurked in the fact
that, just as this new version of the pastoral achieved widespread popularity, so the area of possible coincidence between it and contemporary experience began steadily to contract.

The paradox is a familiar one, of course, because it applies equally
to the Appalachian region in the first two decades of this century, and
to every other part of the country below the Mason-Dixon line. What
we are confronted with in the time and place in which Thomas Wolfe
grew up turns out to be a quintessentially *Southern* case: a basic pattern of change being met with reluctance or active resistance, and
the search for an alternative mythology. There were, as I say, differences in the pattern as it occurred in the highlands—indeed, it would
have been surprising, considering the earlier history of the hill folk,
if there had not been—but these stemmed largely from the fact that

everybody was much more isolated and everything was much more exaggerated in the mountains than it was anywhere else, so the pattern tended to be that much clearer there. It was yet another case of the hills being "the same, only more so." The moment of change, for example, was especially traumatic for the mountain community precisely because it had existed in such a unique state of loneliness and stasis for so long. By comparison the absorption of the rest of the South into the national culture almost assumes the character of a predictable development—the fulfillment, anyway, of tendencies that were already in existence. Similarly, the retreat into nostalgia that this moment precipitated in the hills was exceptional—for its deliberateness, that is, and the self-consciousness with which it was pursued —even in a region long accustomed to imposing unlikely interpretations on the past and then seeking comfort from them. Almost in despair of unearthing an alternative elsewhere in the region, it seemed, admirers of the mountain folk hastily elevated them into relics of bygone, golden days, sturdy farmers crying defiance to progress. Not only that, the mountain folk themselves seemed to conspire with their admirers, by desperately clinging onto their old traditions and habits of thought even while they were being dragged rapidly into the industrial age. This, the fact that the hill folk as a group tended to be even more stubborn in their preservation of familiar ways than any of their outland neighbors, was perhaps a by-product of their customary defensiveness—just one more instance, although a particularly striking one, of their habitual reluctance to follow the example of "foreigners." Be that as it may, it led at first to what one observer has described as a curious "persistence of a frontier type of organization and value-system in an environment no longer suited to either."[35] And it resulted eventually in an even more curious state of affairs, in which the value system itself, altering under the impact of change, began to assume its own ambivalence—to become, in fact, an anomalous mixture of the old and the new in its own right. Everywhere one looked in the hills in the 1920s, the conflict that the entire South was experiencing at the time—between optimism and nostalgia, the pull toward the future and the pull toward the past—seemed to be repeated in a minor but uncomfortably emphatic key. The disease of facing both ways had been brought to what appeared, in effect, to be a terminal stage. This was something that no writer who wanted to deal with that time and place properly could afford to ignore; and, as I see it, Thomas Wolfe— the greatest writer that the Southern hills have produced, and one of the greatest writers the South has produced as well—managed in his own rather uncertain and instinctive way to recognize this from the very beginning. His work demonstrates, I think, an increasing willingness to engage with his locality in terms of the contradictions visited upon it by change—and, on top of that, a growing eagerness to resolve those contradictions. Admittedly, this process of resolution started slowly enough and was never really completed, being cut short when Wolfe died suddenly at the age of thirty-eight. But Wolfe had brought it near, agonizingly near, to completion by the time that he died, and in doing so had devised at the very least a series of notes toward a unique version of "Southern-ness"—something that is as special and yet central to the imaginative life of his region as his own mountain background was to its cultural life.

But to suggest that Thomas Wolfe is in any meaningful sense a Southern writer is, of course, to depart from the consensus opinion about him, to risk sounding downright perverse, since there is an assumption among most critics—regardless of their estimates of the quality of his work—that he shares little with his region other than what Maxwell Geismar once called "the accident of birth." This is not questioned too often, and even when it is, a useful defense for it can usually be mustered out of some remarks made by the writer himself. After all, did not Wolfe *say* that he was "more American than Southern," and then go on to claim "the enormous space and energy of American life as a whole" as his subject? And what about his famous description of his first book, *Look Homeward, Angel,* which was so clearly a personal narrative? "I am telling the story of a powerful creative element," Wolfe explained to a friend, "trying to work its way toward an essential isolation, a creative solitude, a secret life. . . ." That hardly suggests any sense of belonging—to the South, to the mountains, or indeed to anywhere. Most of Wolfe's biographers have in fact taken remarks like these at their face value, ignoring his tendency to leave the line between his own and fictional experience a pretty vague one—as well as his almost Emersonian contempt for consistency, or telling the whole truth on any particular occasion. And so the conventional method of describing his career is to adopt a figure from the writer himself, and say that it demonstrates a centrifugal movement, a flight "outward through a series of pressure chambers—from Asheville to Chapel Hill to Harvard to New York—each widening his horizon and freeing him a little more."[36] Wolfe may have been born in the South, the implication is, and raised in a unique environment; but this impinged upon him hardly at all. The hills were merely one "pressure chamber," a prison from which he had to liberate himself before going on to the discovery of some genuinely creative resource.
The argument is a persuasive one, certainly—but then all specious arguments are. And that this is a specious argument even in the ab-

stract is clear, I think, from the way in which it ignores the principle of definition by rejection: writers, like other people, are defined by the things they reject (or try to reject) as much as anything else. We have only to think of James Joyce, Dublin, and Roman Catholicism to recognize that. More important, its speciousness becomes especially obvious when we apply it to the particular case, the case of Thomas Wolfe and the Southern highlands, to see how well it fits. For it fits, we discover, hardly at all. The situation in Wolfe's novels is much too subtle and complicated to be described in terms of some "either-or" antithesis. Notions of rejection, or acceptance, simply do not apply here and to use them is really to mislead. This is not to say that Wolfe is *unaware* of the impulse to reject, to escape from the embrace of the mountains. Of course he is, and he dramatizes it vividly—not least in this opening description of "Old Catawba" (a fictionalized version of western North Carolina) in *The Web and the Rock*.

> In Old Catawba, the hill boy helps his father building fences and hears a soft Spring howling in the wind. . . . And far away he hears the whistle's cry wailed back, . . . as a great train rushes towards the cities of the East. And the heart of the hill boy will know joy because he knows . . . that some day he will meet the world and know those cities too.[37]

But Wolfe adds to this the rider that neither he nor the hill boy can ever properly escape. Both are, as he once put it, "acted upon by all the accumulated impact" of their ancestral experience and they can no more deny this than Eugene Gant, the hero of *Look Homeward, Angel*, can rid himself of a mysterious "tetter of itch" that appears on the nape of his neck one day—a tetter Wolfe identifies as the outward and visible "sign of kinship" with his ancestors in the mountains. For all of them the past is a part of their blood.

In a way, Wolfe's protagonists seem to acknowledge this involvement with the past and all that it implies by complicating their longing to escape with all kinds of curious reservations. So when Eugene Gant, for instance, does finally board the train for the "golden city" of New York—in *Of Time and the River*—his reactions are not unmixed. Looking out at the last of the Catawba towns on the line, he finds that the expected "feeling of illimitable and exultant power" is uncomfortably tempered by something else as well.

> On everything—trees, houses, foliage, yards, and street there was a curious loneliness of departure . . . this dark and dusty street of the tall trees left a haunting, curiously pleasant feeling of strangeness and familiarity. One viewed it with a queer sudden ache in the heart, a feeling of friendship and farewell, and this feeling was probably intensified by the swift and powerful movement of the train which seemed to slide past

the town almost noiselessly, its wheels turning without friction, sound, or vibrance on the pressed steel ribbon of the rails. . . .[38]

Wolfe once wrote to his editor, Maxwell Perkins, that the "hunger for . . . getting away" and the "desire . . . for home, for permanence, for a piece of the earth fenced in and lived on" were both rooted in his experience; and this passage captures the combination well, I think. It is a combination that reappears in *The Web and the Rock* when the hero, George Webber—who is, like Gant, a thinly disguised *alter ego* for the author—makes *his* departure from the hometown. There is the same conflict between contradictory reactions, a "tension of the nerves" so painful as to make Webber "grit . . . the teeth and harden . . . the jaws." And in the case of both Webber and Gant, the contrast between the train and the land over which it hurries is deliberately used as a metaphor, a way of externalizing the dilemma.

> The boy felt the powerful movement of the train beneath him and the lonely austerity and mystery of the dark earth outside that swept past forever with a fanlike stroke, an immortal and imperturbable stillness. It seemed to him that these two terrific negatives of speed and stillness, the hurtling and projectile movement of the train and the calm silence of the everlasting earth, were poles of a single unity—a unity coherent with his destiny, whose source was somehow in himself.[39]

The train and the earth, the web and the rock: both pairs of opposites are a means of locating the double-sidedness of the author and his heroes and, by extension, the ambivalence of their relationship to their birthplace.

A relationship implies the presence of at least two active participants, even when only one man and his locality are concerned, and Wolfe acknowledges as much by devoting the same attention to his native region as he does to the inner landscapes of his characters. Romantic he might have been, but there is nothing of the romantic egotist in his fidelity to the given particulars of the mountain inheritance—which are as undeniably *there,* contributing to the drama, as Eugene Gant and George Webber are themselves. Needless to say, as Wolfe describes them there is little of the aristocratic in their makeup. He was fascinated by what he called the "dark romanticism" of the lower, more "opulent South," certainly, but his was always the fascination of the outsider. Mrs. Selborne, for instance, a lady from South Carolina who boards at the house of Eugene Gant in *Look Homeward, Angel,* is presented as an alien creature, attractive by very reason of her strangeness. "She moved leisurely with a luxurious swing of her body: her smile was tender and full of vague allurement, her voice gentle, her sudden laughter, bubbling out of midnight secrecy, rich and full." The lush epithets, and the suggestion of mystery, do not leave much doubt as to the nature of Eugene's, and Wolfe's, attitude to the character here. It is one of wonder, the kind of bewildered admiration that might be inspired by a visitant from another world. A similar tone and vocabulary occur even when a more hostile attitude is adopted toward this world, only now the wonder is mixed with horror.

> . . . in South Carolina . . . they have . . . something haunting, soft, and lonely in the air . . . the men . . . get fat about the bellies. . . . They are soft-voiced and drawling. . . . They drawl softly in front of the drugstore. . . . And after a day before the drugstores or around the empty fountain in the Courthouse Square, they go out to lynch a nigger, . . . before they hang him they saw off his nose and his fat nigger lips with a rusty knife. And they laugh about it.[40]

The horror here stems partly from a longing, and an inability, to understand why men behave this way. It is not merely that their actions are cruel but that, in Wolfe's eyes, they are incomprehensible as well —the language of another country that must remain foreign to him. On a different level, the same sense of distance and foreign-ness is implicit in Wolfe's breezy dismissal of the Nashville Agrarians—who, he declares, were just a group of "refined young gentleman of the New Confederacy . . . [who] . . . retired haughtily . . . to the academic security of a teaching appointment, . . . from which they could issue . . . very small and very precious magazines. . . ." This time the failure of understanding is unconscious, I think: Wolfe believes he is telling us the truth about people like Warren and Tate when he is really only guilty of a simplification. Just as much as the description of the lynchers, though, this pen-portrait indicates how estranged he was from large areas of Southern experience and history—from all those areas, in fact, that did not find their equivalents in the hills.

Nothing could be further removed from the opulence and casual violence of the delta country, the land of the higher plantation myth, than the life of the Gants and Webbers. Wolfe tries to capture that life in one word: it is, he says, "homely." Despite contamination by the more sophisticated newcomers from the lowlands, he claims, the hill folk still retain a few traces of their old culture; and those traces betray an overall simplicity, forms of belief and behavior as spare as the environment that helped produce them. The spareness, apparently, is partly a matter of externals; it is witnessed for Wolfe among other things in the "lean, angular, high-boned and loose-jointed" frame that he says tends to identify the native highlander, and in his "utterly common, familiar, plain Scotch-Irish face." But this is less interesting,

I think, than the "narrow . . . dogged and . . . puritan" ethic Wolfe also attaches to the men of Old Catawba. There is a moral rigor about the customary laws of the hills, as he describes them, amounting almost to the sadistic. Exactly how close they can come to sadism is illustrated by George Webber's grandfather, who announces "solemnly and implacably that he 'would rather see a daughter of mine dead and lying in her coffin than married to a man who drank'";[41] and this when actually speaking to his daughter! Part of the significance of what is said, of course, lies in the fact that it is the *grandfather* who says it. For this helps to place the ethic in its pristine form back at least two generations, to the days before the invasion of the mountains by the "outlanders." After that invasion, we learn, the rules started to change, discipline relaxed; and just for once we are tempted to conclude that the change was for the better. In nothing, I think, is Wolfe's realism more evident than in this: that the old ways—as they existed without contamination several generations ago or as they remain now—are by no means seen in a haze of nostalgia. Warts and all, they present themselves to the reader as symptoms of a once living, and consequently imperfect, culture.

Certainly, for documentary accuracy in the presentation of the old mountain ways, or what may be left of them, Wolfe is, I believe, unsurpassed. Nobody has caught as well as he has, for instance, the attitude of the highlander toward violence, which leads him to "kill about a fence, a dog, the dispute of a boundary line." It is, Wolfe suggests, like the attitude of the lowlander in its apparent casualness but fundamentally different in its origins and implications; and a typical example of it is offered to us by Nebraska Crane, a hillboy who befriends George Webber in *The Web and the Rock*. George is set upon one day by a group of local bullies, and Nebraska saves him by cracking one of them over the head with a club. The blow is almost fatal but Nebraska is unperturbed, unshaken in his belief that he has acted correctly.

> "Why that's nothin' to be afraid of!" said Nebraska. "Anyone's likely to get killed. . . . You're likely to have to kill someone almost *any* time! . . . this is America an' we're a free country—an' if someone gets in your way an' bothers you, you have to kill him—an' that's all there is to it! . . . If you have to go to court, it's a lot of trouble an' takes up your time— but then the jury lets you off, an' that's all there is to it!"[42]

The explanation involves a simultaneous appeal to masculine courage, the liberty of the individual, and the supremacy of destiny; and it does not require a logician to see an element of inconsistency here. The inconsistency hardly matters, though, since Wolfe's point is that the principles Nebraska Crane invokes are reconciled in experience, if not in logic, by the simple fact of their all being a part of his system of values. Fatalism and individualism may seem like a strange combination, but hill men such as Nebraska have managed to combine them for generations so as to produce habits of perception that are quite unique. That, I think, is one suggestion Wolfe is making in the passage, and out of this in turn develops a further suggestion; which is that the violent impulses of the hill men—supported as they are by such principles—must be as natural to them as other, more obviously normal aspects of their experience are. They represent not an eccentricity, or a lapse, but something rooted in a common code. This is an ingenious argument and, in addition, a characteristic one. For what Wolfe is doing, effectively, is deprive "feudin' " of the more colorful associations given to it in conventional fictional portraits of the Southern mountaineers—associations, that is to say, that would identify it as thoroughly exotic and strange—and place it in a context where it seems an inevitable part of the life described. The methods of the local colorist are being avoided, in other words, in favor of a strategy at once more sophisticated and more honest, which explains one aspect of a society (however odd it may seem) in terms of the entire structure.

It is also characteristic that there should be no use of direct statement or analysis in the making of all these points. On the contrary, the character is permitted to speak for, and define, himself. Those whom Wolfe called the "rich, juicy . . . people" from the "hills of home" habitually reveal the dimensions of their lives through what they do and, perhaps even more important, what they say—rather than through any larger framework of explanation their creator may give to their activities. The history of the Pentland clan, for instance, the mountain ancestors of Eugene Gant, comes filtered to us through the memory of Eugene's mother, Eliza; and as she remembers that history her own observations, indeed her own manner of describing events, act as a means of evoking the old mountain ways. The process is magnificently illustrated by the monologue Wolfe ascribes to her in his short story, "The Web of Earth." Here, Eliza starts to explain the "voices" which she heard years ago whispering to her the words "Two . . . Two," "Twenty . . . Twenty." But random digressions intervene—so that only hours after she began to talk does she finally describe how, exactly "*twenty* days from that evening" when the voices spoke to her, she gave birth to twins. The procedure may irritate some readers—until, that is, they recognize that the purpose of the monologue is not so much to tell a particular story as to reveal a personality, and a representative personality at that. Certain things are being said about the character of Eliza Gant, and by extension about the mountain character in general, and they emerge from every line of the narrative, making none of them superfluous. Among other things, what Wolfe calls the "Scotch superstition" of the highlander, the superstition, in other words, that prompts Eliza to tell the anecdote in the first place, is implicit in nearly every other story by which she is distracted. Most of them involve spirits, premonitions, and quirks of fate; and the tone of each one of them is set by her claim that life is "pretty strange when you come to think about it,"[43] a claim repeated so often that it soon assumes the character of a motif. Eliza's is a vision that makes ghosts, taboos, and strange prophecies the stuff of everyday experience. As such it prescribes her way of telling the tales as well as the content of most of them.

This is equally true of the other aspects of mountain life that Wolfe discovers in the course of the monologue: they are perceived in dramatic terms, as ideas in action. The stoicism of the highlander, for example, is communicated in an almost imperceptible way—as a lesson to be learned and relearned every time Mrs. Gant recalls the restlessness of her late husband ("They're all alike . . . I never saw a man that could stay where he was for five minutes."), or describes the calmness of her reaction to the disasters his financial adventures bring upon them.

> "Oh Eliza," he said, "We're too old to start again, and we've lost everything." "No," I said, "not everything. There's something left." "What is it?" he said. "We've got the earth. We'll stand upon it and it will save us. It's never gone back on nobody yet."[44]

Passages like this make Eliza Gant's endurance into something we experience while we read the story—which we feel as much as know in a conscious and detached way, because we are not just told about it. And the same procedure, of making us encounter the character directly rather than via explanations, is adopted when Wolfe presents us with what is undoubtedly the most interesting quality assigned to her. I mean by this her extraordinary "lust for debate" and the coincident respect she shows for those with any "command of language." Admittedly, Eliza does make these interests of hers quite explicit. She likes to talk about words and wordspells, and even admits that her love of eloquence is something she shares with most of her neighbors. But these remarks, relevant though they are, are only by way of an aside. What is far more effective, I think, as a method of informing us of this interest is the sheer impact of her speech; a staple idiom, apparently characteristic of hill folk, that is just as "plain, rich, pungent, earthy [and] strong-colored" as Wolfe had claimed—in his letters—

that it could be. It is a verbal equivalent for the best parts of her personality and culture, her vitality, her rigor, and her earthiness.

> "I reckon for a fact that I had the power of Nature in me; why! no more trouble than the earth takes bearing corn, all of the children, the eight who lived, and all the others—all of the children and less married life than any woman that I know—and oh! to think of it . . . he [Mr. Gant] . . . cursin' and tauntin' me and runnin' wild with other women. . . . Lord! Lord! he was a strange man, a wild and savage man. . . ."[45]

Here Eliza Gant has been given a style that helps to reflect her own response to experience, her own vision of life; or at least those elements in her response and vision that draw their strength from the mountain traditions.

That qualification is necessary because even in "The Web of Earth" Mrs. Gant is more than just a reminder of the "good ol' days" in the hills. She talks a lot about the land and the trials it visits upon those who care for it, but she also spends a great deal of time discussing the tourist boom, fluctuations in the stock market, and her own small gambles in real estate. As Wolfe puts it in *Look Homeward, Angel,* she is somebody who has complicated the "visionary fanaticism" of her ancestors with the "hard monied sense" of the speculator. So complete did her absorption in business become during one period, he goes on, that she even abdicated her responsibilities to her family so as to devote all her attention to it. Her children were then entrusted to the care of her oldest daughter, and her husband was left in one house while she tried to run a tourist home in another. She is in fact, as Wolfe intends her to be, like an abstract and brief chronicle of her times—a woman encapsulating in her own experience the mixed values of, and strange distortions wrought upon, her "sleepy little mountain village"[46] by the new spirit of "boosterism." In nothing, perhaps, is Eliza Gant more representative than in this: that the dilemma in which she finds herself, caught as she is between the provincialism of her past and the more cosmopolitan vistas opened out by her future, belongs to her community as much as it does to her. Her life records the other half of the mountain story as well, the half concerned with transition.

Just how representative Eliza is, in this other sense, becomes clear enough when Wolfe transfers our attention from her to the larger canvas of the mountains again. One thing then tends to dominate the scene: change, an invasion of the old by the new so complete that at times it seems as if every person in Catawba is devoted to the business of business. Certainly, few people escape criticism in a situation where exploiters like Mrs. Gant and the exploited are equally identified with the betrayal of an inheritance. Top and bottom dogs alike seem to have surrendered "every principle of personal and communal rectitude," everything of value that they might have learned from their mountain culture, to a growing acceptance of the cash nexus. Indeed, if there is any distinction to be made between the two groups at all, it is only because the failures appear to supply Wolfe with a more incisive demonstration of what has happened. As he describes them, they and their surroundings offer us a vivid physical equivalent for the process of universal corruption. They become the sore that indicates the disease-ridden state of the entire organism.

> No birds sang in that barren world. . . . In summer the heat beat down . . . upon the wretched streets, and on all the dusty, shadeless roads and alleys of the slum. . . . It shone with the same impartial cruelty . . . on a thousand mangy, scabby, nameless little children—hideous little scarecrows with tow hair, their skinny little bodies unrecognizably scurfed with filth and scarred with running sores. . . . And the sun also shone on the slattern women of the district. . . . They stood there at the edge of the ramshackle porch . . . with their gaunt, staring eyes, toothless jaws, and corrupt, discolored mouths.[47]

This is the final stroke in the portrait of the mountain inheritance to which Eugene Gant and George Webber are so ambivalently attached —and a sinister one, if only because it suggests that the inheritance has its own special kind of double-sidedness.

There is a nice irony introduced into the narrative here. Contrary to first impressions, it seems after all that the "piece of earth fenced in and lived on" where Eugene Gant and George Webber are born is not just an emblem of stability. It is compromised as well, involved in the same "hunger . . . for getting away"—or at least getting on— that drives Gant and Webber northwards. The desire for permanence and the longing for movement and change—they are both of them to be found in the homeplace. Few people, it appears, can be free from the contradictions that baffle Gant and Webber any more; they are general and perhaps insoluble. To make matters worse, neither the impulse toward movement nor the impulse toward repose ever seems to offer a viable alternative in its own right. Each tends, when they are separated, to prescribe a course that ends slowly but invariably in frustration. All that progress appears to mean, for example, when worshipped as an end in itself by any of Wolfe's characters, is what, essentially, Eliza Gant takes it to mean: a restless pursuit of "more Ford automobiles, more Rotary clubs, more Baptist ladies social unions." "Growing," too, becomes no more than a euphemism for self-aggrandizement. And all that stability boils down to is just as bad, since it comes to stand effectively for stagnation. The more "stable" mountain folk, in fact, the small number who have managed to evade the pressure toward change, are those who have ceased to develop. Escaping from the difficulties of the present into a desperate reconstruction of the past, their very attempt to keep their inherited culture intact really betrays their failure to understand all that was most vital to it. Here is how Wolfe charts the paradox—of losing the substance of a tradition by chasing its shadow—in one of his books.

> The lives their forebears lived were harsh and new, still seeking and explorative; their own lives often were just squalid, which should have been better. . . . Turned backwards now, world-lost, in what was once new land! Unseeking now, in what their fathers sought! Turned in upon themselves, congruent as a tribe, all intermarried.[48]

The situation resolves itself into a problem with what seem like two equally inadequate solutions: either to go forward, to escape and consequently lose all contact with one's roots, or to stay put and rot. To forfeit the stabilizing influence of an inherited culture, or to be smothered by the past—the paths figured respectively by the train and the earth turn out to be similarly disastrous. But is there another path? Was there a third alternative, an escape route for Wolfe to discover or invent; and could he use it to solve his own predicament—as a writer who felt that he belonged to the hills and mountains of his birth, and yet did not want to be confined by them?

We can, if we want to, put the question in a rather more positive way. Progress, as an idea, was something that a part of Thomas Wolfe genuinely believed in—and a very important part at that. He knew that mountain communities had to change, just as he and his heroes had to change, to grow and to meet new challenges, and sometimes he could even rejoice in that knowledge. But—and this can never be emphasized too much—he knew that there was another part of him, and of human beings in general, which longed for roots; or, to be more accurate, which recognized the value of the past and its legacies along with the future. And how, he wondered, was this to be catered for? Something valuable, it was his belief, could and should be recovered from "Old Catawba" and carried over to subsequent generations—and how was this to be done? No matter how we put the question, though, positively or negatively, it remains clear, I think, that none of Wolfe's novels from *Look Homeward, Angel* to *You Can't Go Home Again* ever provide a satisfactory answer to it. There is no third alternative, no way out: Eugene Gant and George Webber simply continue (and end) as they began—wavering between opposites, dodging and hovering restlessly between two poles. Several critics have described this move-

ment, as it recurs in most of Wolfe's fiction, as Hegelian;[49] and it is true
that Wolfe owed a debt to Hegel for the preliminary definition of his
characters' lives—or, if not to Hegel directly, at least to that version
of Hegel he was taught while at college. But it is necessary, I believe,
to add an important qualification to this. Although Gant and Webber
are certainly confronted with what we might call a "Hegelian situation" during the course of their adventures, in the sense that they are
caught between the "thesis" of their rural background and the "antithesis" of their urban future, there is never ever a hint of their reaching the third stage in the Hegelian process—of a possible *synthesis*
taking place. And because of this, for all the surface activity of their
lives, although they may move and change in other ways, there is one
part of Wolfe's protagonists that can never really grow. I mean by this
that they can never develop *morally,* since the means of such a development—the ability to organize and integrate available values—is
something quite beyond their reach, and apparently beyond Wolfe's
reach as well.

This was a situation that lasted through most of Wolfe's novels,
appearing to be as much a part of them—a characteristic problem as
it were—as his lyrical magniloquence was, or the profoundly autobiographical nature of his protagonists. So it was all the more surprising
when in his last book he made a sudden break with it, or rather moved a
stage forward, building upon what had been done before. The book,
tentatively entitled *The Hills Beyond,* was never completed because
Wolfe died while he was writing it; and perhaps this very incompleteness accounts for the extraordinary lack of critical interest there has
been in it. Whatever the reason, it *has* been neglected; and this is
unfortunate since the new departure Wolfe was making here has never
been properly acknowledged as a result. *The Hills Beyond* is a historical narrative, which is in itself a new field for Wolfe—but that is a
relatively minor point. What is much more important is that it represents a genuine attempt—and as far as it goes a successful attempt, I
think—to reconcile the two impulses figured in the train and the earth.
The reconciliation is made in terms of a few people from what Wolfe
liked to call "the great and marvellous hills of North Carolina"[50]—
highlanders, modeled on some of his own ancestors, whom he elevates
to the status of an imaginative ideal. This is history mythologized, and
mythologized as it turns out with the help of strategies that have
themselves been inherited from the past. For Wolfe's purpose is to
create his own folk heroes, who solve the problems and resolve the
tensions characteristic of their generation; and to do this he adopts
the simple, yet profoundly effective, technique of borrowing from other
folk heroes. Their stories are imitated, their characteristics remem-

bered, but all with a difference so as to create out of heroes of other times a hero for our own.

The Hills Beyond is ostensibly concerned with the early settlement of the Joyner family in North Carolina, and in particular with the lives of William "Bear" Joyner, the first of his clan to settle in mountainous Zebulon County, and his four oldest sons. William, especially, is shown to be deeply attached to his backwoods "web of earth"—so deeply that he becomes its embodiment, its representative hero. His neighbors tell stories of his fighting prowess, for example, which make of him "an almost legendary figure."

> There is the story of his fight with a big blacksmith: a quarrel having broken out between them over the shoeing of a horse, the blacksmith brained him with an iron shoe. . . . As William started to get up again, bleeding and half-conscious, the blacksmith came at him again, and Joyner hit him while still resting on one knee. The blow broke the blacksmith's ribs and caved in his side as one would crack a shell.[51]

In a way this story belongs to the same genre as Longstreet's description of the fight he witnessed in Georgia—but only in a way. For the condescension of *Georgia Scenes* has disappeared; so, for the moment, has much of the critical detachment implicit in *Sut Lovingood*. And what we have in their place is the kind of sympathy between narrator and character—and, ideally, reader as well—that is more appropriate to folklore than anything else. Wolfe intends to construct a *myth*, an expression of the better possibilities of the age, and this requires that he create some sense of community (some limited sense of community, at least) between the people variously involved in the enterprise. They must share in the experiences he describes rather than merely observe them.

The debt, then, is not so much to Southwestern humor as to the folktale, the stories told *by* the people *about* whom Longstreet and Harris wrote (and from whom they often borrowed themes and character types for their sketches). This becomes fairly obvious, I think, once we compare the stories told about Joyner's fighting ability with the legends of people like Mike Fink (the hero of the Mississippi keelboatmen), Davy Crockett, or Daniel Boone. All of them love to fight, and excel at it. Indeed, Mike Fink's characteristic boast might almost have come from the lips of William Joyner after he had conquered the blacksmith: "I can lick five times my own weight in wildcats. I can use Injuns by the cord. I can swallow niggers whole. . . . O for a fight, boys, to stretch these here limbs!"[52] And other parallels between their exploits and his are too close to be merely an accident. Thus, according to legend both Daniel Boone and Davy Crockett proved that they were "mighty hunters" by grappling with wild bears in the wilderness and emerging from the conflict victorious—although horribly mangled. "Bear" Joyner does exactly the same and, we infer, for precisely the same reasons.

> . . . the bear charged him at close quarters and there was nothing left for him to do but fight. A searching party found him two days later, more dead than living—as they told it, "all chawed up," but with the carcass of the bear: "and in the fight he had bit the nose of that big b'ar and chawed off both ears. . . ."[53]

Like Fink, Joyner carries enormous weights on his back, to prove his strength. Like Crockett he is a man of keen wit, who can outwit others in a trade. Like Boone he is most at home in the forests, tracking deer or fishing. Every one of his exploits carries an echo, reminding us of its original in earlier times; and a primary function of these echoes, I think, is to make of William Joyner a representative figure— a fulfillment of the larger possibilities of his community, "its life, its speech, . . . even the clay of its soil." "The spirit of a people," Wolfe observes at one point, "is recorded in the heroes it picks," and his observation is obviously appropriate to a character who acts as a kind of focus for the qualities that his simple mountain neighbors revere.

But this is only one function of "Bear's" exploits (William Joyner is called "Bear" after his fight with the "big b'ar") and the legendary echoes they bring with them: to give him a touch of representativeness —to make him seem like a typical backwoodsman. Another purpose Wolfe has in mind, and a no less important one, is to hedge this representativeness with qualifications; to suggest, in fact, the existence of certain significant dissimilarities between the people and their chosen hero—and so establish his protagonist as special. To an extent these dissimilarities have to do with the actual process of myth making. Wolfe is, after all, unlike the folk who invented the legends of Mike Fink and Davy Crockett in that he is a conscious mythologizer. He is a deliberate artist, aware of what he is doing, and this awareness is taken account of in the narrative.

> "Bear" Joyner . . . was increate with myth, because the very nature of the man persuaded it . . . it is not the Myth that falsifies the true identity of man. . . . The Myth is true. . . . The Myth is founded on *extorted* fact; wrenched from the context of ten thousand days, and rutted roads, the desolations of lost voices long ago . . . the vacancy of unremembered hours. . . .[54]

That is why so many of the anecdotes told about "Bear" begin with the phrase, "there is the story" or are told through the medium of his neighbors: because, like Allen Tate, Wolfe wants to dramatize the myth making process even while he is making his myth. He is remind-

ing the reader that his concern here is with possibility, what might
have been rather than what is. And since the other, ordinary inhabitants of Zebulon County tend themselves to represent what is, they
must necessarily differ from the figure of their hero.

There is another reason for the dissimilarity, however, which is special to *The Hills Beyond* and has to do with its unique purposes. The
mountain folk amongst whom Wolfe places William Joyner are not
pioneers; appearances to the contrary, they are several generations removed from the frontier. For all that, their lives are hardly different
from the lives of pioneers. In fact, as the narrator explains, their patterns of belief and behavior have "scarcely changed at all" since the
first days of settlement. The result of this is a paradoxical state of
affairs in which the originally unconventional behavior of the frontiers-
man has ended up by establishing its own "narrow framework of convention." The people of Zebulon County are, Wolfe suggests, guilty in
some ways of that sin to which too great an attachment to the earth
habitually renders one prone; which is the sin of refusing to acknowledge, and so adapt to, a changing environment—a reluctance to alter
and thereby to grow. Of course, this is a problem that Wolfe has dealt
with before, and for a while we may suspect that he is going to confine himself to the familiar limitations prescribed by the "web and the
rock." But he does not do so this time, and the fact that he does not
is due really to one thing—the introduction of a new element into
the situation represented by William Joyner. Despite his attachment
to his native region, Wolfe insists, Joyner has not stayed still in the
way his neighbors have. He has retained much of the *genuine* spirit
of the settlers, the spirit of the pathfinder "still seeking and explorative."[55] Consequently, when his neighbors compare him—even by
implication—to Mike Fink and Davy Crockett, or some other folk
hero of pioneer days, they are making a comparison that is more
appropriate than they can know—and, by extension, confirming a certain distance between him and themselves.

Still, the comparison between William Joyner and the frontier heroes
is a comparison and not identification. It allows for the sort of differences that are inevitable when a particular set of principles is used
in a different context—when the values of yesterday are engaged directly with the problems of today. The "Bear" is adventurous just like
his ancestors, certainly, but he is adventurous in a new way—which
is, after all, what adventurousness really means. He learns to read
and write at a time when, it seems, it is the convention for people to
be illiterate; and having done this he leaves Zebulon County for Libya
Hill, a new and growing town on the edge of the mountains. There
he becomes to all intents and purposes a townsman, a widely respected

merchant who prospers sufficiently to send each of the sons who move with him to college and then into the professions. Even in this setting his association with his backwoods contemporaries remains unbroken, and his commitment to the values of his ancestors does not waver at all. But, in adapting himself and his values to a culture so utterly unlike theirs, he has added a further, and thoroughly personal, dimension to his character, something which he owes to nobody— original with him.

That dimension is also present in his sons, and perhaps most of all in the oldest one, Zachariah Joyner, who becomes a politician. Zachariah, or "Zack" as the hill folk prefer to call him, is presented as just as much of a hero to his neighbors as his father ever was. But this time Wolfe goes a step further, I think, than he did with old "Bear" Joyner by openly acknowledging the peculiar implications of such heroism—by drawing our attention, more or less directly, to what being a hero in these circumstances really means. The people "over yonder in Zebulon," Wolfe explains, admired Zack for many things:

> . . . among the qualities they seemed most to admire . . . was his . . . smooth dealing. They loved to tell stories to illustrate Zack's smartness, his adeptness, his superior adroitness, . . . and men would wag their heads and laugh with envious approval, as though they wished they could do such things themselves, but knew . . . that they could not.[56]

Zack is presented here as a type familiar to folklorists: the pioneer trader, an American descendant of Hermes Trismegistus the trickster god, whose sharpness of wit in a bargaining session is regarded as proof of his superior mental ability. Elsewhere he is celebrated not so much for this, his intellectual prowess, as for his physical power— as a person very much like his father, whose exceptional stature and amazing strength have turned him into a sort of "Davy Crockett and Paul Bunyan rolled into one." No matter how much the specific character of his heroism may vary from time to time, however, one thing remains constant: the kind of clear-sighted recognition of his superiority—and so of his differences from those around him—that Wolfe allows the people of Zebulon County here. The people of Zebulon, Wolfe says, "wished they could do such things themselves but knew . . . that they could not." That just about sums it up. They have to admit their hero is different from them as well as like them. "No other place on earth but theirs could have produced him," they can claim proudly; but in growing up he has obviously grown beyond them—by becoming "a living prophecy of all that they might wish to be" he has come to define, in a way, all that they are not.

Like his father, Zachariah Joyner has grown beyond his neighbors partly because he is so very much of them, or rather of the pioneer spirit on which their community was founded; his life is "harsh . . . new" and heroic because it draws its energy from the same sources as the lives of the early settlers did. Of course, *he* does not strike out into an uncharted wilderness; he does not even (in the manner of William Joyner) lead an advance guard into another part of the hills. Far from it: *his* discovery of "new land" takes an original and thoroughly contemporary turn. Zack grows up in the towns, where his most vivid impression in his youth is of the sufferings and exploitation of the poor. Appalled by this he becomes their spokesman, "a vigorous and undaunted champion of the common people," and as such steadily acquires more and more political power. Eventually he rises to the position of state governor, the first person of his particular background or persuasion to do so, where he has the means of implementing many of his beliefs. And all this he achieves, Wolfe tells us, not by reneging on the principles he inherits from the hills; but by recognizing their essential thrust, the moral commitments they require, and then using that recognition to guide him in his new environment. What Zack has learned as a "son of the mountains"[57] is accepted by him, and then changed only to the extent that he applies it to a changed series of realities.

Perhaps the importance of William and Zachariah Joyner, and the two or three other characters like them in *The Hills Beyond,* is becoming clear by now. For they represent, I think, the kind of situation or solution that a social scientist might use the phrase "a transvaluation of values" to describe. Two different notions of human possibility, which Wolfe had previously figured for us in the emblems of the train and the earth, are used now not to contradict but to complement and reinforce each other—to produce a moral and philosophical framework for the novel that represents a reconciliation of its originals and a raising of them to a higher power. The spirit of the pioneer is an inherited force for the "Bear" and Zack, as much a characteristic of their mountain background as its forests and mica pits. But it is a spirit, Wolfe reminds us, that encourages them to be "still seeking and explorative": to search and to innovate rather than simply to copy. In turn, the life styles that the two Joyners devise are new and dynamic, expressive of the same energies that drive Eugene Gant and George Webber to leave the South; and yet they owe much of their newness and force, really, to an ethic learned in the hills—to things which have belonged to the mountain inheritance (as Wolfe puts it) "since the beginning," such as the belief in "freedom and the integrity and worth of the individual."[58] *The Hills Beyond* is unlike anything else Wolfe had ever written before, quite simply because the values it cherishes are at once traditional *and* original; the dreams it articulates are both special to particular characters and a recognizable product of community norms. For once, in fact, Wolfe has managed to connect the pull toward the past with the pull toward the future, or rather to create a synthesis out of them so complete that sometimes it becomes difficult to tell where the influence of the one ends and that of the other begins.

Thomas Wolfe was starting, then, to make new use of his childhood environment in his last novel. The mountains had exerted a powerful tug on his imagination throughout his life, and it was as if he was hoping now to work out just what this tug might mean to him—just what in his past might be valuable and worth preserving. It is a profound pity that *The Hills Beyond* was never finished, since as it stands a lot more remains to be said about the possibility of applying the old values in fresh ways. We still need to know, for instance, exactly how the Joyners managed to build what Wolfe calls "a newer, more productive order" in their urban environment, and exactly what form this order assumed. Even in the rather abortive state in which the book has come down to us, though, it represents a significant advance on Wolfe's previous work, something that places its author firmly and squarely in the Southern tradition; and we should not, I believe, allow our recognition of this to be spoiled by any lingering regrets we may have for what Wolfe had necessarily to leave undone. What Wolfe *has* done is, after all, a great deal. Skirting nostalgia for vanished folkways on the one hand, and a sterile rejection of the past on the other, he has finally succeeded in devising the third alternative for which he had searched for so long: a genuine and really dynamic traditionalism in which principle and fact—past and present—are made to exist in a state of creative tension, like the arch and string of a bow. In practical terms, he has portrayed roots as the basis of personality, something that supplies the minimal context necessary for self-definition while at the same time encouraging growth and change; and, like so many other Southern writers before and after him, he has used a form of mythologized history to do all this. This, as I say, is a considerable achievement. And perhaps another novelist from the South, Robert Penn Warren, has provided us with as good a way of summarizing it as any. For in an essay written when Wolfe was only just beginning to tell the story of the Joyners, Warren prophesied, "Mr. Wolfe promises to write some historical novels . . . they may well be crucial in the definition of his genius."[59] That prophecy proved to be a remarkably accurate one, I think. *The Hills Beyond,* the one historical novel that Wolfe managed to start work on before his death, *is* crucial in the definition of his genius; although the reasons why this is so are something that Warren, and perhaps Wolfe himself, could hardly have anticipated at the time.

4. Back to the Old Plantation: The Recovery and Reexamination of a Dream

The preoccupation with history has led Southern writers, like Eliot's Gerontion, along many cunning passages and contrived corridors, into a pretty varied involvement with the past; but perhaps nothing they have done has aroused more excitement and interest than their revival of the dream of the old plantation. Certainly, it is the aspect of their work that is best known outside of the South—so well known, in fact, that one of my aims has been to redress the balance by emphasizing other, equally important aspects. I do not want to imply by this, though, that the legend of the noble planter has been *un*important, has not exercised a profound influence in the past forty or fifty years —because, of course, it has. It is accountable for some of the most characteristic, not to say eccentric, features of modern Southern writing. Very often, too, it has maintained its separate character, uncomplicated by any contact with that other, typically Southern legend associated with the figure of the good farmer. We have already had one illustration of this in the person of Allen Tate, whose work (as I have tried to show) is more or less confined to the world of the plantation. And the writers we are going to look at now (all, strangely enough, women) offer us three more examples. I mean by this Caroline Gordon, Eudora Welty, and Katherine Anne Porter. Like Erskine Caldwell and Thomas Wolfe, these three writers have concentrated in their work on those varieties of the regional experience in which they have been immediately involved themselves—and which have, therefore, appeared to them to be the most significant. Unlike Caldwell and Wolfe, though, this has taken them into the kind of country that is the special preserve of Southern romance: the world of vast cotton fields and black field hands, casual violence and battles long ago where (as one of William Faulkner's characters puts it),

> It's still not yet two o'clock on that July afternoon in 1863, the brigades are in position behind the rail fence, the guns are laid and ready in the woods and the furled flags are already loosened to break out and Pickett himself ... looking up the hill waiting for Longstreet to give the word and it's all in the balance, it hasn't happened yet, it hasn't even begun yet. . . .[1]

The differences between people like Caldwell and Wolfe and these other writers go further than that, however: they are not just a matter of different *interests*. In fact, as it turns out, they have to do with the different *forms* and *directions* these interests assume as well. With Caldwell as we have seen, as with Wolfe, the special problem of the writer has been to reconcile his two different functions as journalist and mythologizer. He has to concern himself closely with what is, along with what might be, because he is working on the assumption that the redemption of the hero and the recovery of the Jeffersonian ideal is a genuine and distinct possibility. The familiar question, "Can the dream be redeemed?" is still at the imaginative center of his books, supplying inspiration and some difficulty. Nothing could be less true of writers like Gordon, Welty, and Porter, since for them the center of interest has shifted radically. In their work the possibility of redeeming the dream, and re-creating it in experience in any recognizable form, is more or less dismissed at the outset. This might seem to suggest that they have retreated into daydreaming, that they have evaded the obvious discomforts of the present day by fleeing into a past exalted by memory and loss—which is, after all, what writers of plantation romance like Margaret Mitchell (*Gone With the Wind*) and Stark Young (*So Red the Rose*) generally do. Far from it: what they have done is, I think, much more interesting and involving than this. They do not confuse the myth of the old plantation with the realities of either the past or the present. Instead, they accept it *as a myth*, a once powerful but idealized projection of the regional identity that has forfeited the allegiance of all save a few diehards. And having done this they then examine this myth in detail to see in what ways, if any, it can supply a means of understanding and controlling their present environment—what possible contribution it can make toward a meaningful, and relevant, criticism of life. The *idea* of aristocratic agrarianism, in other words, becomes the principal focus of attention; the aim of this being to determine what significance such an idea may still possess for a society—*our* society—that can be neither aristocratic nor agrarian.

What significance is this idea found to possess, by people who are as otherwise different as Gordon, Welty, and Porter are? Exactly how does the presence of the plantation legend manage to make itself felt in their work? To ask the question in this way is, of course, to imply that it may be a difficult one to answer; and it is difficult, I believe, if only because individual writers tend—when engaging with any problem—to come up with individual solutions. Differences of personal experience and sensibility lead invariably to different assessments of a myth. Given this perhaps obvious point, though, there is one premise that I think all these three writers share in common, and a fairly significant one at that. This is the belief—implicit in nearly all of their work—that, whatever else it is, the dream of the old plantation is above all a product of what Wallace Stevens once called the "rage for order." They all begin by assuming that the values represented by the figure of the planter form, when combined, a complete and objective code—an elaborate system of belief and behavior that prescribes a specific ritual for each moment of an individual's life, and a significant gesture for his every emotion. Life, according to this prescription, is turned into heroic art—in a way and to an extent that perhaps the historian J. M. Huizinga best described when talking about a comparable impulse felt during the Middle Ages. "To be representative" in such circumstances, Huizinga explained, means

> to produce by conduct, by customs, by manners, by costume, by deportment, the illusion of a heroic being, full of dignity and honour, of wisdom and, at all events, of courtesy. This seems possible by the . . . imitation of an ideal past. The dream of past perfection ennobles life and its forms, fills them with beauty and fashions them anew as forms of art. Life is regulated like a noble game.[2]

Gordon, Welty, and Porter all choose to interpret the aristocratic legend, and the principles it dramatizes, in precisely these terms. As they see it, the plantation world is at once an example and an emblem of a common human impulse, which is the longing to inform experience with a sense of meaning, arrangement, and nobility, the desire—felt by all of us at one time or another—to ritualize and ceremonialize virtually everything we do or say.

Huizinga's description, then, helps us to define the area of consensus between Gordon, Welty, and Porter, the point at which their explorations meet. But it still leaves a lot of questions unanswered. We still need to know, for instance, about the room for personal maneuver that should—as these writers see it—be left by such a code, or the precise tendencies of the ethic expressed in its prescribed ceremonies. And we still need to know as well about the relevance these writers may find in all this for their own, profoundly different, surroundings. That should not be so surprising, though. It stands to reason that to learn about *these* things we shall have to look at their work individually.

Acts of Darkness, Ceremonies of the Brave: Caroline Gordon

The acceptance of myth as myth is a procedure that we are perhaps familiar with already from the work of some of the Agrarians, since at their best people like Robert Penn Warren and Allen Tate tend to treat their Southern legacy in exactly this way. Tate, in particular, uses the inherited figure of the old plantation with extraordinary self-consciousness and skill; and it comes as no surprise, really, to find that at least one of the writers we are concerned with now seems to have learned about the mythologizing process from precisely this source. Caroline Gordon, the novelist, essayist, and critic, was the first wife

of Allen Tate. She was married to him, in fact, when his ties with the
Agrarians were still quite close, and it was through him that she got
to know many members of the group. At one time she even went so
far as to identify herself with their "stand"—or, at least, their stand
as she understood it. That qualification is necessary, I think, because
Gordon has never been particularly interested in the social and economic arguments that form so important a part of the general Agrarian
program. What she cherishes, rather, is the idea of order that she finds
expressed in the image of the old plantation—an idea immediately applicable, as she sees it, to any time or place. Order, decorum, ceremony
—a system of external references by which the inner life must be
carefully guided: these for her are absolutes. She honors them with an
unwavering devotion, and this I believe has a peculiar impact upon
her work. For so concerned is she with the heroic code, apparently,
and the tribute which both she and her characters must pay to it that
every action she describes in her stories tends to assume a certain
rigidity, a certain frozen decorousness, as a result. Her people are
caught in fixed postures, as it were, and sometimes so depersonalized
by the common ritual as to be less memorable than the elaborate
scenic properties surrounding them. At one point near the opening of
her very first novel, *Penhally*, Gordon seems to step aside from the
action for a moment to describe a butterfly fluttering around a room.

> The veinings that ran across the wings to converge at the body were
> silken and glistening, the whole design miraculously exact, conventional-
> ized like the pictures that young ladies paint on glass or on the silk
> covers of albums.[3]

The portrait, brief as it is, is not I think really a digression. For it is
almost as if the novelist is describing the nature and purposes of her
art here, at the outset of her career, and, by transforming a living
organism into a still design, offering us a paradigm of it as well.

"Design" is one word Gordon uses to describe her strictly formalized
version of experience. "Game" is another. It is perhaps just as appropriate, since in a sense what she is arguing for is a traditionalist version of the games philosophy—the philosophy, I mean, whereby man
is presented as a creature who imposes patterns, quite deliberately and
self-consciously, upon his experience. He subdues the chaos around
him (and within him) by regulating everything according to certain,
admittedly fictive, laws. He gives meaning—or at least an artificial
meaning—to his life by playing it according to a set of carefully defined rules. Gordon's second book, *Aleck Maury, Sportsman*,[4] demonstrates this philosophy well, I think. In a way it is not so much a novel
as a fictional diary. Little of major importance occurs in the course of
the narrative—certainly there is no crisis—and beyond the fact that we

are being told about some days in the life of a particular narrator, there
is nothing that can be called a consecutive plot. For all this the book
has none of the apparent randomness of stream-of-consciousness fiction, the positive delight in the arbitrary and spontaneous that we
tend to associate with the diary form; and this is because every detail
of his experience that Maury chooses to tell us about is acted out in
obedience to his code. Aleck Maury, in fact, is not so much a person
who happens to be a sportsman as somebody whose character is defined by his sporting life. The ceremonies he adopts as a huntsman, the
ritual he follows as a fisherman, are both metaphors of conduct—a
way of illustrating his preference for ordering and regulating everything. Maury likes to describe himself as "playing" whether he is fishing, making love, or presiding as magistrate at the local county court,
and the sporting scenes that recur throughout the novel act as a gloss,
a method of explicating this. In a way that is both literal and figurative,
they tell us exactly what Maury means when he says he "plays."

The ceremony of the hunt, described at length in the book,[5] is a
perfect illustration of this. Certainly, even the most casual reader
cannot fail to see that it *is* a ceremony, a series of elaborate gestures
succeeding one another in prescribed, unalterable sequence. The
change into an appropriate costume (clothes changing is, as it is in
The Fathers, an important part of the ritual) is followed by the hunt
breakfast, which is followed by the mounting of the horses upon the
lawn. This in turn is followed by the chase, the capture and killing
of the quarry, and its dissection by the leader of the hunt according to
certain fixed specifications. And so on. Everything is ritualized; every
event seems to have the weight of previous occasions behind it, from
the most solemn, such as prayers before dinner ("Grace was always
said Old Virginia style, everybody standing up with hands on the
chairback"), to the most commonplace and mundane. The scene immediately after breakfast provides us, I think, with a good example of
the latter. One of the huntsmen, a certain George Beckett, always gets
drunk (we are told) just before it is time to start on the actual hunting.
But he will never admit that he *is* drunk. So he invariably spends several minutes trying, without any success, to clamber up on to his horse
—while his companions wait patiently around him, pretending not to
notice his discomfort. They are waiting, we learn, not for him to mount
but for his brother to offer a particular—and implicitly preestablished
—signal, which is to declare, in a rather offhand way and with no
further explanation offered, that unfortunately George will not be able
to "make it" today. Then, and only then, do they feel free to move
off. Of course, the situation is a potentially comic one, and Gordon
does allow a sense of amusement, an appreciation of the humorous

side of the spectacle to seep through into her prose. Her amusement is clearly tempered with affection, though, and even more with a genuine admiration, because, as she knows full well, what she is offering us here is really only another instance of decorum—its procedures, its uses, and its value. As it starts out, the situation offers a great deal of possible embarrassment to all concerned. George Beckett is too drunk to mount his horse, but he is too proud to admit he is. His friends do not want him to accompany them in his state, but they do not want to humiliate him, by pointing out that he is drunk, either. What, then, is to be done? How can the situation be resolved without offending the sensibilities of anyone? The answer, quite simply, is to fall back on ceremony—a ritual in which just enough of the truth is admitted to sort out the problem but not enough to hurt the person who created that problem in the first place. It is the perfect marriage of courtesy—the respect owed to Beckett as a member of the group—and utility, the demands of common sense. And in a way, Gordon suggests, exactly the same could be said about the entire rigmarole of the hunt. It too is rooted in practical difficulties, in this case the difficulties created by the animals that prey on livestock, and has the eminently practical purpose of ridding the coutryside of these pests. This purpose is realized, however, in terms of a ritual that satisfies the minds and hearts of its participants as well as their pocketbooks—a game in which a sense of the practical, the beautiful, and even perhaps the good are all conveniently combined.

This, I think, is one of the more attractive consequences of Gordon's idea of ceremony: that it leads her to give an additional value, a certain stateliness to everything—even the most ordinary things—her characters do or say. There are less attractive consequences, though, stemming from the same source; and the one I take to be least attractive of all is something I have mentioned in passing before. This is the tendency shown by nearly all her heroic characters to dissolve, to fade away behind their own gestures of heroism—to become lost in the paraphernalia of their strictly defined code. Even Aleck Maury comes across to us as a vague, distant figure, although he speaks to us in the first person; and when we turn to Gordon's third (and most famous) novel, *None Shall Look Back*, we find I believe that even the small portion of individuality allotted to him has more or less disappeared. Nominally the book is about one family, the Allards, in the years immediately before and after the Civil War. Like *The Fathers*, it tries to describe a civilization and its decline in and through the story of one house. It turns out to be very different from Tate's book, though, because, whereas Tate manages to invest his account of an impersonal order with an extraordinarily personal intensity—and so maintain a constant tension between the individual life and the social —Gordon hardly seems to be concerned with personality at all. Her obsession with the heroic code is such as to inhibit any great interest in the inner life, and so prevents the creation of forceful or complex characters; and really the leading figure in her novel is not so much a person as a house. Bracketts, the ancestral home of the family and an embodiment of the decorous values the Allards fight for and lose: that is the presence that dominates the story. Its physical appearance and symbolic function are what Gordon is preoccupied with in the opening pages. Its survival seems to be of major concern to most of the characters. And, when at last it is destroyed, this is described with an acute pain, the kind of elegiac regret that we never find in Gordon's presentation of any human death.

> . . . all stood watching the burning house. The smoke rolled low, . . . and then licked by the wind a great flame would rise and tower. Mrs. Allard saw one, a fiery mass that seemed to have fingers to tear the house apart. She watched the dividing walls melt away and suddenly saw revealed in the burning mass a rectangle of glowing logs, a cabin, it seemed, burning inside the house. She touched Cally's arm. "The old house," she said quietly, "the original log house. See it burn."[6]

What is remarkable about this passage, essentially, is the almost human feelings with which the nonhuman is endowed. The inanimate fire becomes an animate force, tearing the house apart with its "fingers." In the face of such violence the house melts away until only the nucleus from which it grew—we might almost say, its "heart" or "soul" —remains to be seen. Meanwhile, standing on the borders of the event, the human beings are left depersonalized: they seem to be no more than an audience, a choric group uttering sounds of lament appropriate to the drama. This, it goes without saying, represents a complete reversal of a normal dramatic situation. The background has been dragged into the foreground as it were, made over into a protagonist, and the actors in turn have been transformed into spectators. And, extreme though it is, it is I think symptomatic of something quite widespread—a general *drift* in Gordon's fiction.

It is, probably, thanks to this—this general drift or inclination—that most of the characters in *None Shall Look Back* resemble the traditional stereotypes so closely. They are, after all, being defined almost exclusively in terms of their local traditions—according to their assumption, however deliberate, of an inherited code. Belonging wholeheartedly to an order, they belong, by definition, to a series of roles as well; accepting the benefits of an established ritual, they accept, along with them, the rigors of a fixed self. So Fontaine Allard, the head of the family and the owner of Bracketts, becomes an emblem more than a person, a more or less faithful reproduction of somebody like Frank Meriwether in *Swallow Barn*.

> [Fontaine] regarded dependence upon and culture of the soil as the proper state and he had a good-natured contempt for a man engaged in business as one who had to resort to what he privately labelled "tricks" and "shifts."[7]

A man who prides himself on his habit of "conducting his affairs in order," Fontaine is circumscribed by his function, both in the sense that he allows code to dictate *all* of his behavior to him and in that he is present in the novel really to illustrate a particular facet of the system. He is there as a type, a private face committed to its public place; and that, for better and worse, is just about all he is there for.

Given that most of Gordon's other characters tend to be as static as Fontaine Allard is, with their personalities absorbed into their roles, it is perhaps inevitable that the action of her novels should resolve itself into a series of set pieces, tableaux with appropriate places for the statues. It is not so much action we are offered in fact as a succession of frozen moments, each with its own prearranged meaning for audience and participant alike: the dinner, the horserace, the ball, the duel. There is no progression, no plot—or at least no more plot, usually, than is implied in the elegiac pattern of decline and fall. The narrative structure is spatial rather than linear, its prototype being the gallery of local color portraits that go to make up *Swallow Barn;* and, as Gordon has found to her cost, this carries some pretty serious problems along with it. The main problem, I think, has to do with the kind of relationships that this structure does and does not allow. *Established* relationships offer no special difficulties, of course, because they can be presented as they stand, with the roles of the people involved supplying the necessary points of reference. But *developing* relationships, the growth of an attachment and the subtle ebb-and-flow of feeling that accompanies it: these are a different matter altogether, since the notion of development does imply the necessity of moving between roles. More to the point, it does suggest the possibility of a halfway stage between one group of loyalties, one set of coordinates and another, and Gordon's commitment to fixed postures must prevent her from dramatizing any such thing. All she can do, in those cases where she does have to deal with any shifts of emotion, is present them as sudden and radical—in effect, to give her characters one role in place of another, with little preparation made or explanation offered for the change. Thus Rives Allard and Lucy Churchill, Fontaine's "cousin" and granddaughter, become lovers during the course of *None Shall Look Back:* but, thanks to the limitations of Gordon's approach, they can never be described in the actual process of falling in love. We

merely see them first as virtual strangers—a young gallant and a
Southern belle walking carelessly in the garden together—and then,
on their next appearance, in the roles of bridegroom and bride. How
they came to fall in love in the first place, or what the nature of their
love for each other is, are subjects that appear to lie beyond the interests of the story—and, we must suspect, beyond its scope as well.

Another way of putting it, perhaps, is this. Conflict by means of
which personalities are altered, and positions readjusted, is impossible
to dramatize in the context that Gordon establishes for most of her
novels, which is unfortunate, because conflict is what they are really
all about—conflict between individuals, between societies, and ultimately between value systems too. On a personal level, this means that
her characters can never seriously argue with each other, in the sense
of engaging and wrestling with one another's opinions, since to do so
would be effectively to test those opinions for a moment, to offer them
up during the debate for possible modification and change. The most
that a person like Fontaine Allard can do, for instance, when faced
with an opponent (or merely someone who disagrees with him), is
either stay completely silent or state his beliefs as a matter of record
and then leave it at that. Even the most crisis-ridden moment of his
life cannot, apparently, force him from the confines of his role. This is
when his estate is overrun by Union troops, his house is pillaged and
burnt to the ground, and he is insulted by the troop commander.

> Fontaine Allard stood looking at the officer. The red had died out of
> his face, leaving it a deathly white on which the engorged, thick-spread-
> ing veins shone purple. His wife gave a cry of alarm and rushed to him.
> He looked at her and the expression of his face was such that she re-
> coiled.
> "Don't," she cried. "Oh, Mr. Allard, don't!"
> He made a gesture as if to push her away, then turned through the hall
> into the parlor. He walked the length of the long room once, then sat
> down on a little sofa.[8]

This is the nearest Allard ever gets to arguing, answering back—and
he never speaks! Debate, and the possibility of *intellectual* growth
it brings with it, seem to be quite beyond him. The title of the book
is surely of some significance here. For the impressions of stoic defiance and obstinate refusal which a phrase like "none shall look back"
brings to mind are, I think, entirely appropriate to an action such as
this, in which the major characters have no room for maneuver when
confronted by a strange situation, and cannot really talk to anybody
who is radically unlike themselves. As one of these characters puts it,
they can see "just two kinds of people in the world"—those who know
the limits prescribed by the game and stick to them, and those who

resign themselves to the chaos consequent upon a suspension of its rules. With the one kind debate is unnecessary, we can infer, and with the other it is utterly impossible.

So it comes down to this: an acting out of more or less unalterable roles. People like the Allards may seem to change as their story progresses—from decorous aristocrats, that is, to unreconstructed rebels— but really it is their environment that does the changing. They, and their commitments, remain essentially the same. Where, then, is the tension in all this? Conflict, and internal debate of the conventional kind are more or less ruled out, it seems; so what, if anything, prevents Gordon's stories from becoming a series of exercises? What is there, in fact, to stop the movements of her characters from degenerating into the dead gestures of dolls? In a way, there are two answers to this question. One, which I have suggested already, is that in comparison with most other novels Gordon's *are* fairly static. She is, as one of her critics has put it, "a painter by avocation";[9] her books are moral landscapes, compositions rather than actions, in which the figures when they move do so only by stealth. Even a composition, though, should have some vitality in it, a focus or implicit principle of tension to bring it into life. And this, I believe, or something like this, Gordon's stories certainly do possess. Just now I used the word "force" to describe the kind of pressure Fontaine Allard was under at a moment of supreme crisis—the temptation, registered in his features, he feels to break loose and depart from his habitual sense of the correct. That word is, I think, exactly right for capturing the burden of the moment. By extension, it suggests precisely how conflict and contradiction enter into the lives of all Gordon's major characters. They do not change if they can help it, nor even lose their self-control, but like Fontaine Allard it costs them an immense and sometimes visible effort to achieve this. If they remain cool, still, and collected it is usually only with the help of an agonizingly deliberate, carefully sustained act of the will.

It is all a matter, really, of awareness: Gordon's sense of what might happen if we step outside the boundaries of the game, and her characters' more or less implied knowledge of the forces—external *and* internal—tending to prise them from their roles. To remain in a fixed posture is necessary, it seems, not simply because the rules of decorum require it, but because the only alternative to this is what one of Faulkner's characters calls "the shifting sands of moral brigandage." We either stand stiffly upright, Gordon suggests, or we topple over into the abyss—"cutting," in the very process of falling, "a ridiculous figure that somewhere must provoke mirth."[10] This brings us to a further and fairly important dimension of Gordon's novels, since books like *None Shall Look Back*, besides being celebrations of order, are

clearly an attempt to chart the geography of this abyss, a way of re-
connoitring the chaos that apparently lies waiting for her characters
just beyond the limits of the old plantation wall. Not only that: because Gordon draws for us the particular map of the abyss she does,
it brings us, I think, to another vein of the Southern tradition—and to
something I have not really had occasion to mention before. For in
choosing a name for evil—in trying to find an exact, figurative expression for it, that is—Gordon falls back once again upon an acquired
vocabulary, what Allen Tate once called the South's "source of available ideas." Southerners have always liked to claim that they know
more about evil than any of their neighbors do. They have nearly
always tried to present it in certain ways, too, ways that might at first
sight seem strange or even repellent to us. Gordon has chosen to follow them closely in both these respects, I believe; and in order to find
out why she, and they, have done this (why, in fact, most Southerners
appear to be haunted by a particular notion of original sin), we shall
have to look, however briefly, at their background—and at some of
the darker, more sinister corners of the tradition to which they belong.

It is a commonplace in the history of ideas that to emphasize past
experience at the expense of possibility is to encourage the growth of a
profound sense of evil. Man, seen in the context of his previous
achievements and perhaps even defined by them, ceases to be the
free and perfectible being of romantic legend and is translated instead
into a creature of radical limitations; somebody who may pine for
what is not, but whose own manifest disabilities—coupled with the
rigorous difficulties of his environment—prevent him from ever turning wishes into facts. Nowhere has this been better illustrated, I think,
than in the aristocratic tradition of the South, which since the time of
Calhoun has been distinguished by what the historian C. Vann Woodward once termed a "preoccupation with guilt"—and a preoccupation
so intense as occasionally to approach the obsessive. Admittedly, Calhoun himself had certain, rather self-interested reasons for insisting
that "there is evil in the world and it is strong." It is that much easier,
after all, to discourage specific changes (such as the reapportionment
of power in the federal legislature or even the abolition of slavery)
if you can convince people somehow that change of any kind involves
a serious and unprofitable risk. But what he said seemed to spring at
least *partly* from a genuine belief in original sin; and in any case,
questionable though some of his motives may have been, his arguments themselves when formulated only seemed to be confirmed by
subsequent events. Defeat in the Civil War after years of hardship

and sacrifice, occupation and all the humiliations visited upon the region in the immediate postwar period, the feelings of disorientation that have inevitably accompanied the South's emergence as an urban-industrial society: these are only a few of the crises in the regional history that have helped turn the experience of tragedy into a commonplace one for Southerners, and so made them feel haunted by the specters of failure and guilt. At the same time, this ghost-ridden, fear-ridden disposition has probably been encouraged (in a very indirect way) by other, characteristically Southern tendencies as well—most notably by those feelings of stoicism and defiance which seem to have become almost second nature to spokesmen for "Dixie." These feelings, more or less explicit in some of the titles Southerners have chosen for their books—like *I'll Take My Stand, Still Rebels, Still Yankees,* or, as I suggested earlier, *None Shall Look Back*—have tended in turn to foster a sense of uniqueness, of not thinking as other men do. And what better course could Southerners have chosen for proving this, really, for showing that in fact they do not think as other men or at least as other Americans do, than the one they *have* chosen—effectively denying the existence of the American Adam? How could they have stood apart from the national tradition more noticeably than the way they have done: by exposing the contradictions, those squirming facts which help make the national ideals of innocence and perfection seem quite ludicrous? Some Southerners, at least, must have reasoned instinctively along these lines, and so, like Calhoun, may have cherished the idea of evil for what are partly polemical or political reasons.

To say all this is of course to risk simplification, a reduction of some pretty complicated events to oversymmetrical patterns. But that, I think, is a risk that any attempt to generalize about historical experience must run, a danger inseparable from the enterprise; and, insofar as any generalizations can hold good, these, about the Southerner's experience of tragedy and consequent preoccupation with sin, surely do. Or at the very least they are symptomatic of certain tendencies that have helped to distinguish the South from the rest of the nation. Naturally, there are difficulties if we try to develop the thesis in too simple-minded a fashion: if, for example, we try too quickly and automatically to equate all Americans outside the South—and all American writers in particular—with the Adamic notion. Exceptions then seem to crop up all over the place, and the "rule" appears to be one of those that are more honored in the breach than in the acceptance. If we just use a little tact, however, in interpreting the idea we can soon see how it applies—and exactly how, as a result, the Southerner differs from his neighbors. For as

R. W. B. Lewis has pointed out in his book on the subject, *The American Adam,* although the experience of evil may be a frequent one in American writing it generally tends, when it occurs, to "draw its compelling strength from a prior notion of original innocence."[11] What distinguishes the American writer in this respect, in other words, is not so much his absolute denial of guilt as his denial of absolute guilt. He may certainly accept the idea of evil, but usually he either counterbalances this with a profound sympathy for the Adamic or Faustian impulses, or he sees the idea within the context of a moral perfection that man is assumed to have lost recently but that, it is hoped, he will eventually recover. Nothing could be further from the truth for many Southern writers, and especially those who have committed themselves more to the aristocratic side of their legacy. In their work, evil, when it appears, is described as radical and indelible; instead of being a quality limited by a framework of alternative possibilities, it becomes the framework within which possibility is defined. Each little life is shown to be bounded by the imperfect in most Southern literature—bounded in such a way, in fact, as to make acceptance of imperfection a necessary preliminary to moral choice—and that really is one of the sources of its uniqueness.

Naturally, this knowledge of evil can assume many different forms. It may, for example, draw its strength from the fundamentalism that remains powerful in many areas below the Potomac, since, although the tenets of the "old-time religion" may no longer be accepted by most writers, and have not been for some time, that religion may still frequently determine the terms of a book's moral debate and even its tone. The "jealous God" of the Old Testament may still lurk behind the formal structures of a narrative, providing it with a convenient figure for the hazardous quality of life. Alternatively, a claustrophobic atmosphere, of hothouse blooms or dense forests, may be used as it is in, say, *The Scarlet Letter,* to suggest that wilderness of random impulses and hidden dangers in which any human decision has to be made. Robert Penn Warren (as we have seen) uses this metaphor, or rather this figurative setting, in precisely this way, and so too does the West Virginian poet, John Peale Bishop.

> The long man strode apart
> In green no soul was found,
> In that green savage clime
> Such ignorance of time.
>
> The green parrot's scream
> Clung to the wild-tree fruit.
> The wild foot tracked a stream.

> What anger could confute
> Green crowns of crashing bough
> When every day dawned Now?[12]

But neither the wilderness setting, I think, nor the system of biblical reference is as important to the *Southern* discussion of evil, as peculiarly characteristic of the region, as a cluster of associations are that gather around another metaphor altogether—the metaphor of *darkness*. There are invariably many reasons for this importance, the almost talismanic power the color black seems to possess in Southern writing, some of which (such as the ancient religious assumption that blackness is a sign of inner corruption) are obviously not peculiar to the region at all. The reasons I would like to emphasize here, however, and which have clearly been uppermost in the minds of most Southerners past and present, *are* more or less unique. And they bring into special prominence a character who otherwise keeps a curiously low profile in Southern literature—somebody who is often conspicuous by his absence from its books, although he is omnipresent in its society. The character I am talking about is, of course, the Negro.

For it is the Negro who contributes an additional dimension to the sense of evil in Southern writing, giving a certain resonance or regional idiosyncrasy to what would otherwise be a fairly commonplace association. He, I think, is the man at the center here. Why is this so? Why, in fact, is the black man equated so regularly with all-pervasive feelings of guilt, danger, and fear? Perhaps we can get the beginnings of an answer by looking, first of all, at a passage where he may be seen performing exactly this function—at, for instance, this brief moment of epiphany in *Act of Darkness,* a novel by John Peale Bishop.

> That afternoon I went to the shed where my grandfather kept his collection. . . . There was a little of everything. . . . Candlemoulds, trivets, ovens for wide fireplaces; spinning wheels, hand-looms . . . a rotting battle-flag, and firearms. . . . The great show was Lord Fairfax's chaise, which he had brought from Clark County. . . . In one corner was an old deer-hide trunk . . . plunging my hand down . . . I pulled up some skirt hoops . . . I held them to my light. . . . They must, I know, have been my grandmother's. . . . I looked up and saw Peter's brown face behind the kitchen window. He caught my eye and pressed his negro cheeks close to the pane. Where he touched the glass were spots of gray. I dropped the hoops and shut the trunk lid.[13]

To some extent, what the black character is doing here is comparable to what the Indians are doing in *The Scarlet Letter:* the mere presence of exiles from the wilderness, African or American, is meant to imply some of the destructive possibilities that play around the closed society described in the action proper. But only to some extent, since in cases like this, where the Negro is called upon to close in on the protagonist, there is a far greater sense of intimacy between chorus and actor than there ever is in Hawthorne's tale. The red man only visits the white community for a while; he remains an outside commentator pure and simple. The black man, on the other hand, lives on the borders of that community whether he likes it or not, carrying most of its burdens and enjoying very few of its privileges. He is partly outside the action and partly inside it, a person whose marginal, ambivalent status enables him to observe the minutest details of his master's life; and this, as the passage I have quoted here shows, I think, has a remarkable effect upon those observed, the white characters. Encircled as they are, people like the narrator of *Act of Darkness* seem to feel that all the things they do, even their most cherished secrets, are being assessed by alien judges and perhaps mocked. A Sancho Panza is on hand, they suspect, to undermine their every heroic pretension. At one point in a more recent Southern novel, *The Confessions of Nat Turner* by William Styron, one of the black characters admits quite simply that "a white man's discomfiture, observed on the sly, has always been the Negro's richest delight." That, I think, is as good a way as any of defining the relationship between black and white fostered by the peculiar institutions of the South. And to make it applicable to its literature—to books like Bishop's, in fact—we need only add to this the gloss that the evident aim of the writer is to make us *see* both the delight and the discomfiture—as a preliminary, that is, to showing us how inseparable the high and the low are. The elegant gesture and the pratfall, the closed society (commemorated here by a collection of antiques) and the surrounding darkness that seems to mock and threaten it: these may be closer to each other than is commonly supposed—a possibility the reader is forced to acknowledge when both are implied in the same movement, or described in the same paragraph.

This is all by way of saying, of course, that the disposition of the Negro character and all that it entails is largely a matter of historical circumstance. He stands on the periphery of the narrative because that is where he has always stood in Southern society. He acts as an observer, and perhaps a parodist, of white behavior for the simple reason that this has been his function, his prescribed role since Negro slavery began. And he can serve as an emblem of darkness, a reminder of the abyss to which both Caroline Gordon and Allen Tate refer so frequently, because he himself has nearly always lived *in* that abyss. As James Baldwin once put it, "the Negro tells us where the bottom is because he is there." All this is only half the story, though. It leaves two simple, but very important facts out of account. These are that the Negro was, after all, consigned to the abyss in the first place by the white man; and that the literature of the South is more or less a *white* literature. There are pitifully few Negro writers who can be called "Southern," certainly nobody of any stature can be included in this category, and such accounts as black people have given us of the South are mostly written from somewhere else in America—and from the standpoint of later, urban migration. This means, really, that the image of the black man we receive in Southern writing is very largely a white image. For all his probable distance from the norms of his community, and so from most of its prejudices, the Southern writer is usually somebody who, at some time in his life, has actually experienced the fear and guilt he is talking about; and this cannot help but affect how he sees the Negro.

The net effect of this shared background, this perspective which nearly all Southern writers have in common by the mere fact of being white, is to confirm them in their willingness to associate black characters with premonitions of danger and evil. The Negro is there in Southern society and its literature, the author knows, because he was sinned against by the white community—in other words, by people like the author himself. His present situation, insofar as it still reflects his previous oppression, serves to compound the sin; and every time he appears he makes it that much more difficult for his white neighbors to deny the omnipresence of sin in themselves and their environment. Seen within the context of white guilt over what William Faulkner called "the old . . . shame" of slavery, black people become a kind of nemesis—a doom-laden chorus to the main action, the general character and purpose of which are perhaps best suggested in some of Faulkner's own novels. I am thinking in particular of that moment in his seventh novel, *Light in August,* when one of the white characters, Nathaniel Burden, takes his daughter to the family graveyard. "Your grandfather and brother are lying there," says Nathaniel, pointing at two of the grave-stones,

> "murdered not by one white man but by the curse which God put on a whole race before your grandfather or your brother or me or you were even thought of. A race doomed and cursed to be forever and ever a part of the white race's doom and curse for its sins. Remember that. His doom and curse. Forever and ever. Mine. Your Mother's. Yours, even though you are a child. The curse of every white child that ever was born and that ever will be born. None can escape it."[14]

The power of this speech depends, I think, on the fact that it endorses a feeling provoked by the entire narrative. The idea of the Negro as the bearer of a curse is at once a preoccupation of the various characters—an analyzable aspect of their beliefs—*and* part of the mythological framework of the story in which they appear. We are asked to witness and inspect the sense of doom, and we are also made to experience it. I shall have more to say later on about this obsession of Faulkner's with the legacy of guilt, the sins of the fathers being visited on their sons. For the moment all I want to emphasize is that this *is* an obsession of *his* and not just an aspect of described behavior: it is something Faulkner has inherited from his region, which he cannot stop from influencing his stance toward reality. What is more to the point, perhaps, it is also something that—as far as origins are concerned, at any rate—he shares with most other Southern writers. The sense of evil in their work may connote a destiny to be embraced, a chaos to be avoided, or (as is more likely) a confused mixture of the two. That all depends on the further perspectives established by its context. What remain constants throughout all this, however, no matter the other variations, are the association of this sense with the figure of the black man—and, as in Faulkner's case, the more or less active participation of the author in the associative process. As a slave and then as the member of an oppressed race, the Negro has worn an articulate mask of doom in the South for over a century; and, for better or worse, it is with this mask *on* that most writers from the region have tended to draw him.

To return to Caroline Gordon: in books like *None Shall Look Back* all the characters and not just the Negroes tend to wear masks, of course, in the sense that they are all defined by a role or function. But in the case of the major white characters, at least, that function is primarily a *social* one. Fontaine Allard and his family adopt roles that have been given to them by their society; and since their adoption of a role is a subject of the narrative, something to which our attention is being drawn, they are endowed even if only by implication with a capacity for choice. We may not see them as individuals during the course of the action, but that, we infer, is because they have deliberately surrendered their individuality. The black characters at Bracketts, however—by which I mean both the field hands and the house slaves—are restricted to a function that is not so much social as *symbolic*. Their roles are dictated by the imaginative exigencies of the story, and Gordon no more draws our attention to this than she would draw our attention to any other aspect of her fictional technique. In the event, they do not emerge as personalities, nor even as people who have consciously repudiated personality in the name of an impersonal pattern: their brief is simply to act as metaphors, to represent those more disruptive areas of experience which the pattern is intended to inhibit. In one of her later novels, *Green Centuries*, Gordon uses a quotation from Flaubert as an epigraph—to establish her theme.

> *Je porte en moi la mélancholie des races barbares, avec ses instincts des migrations et ses dégoûts innés de la vie qui leur faisaient quitter les pays comme pour quitter eux-mêmes.*[15]

In a way that quotation would serve just as well as an epigraph to *None Shall Look Back*, since its Negro characters seem to possess precisely those qualities—the waywardness and strangely familiar tastes of *races barbares*—of which Flaubert is speaking here. Surrounding the action, and uncomfortably reminding their masters of instincts dormant in every heart, the black servants of the Allard family are, in fact, like nothing so much as emissaries from chaos.

As far as the earlier part of *None Shall Look Back* is concerned, this role of emissary is mostly a covert one. The slaves, when we first meet them, are a "furtive and . . . alien" presence at Bracketts, appearing and disappearing like shadows. What makes us notice them, though, and accept them right from the start as prophetic creatures, is Gordon's strategy of presenting them through the eyes of one particular character. The person she chooses for this is Lucy Churchill, Fontaine's granddaughter and an orphan who now lives with her "cousins" on the Allard plantation. It is, I think, a clever choice, since Lucy, when the book opens, is on the verge of adolescence. She is a young girl growing up within the plantation order; somebody whose tastes and values are being formed—even as we watch—in obedience to the limits it prescribes. So, when she receives any hints of forces operating *outside* of those limits, they must be that much more bewildering and significant for her than they would be for anyone whose tastes have been formed already—and whose resistance has as a result been carefully prepared. Fontaine Allard has some imagination of disaster. That is why his efforts at self-control are so measured and deliberate: because, in fact, he knows what is likely to confront him and how he should behave. But Lucy starts out with hardly any imagination at all. All she has, really, is a series of dawning suspicions, the sort of fear and uneasiness that are produced naturally by rumor, and in a way her education is twofold—she is learning in a double sense as she grows up. For, at the very same time that she is being instructed in the proper ceremonies by her white elders, she is beginning, we are told, to form certain "vague pictures" in her mind about "goings on"[16] in the slave quarters. From a clue here, a guess there, she is starting to pick up some idea of a primitive and instinctive level of existence—apparently illustrated by the Negro—which the ceremonies of the plantation house seem designed mainly to evade.

It will be clear from what I have already said, probably, that, although Gordon uses a common regional equation to describe fear and evil, she uses it in her own, rather special way. Evil for her is disorder, chaos: just as good is law and order, or rule. The opposition between black and white is in effect drained of many of its more usual, moral associations (the kind of associations that we find, for example, in *Light in August*) and made to stand, quite simply, for the conflict between anarchy and restraint. Of course, Gordon is not completely unaware of the moral dimension—in other words, of the wrongs done in the name of slavery and the South's consequent feelings of guilt. She even invokes them in the course of the novel by referring briefly to the presence of certain vicious overseers in the neighborhood, and by hinting darkly at possible instances of rape and miscegenation. All the same, her awareness only goes so far. The stories she tells of violence offered to Negroes are largely used as figures or metaphors—to suggest the existence of evil in *any* established order rather than to present us with symptoms of a particular historical injustice. And she never once describes slavery as a sin in itself, a fundamental evil, only as a system that, like all others, permits the occasional commission of crime. Further than that she will not venture, and cannot really, because to do so she would have to admit that the civilization represented by Bracketts is not the sanctuary of peace, ceremony, and order she claims it to be—but seriously, much more than usually flawed. Just what this suggests about her own limitations, and the dangers inherent in the general practice of mythologizing history, is something I shall return to later. At present all I want to point out is that this, a conflict between rule and misrule, is how she prefers to see the white/black contrast; and that her preference has important repercussions for her actual portrait of the Civil War.

One result of Gordon's particular bias is that she seems to redefine the general significance of the war. True to her habit of turning every historical event into a metaphor, pure and simple, the conflict between North and South becomes little more than an occasion or figurative setting. The old order, when it dies in *None Shall Look Back,* seems to do so less as a direct consequence of the military struggle than because that struggle provides an appropriate moment for the forces of anarchy to loose themselves upon the world. As the Allards' grip on themselves and their surroundings weakens under pressure, the slaves seize the opportunity for which apparently they have always been waiting—to take command and become manifest, dominant pres-

ences rather than covert ones. Suddenly, as the harbingers of confusion, they are everywhere. The roads and rivers seem "black with
throngs" of them, and they talk almost obsessively about insurrection.
If they are not discussing news of possible revolts, they are spreading
rumors of Union victories or wandering around the countryside col-
lecting loot and looking for the invader. All their activities have a
certain random, directionless quality to them: in complete contrast to
the Allards they are constantly on the move, and they act impulsively,
with no deliberation whatsoever. And again, just as in the earlier part
of the book, it is Lucy Churchill who provides us with a perspective
on all this, as a guiding consciousness whose original uneasiness has
now been quickened into a clear awareness of change. Events, Lucy
realizes, have finally conspired to destroy the certainties in which she
was raised, and her initial reaction—an understandable one, really,
from somebody who is still quite young—is complete and unqualified
joy. This, for example, is how she takes the news that a nearby town
is being pillaged.

> She had been standing there, silent as befitted a young person in the pres-
> ence of her elders, but her vivid imagination had been busy. She saw the
> town in . . . panic and confusion, . . . visualized the river front swarming
> with negroes, the warehouse looted, the houses along Second Street de-
> serted or filled with terror-stricken people. She pictured it all but she got
> from it not a sense of confusion and terror but a feeling of new, up-spring-
> ing life.[17]

Now that the system is disintegrating, Lucy senses, the roles to which
she has been confined will no longer apply. She may perhaps be free
to do what she wants to do, go where she wants to go—in fact, to
embark upon a newer, more open kind of life. It is a natural reaction,
perhaps, certainly a sympathetic one—but, Gordon insists, it cannot
last.

The reason why it cannot last is very simple: it is based on a misunderstanding. The death of the old plantation order is just that, evidently, a death—it involves no rebirth, or act of new life. The turmoil
that accompanies its departure is chaos, total and irredeemable anarchy, not the raw, unformed matter out of which new forms of being
may spring. All this Lucy has come to understand by the time the
Civil War is over; it is something, we might say, she has been made
to learn under her creator's careful supervision. Characteristically,
though, no sense of continuity is given to the process of learning: indeed, the way Gordon presents it, it seems somehow inappropriate to
describe it as a process at all. Lucy has one opinion about the repercussions of the war, and then she has another, and that is that: there
is a simple volte-face. We are back effectively where we were before,

in the white world of frozen gestures and still tableaux—where different scenes, displaying separate stages in a character's life, are offered
in juxtaposition rather than sequence. If Gordon were interested in
Lucy Churchill as a psychological specimen this would be a curious
and unsatisfactory procedure. But, of course, she is not: she is no more
interested in the workings of Lucy's mind than she is interested in the
inner lives of any of her characters. Like all the rest of the Allard family Lucy acts as an emblem, a locus for representative attitudes, the
only (admittedly important) difference in her case being that these
attitudes have as much to do with what she sees as with how she behaves. The generalizing tendency is preserved, in fact, even while the
emphasis on externals is qualified. This is particularly well illustrated,
I think, by the scene in which Lucy does finally recognize the truth
about the change in her circumstances. Appropriately enough, it is
set in the slave quarters—the only time in the novel when the reader
is allowed to go in there.

> . . . the scene was one of extraordinary confusion. The negroes had de-
> parted in great haste. It was apparent that they had tried to take some
> of their belongings with them and then had abandoned the effort as too
> great. A feather pillow was tossed into a bed of hollyhocks, a rocking chair
> sat forlornly under a tree, a child's wagon beside it. Lucy saw something
> shining at her feet and stooping found a little pocket mirror she had given
> to one of the maids, . . . its glass shattered, its pretty embroidered case
> fouled by mud. She went on down the street and stopped before the
> door of Aunt Mimy's cabin. The hearth was cold and the room in dis-
> order. . . . Lucy stood looking . . . with an astonishment almost child-
> like. . . . The sight of the gaping dresser drawers, the tumbled mattress,
> all increased the sadness which was already upon her.[18]

This, the central intuition of chaos in the story, is presented in a
familiar way, as a kind of impersonal ritual, a frozen moment in time.
The stillness of the scene invites Lucy to acknowledge a truth, and
Lucy, acting now as a humble acolyte should, makes the required response. The controls have been lifted, she must recognize, the power
of darkness released; and the feelings of sadness that come upon her
at this moment, of loss and acute melancholy, are really the only ones
possible for someone who has come to accept the claims of order as
absolute. They are feelings shared by all the members of the Allard
family, once the significance of what has happened to them is grasped,
and Lucy is special only in the sense that it is given to her—or, rather,
to the scenes in which she appears—to articulate them.

Not that these feelings of desolation ever really stop any of the
Allards, including Lucy, from struggling to reassert control: far from
it. Their "visible efforts at self-containment" continue, the game is

played on—only more frenetically now, because so few other people appear willing or able to join in. The heroic code has been put in jeopardy, its controlling principles denied and the way of life that supported it more or less destroyed; and so, although Fontaine Allard and his family may still try to behave correctly, they find their attempts meeting with steadily less and less success. It is during this part of the story, in fact, that Lucy refers to plantation society as a "sinking ship," and in a way the whole atmosphere of these closing pages makes it seem just like that. The Allards, still following an unchanging ritual while everything about them has changed, behave exactly as the captain is traditionally supposed to when the ship goes down: they stand by the helm, screwing their courage to the sticking place in a manner that seems noble, pathetic, and just a little absurd, all in one. By this time their decorous conduct has become more a matter of nervous defiance than the product of conventional self-discipline; and, as the threats to their precious order increase day by day, they have, apparently, to start encouraging one another. They begin reminding each other to stick to the normal routines, for fear of what might happen otherwise. Significantly, I think, when this fear is openly expressed— as it is now, several times—it is couched in terms of what the *Negroes might do* otherwise. Here, for example, is how Lucy's Aunt Cally advises her to behave when the slaves return to the plantation from their wandering.

> . . . terrible things were happening every day . . .—men . . . were being killed . . . or suffering tortures. . . . The chief thing was to keep your head, not to forget the duty that you owed to others. . . . The negroes were coming back—soon they would probably all be at home. The problem was to keep them in order. The best way to do that was by disciplining your own thoughts. . . . Lucy must . . . never show any fear before the servants. . . . The thing was never, even for a moment, to give way to the panic in yourself.[19]

It is, really, symptomatic of everything that has happened that this advice has to be given at all. The dangers involved in losing control and the dangers latent in the power of blackness, the need to adopt a role of some kind and the sheer difficulty of doing so in a world where nearly everything is on the side of the forces of disorder: all this is made explicit now, because in an utterly desperate situation like the one facing the Allards after the Civil War it has to be. There is no room for the tacit understandings and almost automatic assumption of parts characteristic of more congenial (that is, relatively more congenial) times. This, of course, adds to our understanding of the novel's theme: at the very moment of collapse, the structure and purposes of the plantation order become starkly clear because they are articulated,

insisted upon by those members of the old guard who stubbornly re-
fuse to give them up. They are turned, almost, into a set of injunctions
rather than a series of assumptions. By now it does not take an unusually perceptive reader to see what Gordon is getting at, nor to
recognize, perhaps, that the costs of the heroic code which her characters sacrifice themselves for and then lose tend to run terribly, even
painfully high.

I am talking about the costs for Gordon herself, of course, as well as
those incurred by the people she describes. For it is fairly clear, I think,
that one result of her preoccupation with impersonal standards, and of
her use of the mythologizing process in general, is a radical simplification of life. Admittedly, her awareness of what she is doing enables
her to avoid the simpler kinds of confusion between legend and fact
that we find, for example, in the novels of John Pendleton Kennedy or
(to bring the illustration up to date) in the verse of Donald Davidson.
And certainly she always manages to inject at least some of this awareness into her characters. She is never less than deliberate about her
presentation of the myth of the Old South as myth, and they are never
less than deliberate either. So the more rudimentary forms of nostalgia
—the naïve assumption that, for instance, the past *was* as the writer
chooses to describe it, or that the South *was* everything it claimed itself
to be—these, at least, are avoided. There are, however, other dangers
to which anyone writing about history and the past lays himself open,
dangers some of them of a more esoteric or intellectual kind; and it is
to these, I believe, that Gordon eventually succumbs. No matter how
much we may try to gloss over it, by referring to the adroitness of her
fictional techniques or the deliberateness of her purposes, we cannot
actually get around the fact that what she does in her novels is *escape*
—and escape just as Kennedy and Davidson do, into a place where
fancy is allowed to roam more or less unhampered by any damaging
contact with historical fact. This place, unlike Kennedy's or Davidson's,
is a conscious fiction—somewhere that wears its ideal status upon its
face—but that hardly excuses the drastic exclusions its creator practices; the chief among which, really, is her exclusion of the possibility
of growth. There is no chance of any genuine development occurring
in books like *None Shall Look Back,* no room for maneuver, or for the
sort of changes that could alter the existing order without destroying
it. All that Gordon offers us—the most that is available within the
terms of her own invention—is stalemate, a choice between the rigid,
constricted patterns of white life or, alternatively, the self-destructive
chaos of the black.

This brings us back to the limitations implicit in Gordon's treatment
of Negro characters, limitations that, as I see it, are partly held in

common with other Southern writers[20]—and are partly the result of her own bias. As the representatives of unpatterned experience, every area of life that falls outside the scope of the rules, the slaves are given what is—in a moral sense, at least—a peripheral status. They are like shadows hovering on the borders of the narrative—something that the white characters, under the tutelage of their creator, view with the utmost distrust and do their best throughout their lives to avoid. In this capacity they provide us with a vivid illustration of what the power of darkness means to the average Southerner, but they can do nothing more than that. There is clearly no suspicion on Gordon's part that their mnemonic function might be a valuable one—that to be reminded of the restrictions inherent in any game, or to be forced to confront uncomfortable facts, might be useful exercises. Nor, for that matter, is there any indication that Gordon knows why she treats her black characters in the way she does. She may equate them with the sense of evil and with chaos: she will not, though, place this equation in a context that satisfactorily explains it. There is nothing in any of her fiction comparable to the strategy I mentioned in connection with Faulkner's work, of locating and criticizing an aspect of inherited belief even while it is being used. The idea of the black man as a carrier of doom is just employed without comment—and employed, we may reasonably suspect, without its ever being properly understood.

There is an irony contained in all this, of course, which is that, as it turns out, Gordon's awareness—that extraordinary self-consciousness that seems to color everything she ever does—only extends over certain areas. Like Allen Tate and Thomas Wolfe she is perfectly aware of the mythologizing process, the ploy of selecting and abstracting from the historical past such detail as is necessary to create a system of value for the present. But unlike them she cannot develop this awareness further, so as to take account of facts that bulge outside of her system, that conflict with it and require of it constant adjustment and modification. An index of this difference is that, whereas "ceremony" has an inclusive function in *The Fathers* in the sense that it enables people like Major Buchan to deal with all kinds of different emotions and appreciate them properly, its principal use in *None Shall Look Back* is an *ex*clusive one. It becomes a technique of evasion, or suppression, more than anything else. Perhaps it is useful, as a way of understanding the tendencies of her work, to know that in her more recent novels Gordon has espoused a profoundly conservative form of Catholicism that rejects present circumstances as irremediable and finds perfection, if anywhere, only among those people who have retreated entirely from the world. The gentleman is then transformed into Christ; the black man, into the Black Man, or Devil; and the order of the old plantation, into the rituals and ceremony of the Holy Church.[21] Perhaps it is useful to know this—but, I think, it is hardly necessary. For the earlier and better-known fiction tells us all we really need to know about the otherworldliness of her standpoint, and the unfortunate substitution it implies of the heroic and ceremonious for the human.

A Dance to the Music of Order: Eudora Welty

Caroline Gordon has never really altered her sense of how life should be, despite changes in her immediate loyalties, and much the same could be said of another writer from the South who is almost her exact contemporary, Eudora Welty. There is the kind of consistency of argument in the work of both that makes it comparatively easy for commentators to define their oeuvre in terms of a few specific principles: in the best sense possible, they both demonstrate the predictability of the committed. For all this likeness, though, which has to do with the way they stand fast by their beliefs, the radical dissimilarity of the things they believe in prevents the comparison from being too pat. In a book like *None Shall Look Back*, the values endorsed are essentially fixed and impersonal because the individual is described as a being who receives his every satisfaction from a properly ordered society. He has no life outside of the code, and he does not need or want one outside of it either. By contrast, the fiction of Eudora Welty has never ceased insisting on the existence of conflict—an irrepressible struggle between the individual, irrational nature of man and those structures, or principles of order, which man uses to arrange life for him. The human personality, as Welty sees it, is defined by its spontaneity and consequent unpredictability; and this means that no forms, including those supplied by the myth of the old plantation, can ever contain or express it completely.

This conflict between the dynamism of personality and the forms devised to control it is perhaps presented at its clearest in a piece in Welty's second collection of stories, entitled simply "A Memory." In it the narrator, a thinly disguised version of the author herself, recalls one of the days of her childhood, when she lay by a lake in the local park, making "small frames with [her] fingers, to look out at everything." The gesture, casual though it is, is a significant one, for within the compass of these frames the people around her tend to assume "fixed attitudes." They become as rigid and hieratic, almost, as the characters populating *None Shall Look Back*—but with the difference that their rigidity has been imposed on them by an observer, and is the product of *her* innocence and fear more than anything else. As the narrator explains later on in the story,

> I was at an age when I formed a judgment upon every person and every event which came under my eye, although I was easily frightened. When a person, or a happening, seemed to me not in keeping with my opinion, or even my hope or expectation, I was terrified by a vision of abandonment and wildness which tore my heart with a kind of sorrow.[22]

And her behavior in the park is obviously a physical equivalent for this habit, a figure for the ordering tendency, which carries its own serious criticisms of that tendency along with it. As the narrator describes them—through scenes recollected in tranquillity—her attempts during childhood to reorganize her perceived world were genuine enough and perhaps necessary, but they were very much the attempts of a child, having their origins in certain invariable limitations of vision and sensibility.

Just how limited this particular idea of order is, is confirmed by the scene in the park a moment later, after everything has been set in "small frames." Suddenly, a new group of characters appears by the lake, "loud, squirming, ill-assorted people who seemed thrown together by the most confused accident." Pinching, kicking, and laughing at each other, communicating by what seem like a series of "idiotic sounds" rather than a comprehensible language, they offer a definitive threat to the structured vision of the child. She cannot contain them—as she did the previous tenants of the scene—within her prearranged system. All she can do is watch helplessly while the vision of chaos they supply rushes toward its climax—as one member of the group, a man, begins to scoop sand over the legs and body of his companion.

> I saw the man lift his hand filled with crumbling sand, shaking it as the woman laughed, and pour it down inside her bathing suit between her bulbous descending breasts. There it hung, brown and shapeless, making them all laugh. . . . The man smiled . . . and looked at me, and included me. . . . I closed my eyes . . . when I looked looked up, the fat woman was standing opposite the smiling man. She bent over and . . . pulled down the front of her bathing suit, turning it outward, so that the lumps of mashed and folded sand came emptying out. I felt a peak of horror, as though her breasts themselves had turned to sand. . . .[23]

At this moment, the framework established by the child gives way completely. The strategy of her creator, in fact, has been to allow her only a brief while to arrange the scene before showing just how incomplete her arrangements are, and then demolishing them.

Two things, I think, are especially worth mentioning about this story. One is that this movement from order to confusion is character-istic of Welty's fiction: a particular order—maybe a child's, maybe a man's or a whole society's—will be described, its limitations or simple impermanence discussed, and then life will somehow break in to de-stroy it. And the other is that, whatever the specific nature of this order, however restricted or unimaginative it may appear to be, Welty always presents it as she does here—in such a way, that is, as to maintain a balance of loyalties, to make us respond critically and sympathetically at one and the same time. Certainly the child in "A Memory" is rebuked for her naïveté, and for the inadequacy of the frames she constructs for interpreting the real. That, after all, is implicit in the entire presen-tation of the tale—which is offered as a kind of initiation ritual, part of the process of growing up. But the rebukes are never carried too far. Welty hedges them about with reservations, because as she sees it the child—like any other person—needs some sort of frame at every stage of her development. She has to have some way of arranging her circumstances before they can even begin to make sense to her. The only alternative to this, it seems, is pure anarchy. The consciousness is either building and rebuilding systems all the time, no matter how incomplete or provisional every one of them may turn out to be, or it is consigned to oblivion: that, essentially, is the message that comes through to us from the realized vision of oblivion supplied by the woman in the bathing suit and her friends. Like the figures in a nightmare they offer a terrifying contrast to the daydreams spun by the young girl who observes them; in the process they force the author, the narrator, and ourselves to remain poised between choices in the knowledge that neither fixity nor flux is in itself enough.

"The novelist is always seeing double," Welty declared in one of her essays on fiction, "two pictures at once . . . and he . . . works in a state of constant and subtle and unfooled reference between the two."[24] As always when she was being most interesting about the writer and his vocation, the immediate source of her observations was the experience of her own work. Those of her characters who, like the child in "A Memory," try to prescribe roles for others (or simply adopt them for themselves) are both admired and gently ridiculed—until the patterns they have imposed on experience finally collapse. In turn, those who are activated by nothing more than impulse are at once praised for their spontaneity and quietly scored for their irresponsibility, their failure to accept the other, and usually more public, side of their hu-man function. They free themselves from bondage, their creator ad-mits. But, she adds, they do so at the expense of others; and insofar as they are social, rational creatures, needing to find structure and meaning in their lives, at their own expense as well. The vacillation between poles, the habit of looking at the rage for order from two, completely opposite directions is nearly always there in Welty's writing; and, in the best of it, it is not so much a vacillation *between* individuals as one occurring *within* them. It ceases to be a matter of allegory, in other words (the kind of allegory that we find in "A Memory"), and assumes the more complex and in a sense more realistic dimensions of an internal drama, something that turns each major character into a field of warring inclinations—a chameleonlike being, every moment of whose life is expressive of conflict and change. This is perhaps best illustrated by *Delta Wedding*, the novel published in 1946 that more or less established Welty's reputation. Set on a Mississippi plantation during the early years of this century, it was one of her first pieces of long fiction. It was and is also, I think, one of her finest, not least because it places her interests within a framework of metaphor that takes us right back to the heart of her Southern inheritance—and in doing so reminds us of the forces largely responsible for giving her those interests in the first place.

As *Delta Wedding* opens, the central character, Laura McRaven, is on her way to stay with her cousins the Fairchilds at Shellmound, the plantation where they have lived for several generations. The journey, which is taken by train, is described in some detail, and the description serves, I think, as an ideal prologue to the story that follows.

> In the passenger car . . . a breeze blew through, hot and then cool, fragrant of the woods and yellow flowers and of the train. The yellow butterflies flew in at any window, out at any other, and outdoors one of them could keep up with the train, which then seemed to be racing with the butterfly. . . . Thoughts went out of . . . [Laura's] head and the landscape filled it. . . . The land was perfectly flat and level but it shimmered like the wings of a lighted dragonfly. It seemed strummed, as though it were an instrument and something had touched it. . . . Sometimes like a fuzzy caterpillar looking in the cotton was a winding lane of thick green willows and cypresses, and when the train crossed this green, running on a loud iron bridge, down its center like a golden mark on the caterpillar's back would be a bayou.[25]

To some extent, the felicity of this description is something that any reader can appreciate at once. The immediate subject is an adolescent girl traveling into strange territory, and it is obviously the author's intention to capture the excitement, mingled with a touch of fear, that is natural to any young person at such a time. That, after all, is one reason why the sense of movement is emphasized here, why sense impressions are confused and spatial dimensions altered at will: because the urgency of the prose helps reenact Laura's own excitement, while the effects of synesthesia and the rapid variations of perspective can provide a sort of imagistic equivalent for her feelings of dazed expectancy. But beyond this specific and fairly local purpose Welty clearly has other aims in mind, which can really only be understood in terms of the whole narrative—when, in fact, we have finished reading the entire book. For she is introducing us not merely to one particular character, albeit a major one, but to the novel's controlling theme: what is said here, and even more important *how* it is said, will come to our minds throughout the story, gathering new dimensions and meanings as it does so. The passage describes something like a faery realm, an evanescent medium in which things are constantly melting into one another or dividing their identity between different levels of experience. The mind absorbs the landscape and then the landscape absorbs the mind. The train moves and the land stays still; subsequently the roles are reversed, and the land seems to move while the train remains stationary. Thanks to Welty's way with descriptive detail, the senses become confused as well, so that the engine appears to be racing with a tiny insect and the shimmering countryside sounds with heat. Everything, as the author presents it, is animate and apparently capable of numerous metamorphoses: so much so that the metaphors lacing the description hardly seem like metaphors at all, but literal accounts of a magical environment. All is shifting, all is clear and yet somehow fluid, intangible; and all this, as we find out eventually, is the perfect ticket of entry into the world that Welty is going to create—where character is seen, essentially, as a series of tensions very much like the ones outlined here. Most of the people Laura McRaven is going to meet at Shellmound are caught, exactly as the components of this scene are, between the energies of their personal being (what earlier writers might have called their "animus," or spirit) and the fixities and definites of their environment. They seem just as capable as the train, landscape, and insects are of continual transformation, adopting one role for a moment only to discard it—under the pressure of changing need—for another one, slightly different. The figure of the butterfly racing in and out of Laura's carriage will seem, when we have come to know them, to express their lives in miniature— and (especially if we compare it with the equally figurative description of a butterfly with which Caroline Gordon begins *Penhally*) will serve to remind us, I think, just how far any of them are from being tied down to a fixed identity, or constrained by the exigencies of a still design.

Laura begins to recognize all this as soon as she meets the Fairchilds: they are, she senses, bound together in the "closest intimacy" by their group order and yet separated out into the "greatest anonymity" by the pressures of their subjective lives. Like the butterflies she saw in the train carriage, they seem to move rapidly in and out of the containing structures fashioned by men, never staying still long enough to be thoroughly defined. One pivotal event focuses the paradox on which their lives turn. It is when George Fairchild, the son of the owner of Shellmound, risks his life to save an idiot child from being crushed by a train. The child, Maureen, is the daughter of George's dead older brother, Dennis, and the rest of the family, who are out taking a walk with George at the time, witness the event. Indeed, they act almost as a chorus, observing what happens as a unit and then immediately drawing certain shared conclusions from it. "He did it for Dennis," the general opinion is. For all of the family George's rescue has this common meaning: that it demonstrates his courage and self-lessness, his concern for another Fairchild, his care above all for his more dependent cousins and friends. And, to the extent that it *is* held in common, this meaning acts, I believe, as a revelation of their close-ness—the bonds binding them together in companionship and giving them a sort of collective identity. They can, at least to begin with, reciprocate value judgments and share in each other's reactions; and insofar as they can do so they are, just as the Allard family in *None Shall Look Back* are, more of a community, an homogeneous group than a random collection of individuals.

As soon as Welty starts to delve further into some more personal reactions to the event, though, this apparent unity is suddenly qualified and differences between the Fairchilds and Gordon's Allard family become patently clear. In fact, it is an index of their differences that Welty delves further at all, since Gordon tends, for her own reasons, to avoid anything more than the most cursory examination of the inner lives and private responses of her characters. She would never, for instance, have permitted any of the Allards to dwell on the more macabre possibilities of an event in the way that Orrin Fairchild, George's younger brother, is allowed to. Nor would she really have been able to include the complications that another younger relative, George's sister India, adds to the affair. In India's case admiration is tinged with a certain amusement, an Austenian relish for the ludicrous details of even the most serious occasion—and the note of irony this introduces would, I think, have been irrelevant, not to say positively damaging, to the single-minded purposes of *None Shall Look Back*.

> "It was late in the afternoon," cried India. . . . "Maureen caught her foot. She was dancing up there and . . . she . . . caught her foot good. . . . The whistle was blowing . . . but the Dog [the train] was not coming very fast. . . . Maureen said 'Litt-la train-ain can-na get-la by-y,' and stuck her arms out. . . . Maureen and Uncle George kind of wrestled with each other and both of them fell off, and . . . the Dog stopped . . . and we all went home. . . ."[26]

The point about this is not that it demolishes the group version of the scene, since India respects George and his heroism as much as anybody does, but that it adds a further perspective to it. The seriousness and danger of the event are both registered still, but they are accompanied by a quiet yet firm refusal—which is India's refusal, a product of her own sprightly intelligence—to be oversolemn about any human affair. The reader is being asked in effect to accept the public interpretation of the rescue, held in common by all the Fairchilds, *and* the private meaning that India finds in it all at one and the same time. By following this request he can, perhaps, share for a moment in the double-sidedness of her existence—and enjoy something of the tension and sense of vitality that are its practical issue.

The situation becomes even more subtle and interesting with the other members of the family, because unlike India (and Orrin) their relationship to the rescue tends to be two way. They are affected by their memories almost as much as they affect them; recollection, far from being just a means of exposing their characters, becomes an agent of character development, a catalyst for new modes of thought and sensibility. Shelley Fairchild, another younger sister, offers a perfect illustration of this—the very way in which she remembers what has happened helping, really, to explain its effects upon her.

> . . . her memory arrested the action and let her see it again and again, like a painting in a schoolroom, with colors vivid and thunderclouded, George and Maureen above locked together, and the others below. . . . The engine . . . was upon them, coming as it would. George was no longer working at Maureen's caught foot. Their faces fixed, and in the instant alike, Maureen and George seemed to wait for the blow.[27]

The scene, as Shelley draws it in memory, is a sort of heroic portrait. Action is frozen into an illustrative emblem, people cease to be people and become strange, superhuman creatures living outside the world of time and change; as Welty suggests, they are rather like figures in a classroom painting—of Caesar crossing the Rubicon, perhaps, or Horatio defending the bridge. Of course, the impetus toward a heroic interpretation of this type has come from the rest of the Fairchilds, since they all like to think of George as a legendary being, an embodiment of the family virtues. Shelley has been driven by it much further than anyone else has, though—so much further, in fact, that nearly all sense of contact with ordinary human existence has disappeared from her recollections of the event. Why has this happened? Because, as Welty explains later, "there were things in that afternoon [of the rescue] which gave Shelley an uneasiness she seemed to feel all alone." George's act, we learn, forced her to recognize her own timidity for a moment—her fear, not merely of heroic endeavor, but of positive,

adult experience of any kind. Her more or less conscious attempts to
suppress that recognition have now in turn colored her memories of
what occurred. For what Shelley has done, effectively, is to distance
the rescue in order to offset the challenge it offers. She has translated
it into a dream, something existing at a considerable remove from
genuine human possibility, so that it will present as small a threat to
her own security as it conceivably can.

It does not require too much imagination, I think, to see that—
quite apart from her interest in an individual character here—Welty
is making another point as well, which involves an attack on the heroic
tendency in general, a radical criticism of the sort of epic posturing
or absolute acceptance of the public function that Shelley attributes,
with such care, to her older brother. Significantly, the only person in
Delta Wedding who really *is* imprisoned within his heroic, public role
in the way that Shelley imagines George to be is the oldest son of the
family, Dennis Fairchild—who is dead. "Not at large," as Welty puts
it, "not in transit any more, as in life, but fixed—tied to a tree," only his
role is remembered; and the man who filled it, some of the time, is no
longer around to remind us of its necessarily partial and provisional
nature. With the other Fairchilds, including Shelley herself, to move
in and out of their customary parts becomes a way of demonstrating
that they are alive, that they have the kind of energy that makes them
larger than any position or function given them by their society. Battle
Fairchild, for instance, the owner of the plantation, often seems to be
an exact copy of Kennedy's Frank Meriwether or Gordon's Fontaine
Allard, a patriarch those tastes are defined by the limits of his holdings
and the responsibilities of his vocation. But every now and then
glimpses of another, completely different person will peep through:
"a rushing, mysterious, laughing man," his creator says, who "could
put on a tender, irresponsible air, as if he were asking . . . 'Look at
me! What can I do? Such a thing it all is!'" Similarly, his wife will
occasionally break out of her role of plantation matriarch and relive
the excitement of her youth, when she was "a town-loving, book-lov-
ing young lady" with no responsibilities to anyone. At such moments
she, as much as her husband, seems to possess the kind of freedom
or expansiveness of being, and consequent amusement with an assigned identity, that Walt Whitman described so well in "Song of Myself."

> Apart from the pulling and hauling stands
>   what I am,
> Stands amused, complacent, compassionating, idle,
>   unitary,

Looks down, is erect, bends an arm in an
    impalpable certain rest,
Looks with sidecurved head curious
    what will come next,
Both in and out of the game, and
    watching and wondering at it.[28]

This freedom possessed by nearly all the Fairchilds, their capacity for being as Whitman puts it "both in and out of the game," inevitably has some impact on the scenes in which they appear—or, to be more exact, on the rituals in which they are made to participate. Like any other, more conventional plantation novel, *Delta Wedding* is organized around a few crucial episodes—tableaux, really, which illustrate different facets of the society and its culture. But because Welty's people are so extraordinarily elusive, and can never quite be confined to their social functions, these episodes have a peculiar edge and sense of movement here that they rarely have elsewhere. A writer like, say, Caroline Gordon tends to see plantation life as a series of still moments: she describes the tribal rite, dwelling above all on the feelings of unity and symmetry that accompany it, and then leaves it at that. Welty, on the other hand, will almost invariably describe the moment *and its passing;* there is a continual fluctuation, in her work, between her respect for ceremony and her love of what she calls the "iridescent life" playing beneath the surfaces of every ceremonial occasion. The dance that concludes the action is a vivid illustration of what I mean.

. . . the dancers . . . all looked alike, all . . . alike smooth and shorn, all faces painted to look like one another. It was too the season of changeless weather, of the changeless world, in a land without hill or valley. . . . Then in a turn of . . . India's skirt, as she ran partnerless through the crowd . . . the dancers become the McLeoud bridesmaid, Mary Lamar Mackey . . . become Robbie, and . . . Shelley, each different face bright and burning as sparks of fire . . . more different and further apart than the stars.[29]

The turnabout here, beautifully introduced by the eruption of India, partnerless, vivacious, and mischievous, into the decorous dancing scene, suggests I think the tension on which the entire narrative depends. So, too, does the rapid alteration of verbal and imaginative reference that follows it. For the keywords "all" and "changeless" are substituted, quite suddenly, the terms "each" and "different." The generalized portrait of a land "without hill or valley" is succeeded by the invocation of the bright, particular stars above it. In the space of a few, brief seconds, "sparks of fire," those traditional images of the individual soul, are shown burning beneath the smooth and painted appearance of each member of the dance, so that the reader is reminded almost at the same moment the ceremony reaches its climax of just how much it tends, at its own cost, to exclude.

We can, if we want to, put all that I have said about *Delta Wedding* so far in another and perhaps more familiar way, by saying that what Welty has done here in her portrait of the Fairchilds and their world —that world which Laura McRaven is entering at the start of the novel and from which, subsequently, she learns so much—is simply to *use* the emblems of order transmitted to her by her region. She has taken the figure of the old plantation and given it her own, fresh meanings—just how fresh we can tell, I think, if we compare Shellmound with Gordon's Bracketts, Tate's Pleasant Hill, or Kennedy's Swallow Barn. Certainly, the place Welty describes is like those other landscapes of the mind in some ways: the very name, Shellmound, with its connotations of enclosure, control, and discipline suggests as much. But there is another side to it that they lack completely, making the Fairchild estate seem sometimes, Welty says, like "a nameless forest, wherein many . . . lives lived privately, each to its own lyric pursuit." This is a side that Laura notices as soon as she arrives there. Shellmound, she discovers, is something more than a communal center or point of stability. It is a place of some mystery as well, where people can hide from one another and remain in a measure unknown.

> She thought of the upstairs hall where it was twilight all the time from the green shadow of an awning. . . . They could play an endless game of hide-and-seek in so many rooms up and down the halls that intersected and turned into dead-end porches and rooms full of wax begonias and elephant's-ears, or rooms full of trunks. . . . A dizziness rose in Laura's head. . . . She remembered life in the undeterminate number of other rooms. . . .[30]

As this passage suggests, there is even a touch of the House of Usher about Shellmound, in the strangeness of its dimly lit rooms and the elaborate, exotic clutter with which it is furnished. At once a mansion and a labyrinth, a dwelling and a kind of maze, it reflects the ambivalence of Welty's allegiances as much as its inhabitants do, making it seem only natural that the Fairchilds should have such an affection for it—that, to adopt a phrase Welty uses elsewhere in her writings, their feelings should be so intimately "bound up in place."

The first time Welty used this phrase was, as far as I know, in one of her essays on fiction; and I would like to quote something else, a slightly longer passage from that essay because what she says there— about place and people—is, I think, very pertinent not just to *Delta Wedding* but to all of her work. "It is by knowing where you started," she says,

that you grow able to judge where you are. Place absorbs our earliest notice and attention, it bestows on us our original awareness, and our critical powers spring up from the study of it and the growth of experience
inside it.[31]

It is not difficult, really, to see how this applies to Welty's own intimacy with her region, since it has been just as she suggests here, by
testing herself against the norms of her environment, that she has been
able to develop her art. The South's love of ceremony, which in turn
can be seen as one example of man's rage for order, has been explored reverently but critically in nearly all of her work; and in some
of it the South's own myths, above all the myth of the old plantation,
have been used as well—as tools, or appropriate means of exploration.
Welty is not just talking about herself in this passage, though, or even
just about other writers. She is talking about people in general: the
need everyone has for background, something against which they can
define themselves, and roots, something from which they can grow.
And it is at the moment when we recognize this, I believe, that a curious gap seems to open up between the kinds of connections with place
she is advocating—and that are implicit in her own regionalism—and
the kinds of connections that most of her people, her characters enjoy.
For people like the Fairchilds do not grow in the way Welty describes
here. They may leap about between roles, but they never seem to be
seriously affected by the process; nor are the roles or codes they adopt
affected to any significant extent, either. Welty herself may have
established a genuinely dialectical relationship with her surroundings,
out of which can develop a third thing, that special world or South
with a difference which is the setting for most of her stories. But not
so Battle Fairchild and his kind: their fragile and evanescent selves
and the collective order to which they belong remain two stationary
principles, neither of which is very much changed by any contact or
conflict that may occur between them. So by an extraordinary (and, of
course, totally unintended) stroke of irony a book like *Delta Wedding*
ends, I think, by posing a criticism of itself, or at least of its apparent
heroes. Its status as a regionalist work, in other words, and the nature
of its relationship to the Southern tradition, offer a subtle commentary
on the ideas of traditionalism, regionalism, and Southern-ness that
are expressed in its characters' lives. As far as this goes, Welty too
seems a bit like the "amused, complacent" creature Whitman describes
in "Song of Myself": a writer who stands apart from her writing just
a little, "watching and wondering"—vaguely aware, perhaps, of a discrepancy between what *can* be done, what *she* has done in laying the
foundations of her imaginative world, and what her people (the apparent bearers of her message) say and do.

The Grace of Pure Awareness: Katherine Anne Porter

Silenced, she sank easily through deeps under deeps of darkness until she lay like a stone at the farthest bottom of life, knowing herself to be blind, deaf, speechless, no longer aware of the members of her own body, entirely withdrawn from all human concerns, yet alive with a peculiar lucidity and coherence; all notions of the mind, the reasonable inquiries of doubt, all ties of blood and the desires of the heart, dissolved and fell away from her, and there remained of her only a minute fiercely burning particle of being that knew itself alone, that relied upon nothing beyond itself for strength; not susceptible to any appeal or inducement, being itself composed entirely of one single motive, the stubborn will to live. This fiery motionless particle set itself unaided to resist destruction, to survive and be in its own madness of being, motiveless and planless beyond that one essential end. Trust me, the hard unwinking angry point of light said. Trust me. I stay.[32]

The words, from "Pale Horse, Pale Rider," are those of Katherine Anne Porter; and the belief they express, in a central and independent consciousness that steers the individual through any difficulties confronting him, is one basic to nearly all of her fiction. Many of her short stories, in fact, have as their subject the actual growth of this consciousness, the education of a character into the duties and possibilities of his own intelligence. The tutored sensibility is the closest thing to an absolute we will find in Porter's work; by contrast, the system of law and order that Caroline Gordon holds so dear is entertained only to be rejected. Perhaps it would be more accurate, though, to say dissected: Porter does not so much dismiss the entire framework of law as subject it to a radical analysis—this as a preliminary to reconstructing it as a living, growing thing within the minds of her protagonists. Her strategy is nearly always the same: an objective myth or order is examined and its inadequacy exposed by comparing it, and the restrictions it imposes, with the needs of a developing consciousness. It then becomes the task of this consciousness, not, as in the stories of Eudora Welty, to find some sort of provisional satisfaction in the given rules—accompanied, perhaps, by the occasional escape into a more liberated zone—but to evolve a subjective world that represents a reconciliation of rule and freedom, value and raw experience. So precisely that kind of dialectic emerges that books like *Delta Wedding* never really manage to enact. As Porter describes them, the demands of an impersonal code work productively with the energies of the self to produce a third thing—a new kind of order that (to quote one of her most perceptive critics)

is internal, its terms the terms of consciousness, its relations those of time rather than space, its value the freedom conferred by understanding, the grace of pure awareness.[33]

The stories that Porter has gathered together under the title "The Old Order" provide as good an example as any of exactly how this "grace of pure awareness" is arrived at, and what its more detailed characteristics are. Semiautobiographical in their origins, these stories have as their subject a young girl called Miranda Rhea, growing up in the South in the early years of this century, who learns simultaneously about the limitations inherent in the code transmitted to her by her family and about the scope of her responsibilities. Eventually these two levels of the narrative, the examination of impersonal myth and the theme of personal development, become inseparable; since the static and disciplined world into which Miranda is born is seen to be typical both of the Old South and of childhood, while Miranda's gradual freeing of herself from her environment and the forms of behavior it dictates is, we are told, as much the consequence of its general decay as of her own increasing maturity. Becoming an adult, she becomes less of a conventional Southerner; forsaking childhood and childish things, she forsakes along with them the codes and ceremonies of the old plantation. This, I think, adds a special dimension of irony to the criticism of the South and its traditions running through every tale. For what Porter is clearly suggesting, by equating Miranda's growing up with her escape from the plantation system, is that this system—and the sort of objective order it represents—is not (as Caroline Gordon would have us believe) a valid moral agency at all. It simply offers a means of ignoring moral problems, above all the problem of choice. It continues the restrictions of childhood into maturity, by denying the demands and supplanting the responsibilities of the adult, and as such is more a tactic of evasion, a way of protecting oneself against reality, than anything else.

Just how evasive the old order can be is illustrated by the earlier stories in the series, which trace Miranda's growing uneasiness, her emerging suspicion that her sympathies, and perhaps her intelligence as well, separate her from the rest of her family. They—her parents, her grandparents, and her "cousins"—still subscribe to the official Southern version of the past, peopled by fine gentlemen and happy darkies. In a sense they have to, because it provides them with a historical confirmation of their code, a myth to reassure them as to the validity of their own life style. Miranda, however, cannot help feeling that another image of the past is far more credible, the one supplied to her by the field hands and black servants of the household, which emphasizes violence, cruelty, and deprivation above all else. The nightmare of the chained and beaten slave will keep returning to haunt her; and, every time it does so, it

forces Miranda to adopt a more critical attitude toward her elders and
the dreams they spin. Needless to say, it does not lead her to accuse them
of bad faith or self-deception; she is still too young and tentative in
her opinions for anything like that. But it does make her suspect that,
in some ways, she knows more than her family does, and so prevents
her from feeling full identification with them. Qualifications enter into
her acceptance of their authority that, sooner or later, must develop
into a deep sense of estrangement. And they do so, curiously enough,
during a visit to the circus, when Miranda finds her reaction to the
performers—and, in particular, the horror that the chalk-white faces
of the clowns inspires in her—unshared and even misunderstood by
her relatives. It is then that she has to accept her difference, the enormous distance separating her from them. She is terrified by what she
sees; her brothers and sisters are not. Worse still, they are incapable of
understanding why she *should* be terrified, so their concern for her
can be no more than mocking, their sympathy a thin disguise for
contempt.

> The other children told Miranda what she had missed. . . . The other
> children . . . moaned over her with sad mouths, their malicious eyes watch-
> ing Miranda squirm. . . . "Can you *imagine* being afraid of that funny old
> clown?"[31]

Miranda may be growing aware of how alienated she is from the
people around her, and the system into which she was born, but she
still has to learn to trust herself a little more. She has to become, in
fact, not merely separate but self-sufficient. And this she is beginning
to do, in her own very quiet way, in what I think is one of the finest
stories in the sequence, "The Grave," which describes her initiation
into the mysteries of birth and death. As the story opens, she and her
brother Paul are on their way to visit the spot where most of their
ancestors are buried. Arriving there, they play among the gravestones
for a while, and then go hunting, and manage to catch and kill a rabbit. Paul insists on slitting the rabbit open, in obedience to the rituals
of the "chase," and in its stomach they find some embryos—"a bundle of
tiny rabbits, each wrapped in a thin scarlet veil." These Miranda insists on examining closely.

> Miranda said, "Oh I want to *see*," under her breath . . . she wanted
> most deeply to see and to know. Having seen, she felt at once as if she
> had known all along. . . . She understood a little of the secret, formless
> intuitions in her own mind and body, which had been . . . taking form, so
> gradually . . . she had not realized that she was learning what she had
> to know.[35]

Obviously, what Miranda is discovering here is important, but so also is the way she is discovering it. For as the conjunction of "see" and "know," and "body" and "mind" suggest, Miranda is taking nothing on trust. The knowledge she is acquiring is not the sort of predigested information that Miranda's family would have her accept but knowledge that is experienced directly, felt upon the pulses. Independence, the habit of finding things out for oneself, is its hallmark; and it requires no particular effort, really, to see how destructive of established rules and rituals such a method of learning must be.

The innate deficiencies of the inherited legend and the resistance offered by the developing consciousness to any kind of imposed discipline: these are two reasons why conflict between Miranda and the old order seems to grow during the course of the story sequence. There is, I think, a third—which is that whatever the original power of the plantation system, however effective it might once have appeared to be as a way of organizing experience, it is now in a state of decline anyway. The struggle between code and personality is all the more inevitable, we learn, because that code is so clearly antiquated and weak. This is indicated, among other things, by the characters who are taken to be the purest representatives of the plantation order, who are either the dead, surviving in memory, or those whose real allegiance is to yesterday. Miranda's Grandmother Rhea and the grandmother's former body slave, called Nannie, are good examples of the latter, two women who despite their obvious, superficial differences are (as the similarity of their names is probably meant to suggest) very much alike. Both have had specific functions assigned to them since birth and have accepted those functions wholeheartedly. Both, in the few years that Miranda knows them, spend all their time sitting on the front porch "cutting scraps of family finery . . . and fitting them together again"— an apt metaphor, as it turns out, for their desultory and invariably nostalgic conversations. Belonging to another era, and to all intents and purposes living in other eras, neither woman can offer Miranda much except a warning, a way of measuring the obsolescence of the old controls. And when at last Grandmother Rhea collapses into senility and then dies, all that Nannie can do, having lost her accomplice, is retreat still further into the past—discarding her role of "faithful old servant" for that of "an aged Bantu woman, of independent means."[36]

From what I have said so far about "The Old Order," it might be assumed that its author is entirely on the side of her isolated protagonist, and the forces contributing to the disappearance of the plantation code. But this assumption, I think, would be a mistake, a simplification of what is essentially a very subtly presented case. Admittedly, Porter's interest in the growth of the individual consciousness, and its liberation from the restraints of childhood, leads her to place major emphasis on Miranda and the *positive* nature of her struggle against closed forms. This does not prevent her, though, from acknowledging what is good and valuable about those forms, or at least the impulses that brought them into being—from recognizing, in her own way, that the customs and ceremonies of the old plantation are the product of need, reflecting an important part of the human personality and its response to life. Even in the earlier tales this tends to be so, because Porter does not deny some original worth to the plantation code and its representatives; a feeling of sympathy—implicit, for instance, in the elegiac atmosphere surrounding Grandmother Rhea and Nannie—helps to qualify the dominant strategy of attack. And in the last, longest, and undoubtedly the finest of the stories in the sequence, "Old Mortality," this sympathy becomes much more prominent, so as to provide the necessary starting point for Miranda's own quest for order: she has to learn now the few things her inheritance has to offer her, and how to separate them cleanly and completely from all that she has had to reject.

The title of "Old Mortality" is, of course, borrowed from Sir Walter Scott, the person whom Mark Twain, in a famous passage in *Life on the Mississippi,* blamed more than anybody else for the self-destructive romanticism of the Old South; and the sort of dry irony or edgy wit that probably prompted this borrowing is also there, I think, in the opening paragraph of the story. It describes a photograph of Amy Rhea, an ancestor of Miranda's who lived at a time when plantation society was at its most secure—and who, since her death many years previously, has acted as a focus for the family's nostalgia. Once she was subject to the restrictions of the heroic code; now she has been turned into its commemorative emblem, and the portrait Porter presents of her here (or rather of her figure frozen by the camera) helps to suggest just what both of these things involve.

> She was a spirited-looking young woman, with dark curly hair cropped and parted on the side, . . . and a large curved mouth. A round white collar rose from the neck of her tightly buttoned black basque, and round white cuffs set off lazy hands with dimples in them, lying at ease in the folds of her flounced skirt, which gathered around to a bustle. She sat thus, forever in the pose of being photographed, a motionless image in a dark walnut frame . . . her smiling gray eyes following one about the room.[37]

The feeling of life and energy, the sense of Amy's simple vitality that this description arouses is, I think, indisputable. It is caught in the sensuous quality of the details picked out for emphasis, in Amy's "large curved mouth" and "lazy hands with dimples in them"—and in the habit of lively curiosity expressed by her eyes. But this feeling is profoundly qualified by another system of references, which suggests containment and restriction: the "round white collar" and "tightly buttoned black basque," for instance, which used to hem Amy in, or the "dark walnut frame" in which she seems to be captured now. The net result of all this, really, is to establish a witty series of criticisms of the legend even before its presence has been openly admitted. A lively young woman has been imprisoned, it seems, within a series of stationary and essentially artificial forms. She has been reduced to a "motionless image" by convention and later by memory, her motionlessness offering us one criticism already, one way of measuring the deficiencies of that timeless order to which, apparently, she belongs.

The criticism is carried a little further in the scenes immediately following this, which cover roughly the same period as the previous stories in the sequence—that is, Miranda's childhood and early adolescence. It is while Miranda is still fairly young, for instance, that she and her sister overhear their father talking in reverential terms about Amy and, by extension, all the ladies of the Rhea household, larding them with effusive and patently inaccurate praise, which ends in the blank assertion, "There were never any fat women in our family, thank God." Listening to him, the girls cannot help wondering what he means. There *were* fat women in the family, they remember, many of them—among them a great-aunt "who quite squeezed herself through doors" and an Aunt Kezia who was so big that her husband refused to let her ride on his horses. In particular, the two girls recall how Kezia's husband expressed his refusal—by declaring, "My sentiments of chivalry are not dead . . . but neither is my common sense."[38] And they note in this apparently simple formula a clue to the dilemma in which they now find themselves placed. Are they, they wonder, to do as their father does—to follow the dictates of chivalry no matter how far from reality this may carry them; or should they take their stand on the plain, unadorned facts? Must they, like their great-aunt, try to squeeze themselves into the spaces prepared for them, or should they try to escape to some freer environment elsewhere?

The answer to these questions is not as obvious as it might seem to be at first, because as the story goes on Porter begins to qualify her original opinion. The mythologizing impulse, she implies, is never merely perverse; it has its sources in positive feeling, the kind of motives we can all understand. Interestingly enough, this turn in the tide of comment occurs when she tries to explain Mr. Rhea's apparent blindness to the size of some of his "cousins."

> This loyalty of their father's in the face of evidence contrary to his ideal had its springs in family feeling. . . . Photographs, portraits . . . and the festival garments folded away in dried herbs and camphor were disappointing when the little girls tried to fit them to the living beings created

in the mind by the breathing words of their elders. Grandmother, twice a year, . . . would sit beside old trunks and boxes . . . unfolding . . . small keepsakes, . . . unwrapping locks of hair and dried flowers, crying gently and easily, as if tears were the only pleasure she had left. . . . The little girls examined the objects . . . and did not find them . . . impressive. Such dowdy little wreaths and necklaces, . . . faded things . . . yellowed . . . and misshapen. . . .[39]

The sheer difference in tone and attitude between this passage, and the earlier description of Amy's photograph, is remarkable. For here it is the *legend* that is seen as something vital, in that it had its origins, Porter says, in living emotion. It was created out of "breathing" words, to give value and dignity to life. In turn, the reality it had to subdue is now described as essentially lifeless, a series of cruelly impoverished particulars like the "dowdy little wreaths" the girls discover or the "dried herbs and camphor" in which the various relics of the family are kept. The real seems, in effect, to need some sort of legendary habiliment to make it tolerable, an appropriate context for the moral life, to be enriched by chivalric fictions rather than spoiled by them. Admittedly, Porter's volte-face is not complete. She still retains a trace of that irony which characterized her earlier approach—for example, in her wry, dry description of Grandmother Rhea's rather self-indulgent grief. But enough of a change has been made to deny our initial expectations, and in doing this to establish a balance, a measure of equilibrium between our sympathy for the myth-making impulse and our recognition of the recalcitrant facts.

This balance is maintained throughout the rest of the first section of the story, so that nearly everything the narrator says turns out to have a double edge. A good example of this occurs toward the end of the section, when we learn about Amy Rhea's love affair with a young man called Gabriel. This, apparently, has become a part of the Amy legend too; a story told so many times, Porter says, that it has assumed something of the quality of "poetry or music . . . the theater," and seems to belong to another and more heroic world altogether, "the world of personages taller than human beings." To an extent, I think, all these observations are intended quite seriously since, like Caroline Gordon, Porter wants to emphasize the element of game or artifice in Southern culture. The Rhea family are trying to elevate Amy's life in memory, to give it symmetry and significant proportion, and in this —the author suggests—they are not so very different from the poet, the heroic dramatist, and the composer. The seriousness is obviously edged with a great deal of irony, however, because such comments do also imply the element of duplicity inherent in the attempt (the family, like the artist, tell lies that only *resemble* the truth); and, much more important, because they help measure the weakness of the Rhea's fabrications—and, by extension, the relative poverty of their collective fantasy. In any comparison with the vision of the Good Life expressed in art, in lyric poetry, say, or heroic drama, the story of Amy Rhea obviously pales into insignificance. It betrays the conventional minds, the limited emotional range and captive imaginations, of those who cherish it; and we have only to do as Porter does later, to set it beside such things as "the Vita Nuova, the Sonnets of Shakespeare, the Wedding Song of Spenser,"[40] to see just how much it excludes. A still further irony is added to the situation when we discover that Amy, as the details of her love affair show, occasionally rebelled against the very community that adores her memory: once she cut her hair short in defiance of her elders, we are told, and she only agreed to marry Gabriel after he had lost his fortune and so was ineligible for marriage according to the code. Miranda, growing up when she first hears these tales but still something of a child emotionally, says that she wants to be like Amy now—and this additional information can only make her aim seem a peculiarly ambivalent one. Is it Amy the rebel she is thinking about when she says this, we wonder, or Amy as she is chiefly remembered, a model of refinement, old world courtesy, and obedience?

By the time the second section of the story opens, Miranda's hopes of becoming a beauty like Amy have diminished a little—although her respect for Amy herself remains undimmed—and she has a new ambition, which is to be a jockey. That is one reason why, when her father proposes that he, she, and her sister spend a day together at the races, she greets his proposal with conspicuous enthusiasm. Another is that Gabriel, Amy's widower, will be there because his horse is running in one of the events, and this will be the first chance she has had of meeting someone who is directly involved in the family legend. Predictably enough, perhaps, the day does not come up to Miranda's expectations. Gabriel's horse wins, but the glamour of victory (and of racing in general) is shattered when she notices that it is bleeding at the nose from the strain. Worse still, Gabriel is nothing like the "handsome, romantic beau" of hearsay—just "a shabby fat man with . . . sad beaten eyes, a melancholy laugh."[41] He is ordinary, Miranda has to admit, and rather pathetic, and her disenchantment with him cannot help but damage her confidence in the story with which he has always been connected.

The legend has proved something of a betrayal then, by the end of the day, but the unembellished facts, events stripped of their fictive covering, do not come all that well out of it, either. For things do not stop there, with the last race. Gabriel, flush with victory, insists on taking his relatives home to his squalid lodgings on the other side of town for a small celebration. There, waiting for them all, is the woman Gabriel married after Amy died, whose name, Miss Honey, is a rather clumsy piece of irony, I think—because as soon as we meet her it becomes obvious that she is anything at all except sweet. Unconventional and hard-headed, she counters Gabriel's every attempt at optimism with her own cruel brand of mockery. She derides him in front of his visitors for his naïve delight in victory and his roseate visions of the future; and, not content with this, she insults her visitors as well by stubbornly refusing to allow them the ordinary forms of politeness. Seeing things only for what they are, and calling them by exactly their right names, she is realistic in the most thoroughgoing sense possible—and, as Porter intends, she is contemptible. Neither Miranda nor the author make any bones about it. She has allowed herself to be circumscribed by the particulars of her environment, and in doing so has become as depressing and repellent as they are.

> There was a big lumpy bed, with a grayish-white counterpane on it, . . . grayish coarse lace curtains . . . and two trunks, standing at odds. . . . Everything was dingy and soiled and neat and bare. . . . "We'll move to the St. Charles tomorrow," said Uncle Gabriel. . . . Miss Honey's nostrils pinched together . . . "I'll just stay where I am, thank you. I prefer it to moving back here in three months. . . . I feel at home here," she told him . . . her pale eyes kindling with blue fire, a stiff white line around her mouth. . . . "She loathes and despises everybody in this room," thought Miranda. . . .[42]

If the portrait of Miss Honey's room sounds familiar, it is, of course, because it recalls the description of the "dowdy keepsakes" that Miranda and her sister found in the attic, the stuff out of which the Rhea family wove their dreams. Together this room and those "faded things" seem to offer a visible measure of the inadequacy of the unadorned fact; and a way of charting the failure of that attitude—call it realism, materialism, positivism, or what you will—which would elevate facts as a species into the sole standard of human judgment.

Several years have passed when the third and final section of the story opens, and in the meantime Miranda has got herself married without the consent of her parents. We see her now returning home for the first time since her marriage. On the train she meets her cousin Eva, a woman she has hardly spoken to before because relations between Eva and the rest of the family have always been so extremely strained. Eva is, in fact, an outsider—somebody who has escaped the influences shaping Miranda's childhood and early adolescence and whose personality and beliefs, formed in virtual isolation, make her seem like a reincarnation of Miss Honey. She has the same withered appearance that Gabriel's second wife had, the same opinion of the Rhea family, and the same tone of ferocious sarcasm when expressing it; even her surroundings on the train, "stuffy . . . dusty" and acutely depressing, revive memories of that dingy hotel room Miss Honey liked to call home. If there is a difference between the two women it stems simply from the fact that Eva, once she knows who Miranda is, is more open and direct in her attack on the family legend than anybody, including Miss Honey, has been up until now. As she describes it the story of Amy Rhea, and in particular the story of Amy and Gabriel, is a tissue of cunningly contrived lies from start to finish that need to be exposed for the benefit of future generations. Amy, Eva insists, was never anything like the Southern belle she has become in the family memory. She was unfaithful and made Gabriel miserable. Like all her contemporaries she was "sex-ridden," but, knowing nothing "about that," she "simply festered inside"[43] until she was permanently damaged. Her beauty, Eva goes on, was not all that it was supposed to be, either: she was too thin when she was young, too fat when she was older, and the few attractive features she did possess —such as her fine complexion and delicate features—were really the visible effects of tuberculosis. Eva spares nothing from the assault, and Miranda comes away from the conversation, or rather the monologue, feeling as she did after she had noticed Gabriel's horse was in agony or watched Gabriel himself being humiliated—that she has witnessed an almost iconoclastic act, the desecration of a once cherished and reverenced object.

The desecration is so complete, in fact, that Miranda will not accept it. Eva seems just as alien to her as Miss Honey did, her brand of realism just as unconvincing—and this time, because she is older, she can begin to see why.

> Miranda found herself deliberately watching a long procession of living corpses, festering women stepping gaily towards the charnel house, their corruption concealed under laces and flowers, their dead faces lifted smiling, and thought quite coldly, "Of course, it was not like that. This is no more than what I was told before, it's every bit as romantic. . . ."[44]

"Every bit as romantic": that is Miranda's verdict on the supposedly unadulterated version of events offered to her by her cousin. What she means by this, I think (and what Porter means as well), is that to emphasize raw experience at the expense of all that the human consciousness can do to give it shape and significance is really to oversimplify. The cynic, after all, is no more than a betrayed idealist who simply repeats the idealistic error by reversing it; apotheosizing events and denying the possibility of a legendary dimension, his version of life must be as limited as that of the man who celebrates the myth and ignores the facts. A common allegiance to romantic half-truths, Miranda suspects—the same blindness to the fact that there are two sides to the historical equation—draws skeptic and sentimentalist together despite their apparent differences, a suspicion that is confirmed, with beautiful irony, right at the end of the story when the long journey home is over. There at the station waiting to welcome the travelers is Miranda's father, one of the arch-dreamers of the family. Nominally he is there to greet both Miranda and Eva, but, it soon becomes obvious, all the warmth of his greeting is reserved for the latter. Mr. Rhea and Eva greet each other affectionately, even passionately. Then together the two of them, the myth maker and the myth destroyer, walk off arm in arm—for all the world, as their creator puts it, like people who occupy "their place in this world, . . . arrived at by paths familiar to them both." Miranda meanwhile walks behind them like an exile, ignored by them both and excluded from their conversation as effectively as if she spoke a different language.

So Miranda's isolation, which has been growing steadily since the first story in the sequence, is now more or less complete. The family she grew up in, the people she knew have become strangers to her and she has, apparently, no new friends or community to replace them with. Even her marriage, which has established the final barrier between her and her relatives, is clearly a means of escape rather than fulfillment, and by the time of her visit home (to renew *formal* acquaintances with her father and mother) she is already contemplating flight from this as well. She is alone, utterly alone, or as Porter would prefer to put it, she is independent. Turned in upon herself (that "fiercely burning particle of being" described in "Pale Horse, Pale Rider"), Miranda can "look at the world with her own eyes"[45] from now on, and *use* what she has learned from her elders rather than be controlled by it. Naturally she will make mistakes: she knows this and the author suggests as much by reminding us how close her hopefulness and independence are to ignorance. But at least any mistakes she makes now will be her own; no matter how tenuous and provisional any version of experience she fabricates may be, it will have some value for her precisely because it is hers and not somebody else's. And perhaps, Porter adds, it will not be as fragile as all that, thanks to the education Miranda has gone through in these stories. She has, after all, learned about the crucial things, the problems inherent in accepting a myth at its face value and the dangers implicit in sticking to the unvarnished facts. All she has to do now, really, is weave her way somewhere in between these two extremes—creating new syntheses out of them as she goes along, new visions of order for every minute she remains alive.

Miranda has learned the need for a technique, then, rather than a code. Not only that, she has learned what this technique requires—just as we the readers have, even though we may be hardly aware of it. For the qualities that Porter sees as basic to her new kind of order—self-knowledge, understanding coupled with affection and sympathy, above all "the grace of pure awareness"—are exactly the ones her heroine has acquired in the course of growing up; *and which have been there right from the first in Porter's narrative,* as the distinguishing features of her approach and style. The precision of her judgments, the limpidity and subtlety of her phrasing, her wit, her pity, and her irony: in everything the author says or does in "The Old Order," she tries to demonstrate that agility and luminosity of mind apparently so essential to travelers along what she calls "the downward path to wisdom." This strategy—whereby all the characters need to guide them through their lives is shown to be there in the controlling intelligence of the story—must, I think, be counted among Porter's major achievements; and if we want a good description of it, how it works and the sort of conclusions it helps lead to, I know of none better than the one Robert Frost gave when trying to explain "the figure a poem makes." Frost, needless to say, had his own writing in mind at the time, but he might just as easily have been describing the movement of a tale like "Old Mortality."

> It starts in delight and ends in wisdom. The figure is the same as for love. No one can really hold that ecstasy should be static and stand still in one place. It begins in delight, assumes direction with the first line laid, it runs a course of lucky events, and ends in clarification of life—not necessarily a great clarification, such as sects and cults are founded on, but in a momentary stay against confusion.[46]

That, exactly, is the type of order that emerges from Porter's stories: "a momentary stay against confusion," created out of the incessant coupling of event and myth—and involving, among other things, both the active intelligence and the sympathetic heart of the writer. It is a far cry, of course, from the idea of order enshrined in the legend of the old plantation, and Porter never tires of reminding us of that fact by delivering a few glancing blows at the Old South and its image of itself along the way. All the same she is clearly indebted to the plantation myth for interesting her in such matters in the first place—for the questions it asks about custom, ceremony, and the patterns men try to find in experience if not usually for the answers it offers. Like her own heroine, in fact, Porter remains very much *of* the South even while no longer appearing to belong *in* it; her sympathies may have carried her over the Mason-Dixon line, literally or in imagination, a long time ago —but its obsessions remain hers in spite of that, and she bears its marks upon her brain and memory.

5. The Individual Talent: William Faulkner and the Yoknapatawpha Novels

~~~~~~

"Loving It Even While Hating Some of It": Faulkner and the South

> "So it takes two niggers to get rid of one Sutpen, don't it?" . . . Shreve . . . continued almost without a pause: "Which is all right, it's fine; it clears the whole ledger, . . . except for one thing. . . . You've got one nigger left. One nigger Sutpen left. . . . You still hear him at night sometimes. Don't you?" "Yes," Quentin [Compson] said. . . . "Now I want you to tell me just one thing more. Why do you hate the South?" "I don't hate it," Quentin said, quickly, . . . *I don't hate it*, he thought, panting in the cold air, the iron New England dark; *I don't. I don't! I don't hate it! I don't hate it!*[1]

This is how *Absalom, Absalom!* ends. It is the conclusion to what is perhaps William Faulkner's finest novel, certainly his definitive treatment of the South; and the conclusion is an enigma. Does Quentin Compson love the South or does he hate it? He does not know. All he can do is deny hatred in a way that at once rejects it as a fact and admits it as a possibility. Love there may be as well, but it is too tentative and confused to be included except by implication. Feelings are so mixed and provisional, in fact, and yet so extraordinarily intense that they can only issue in the kind of uncertainty Quentin expresses here. Like Poe's febrile and obsessed young protagonists, or some of Goethe's and Byron's heroes, Quentin seems to receive the world at his nerve ends—and experience too much too immediately ever to be able to put his house in order.

Quentin Compson is not William Faulkner, of course, and it would be quite wrong to identify his attitude toward the South, his homeland, with that of his creator. The fact that Faulkner can actually talk about the South, whereas Quentin is reduced to a series of outraged negatives, is proof enough of that. But that should not prevent us from seeing that what is said here *by both Quentin and Shreve* owes a great deal to Faulkner's special relationship with his region—and, because of this, can help us to understand just what this relationship involved. Contained within this exchange between the Southern boy and his roommate at Harvard are clues about Faulkner's "Southern-ness" that it would be wrong to ignore. Let us look at the clues offered by Quentin himself first, since it is he who makes the more immediately striking impression.

Quentin, as we have seen, cannot understand the South, its history and the nature of his own communication with it: the only way he can express himself, when he thinks about these things, is in contradictions and paradoxes, which gradually lapse into silence. He dislikes and even despises the South, he tells us several times, and yet he is irresistibly drawn toward it. He has tried to escape from the claustrophobic pressures of home and family, but he has succeeded only in taking those pressures with him wherever he goes. Another, earlier book, *The Sound and the Fury*, helps us to understand this problem of his a little more clearly, I think, because it describes his actual attempt at escape— and then goes beyond that to examine its disastrous consequences in detail. Like many other Southern boys before and after him, Quentin leaves his homeplace for the North. We are not told why, really, but we can guess: he is seeking personal freedom, a fresher and wider world than the one he has known in his youth. Unfortunately, though, a strong sense of doom seems to accompany him on his journey; and once arrived at his destination, in Cambridge, Massachusetts, he spends most of his time looking backward, acting out old memories even while they carry him irrevocably toward his death.

Examples are always more helpful than generalizations, so let me offer as an illustration of this Faulkner's account in *The Sound and the Fury* of Quentin's relationship with another young man he meets at university, Gerald Bland. Bland is the sort of character that is often supposed to be beyond Faulkner's scope—a delightfully comic figure, an American version of somebody like Jane Austen's Mr. Collins or George Meredith's Sir Willoughby Patterne, whose every gesture becomes an index of his social pretensions. With the help of endless, adoring comments from his mother—who is his constant companion— he tells us all we really need to know about the desperate pursuit of the genteel. Here is how Quentin, acting as narrator, introduces us to him.

> Bland . . . wore flannels, a grey jacket, and a stiff straw hat. Either he or his mother had read somewhere that Oxford students pulled in flannels and stiff hats, so early one March they bought Gerald a pair shell and in his flannels and stiff hat he went on the river. . . . They said his mother tried to make him give rowing up . . . but for once he was stubborn. If you could call it stubbornness, sitting in his attitudes of princely boredom, with his curly yellow hair and his violet eyes and his eyelashes, while his mamma was telling us about Gerald's horses and Gerald's niggers and Gerald's women.[2]

Mrs. Bland, Quentin goes on to tell us, approves of Gerald associating with him, "because I at least revealed a blundering sense of *noblesse oblige* by getting myself born below the Mason and Dixon line." But he, Quentin, is less than enthusiastic about the association. The reason why this is so is, I think, obvious enough: it is because Gerald reminds Quentin rather too uncomfortably of himself. Gerald's pretensions to gentility, it turns out, are a reflection of Quentin's own, comically exaggerated just enough to turn resemblance into parody. Gerald plays the gentleman and so does Quentin as soon as he reaches Harvard— with his companions, with the Negroes he meets on the streets of Cambridge and tries to patronize, and with the women whose honor he regards it as his duty to defend. On one level he is a sort of latter-day Don Quixote, a living anomaly: "the champion of dames," as his friend Spoade addresses him, "Bud, you excite not only admiration but horror." Small wonder, then, that the Blands are inclined to iden-tify Quentin with Southerners of the old school: Quentin himself, even though he may sometimes be amused by their opinion of him, acts in a way that seems precisely calculated to excite such an identification.

That is not the only reason for Quentin's reluctance to associate himself with Gerald, though. Quite apart from any conscious motives he may have for refusing the intimacy that both the Blands, but es-pecially the mother, appear to offer him there is the simple fact that Quentin could never relate to Gerald even if he wanted to because he keeps confusing him with somebody else. Try as he will, Quentin cannot help mistaking Gerald Bland for Dalton Ames, who was the lover many years ago of his sister Caddie. Quentin is always liable to drift away from the present into recollections of the past and, when-ever he is with the Blands, that liability seems to become a necessity. At such moments he acts like a sleep-walker; with his body existing in one dimension of time and his mind operating somewhere else, in another. Eventually he even strikes Gerald, under the impression that this is the seducer of his sister, and gets beaten up and knocked out for his pains. It is this episode, in fact, which prompts the remark made by Spoade that I have just quoted: despite all his efforts, Quentin re-mains a "champion of dames"—a perfect gentle knight in an age that has no use either for knights or chivalry. Borne back ceaselessly into a past compounded equally of childhood memories and legends of old times before the Civil War, he has about as much chance of under-standing his inheritance as a prisoner has of understanding his chains. He is too near the South, really, to make an objective assessment of it; which is why—to return to my original point—his silence, which con-cludes *Absalom, Absalom!*, seems such an inevitable response.

But if Quentin is too *near* to the South and the legacy it bequeaths, then Shreve, the other person involved in this final scene, is much too *far away*: that is the second inference we can draw from their ex-change. Quentin, as Shreve himself might have put it, is right in there, immersed in the legends he has inherited. Shreve, on the other hand, is so detached from them that he can end by reducing the entire story of Thomas Sutpen—the story, that is, which encapsulates the Southern past for both of them—to a kind of mathematics. It is a curious kind, because Shreve seems to be mocking the rigidity of his conclusions even while he formulates them. But that, when we look at it closely, turns out to be a further symptom of his detachment: he is so much the indifferent, distanced spectator, it seems, that he can stand back not only from the South but from his attitude toward the South as well—smiling at it and suggesting its possible limitations. It is as if suddenly one of Nabokov's or John Barth's heroes (Kinbote, say, in *Pale Fire* or Jake Horner in *The End of the Road*) had been asked to pass judgment on the regional myth and had succeeded in reducing this, along with everything else, to the status of an exercise—anthropologically interesting, perhaps, but not worthy of any genuine commitment. At best, the legends are theater, a spectacle exciting our amazement and applause ("Jesus, the South's fine, isn't it," Shreve says at one point in the book. "It's better than the theater, isn't it.");[3] and at worst, a shabby piece of self-deception. Either way, they are not something to be taken too seriously. That is Shreve's final verdict, I believe, and it might seem an attractive one initially—until, however, we remember that these legends *have* been taken very seriously in the past, seriously enough to affect the course of history, the way men think and nations behave. Unlike theater, they have helped shape the circumstances in which people live; they have cost lives and blood, and maybe still do.

What has all this got to do with Faulkner, though, and *his* relationship with his region—which is, after all, the subject we are concerned with now? The answer, I think, is very simple. Quentin Compson and his friend Shreve end up in equal difficulties: Quentin because he is too involved with the South ever to acquire satisfactory knowledge of it—he cannot stand back from it and see it whole—and Shreve because he stands back too far—from a distance the legends of the South may assume shape and completeness, but they are drained of all ordinary feeling. These are the different routes followed by the two friends; and in a way the problem of their creator, William Faulkner, has been to steer a course that improves upon them both—in pursuit of a third alternative that encompasses the attitudes both men adopt and then goes beyond them. The passage that ends *Absalom, Absalom!*, in other words, is much else besides, but on one level it belongs with poems like Yeats's "Ego Dominus Tuus" or John Berryman's "Dream Songs"; or with the kind of verse Wallace Stevens was thinking of when he said,

> . . . an invisible audience listens,
> Not to the play, but to itself, expressed

> In an emotion as of two people, as of two
> Emotions. . . .[4]

Quentin and Shreve are just like the two different people, the two masks expressing alternative possibilities, that Stevens describes here, and together they pose a single question—which is, how can one share in an experience (as Quentin does) and judge it (as Shreve does) as well? How can we be "in" history and "outside" it at one and the same time? The problem that dogged Faulkner throughout his career can be stated as simply as that, but not his answer to it—because, of course, the answer does not lie in this expressed opinion or in that but *in the imaginative discovery of Yoknapatawpha County.* Loving his inheritance and hating it, involved with its mythology and yet well aware of the difference between history and myth, Faulkner was in a sense obliged to create his fictional world—a paradigm of his region existing beyond established categories, where all that he had found in the South and felt about it could be absorbed into a coherent form of knowledge.

"Loving and hating": that phrase has cropped up several times, to describe a possible attitude toward the South, and with good reason. For whenever in his later years—when he was inclined to be more expansive on such matters—Faulkner was asked to talk about his home and his relationship to it, those two words, "loving" and "hating," came up almost inevitably, closely linked together. The article called "Mississippi," for instance, which he wrote for a travel magazine and then drastically revised, is more or less built around their opposition. Here is a typical passage.

> Home again, his native land; he was born of it and his bones will sleep in it; loving it even while hating some of it: the river jungle and the bordering hills where still a child he had ridden behind his father on the horse after the bobcat or fox or coon . . . most of all he hated the intolerance and injustice: the lynching of Negroes not for the crimes they committed but because their skins were black, . . . the inequality: the poor schools, . . . the hovels. . . . But he loves it, it is his, remembering . . . being waked . . . to have breakfast by lamplight in order to drive by surrey into town . . . to take the morning train for Memphis. . . . Even while hating it . . .[5]

The "he" mentioned here is the author himself, only very thinly disguised, and in fact the main interest of this article lies in its clearly autobiographical nature. It represents one of the few times Faulkner talked about himself, almost directly and at length. Characteristically, the personal facts are mixed with a great deal of fiction: Faulkner sets himself, variously described as "the young man," "the middleaged," or "the old man," in a place he prefers to call Jefferson rather than Oxford, Mississippi, and he populates this place with characters from his fiction rather than their real-life models whom he knew. But this in itself is significant, suggesting that (as I have said) he could only understand his inheritance in terms of the fictional masks which he devised for it—and which helped him to distance himself from it just a little: he needed Yoknapatawpha County in order to know Mississippi thoroughly, just as Twain needed St. Petersburg and Dawson's Landing in order to know his hometown of Hannibal, Missouri. And, in any case, it still leaves us with the initial pattern of autobiography unimpaired. The detail, the names and some of the anecdotes, may have been altered in the telling. But the sense of personal reference remains; and this, backed up with what little we know about Faulkner's life from other sources, can provide us, I think, with some further clues to the nature and implications of his "Southern-ness."

Faulkner was born, he tells us, of a family long settled in Mississippi and immersed in its legends. Indeed, his own great-grandfather William Clark Falkner (the "u" was added later to the family name by the author) was really a legend in his own right. Among many other exploits, he helped save a condemned murderer from a lynch mob. The murderer was so grateful, apparently, that he told his rescuer his life story; which was promptly written up, published, and then sold by the hundreds on the day of the official execution. That was not William Clark's only venture into the world of letters: he also wrote a romantic novel, called *The White Rose of Memphis*, which became a national best seller. He killed two of his enemies in violent quarrels and was himself killed, eventually, by a third enemy—who gunned him down on the streets of his hometown in broad daylight. He raised his own company, the Magnolia Rifles, during the Civil War, and after disagreements with his men returned home to recruit another. Then after the war he helped organize the construction of a railroad from Tennessee into his own part of the state. Violence and glamour were the peculiar features of his life and, exaggerated by the stories of several generations, provided the young Faulkner with a personal equivalent for the larger public myths: to the pantheon of regional heroes could be added the local figure of Colonel William, an intimate reminder of all that the South regarded as most captivating about its past. Not only that, the fact that the Colonel had been responsible for bringing the railroad to northern Mississippi meant that he, and by extension his family, were also implicated in the change from Old South into New. The Colonel had introduced the machine into the garden in his small corner of the world, and prepared the way for all the forces that were to make his own style of life an anomaly. So the awareness of new directions, along with the memory of dear dead days beyond recall, became a special property of the Falkner clan; on both counts it could find a regional commonplace confirmed in personal, or rather familial, experience.

William Faulkner himself grew up in the town of Oxford, Mississippi, to which his parents had moved a few years after his birth. Oxford at that time was a curious place, if only because it seemed to exist in several different worlds at once. As the home of the state university it had at least some pretensions to culture and learning, which was suggested by the presence within its boundaries of people like Phil Stone, a graduate and amateur man of letters who helped encourage William's interest in literature. But it was still a small town in the Deep South, and could not help being affected by that fact. Nor could it help being affected, I think, by the baffling richness and variety of the surrounding countryside—where, as Faulkner puts it in his essay, "the . . . sons of Virginia and Carolina planters" lived side by side with "the tall man roaring with Protestant scripture and whisky"[6] and the great landowner looked out over his holdings to the fields of the poor farmer, white or black. Oxford, Faulkner tells us, was close to both plantation and backwoods at the beginning of the century. It bordered on the world where cotton was king and the world where the poor man scratched a meager living from the soil; and the two met, even if they did not mingle, on its streets. What is even more interesting, as a boy Faulkner was largely unprotected from either of these worlds, or for that matter from the life of the ghetto, because his immediate family, apparently, were considerably less wealthy than their predecessors had been. Murry Falkner, William's father, was an impractical, lackadaisical man who spent most of his time drifting from one occupation to another, only to sink finally and with some relief into the post of business manager at the university. This job might have been pleasant enough, certainly there were no arduous duties attached to it, had it not been for the fact that then as now the state of Mississippi paid its public servants as little as it possibly could for their labors. So the life Murry offered to his children continued to be what it had always been, one of more or less genteel poverty. It could give them little shelter from their surroundings; in a sense, because it was so fluid and uncertain, it even seemed to reflect those surroundings. There was no chance of that fairly cloistered upbringing that, say, Thomas Wolfe or—at another point in the social scale—Katherine Anne Porter experienced. While he was growing up, Faulkner found himself exposed to all the forces and changes operative in his neighborhood; of necessity he knew both rich and poor, as well as those in between, both Negro and white—and, as things turned out, it was to the distinct advantage of his work that he did.

Even as a young man, Faulkner's relationship with the South was not simply a passive one, though: he was not just a blank sheet of paper to be stamped with the imprint of his locality. In fact, by the time he was old enough to be really interested in literature, he had adopted a stance of conscious rebellion against both the legends of the Falkner clan and the small-town mores of Oxford, Mississippi. His earliest creative work, some of it published in the university magazine, illustrates this. It smacks of conscious defiance, a deliberate attempt to shock his elders and shrug off the traditions they wanted to hand down to him. The prose pieces recall the writers of the nineties whom Faulkner was reading avidly at the time, people like Oscar Wilde and Walter Pater, the sketches are pale imitations of Aubrey Beardsley, while the poetry, which makes up much the largest portion of this work, sounds like the Symbolistes at their very worst.

> I follow through the singing trees
> Her streaming clouded hair and face
> And lascivious dreaming knees
> Like gleaming water from some place
> Of sleeping streams, or autumn leaves
> Slow shed through still, love-wearied air.[7]

Verse like this, mellifluous, occasionally bizarre, breathing an atmosphere of languor and decay, is virtually a parody of the writers the young Faulkner admired so much: but it had its importance, I think, in providing him with the sort of verbal equivalent he needed for his confused feelings of revolt. It was on a par with his playacting among friends and relatives—the role of literary eccentric, born out of his due time, which he went about earning for himself with a quite painful deliberateness. He wore the most flamboyant clothes he could find, complete with walking stick (which he is said to have introduced to the Mississippi campus); later, he assumed an air of almost aggressive laziness in his job as university postmaster. And he soon received an appropriate reward for his pains by being dubbed "Count No Count" by his neighbors. When to this notoriety was added his membership of the local "fast set," such as it was, then his break with Oxford seemed just about complete.

It *was* apparently complete a few years later, when Faulkner left his hometown to go first to cosmopolitan New Orleans and then subsequently to Europe. There he met people who had never even visited Mississippi, let alone been influenced by it, and in their company the prospects for liberation from that faraway country seemed greater than ever before. Of particular help to him among these new acquaintances was the novelist and short-story writer Sherwood Anderson, because his work was actually about liberation, the escape from the stifling atmosphere of home—which in his case meant the Midwest. Anderson encouraged Faulkner to devote himself to fiction and at the same time introduced him to some of the new directions being taken in the literature of the twenties: the sense of disillusionment that was fast becoming a commonplace among American writers, for example, their disgust with their country and, more particularly, with the norms of the small town. Faulkner, an eager pupil, learned quickly and worked hard, and in 1926 his work bore fruit with the appearance of *Soldier's Pay,* his first novel. Not surprisingly, the book showed distinct traces of Anderson's influence. There were the same feelings of weary self-pity that characterized many of Anderson's stories, the same vague longing for a better life than the one offered within the confines of the imagined place. The characters in *Soldier's Pay* recalled Anderson's, too, suffering as they did from strange disabilities that reduced them to half-beings in a half-alive world. All the clues were there, to indicate the school to which Faulkner had gone and the man who had been his teacher, but within a few short months following completion of the book they had already become misleading. For about the time *Soldier's Pay* was published, to sink quickly into oblivion, Faulkner broke with Anderson, emphasizing the break by contributing a cruel parody of his work to *Sherwood Anderson and Other Famous Creoles.* Not only that, he rejected the cosmopolitan life and even the cosmopolitan pose to return home to Mississippi for good.

Faulkner was back in his home state, and even before his return he was beginning to write about it in what was, for him, an entirely new way. Its story now fascinated him—what he called its "glamorous fatality" as well as other, more earth-bound qualities which he had once rejected in favor of cosmopolitanism. His third novel, *Sartoris,* published in 1929, witnesses the change. Faulkner said about it later:

> Beginning with *Sartoris* I discovered that my own little postage stamp of native soil was worth writing about, and that by sublimating the actual into the apocryphal I would have complete liberty to use whatever talent I might have to its absolute top. It opened up a gold mine of other people, so I created a cosmos of my own.[8]

With *Sartoris,* in fact, began the chronicles of Yoknapatawpha County. They did not, of course, spring full grown from Faulkner's head: he built them up slowly, adding a character here or altering a detail there, so that they have a repetitive, incremental pattern rather than a strictly chronological or logically consistent one. We need not infer from this, though, that (as some critics have argued) Faulkner was ever unaware of what he was doing *in principle*. Far from it, his aims— if not their detailed consequences—were, I believe, quite clear to him from the first; he was trying, as he knew, to create a microcosm of history. By this I mean he was attempting (in an infinitely more ambitious way than in his article on Mississippi) to capture the essence of his region, its story compounded of legend and fact and the nature of his own involvement with it. Certainly, he may have kept returning to the same episodes while he was writing the series, often changing his interpretation of them as he did so. But this, instead of working against his general aims, actually helped him to fulfill them: because he was thereby adopting the classic procedure of the kind of historian he wanted to be—which is that of continually reenacting and recomposing the past. One reason why the story of Yoknapatawpha is such a convincing imitation of the story of the South, in other words, is precisely this, that it *does not have a predetermined, linear pattern*. Thanks to Faulkner's habit of writing and revising it over a number of years, it is founded—much more clearly than the work of any other Southern writer—on a dialectic between today and yesterday, a sustained engagement of event with memory.

But why was Faulkner suddenly so concerned with the South? What had provoked this change of interest? Really, we have to guess here, since there is not enough known about his inner life, at this or indeed at any other time, to provide us with a definite answer. We cannot know for certain why he ever did what he did: but surely it is reasonable to suggest that (as he hints in "Mississippi") Faulkner came back to his homeplace because he had never been as alienated from it as he had liked to think, and a prolonged stay elsewhere had helped him to realize this. He left Mississippi and, for a while, the South only to learn that, if he belonged anywhere at all, *that* was where he belonged; in becoming an exile for a while he discovered a part of his inheritance. The experience, as we know already, was not an uncommon one. Most of the Agrarians were going through it at about the same time Faulkner was; and, if Faulkner differed from them at all, it was only in the intensity of his reaction. Unlike Ransom and his colleagues he returned to the South hardly to venture out of it again, except for such necessary excursions as his visits to his publisher in New York, or his trips to Hollywood to write a film script. It even became something of a habit with him to claim that he was a farmer rather than a writer—one of the locals who enjoyed hunting, fishing, and working in the fields more than anything else. Such claims should not be taken too seriously, of course—any more seriously than Congreve's insistence that he was a gentleman first and a dramatist second. But they do

help to indicate how aware Faulkner had become of his attachment
to his place, and just how much he felt like shedding his earlier role
of rootless bohemian.

We may seem to have come a long way from the original problem
posed, in that passage I quoted from *Absalom, Absalom!*, by Quentin
Compson and Shreve. But what I am trying to suggest about Faulkner's biography is briefly this: that his own life provided him with a
means of solving that problem, or at least with the *beginnings* of a
solution. During his lifetime he encountered virtually everything
there was to encounter in the South, its poverty and its wealth, its
nostalgia and its ambitions for the future; and in reacting to all this he
experienced the extremes of detachment and participation. He even
invented roles for himself to cope with these extremes and express
them in a rather simplified fashion: first that of the young cosmopolitan with no fixed abode, and then that of the crusty provincial. True,
the roles were acted out separately. But that was because they were,
as I say, simplifications. There is no reason to suppose that Faulkner
was incapable of entertaining both, or at least some of the attitudes
that dictated both, at one and the same time—and of *using* both when
it came to writing the Yoknapatawpha novels. He knew what it was
to be an observer, a detached analyst of his region and what it was
to belong, to share in the memories and dreams of his neighbors; and
probably, when he wanted to, he could adopt the two stances simultaneously. He could (and perhaps had to) see himself as at once a
stranger and a brother to the South, an outsider with roots deeply
embedded in its history—which is why, I think, in the books he wrote
about his "own little postage stamp of native soil" he could place
people like Quentin and Shreve in terms of something better.

There is another reason for thinking that Faulkner had this special,
double-edged relationship with his locality, and recognized he did:
which is simply that the kind of paradoxes it could create are re-
produced, many of them, in his characters. The people he describes
in his fiction are often cut off from their neighbors—thanks to their
superior intelligence, perhaps, or more simply their eccentricity—and
yet they still manage to perform a representative function. They are
tied by indissoluble bonds to Yoknapatawpha society because they
share in and dramatize some of its beliefs, but they never fully belong
there. Thomas Sutpen, the great, ante-bellum planter commemorated
in *Absalom, Absalom!*, is the sort of character I am referring to; and
so is Nathaniel Burden, whose speech about the "curse" of the Negro I quoted in an earlier chapter. Both remain outsiders throughout
their lives and yet are somehow *of* the South: like Nick Carraway in
The Great Gatsby, they are within and without, simultaneously a part

of and apart from the imagined community. Or there is Drusilla Hawk, the curiously manlike figure who dominates some of the stories in *The Unvanquished.*

> . . . Aunt Louisa was trying to tell us how . . . when Gavin Breckbridge was killed at Shiloh before he and Drusilla had had time to marry, there had been reserved for Drusilla the highest destiny of Southern woman— to be the bride-widow of a lost cause—and how Drusilla had not only thrown that away, she had not only become a lost woman and a shame to her father's memory but she was now living in a word that Aunt Louisa would not even repeat . . . then we found out what it was: how Drusilla had been gone for six months and no word from her . . . and then one night she walked into the cabin . . . *in the garments not alone of a man but of a . . . soldier . . .*[9]

Drusilla is a good example of social ambivalence in Faulkner's work, "belonging" and yet "not belonging," because her estrangement from her community is a direct result of her commitment to one of its obsessions. She is devoted, as this passage suggests, to the militaristic spirit of the South and the soldier's code of honor and chivalry. What makes this devotion queer in her case, of course, is the simple fact that she is a woman. By adopting a role that, although time-honored, is considered utterly inappropriate for *her,* she becomes a conformist and rebel at one and the same time; as her stepson Bayard Sartoris II, who is the speaker here, suspects, she manages both to represent and defy inherited norms.

But it is not necessary to labor the point by citing endless examples now. Others will occur to us naturally as we go along, looking at some of the major novels in more detail. For the moment all we need remember is how, and how very much, Faulkner's personal experience fed into his work: the paradoxes of his life and character, and the sheer range and variety of his inheritance, enabled him to know more about his region than almost any of his contemporaries—and they also helped him to adopt a stance that, while it might be full of contradictions initially, was also rich in creative possibilities. It did not, of course, provide him with all the answers he required. Only his imaginative discovery of Yoknapatawpha even approached doing that. But it gave him the raw material he needed for a more or less complete version of the South and clues as to how, ideally, it should be treated. Faulkner said once, in an interview, that what he wanted to do in his fiction was "reduce . . . [his] one individual experience of the world into a compact thing which could be picked up and held in the hand at the same time";[10] and one way of measuring the scope and importance of the "individual experience" he refers to here is to say that it was this, above all, which made his task as a writer so difficult and yet, in the history of Southern literature, so very central.

"One Inimical, Irreconcilable Square of Dirt": The Farmer in Yoknapatawpha County

Not so very long ago, when William Faulkner first began to claim the serious attention of critics in fact, it was fashionable to describe him as a man in love with the dream of the old plantation. Admittedly, he had raised the conventional genre of plantation romance to a higher level, by avoiding the easy nostalgia of John Pendleton Kennedy and the confused idealism of some of the Agrarians, but, it was argued, he still subscribed to many of the beliefs implicit in that genre. His basic strategy was roughly the same as his predecessors' was, and so, really, were his prejudices. George Marion O'Donnell, in an essay written for John Crowe Ransom's journal the *Kenyon Review,* provided what was perhaps the most influential expression of this point of view.

> William Faulkner is . . . a traditional moralist. . . . One principle holds together his . . . books. . . . That principle is the Southern social-economic-ethical tradition . . . his novels are, primarily, a series of related myths . . . built around the conflict between traditionalism and the anti-traditional modern world. . . . On one side of the conflict there are the Sartorises, recognizable human beings who act traditionally. Against them the invading Northern armies and their . . . allies. . . . The invaders are unable to cope with the Sartorises; but their invasion provides another antagonist with an occasion within which his special anti-Sartoris talent makes him singularly powerful. This antagonist is the landless poor-white horse trader, Ab Snopes: his special talent is his low cunning . . .[11]

The essay was called "Faulkner's Mythology"; and if we take "mythology" in its commonplace, colloquial sense, meaning a fairy tale or flight of fancy, then I think the title has a certain kind of inadvertent appropriateness. For despite the praise O'Donnell showered upon Faulkner, all he actually did when it came to describing his books was reduce them to tales of cavalier heroics. In looking at the Yoknapatawpha series, he saw only what he chose to see there—which was well-worn allegory, a contrast between gallant aristocrat and corrupt poor white that hardly made up in neatness and boldness for what it lacked in originality.

Some of the things that O'Donnell, and others like him, failed to notice have been pointed out by more recent commentators, among them Edmond Volpe, who argued quite rightly that Faulkner could be almost savage in his criticism of the Sartorises and the legends gathered around them when he wanted to be, and Cleanth Brooks, who has described the social diversity of Yoknapatawpha in some detail.[12] This has gone some of the way toward correcting earlier misconceptions. But in spite of that there is still a fairly common tendency, among both professional critics and readers in general, to associate Faulkner with the aristocratic strain in Southern thought; and to assume that the part of his fiction that deals with old Southern families and decaying mansions more or less accounts for the whole. Very often, if we were simply to read discussions of Faulkner's work rather than the work itself, we would be left with the impression that his real interest lies with the privileged, the powerful, or those once powerful who have fallen on hard times, and that he is concerned with the lives of the poorer inhabitants of his region only in so far as they are relevant to this.

No impression could, I think, be more misleading. To accept such an interpretation of Faulkner's work it is necessary to ignore a good half of it, and to forget that the barriers that Yoknapatawpha society erects between the privileged and the dispossessed are fairly easily surmountable. There is an extraordinary richness and fluidity about Faulkner's portrait of his environment, even on the simple journalistic level of reporting what he has seen, and that necessarily means an avoidance of the kind of mythologizing that would identify the Sartoris family with tradition first and last, or their homeplace with the entire South. Existing alongside the plantation order the Sartorises represent, sometimes mingling with it but always retaining its separate identity, is another world altogether that has nothing at all to do with vast cotton fields, slaves, or bold cavalry charges against the Yankees. We are reminded of it, briefly but eloquently, when Faulkner describes the life of one, minor character in *The Hamlet.*

> . . . at home there was that work waiting, the constant and unflagging round of repetitive nerve-and-flesh wearing labor by which alone that piece of earth which was his mortal enemy could fight him with [sic], which he had performed yesterday and must perform again tomorrow and tomorrow, alone and unassisted or else knock under . . . —this until the day came when (he knew this too) he would stumble and plunge, his eyes still open and his empty hands stiffening into the shape of the plow-handles, into the furrow behind the plow, or topple into a weedy ditch . . .[13]

The sheer sense of effort generated here, among other things by the contorted syntax and the repetitive, polysyllabic vocabulary, establishes the difference between the life of this one anonymous man and the leisurely habits of the Sartorises. For this is the domain of the small, and usually poor, farmer, with its own dangers and its own sort of heroism—the sort, perhaps we could say, that stubbornly confronts the ordinary instead of attempting to transcend it. Clearly, it lacks the glamour of the old plantation, but, for all that, it—and the values it embodies, the way of life it consecrates—forms as honorable a part of the Southern tradition as the planter's world does.

Before we get completely carried away, though, and transform every poor farmer Faulkner has ever described into an emblem of stoic fortitude, it is as well to remind ourselves that this is only one man; with certain representative features, maybe, but otherwise possessing qualities that help distinguish him from all of his neighbors. He does not account for the whole of Faulkner's estimate of the farmer, any more than the Sartorises account for his total assessment of the South. One reason for this will seem obvious, really, as soon as it is mentioned: there *are* particular virtues Faulkner ascribes to his farming characters, perhaps, but they are discovered in the individual, imagined situation rather than imposed upon it. Full credit is always given to the complexity of the personal case. Another reason, though, that is just as important is probably less self-evident, since it depends not only on how Faulkner treats the inherited legend but on the nature, the established range and scope, of the legend itself. Long before Faulkner began work on the Yoknapatawpha novels, the Jeffersonian argument had (as we have seen) assumed a number of very different literary forms: in particular it had been responsible—that is, supplied the ideological basis—for epic narratives like *Barren Ground* (where the farmer was seen as a noble creature, who had at least achieved a moral victory over his surroundings) and also for comedies such as *Sut Lovingood's Yarns* (where humor was used, essentially, to measure the extent of the poor farmer's defeat). Faulkner's special achievement, I think, was that he opted not for one or other of these extremes but for both; in other words, that his version of the farming community and the Jeffersonian myth was based on a full acknowledgement of their latent contradictions rather than the more usual, and more convenient, attempt to neglect them. Certainly there are people in his work, like that minor character in *The Hamlet,* who recall Kennedy's Horse-Shoe Robinson or Ellen Glasgow's farmers more than anybody else, because they have the same courage and capacity for endurance that those earlier heroes have, and possibly the same general ability to set will above circumstance. But just as many of his characters must remind us of Sut Lovingood and other peasant grotesques; even more to the point, there are a few here and there who manage to seem victorious and defeated, heroic and comic, at one and the same time.

But let us go back to the heroic dimension of Faulkner's portrait for a moment, since there is a lot more to be said about it than I have said so far. Even in his most idealized form, which is rare in the Yoknapatawpha series, Faulkner's yeoman is quite unlike his previous avatars because he is neither as uncomplicated nor as insubstantial as they normally are. Take Virginius MacCallum, for instance, a mountain man who appears in several of the short stories and novels. At first sight, he seems to have stepped straight out of folk tale or legend to illustrate the best that was ever thought and said about the man who owns his own land.

> In 1861 he was sixteen and he had walked to Lexington, Virginia, and enlisted, served four years in the Stonewall brigade and walked back to Mississippi and built himself a house and got married. His wife's *dot* was a clock and a dressed hog; his own father gave them a mule. His wife was dead these many years, and her successor, . . . but he sat now before the fireplace at which that hog had been cooked, beneath the roof he had built in '66, and on the mantel above him the clock sat, deriding that time whose servant it had once been.[14]

This, like the passage quoted earlier from *The Hamlet,* hovers dangerously close to sentimentalism or strained heroics: but it hovers near them with a sort of conscious bravado, I think, only to evade them. Faulkner is always taking the kind of risks, with language and feeling, that most of his contemporaries (both inside and outside the South) would never dare take. What saves him usually, though, is his respect for the hard edges of the real—his recognition, among other things, of the commonplace, grim details of his characters' lives. Here, for example, our attention is concentrated finally on a few small things, a log cabin, a clock, a hog, and a mule. These particulars surround and in a sense define Virginius MacCallum's existence. Together with some memories of times out of the ordinary, they describe the limits within which his heroism is exercised and beyond which it cannot go; and in doing this they also help anchor that heroism firmly in our world, in a tangible, historical time and place.

This, as I say, represents one extreme in Faulkner's portrait of the poorer members of his community—an *experienced* form of heroism, a type of courage or if you will nobility that is felt and located rather than merely invoked. The other is suggested by characters who appear, when we first meet them, to be just like Erskine Caldwell's—until, that is, we discover that Faulkner's attitude toward these people is much more complicated than Caldwell's ever could be. Caldwell (as we saw in an earlier chapter) takes the distancing tendencies he finds in Southwestern humor and then exaggerates them, so as to turn his people into problems. He wants us to stand back from his characters, recognize their suffering, and then consider possible means of rehabilitation; and to achieve this his chief guide is George Washington Harris, a writer coming almost at the end of the humorist tradition who emphasizes the deprivations and stunted potential of his country folk. Faulkner is aware of this strategy and employs it too, but, unlike Caldwell, he does not allow it to dictate his entire approach. He uses folk humor, not merely to criticize and place, but to celebrate. What he is after besides historical analysis is some sense of involvement in peasant life—its raw energy and the excitement that can occasionally spill over into violence—and for this his models are the people at the beginning of the humorist tradition rather than those at the end, whose undeclared purpose it was to honor the gusty pleasures of the life they described. They include, in fact, all those anonymous balladeers and amateur story tellers, firmly allied with the folk, on whom Longstreet and his successors depended for much of their material.

Perhaps Faulkner's achievement here will be clearer if we look at one example of his use of the Southwestern tradition: at his treatment, say, of the theme of barter—the cunning trader who outwits his neighbors in some apparently fair exchange of goods. The theme is a common enough one in folk tale, dating back to the time of the ancient Greeks and finding expression nowadays in the slightly bastardized form of jokes about commercial travelers and used-car salesmen; and in America, the land of opportunity and the fast buck, it has been so popular that it has become virtually a separate genre. Of course, its very popularity has stemmed largely from the fact that it can be used for various purposes, and mean different things to different people. But among the folk of the old Southwest, at least, there was one attitude more commonly associated with it than most, which was that of wonder—a sort of naïve envy of the trickster, springing from a genuine admiration for his gifts. This reached its apotheosis in the story of the horse swap, where the trader was shown using his Odyssean cunning to exchange a bad horse for a good one. The reasons why this particular type of story should find such favor among frontier people are, I suppose, fairly obvious. A horse swap was the kind of exchange that would really seem important to both the story teller and his audience because a horse was a sure sign of wealth, security, and mobility in those days, an asset more tangible and necessary than any bank account could be. On top of that, the dressing up of a bad horse to make it look attractive was something that would appeal to the folk as an art, an intriguing end in itself as much as a means to personal gain. Any possible uneasiness the trickster's lying aroused could, consequently, be allayed, dissolved into a pleasurable interest in his sleights of hand and inventions, the various and invariably elaborate forms this lying assumed. The trickster was not just seen as a trickster, in fact, but as a magician or a joker—somebody who had profit only as one of his motives.

Characteristically, most of the humorists used this folk-theme of horse swapping somewhere in their work. Longstreet for example, the first of them, has a story that is actually called "The Horse-Swap" in his *Georgia Scenes*. The tale it tells is a familiar one: a horse-trader who does not even try to conceal his delight in his own cunning is outwitted by another member of his fraternity who poses as a simpleton. What raises it slightly above the commonplace, though, is the way in which Longstreet describes this event—as a ritual, a contest of skill that attracts the interest of the entire community because the skills being tested are held in general esteem. The enjoyment of the folk, in other words, becomes an actual subject of the story rather than a given condition of its being. The audience is there as a participant in the action.

> The removal of the blanket disclosed a sore on Bullet's [the horse's] backbone that seemed to have defied all medical skill. It measured six full inches in length and four in breadth, and had as many features as Bullet had motions. . . . The prevailing feeling . . . was that of mirth. The laugh became loud and general at the old man's [the worsted trader's] expense, and rustic witticisms were liberally bestowed upon him and his late purchase. These Blossom [the other trader] continued to provoke by various remarks. . . . He declared most seriously that he had owned that horse three months, and . . . never discovered . . . that . . . sore back, "or he should never have thought of trading him," &c, &c[15]

If this passage shows something of Longstreet's achievement in the story it also, I think, suggests his limitations. The spectators may share in the excitement of the contest, but *we* are hardly allowed to because the voice of the narrator, polite, genteel, intent on placing his subject, establishes an unbridgeable gap between them and us. In one way this may be no bad thing since, of course, a gap does exist and it would be useless to ignore it: they are "the folk," operating as a cohesive, established group, and we are literate, and probably town-dwelling outsiders—who know as little about the rules of barter as they or rather their real-life counterparts would know about present-day laws of purchase and credit. But in another sense this detachment Longstreet forces us into *is* unfortunate because, thanks to it, we are prevented from understanding his characters properly, from enjoying the kind of knowledge of them and their customs that only an act of imaginative sympathy can give. Such knowledge would not (indeed should not) obliterate the sense of difference, but it would help us to see these people in their own right, as men and women rather than anthropological specimens, and to understand exactly how their experience relates or is relevant to our own.

Where Longstreet failed, Faulkner succeeded. Faulkner deals with the horse-swapping theme in a novel I have mentioned already, *The Hamlet,* the first part of the Snopes trilogy and the one most deeply involved in peasant life; and not content with one stab at it, he has two. The first example of horse trading occurs very early on in the book. It concerns the time when Ab Snopes crossed swords with Pat Stamper, a man who has the reputation of being one of the slickest traders in the state. Ab, we are told, tried to sell Pat a horse which he (Pat) had sold to Ab some eight years earlier, offering the best mule in the Snopes family's team as a sort of lure or bait. He succeeded, but received by way of payment a pair of mules that stood up only long enough to get him halfway home. Returning to the scene of the exchange, he swapped mules with Stamper again, this time acquiring a fine-looking bay mare together with a worn-out, fly-blown mule as makeweight. Too late, he discovered he had been fooled a second time (or, if we care to go back eight years, a third): the mare, as it turned out, was the very horse he had sold to Stamper in the first place— which Stamper's Negro stable-boy had disguised with the help of a coat of brown paint and a bicycle pump inserted in its belly to make it swell up. Ab was left at the end of the day with the horse he had been trying to get rid of, plus a poor mule in exchange for his good one! These are the bare bones of the story, involving the familiar idea of the trickster being hoist on his own petard. But what gives these bones life and flesh—what distinguishes this story from, say, "The Horse-Swap"—is Faulkner's choice of narrator. V. K. Ratliff, the itinerant salesman who acts as unofficial reporter and historian to the poor folk of the county, tells us everything that happened. And his voice, which is that of a man speaking to and about friends, colors the entire incident.

> "But that nigger [Stamper's stable-boy] was a artist. Because I swear to God them mules looked all right. They looked exactly like two ordinary, not extra good mules you might see in a hundred wagons on the road. I had done realised they had a kind of jerky way of starting off, . . . but then Stamper had just told us they were a matched team; he never said they had ever worked together as a matched team. . . ."[16]

This, really, is the edge Faulkner has over most of his predecessors here, the other writers who have used the trickster theme. Ratliff, the story teller, is telling us about his own people, with whom he shares a certain idiom and a distinct system of values—which is why his comments reveal exactly that sense of humor, humanity, and respect for native cunning ("he never said they had ever worked together") probably responsible for the popularity of horse-swapping tales among his neighbors. Just by speaking he reminds us of the folk community, invokes its traditions. And by speaking *to us*, by drawing us into the special world of his language, he seems to be asking us to become part of that community for a moment. As participants, members of the audience along with the people of Frenchman's Bend, the experience of the folk becomes ours temporarily—or, if not ours exactly, something with which we can feel a real, deep sympathy.

Faulkner works a similar effect upon his readers, of being at once inside and outside the action, in his second tale about horse swapping, which is the famous episode of the "spotted horses." Here the trickery takes place on a much larger scale because the entire neighborhood appears to be duped. One day, we are told, Flem Snopes drove into Frenchman's Bend accompanied by a stranger from Texas and leading a string of wild ponies behind him. With the entire day given over to the auction, the Texan then proceeded to sell these ponies to half the local community while the other half looked on with mingled feelings of excitement and envy. Finally, when the sale was completed and people came forward to collect their purchases, the horses suddenly broke loose from the corral, galloped through the hamlet creating havoc wherever they went, and then disappeared—returning presumably to the place from which they had been taken. The account of the day (although not of the subsequent litigation) ends with a description of this stampede.

> . . . the men whirled and ran before a gaudy vomit of long wild faces and splotched chests which overtook . . . them and flung them sprawling aside . . . to crash through the gate which the last man through it had neglected to close, leaving it slightly ajar, carrying all of the gate save the upright . . . with them, and so among the teams and wagons which choked the lane, the teams springing and lunging too. . . . Then the whole inextricable mass crashed among the wagons . . . and rushed down the lane. . . .[17]

Again, it is Faulkner's use of language that determines how we respond to these events. Its energy is a verbal equivalent for the energy of peasant life, its raw violence and color such that we are reminded possibly of the paintings of Brueghel. But V. K. Ratliff is not the narrator this time; he hardly appears during the course of the action, and when he does it is merely as one of the spectators, passing his comments along with the rest. Nor is any other, individual character. Instead, the basic story is told to us by a voice that bears the accents of Frenchman's Bend but remains unassigned. It is the voice, in fact, of the community; the tale of the Texas ponies is part of the common history, the collective memory of the folk, and it is as such that we hear about it.

Put like that it may sound as if we are told everything in a strictly impersonal way, as in a ballad. That is not the case, though, and the reason for this is that Faulkner, as he goes along, manages to add other and quite different inflections of speech or dimensions of commentary to his story. At the very beginning of the tale, for instance, he places us firmly within the *ambiance* of Frenchman's Bend by a very simple device: turning from the anonymous narrator for a moment he allows the conversation and comment of a few bystanders to establish a perspective on Flem Snopes's arrival. The result is rather like those moments in Hardy when we are asked to stand back with the locals—people who have never left Wessex and are never likely to—to witness the appearance of an invader; necessarily, we are drawn closer to them, because we share in their reactions and their sense of distance from the man they describe.

> A little before sundown the men lounging about the gallery of the store saw, coming up the road from the south, a covered wagon drawn by mules and followed by a considerable string of obviously alive objects which in the levelling sun resembled vari-sized and colored tatters torn at random from large billboards. . . .
> "What in hell is that?" one said.
> "It's a circus," Quick said. . . .
> "Hell fire," the first man—his name was Freeman—said. "It's Flem Snopes."[18]

The comments pass back and forth, question and answer, statement and response, and slowly a portrait is built up—an intimate portrait, seen from the inside, of that community which is equally the admiring witness and the amazed victim of the horse trade. Some of this intimacy then in turn carries over into those moments when the individual vantage point is lost and we are returned to the anonymous narrator— since, even without the help of Quick and Freeman, the auctioneer is still usually seen as "the stranger" and the horses he brings with him remain subjects of wonder. A sense of communion is sustained because the voice, or at least the perspective it establishes, does not necessarily change even when its source does.

Communion there may be, but it is never quite perfect; the feelings of intimacy aroused by the story are always less than complete. Why? Because, really, of what I have suggested already: Faulkner's intention is not to reject all sense of difference between us and his folk characters, but to make us respond with them *even while we are aware of our separateness from them*. We must, he feels, know them for their relevance as cases—representative types of the rural life, and the traditions it fosters—quite as much as for their close connections with ourselves; and his way of ensuring that we do this is to use language occasionally to *draw us back* from the scene. Every now and then another idiom will be employed, quite different from the ones I have mentioned, more elegant and self-consciously sophisticated, which establishes our status as spectators as effectively as a camera moving away from close-up into long shot. Here is an example of what I mean. It occurs about halfway through the story.

> "That's a fact," Ratliff said, "A fellow can dodge a Snopes if he just starts lively enough. . . . You folks ain't going to buy them things sho enough, are you?" Nobody answered. They sat on the steps, their backs against the veranda posts, or on the railing itself. Only Ratliff and Quick sat in chairs, so that to them the others were black silhouettes against the dreaming lambence of the moonlight beyond the veranda. The pear tree across the road opposite was now in full and frosty bloom, the twigs and branches springing not outward from the limbs but standing motionless and perpendicular above the horizontal boughs like the separate and upstreaming hair of a drowned woman sleeping upon the uttermost floor of the windless and tideless sea.[19]

The distancing movement is beautifully graduated here, I think. We move, quickly but in a smooth, uninterrupted way, from the dialect of individual folk characters to a more neutral style and then on to the kind of densely figurative, "high profile" language which, by calling attention to itself, places everything it describes at several removes from us. At the end, the sense of detachment is unavoidable; thanks in particular to the baroque image of drowning, which is about as remote from the world of Ratliff and his kind as the idioms of Quentin Compson and his father (both of whom might well have used such an image in thought or conversation) are. Words act finally as a screen separating us from the characters, and the sort of screen which seems intended to remind us of our own comparative sophistication by parodying it. On both counts, we are prevented from making a sentimental identification with the inhabitants of Frenchman's Bend—breezily ignoring the necessary distinctions of class, time and place. We can share in the humor of the folk, Faulkner implies, and consequently learn something about their traditions, but we cannot dissolve our identities, our experience and language, into theirs. Not only cannot but should not, since in order to know these people thoroughly we *must* apparently stand apart from them sometimes; we must participate in their history and also step aside from it occasionally so as to take a larger, more inclusive view. That seems to be the belief implicit in Faulkner's handling of the horse-swapping episodes in *The Hamlet,* and his excursions into folk comedy in general; and it is perhaps one of the reasons for their unique character and success.

The trouble with trying to define anything in Faulkner's novels is that sooner or later the definitions begin to break down under the pressure of the accumulating evidence; for all their apparent accuracy, they have to be qualified as soon as they are invoked. The moment, for example, that we really try to explain what Faulkner wants us to feel about his folk characters, the sort of response he is hoping to elicit, we find that conventional classifications are far too restrictive and we are forced to use apparently self-contradictory phrases like "sympathetic detachment." Equally, when we try to work out just what Faulkner understands by the term "small farmer," we discover that it includes radically different types: the patriarchal, independent figure of Virginius MacCallum jostles with the peasants of Frenchman's Bend and genuine "po' white trash" like Ab Snopes for our attention. No distinction can hold still for very long after it is applied to the world of Yoknapatawpha, and this for the simple reason that Faulkner's work seems to depend for much of its excitement on the actual engagement between the closed world of definitions and the open spaces of raw experience. Any category he uses (and which, subsequently, we may use to understand his work) serves him only in a provisional way; once adopted it is continually being modified or subverted—changed, in fact, by the mass of conflicting particulars that Faulkner feeds into it. To some extent, this could provide us with an explanation for Faulkner's special use of language—that is, if we accept the fairly commonplace notion that language contains within it its own implicit values and categories, a certain way of structuring the world. Faulkner, we could say, stretches words and syntax to the limits for the same reason he stretches categories: so as to squeeze new meanings out of the conflict between the rules and the occasions which those rules are meant to (but do not quite) circumscribe. All I want to do for the moment, however, is to point out how this general principle of Faulkner's—of never letting anything stay undisturbed by its contrary—applies as much to his use of the comic and heroic versions of the folk character as it does to anything else. Of course, the two versions are there to be distinguished; Faulkner necessarily learned them from different people anyway (probably from favorite authors like Ellen Glasgow, George Washington Harris, and Longstreet). But each of them, the low note of peasant comedy and the higher note clearly echoing Jefferson, is there usually just as every received element in his work is there: to be quickened into life by contact with individual experience—and to acquire form and strength in the same way the rib of a Gothic arch does, from the counterthrust of its opposite.

Let me offer, as an illustration of the kind of tension I am talking about now, a major character in *Light in August* called Byron Bunch.

On first reading, he comes across as something of a conventional figure: the comic lover, forlorn and a little self-conscious, who is subjected to daily humiliations by his mistress. This, for example, is the last we hear of him in the novel, when he is trying yet again to conquer the object of his affections, Lena Grove—whom he has decided to accompany on her journey around the South in search of the father of her child.

> '. . . she [Lena] went and climbed into the truck and after a while . . . I knew that she had done got fixed to sleep. . . . I heard him [Bunch] come up, quiet as a cat. . . . I wasn't worried about him doing her any harm she didn't want done to her. In fact, I was pulling for the little cuss. . . . I just watched him climb slow and easy into the truck and disappear and then didn't anything happen for about while you could count maybe fifteen slow, and then . . . she says, not loud neither: "Why, Mr. Bunch. Ain't you ashamed. You might have woke the baby too." Then . . . I be dog if I don't believe she picked him up and set him back outside on the ground like she would that baby if it had been about six years old. . . .'[20]

Byron is very much a figure of fun here, the lover placed in the role of naughty boy to be lectured and then dismissed from the premises. But what makes him comic, I think, also helps make him heroic—or, if not exactly heroic, somebody we are inclined to respect as well as laugh at. I am referring, of course, to the narrator Faulkner chooses for the episode, who is a specific though anonymous countryman very much like Bunch himself. He may be amused by Bunch, but, as this passage shows, he also admires him for his perseverance. He even tends to sympathize with him; in fact he was, he tells us, "pulling for the little cuss" at the time. The reason for this sympathy is really suggested by his own immediate situation. For he is, we learn, telling this story to his wife as they lie in bed together after making love; and as he tells it he cannot help sensing the presence of a connection between Byron's predicament and his own. Or rather he is half-aware that Bunch has become a figure for all men, forced into absurd postures in their pursuit of Woman. The story is, in its essentials, an old story told many times (that is why its every detail has a feeling of inevitability about it), and Byron in a way is Everyman: someone in whom the narrator finds mirrored his own clumsiness and stupidity, certainly, but also his own doggedness—his ability to pursue an appointed aim without allowing himself to be distracted by any false considerations of pride. A brave madman—a man whose bravery is the bravery of the mad, and whose madness is the madness of the brave —Byron Bunch is more an affectionately ironical image of ourselves than he is any sort of folk stereotype; and as such he provides a perfect demonstration of Faulkner's ability to give life to apparent paradox.

But perhaps Faulkner himself has described this ability of his better, more memorably, than anybody else can. "There's not too fine a distinction between humor and tragedy," he said once in one of his talks at the University of Virginia, "even tragedy is in a way walking a tightrope between the ridiculous—between the bizarre and the terrible."[21] With very little alteration those words could, I think, be used to describe the kind of tension I have been talking about here: "walking a tightrope," achieving a balance between different perspectives, is precisely what Faulkner is doing in his portrait of somebody like Byron Bunch. They also bring us back, though, to another problem altogether—since clearly they have a larger frame of reference than just the people of Frenchman's Bend—which is, the relevance of all this to Faulkner's *general* criticism of experience. What does his treatment of the folk tradition have to do with that? How do his versions of the poor farmer fit into the total imaginative structure of his work—if, really, they can be said to fit in at all? Obviously, to ask this question is to move beyond consideration of any local, intrinsic interest Faulkner's portrait of the South may possess and to start thinking about its representativeness, the use of Yoknapatawpha society as a model for the study of social and historical relationships in general. To use Allen Tate's valuable distinction, it is to pass from the provincial context to the regional. And possibly to answer them it would be a good idea, not to resort to generalizations, but to see what the farmer's place is in one specific example of Faulkner's imaginative world—that is, in one particular novel. Faulkner's books are, after all, all self-contained narratives, although they may contribute to an accumulative store of legend, and maybe the paradigmatic method—of exploring the larger organism in the smaller—will be as useful for us as it was for him.

The book that, I think, could act best as a paradigm here is *As I Lay Dying*. One of Faulkner's four or five finest novels, it is almost entirely concerned with the Bundrens, a family of poor whites, and the journey they take to Jefferson where they have promised their mother Addie Bundren she will be buried. According to Faulkner, the book was written while he was working night shifts at a local power station; in fact, he claimed it was written between shifts. We need not take this claim too seriously, any more seriously than we need take his description of *The Sound and Fury* as a book that grew, almost inevitably and without much conscious intervention on his part, out of a childhood memory. There is nearly always a discrepancy between Faulkner's tributes to pure inspiration and the elaborately "made" quality of his work, which we can explain possibly by saying that he no more liked the *idea* of hard labor, or what is often called the Puritan work ethic, than many other, self-respecting Southerners have. His manuscripts bear witness to the care he actually took in revising his books, and even if they were lost there would still be the evidence provided by the books themselves. *As I Lay Dying*, for instance, gives the impression of having been written and then painstakingly rewritten. It is—in the best sense possible—a highly wrought work, a complete and coherent whole that is nevertheless so complex that it seems to defy analysis—which is one reason why, perhaps, so few critics have ever been able to agree about it. According to one group of commentators, the Bundrens are "Bumblies" and their world is a nonsense, absurdist one; while for another the theme of quest implicit in their journey helps turn them into heroes—and their story into a kind of epic, inviting comparisons with the legend of Jason or the search for the Grail. Still others, taking a different tack altogether, see the book as a study in family tension as harshly realistic and supremely modern as some of Ibsen's earlier dramas.[22] And what is even more extraordinary, nearly every one of these people has been able to quote something said by Faulkner somewhere which appears to support his particular interpretation!

Disagreement is not a new thing among critics, of course; it is as old as criticism itself. But it has always been peculiarly rife among Faulkner's commentators. *The Sound and the Fury, As I Lay Dying, Light in August, Absalom, Absalom!*: each of his greatest novels, especially, has drawn almost as many interpretations as it has commentaries. There are several possible explanations for this, but one, and perhaps the basic, reason has to do with something I have mentioned already. Faulkner, as I have suggested, is a writer who thrives on contraries, contraries that are reconciled if at all only in the act of writing. As a supreme example of the artist who communicates before he can be understood, Faulkner does not "think" in the sense of having certain ideas, which he then sets about putting into words—that is, in his best work he does not. On the contrary, such ideas as his novels may contain are a product of the words themselves—a specific imaginative language that attacks, and at the very least drastically reworks, established concepts. So any commentary on those novels must tend to misinterpret because it uses different words—and misinterpret the more it depends on the sort of concepts Faulkner is attacking. The critic uses one style, Faulkner another, and since Faulkner's meaning is discovered in *his* style the difference between the two must be one measure of the scope for possible distortion. Are the Bundrens fools, most people ask when they try to "think about" or explain *As I Lay Dying*, or are they heroes struggling (as Faulkner once put it) "against God in a way"?[23] The proper reply to this, I think (which is the same as for Byron Bunch), is that the question itself is misconceived because it presupposes an either/or situation where none exists. The Bundrens are fools *and* heroes, and any inquiry which is so phrased as to ignore this paradox begins on the wrong foot immediately. It is scenting a false trail right from the start.

We are, I hope, fairly familiar by now with one particular form this tendency toward paradox, this attack on conventional definitions assumes among people like the Bundrens—which is a combining of the two major sides of the populist tradition. The old vein of knockabout comedy, for example, in which there is nothing quite so funny as a man injuring himself, is brought to our minds again and again in the story; even its basic premise—involving the transportation of a corpse, growing smellier by the minute, past a gallery of variously shocked and amused spectators—is like a graveyard joke out of one of the cruder folk tales. While the Bundrens' stoicism, the sheer tenacity they show in fulfilling their promise in defiance of fate, fire, and flood, only needs mentioning to remind us of Southern characters in another and more heroic mold. The journey that forms the spine of *As I Lay Dying* is a trial, among other things, a way of testing strength and endurance; and the qualities the different members of the family reveal during the course of it seem intended to invite our respect along with our laughter. We are pained, impressed, and amused—occasionally even at one and the same time, as we are at that moment in the book when Cash Bundren (one of the sons) has a cast removed from his leg. The cast, which the family improvised when he broke a bone, is made out of cement, and it is the doctor who removes it who describes the incident.

> "Don't you lie there and try to tell me you rode six days on a wagon without springs, with a broken leg and it never bothered you."
> "It never bothered me much," he [Cash] said.
> ". . . And don't tell me it ain't going to bother you to lose sixty-odd square inches of skin to get that concrete off. And don't tell me it ain't going to bother you to have to limp around on one short leg for the balance of your life—if you walk at all again. Concrete," I said, "God Amighty. . . . Does that hurt?"
> "Not to speak of," he said, and the sweat big as marbles running down his face about the color of blotting paper.
> "Course not," I said. ". . . If you had anything you could call luck, you might say it was lucky this is the same leg you broke before. . . ."
> "Hit's what paw says," he said.[24]

The doctor's remarks suggest another characteristic strategy of

Faulkner's that is exploited to the full in the story, by which I mean, of course, the device of the multiple narrator. Faulkner's explanation of why he adopted this device so often is illuminating, and suggests how his use of it differs from, say, Smollett's or George Eliot's.

> I think that no one individual can look at truth. . . . You look at it and see one phase of it. Someone else looks at it and sees a slightly awry phase of it. But taken all together the truth is in what they saw though nobody saw the truth intact.[25]

The Bundrens are presented to us in a variety of mirrors, as it were, which are meant to encompass them and to reflect eventually the "truth" about them. Voices join to tell us about their lives, to agree, to present evidence, or just to argue. No one voice can be regarded as authoritative but equally no voice can be discounted either; consequently, during the course of the debate, each member of the Bundren family tends to assume a multidimensional personality. He or she becomes as rich, edgy, as protean, and occasionally as baffling as somebody we might know from our own intimate experience. Take Dewey Dell, the one girl in the family, who is young, unmarried, but with child: she is seen differently by every character who talks or even thinks about her. Her youngest brother Vardaman, for instance, regards her as a replacement for Addie and so practically worships her. What she says must be right, he feels, because *she* says it.

> The hill goes off into the sky. . . . In Jefferson it is red on the track behind the glass. The track goes shining round and round. Dewey Dell says so.[26]

Anse Bundren on the other hand, the head of the family, sees Dewey Dell more as a thankless child—someone who will never allow anything he does, however slight, to pass without criticism. She is the guardian of the law for him as well, perhaps, but it is a law seen more as a nuisance than a need—the law, we might say, as understood by the habitual lawbreaker.

Still, for all their differences, there is an obvious connection between the assessments of father and brother; the woman, we feel, remains the same in principle—only the judgment passed on that principle, the light in which it is seen, is changed. This can hardly be said of a third image of Dewey, offered to us by a boy who seduces her during the course of the journey. The story of his seduction sounds as if it could have come straight out of folk comedy, although folk comedy of a broader, more robust kind than anything we are likely to come across in nineteenth-century America. As assistant to the chemist in Jefferson, and therefore somebody who has acquired a bogus medical reputation from his surroundings, the boy—called MacGowan—persuades Dewey

Dell that the only way she can end her unwanted pregnancy is with "a hair of the dog" that bit her. One copulation, he advises, will cancel out another, and he is ready to perform the service free of charge when the shop is closed. He evidently has no qualms about telling her this, not the least sense of guilt over his act of deception, and for a very simple reason: he just never thinks of Dewey Dell as a person. She is merely a type for him, a nice, juicy country girl who almost deserves to be deceived as a punishment for her ignorance and seductive good looks.

> She looked pretty good. One of them black-eyed ones that look like she'd as soon put a knife in you as not if you two-timed her. She looked pretty good.[27]

From the moment Dewey Dell walks into the chemist's shop she enters a world quite different from the one in which we have mostly seen her up until then, a world where a different set of relations apply effectively turning her into a different person. It is like meeting an old friend unexpectedly in a new place, perhaps, or with a new group of acquaintances. A side of him or her we had never noticed before is suddenly exposed, and we are forced to reassess our previous intimacy.

Vardaman, Anse Bundren, MacGowan, and all the other people like MacGowan who watch things from the sidelines: that still leaves one very important source of evidence unaccounted for—which is Dewey Dell herself. The entire structure of *As I Lay Dying* is dialectical, involving a continual and fructifying movement between inner world and outer, and this means that somebody like Dewey can carry her own sense of personal identity into the debate. She can tell us about dimensions of her personality that no outside observer can properly know. Of course, her "voice" does not always operate at this submerged level. Very often all Faulkner does when he allows her to speak, think, or talk to herself is remind us, in and through the use of the vernacular, that she is a country girl, a being defined on one level by her geographical and social surroundings. At such times, she comes closest to the kind of person MacGowan describes.

> The first time me and Lafe [her first lover] picked on down the row. . . . We picked on, . . . the woods getting closer . . . and the secret shade . . . with my sack and Lafe's sack. Because I said . . . if the sack is full when we get to the woods it won't be me. I said if it don't mean for me to do it the sack will not be full . . . but if the sack is full, I cannot help it. . . . And we picked on toward the secret shade and our eyes would drown together. . . .[28]

This is not quite colloquialism, though: that last phrase, "our eyes would drown together," hardly belongs with the ordinary, everyday idioms of country speech. With its help we are moving toward a different level of experience, and of Dewey Dell's personality, and a purely subjective one at that. Here, words act as objective correlatives for the unarticulated and otherwise inarticulable impulses running through the character's mind; they are used as symbolic gestures rather than naturalistically.

I doubt if it is possible to exaggerate the importance of this, the almost dreamlike way in which the reader is tumbled down into deeper and deeper levels of a character's mind. Just when we think we have a clear picture of somebody like Dewey Dell, and can place her as an attractive, emotionally generous, but rather simple-minded farm girl, our assumptions are suddenly undermined—our snobbish detachment shown up for what it is—by the revelation of her inner fears and misgivings. We move in beneath the equable surfaces of her behavior to something else, a terror or sense of disaster by no means simple or simple-minded, that can only be expressed in the sort of language that lies completely beyond her personal reach.

> I heard that my mother is dead. I wish I had time to let her die. I wish I had time to wish I had. It is because in the wild and outraged earth too soon too soon too soon. It's not that I wouldn't and will not it's that it is too soon too soon too soon.[29]

And that is not all. In case we should now begin to feel secure, when Dewey Dell's conscious fears have been expressed, Faulkner will occasionally offer us a further jolt. Without any warning, he will take an abrupt step down beyond this toward a more incantatory and imagistic level of expression that is meant, clearly, to recover Dewey's *sub*conscious for us—the secret, subliminal impulses that help make her what she is or prompt her to do what she does. Here her dimly realized fear of losing her identity, which includes her fear of death but goes beyond it, becomes the controlling factor.

> The dead air shapes the dead earth in the dead darkness, farther away than seeing shapes the dead earth. It lies dead and warm upon me, touching me naked through my clothes. I said You don't know what worry is. I don't know what it is. I don't know whether I am worrying or not. Whether I can or not. I don't know whether I can cry or not. I don't know whether I have tried to or not.[30]

The main effect of all this, I believe, is to make us wonder if there is any end to the process of character exploration, whether we can ever reach bedrock certainty when we are thinking or talking about someone. More fruitfully, it is to make us feel that the answer to this must be no, there is no end because the personality—any personality, including Dewey Dell's—is too dynamic for any particular definition to satisfy for very long. Just as certain aspects of Dewey Dell lie beyond the reach of her own words or the words of her companions so, we must suspect, the full scope of her character developing and changing in time is something that no language can properly contain.

If this sounds at all plausible as a way of explaining the effect Faulkner's narrative technique has on us it is, I think, because the gap between language and experience I am talking about now is something to which the entire novel testifies—in its plot, its assignment of motives, even its stated "message." Really, what words *are* adequate to explain Anse Bundren's reasons for traveling to Jefferson? How, if and when we try, *can* we describe his motives for doing what he does when he gets there? Of course, he goes to Jefferson to honor a promise he made to Addie when she was dying, but he also goes there to buy a new set of false teeth and, with the help of his improved appearance, to acquire a second wife. In marrying again once he arrives in Jefferson, Anse finds the sort of helpmeet or rather drudge his own laziness requires, a quick replacement for Addie, but he also obtains by way of a dowry the gramophone for which his oldest son Cash has always pined. His motives are an extraordinary mixture of unselfishness and self-interest, care for others and concern for his own welfare; and so, as it turns out, are those of nearly every other member of the family. They seem to exist beyond explanation, defying any outline we may try to draw of them; and that is why, obviously, one of the classic strategies of comedy, which involves raising expectations only to reverse them, often dictates the movement of the book. It is as though the writer were trying actively to lure us into a particular opinion, a certain way of looking at his characters and their behavior, so that the lesson he is bent on giving us can then be carried to us on the backs of our own shattered preconceptions. We learn, partly, by being taught a system and being told afterwards how constricted that system is. Do we think the Bundrens are engaged in a latter-day quest worthy of being described in Homeric terms? One comment by an observer, comparing the Bundren wagon as it enters town to "a piece of rotten cheese coming into an ant-hill,"[31] is enough to tell us we are wrong if we do. So can we assume the observer is right? Hardly, because no sooner has he spoken than we are back with the family again, sharing in their journey and in the agony that gives it almost epic proportions. One vocabulary is suddenly discarded for another one quite different, and then, almost as soon as we have come to accept *that* as accurate, it too is discarded in favor of something else.

We are gradually returning, of course, to something I said earlier about Faulkner's style: that it exists, as one of his critics has put it, at the extreme "edge of order"—exposing the inadequacies of language and grammar by pushing both to their limits. And return to it we must

because words, I think, are the ultimate category in *As I Lay Dying,*
the prime example of the human need to classify experience. One passage in the novel, in particular, emphasizes this point: it is given to
Addie Bundren, the mother, when she is already dead. Briefly, in a
soliloquy that provides a kind of still center to the narrative, Addie
rehearses her past life—her childhood, her experiences as a teacher,
her marriage to Anse—and then tries to explain what it has all taught
her, the lesson that somehow she now wants to pass on. Issuing as it
does from a coffin out of the mouth of a corpse, what she says here
seems to have an oracular weight and authority to it—which is appropriate, really, since this is the closest Faulkner ever dares come to
stating the "message" of his book.

> . . . I learned that words are no good, that words don't ever fit even what
> they are trying to say at. When he [Cash] was born I knew that mother-
> hood was invented by someone who had to have a word for it because
> the ones that had the children didn't care whether there was a word for
> it or not. I knew that fear was invented by someone that had never had the
> fear; pride, who never had the pride . . . so when Cora Tull would tell
> me I was not a true mother, I would think how words go up in a thin
> line, quick and harmless, and how terribly doing goes along the earth,
> clinging to it. . . .[32]

There could hardly ever have been a more devastating assault on the
harmful effects of language, the way in which it can castrate the personality and reduce experience to a series of rules. We talk, Addie
suggests, and as we do so more than likely we impoverish and distort
what we are talking about. Life, instead of being as Wallace Stevens
once described it, like a revolving crystal, multifaceted, various, constantly changing, is turned into a fixed quantity, something made up
out of the patterns of our syntax, the distinctions implicit in our vocabulary—in short, out of our own painfully limited and limiting stock of
"words."

All that I have said so far about the soliloquy, though, tends to ignore one important and supremely obvious point: Addie is talking,
telling us this. She herself is using words to describe the deficiencies
of words, and she is not just using them as, say, Samuel Beckett might
do—in a negative way, that is, to locate their essential futility. She is
actually trying to explain and define, to shape language into a means
of positive communication. In her own modest fashion she is struggling to create an adequate style—which, of course, relates what she
is doing here to what Faulkner is aiming at on the larger canvas of
the narrative. As I understand it, neither the author nor his characters
is dismissing categories entirely, although admittedly they come pretty
near to it. Rather their intention, as expressed in the sum total of their

actions, is to make categories as open and provisional as they can; "words" and "doing" are not seen as warring interests really, but as the two sides of a mutually profitable partnership, involved in a process of exchange that must last as long as the possibility of an absolute explanation or terminal vocabulary is excluded—in other words, indefinitely. A continuing transvaluation of values of every kind: that I think is what *As I Lay Dying* is arguing for, with the main emphasis resting on the idea of continuance. And this in turn would explain why the book itself does not seem to finish but merely stops short with the arrival of a new character, the second Mrs. Bundren, trailing a fresh set of possibilities in her wake—because its procedures are meant to be a demonstration of its "message," right down to the very last incident described on the last page. The best books, Faulkner appears to be saying, are like the best men: they do not stay still, ever. Living in a state of constant interchange between categories and raw experience, they must always be on the move, altering by leaving themselves open to strange influences and fresh conditions. Look, he seems to add with a touch of characteristically well-placed arrogance, here is an example of the sort of thing I mean—right here in the book I have just written.

We may seem to have come a long way from the original subject of Faulkner's contacts with the folk/popular tradition, but really, I think, we have never left it at all. All we have done is move from Faulkner's use of that tradition as a specific *fact* to his use of it as an *idea;* we have merely shifted from the question of how he relates to his locality to something more interesting and difficult—the question of how he defines and eventually celebrates that relationship. Let me explain what I mean. Faulkner, as we have seen, begins with a complex of associations and concepts gathered around the figure of the poor farmer. The complex is a vast one, bounded at one end by the peasants of folk comedy and at the other by those heroic tillers of the earth which the more sophisticated agrarian theorists liked to dream about. But it is to Faulkner's credit that he manages to encompass most of this and draw a series of portraits in which the old stereotypes come alive, mesh and conflict with one another: one secret of Byron Bunch's vitality, for example, and Dewey Dell's is that they are neither comic peasants nor epic heroes but both. Not only that, Faulkner manages to use all the imaginative resources at his disposal (which—need it be said?—are considerable) to bring these characters of his into contact with the varieties of present experience—to make them change. We see the Bundrens or V. K. Ratliff and his companions from all kinds of different perspectives, close up and far away, we share with them the different dimensions of their lives; consequently they become people in motion for us, as casually unpredictable and yet as *known* as our own friends and relatives are.

This, we might think, would be enough for any writer, but having done this Faulkner then does something else as well—which is to offer the actual processes of his traditionalism, the way in which he involves the notions of the past with the exigencies of the present, as a design for living. As I have tried to explain, the "words" that Addie Bundren criticises so vehemently in *As I Lay Dying* are used essentially as a synecdoche. They refer us to all the forms, linguistic, moral, and social, which the human intelligence devises for dealing with experience. Behind her monologue lies the belief that there are certain intricate patterns implicit in everything ordained by a particular culture, including its language, which tend to systematize and inhibit its members' thoughts—somebody intent on turning her perceptions into theories, a linguist say or a social anthropologist, would probably use the term "structures" or "codes" to describe what she means; and far from inventing these patterns, Addie suggests, the individual may hardly be aware of their existence. They are inherited, imposed on him perhaps without his conscious knowledge, and since they are largely cultural (rather than biological) they can be included, most of them, under the familiar heading of *tradition*. This brings us back to Faulkner. With Addie's help he argues for a dialectic, a marriage between these "words" and "doing" so that the individual can reap the benefits of his culture without becoming completely enculturated. And it does not take a very great deal of effort, I believe, to see that what he has in mind in pleading for this is exactly the sort of contact with tradition on which his own work is based. Does he say that we should be aware of the contradictions implicit in the "words" we use, and the limits they impose? That awareness is precisely what is responsible for the rich paradoxes of his characters. Does he insist that our vocabularies must change, that there should be an incessant coupling of "words" with reality? This, after all, is what makes the story of the spotted horses and the story of the Bundrens' trip to Jefferson seem so familiar and yet so utterly strange and new. The medium is the message in more than one sense in Faulkner's best novels, and this because his own relationship to his past (that is—it is worth repeating it—the relationship to inherited forms which makes such novels possible) supplies him with a sort of blueprint, an original basis of judgment. I do not want to make too much of this at the expense of some of Faulkner's other achievements: it should never lead us to forget, for instance, about the sheer historical accuracy of his renderings of folk dialect or the close acquaintance he reveals with the smallest details of country life. But it is still, I think, decisive evidence of the scope and weight of his attachment to his region: that, when all the accounts are in, he can actually use his own "Southern-ness" as a means of assessment. He can make something out of being born in a specific time and place, with a particular set of beliefs and practices to hand; and then afterwards, not content to stop there, he can make something out of this, the nature of his own encounters with the South, as well.

"Maybe Nothing Ever Happens Once": The Plantation Myth and the Past

Faulkner's first novel set in Yoknapatawpha County, *Sartoris*, ends with what is—deservedly, I think—one of the most quoted and best-known passages in all of his writing.

> . . . the dusk was peopled with ghosts of glamorous and old disastrous things. And if they were just glamorous enough, there was sure to be a Sartoris in them, and then they were sure to be disastrous. Pawns. But the Player, and the game He plays . . . He must have a name for His pawns, though. But perhaps Sartoris is the game itself—a game outmoded and played with pawns shaped too late and to an old dead pattern. . . . For there is death in the sound of it, and a glamorous fatality, like silver pennons downrushing at sunset, or a dying fall of horns along the road to Roncevaux. . . .[33]

A land haunted by memory—that probably is what most of us think of first when anybody makes a reference to Yoknapatawpha. Certainly it is what Faulkner is brooding over here: a still and silent land where the ghosts often seem more real, more alive than the people who conjure them, and the prevailing mood is one of elegant despair. We know it, we feel, because Faulkner invites us back into it again and again and it is home for many (perhaps most) of his more famous characters. But do we really know it? For all our familiarity with it, do we understand what makes it tick; and even if we do, have we any clear idea of how Faulkner himself feels about it and what he expects our opinion of it to be?

In a sense these are the same questions I asked about Faulkner's peasant characters, and offer similar difficulties when we try to answer them. If we look to Faulkner's critics for a lead for instance, a clue as to his possible attitudes, we find much the same confusion here as we found over books like *As I Lay Dying*. Just compare what George Marion O'Donnell says about the Sartorises and the Old South—in that passage from "Faulkner's Mythology" I quoted earlier—with this concluding statement from Olga Vickery's *The Novels of William Faulkner*, which is one of the best recent studies of the subject.

Far from idealizing the Old South, Faulkner sees in it, as in the army,
an instance of the paralyzing influence that a rigid caste system and a
closed society can exert on the individual.[34]

Again, the commentators are at odds; and, on the basis of the evidence, again we must conclude, I think, that neither is completely right
or completely wrong. Faulkner does admire the courage and glamour
of the Sartorises just as O'Donnell says he does: only the admiration
is hedged about with irony and even the occasional touch of scorn.
Equally, he does mock the aristocratic pretensions of the older Southern families and criticize their rituals just as Vickery suggests, but
that does not prevent him from sympathising with them and their
slightly shop-soiled romanticism at the same time. In fact, he manages
—in a way that must be becoming familiar to us by now—both to
praise and to condemn, to draw us a portrait of the plantation world,
or rather what remains of it, so elusive that it appears somehow to
resist our intelligence and the need all of us feel at some time or
another to select and edit in order to "know."

Some of this elusiveness I am referring to is present, I think, in the
elegy to the Sartoris family I quoted just now. Admittedly, the elegy
bears traces of the *fin de siècle* writers whom the young Faulkner
admired so much—in the obvious world-weary elegance of certain
phrases, for instance, and the tired, semiphilosophical references to a
"Player" God—but these are more than compensated for by its antici-
pation of his later style, the sheer sense of surprise it arouses when
we read it through carefully. Look again at the opening sentences:
there is an ambivalence here, a double-edged attitude toward the
Sartorises and all they represent that is caught best of all perhaps in
the repetition of the two words "glamorous" and "disastrous"—where
the harmony of sound serves merely to emphasize the dissonance of
meaning. After that, it looks for a moment as though a simpler judgment is emerging. The Sartorises are dismissed with bitter wit as
pawns played in an "old, dead game," and the harsh, guttural, mono-
syllabic prose used here helps to reinforce the feeling expressed. This
does not last for long, though; little by little a sense of admiration
reappears, signaled by the recurrence of the word "glamorous." Certainly, we are not allowed to forget about the skull hidden beneath the
fine skin of all the Sartoris family, but any reference Faulkner makes
now to death or the waiting grave is radically qualified by his return
to a more colorful, romantic idiom—and by his richly nostalgic evocation of old, forgotten, far-off things and battles long ago. Darkness and
light, despair and glamour seem to meet in the closing sentence—an
appropriate finale, really, for a passage in which abrupt transitions of
tone and vocabulary (or what one of the analysts of Faulkner's mature

style has called "the juxtaposition of elements which do not fit to-gether")[35] have been used to carry the subject far beyond ordinary praise or blame.

But perhaps I am beginning to read too much into the passage now, at least as it exists in isolation, since its suggestiveness is partly a product of its context; it owes a great deal of its interest and mystery to the narrative preceding it, where Faulkner indulges in his familiar strategy—of interpreting something from every possible angle—so as to make us register several different opinions about the Sartoris world at once. His treatment of Bayard Sartoris I, known sometimes as the "Carolina Bayard" (because that was where the family used to live), is a good illustration of this. Bayard, we are told, died during the Civil War while serving as aide-de-camp to the Confederate military leader Jeb Stuart and as the book is set in the early twentieth century we never actually see him while he is alive; rather, he comes to us as a series of memories, via the stories told about him by his descendants. He is remembered in particular at the moment of his death, when, according to legend, he rode into the enemy camp in broad daylight to capture a consignment of anchovies. No romantic, picturesque de-tail is omitted from the incident; the gaiety of his manner, the fear he inspired in the Union camp by the sheer audacity of his behavior, the admiring almost adoring comments of his comrades ("What is one man," says one of them after hearing of his death, "to a renewed belief in mankind?")—none of these things is forgotten. But—and this is what makes our reaction to the young aide-de-camp rather more com-plicated—the utter ordinariness of his end is not forgotten either (he is shot in the back by a frightened cook) or what other people less in sympathy with the chivalric code said about him at the time. "No gentleman has any business in war," declares one Union officer even before Bayard sacrifices himself. "He is an anachronism, like ancho-vies"[36]—the anchovies, we hardly need reminding, for which the sacri-fice is made. The effect of adding such comment to the story is curious, I think, because it tends both to qualify and to confirm our admiration. We are forced to recognize the complete futility of what Bayard does—he offers up his life for something that neither he nor anybody else really needs—and yet to feel somehow that this very futility, the fact that his action has no practical purpose whatsoever, makes it more attractive, elevates it, in effect, to the status of an unadulteratedly romantic gesture. Like the horns and silver pennons invoked at the end of the novel, Bayard's act does not belong in the world of nicely calculated less or more, and in making this point Faulkner seems to be offering both a criticism and a defense.

Our reaction to the "Carolina Bayard"—and the entire Sartoris legend—is complicated still further, I believe, when we see his story in terms of the subsequent history of the family and, in particular, when we compare him to his great-grandnephew Bayard Sartoris III. As several critics have pointed out, this later Bayard is a kind of lost soul, a character suffering from the same strange malaise as Edgar Allan Poe's heroes, say, or some of Melville's. In his case, the lostness is a product of drift: he is alienated from his ancestral culture (which haunts him precisely because he cannot establish a positive relationship with it), and this alienation expresses itself in his activity, which is desultory and purposeless. On his return home from the First World War, the first thing he does is buy himself a car, and he then spends most of his time driving it recklessly around the countryside until, eventually, an accident results in the death of his grandfather. Badly shaken by this, he leaves home again, this time for the place which Faulkner like most Southern writers of the twenties and thirties regarded as the ultimate retreat of the exile, California, the West, where he gets a job as a test pilot flying crackpot experimental planes. It is not long before the inevitable happens: one of the planes crashes and he dies—indeed, it is almost as if he commits suicide, wills his death so as to escape the emptiness of his life. Clearly, Bayard III is meant to provide something of a contrast to Bayard I, a man who enjoys the very thing his namesake lacks—a conviction learned from his ancestors and shared with his contemporaries that his experience has meaning. Dreams, ideas of heroism inform nearly all of the "Carolina Bayard"'s actions, helping to give them what Faulkner calls their "histrionic" or "finely tragical"[37] character. Equally clearly, though, we cannot leave it at that, because the two men also have some things, certain traits and weaknesses, in common. Bayard Sartoris I could, after all, be just as heedless and reckless as his great-grandnephew when he wanted to be: riding madly around the countryside—in his case, of course, upon a horse—and on one occasion showing that he too had an anarchic streak in him by driving a pack of foxhounds into the local church during a service. Even his death betrays a curious parallel: it too verges on suicide, or at least the expression of a death wish, in the sense that there was no pressing reason for his invading the enemy camp—and annihilation when it came was willingly, even eagerly, embraced. Admittedly, any belief the aide-de-camp and his friends may have had in the nobility of their behavior does tend to weaken such parallels a little—Bayard Sartoris III, by contrast, never even begins to think of himself as noble—but it does not really destroy them. In some ways the hero of the Sartoris clan *was* like the young test pilot and his kind; consequently he *is* involved in the criticisms leveled at them. Each episode on which the legend of the

"Carolina Bayard" is founded offers certain resemblances to a more recent and obviously desperate generation as well as differences; there is an elaborate network of comparison, and this has to be taken into account along with everything else when any assessment of that legend is about to be made.

It would be possible, I think, to go on discovering other angles from which we are forced to see the Sartorises, all of which contribute to the shifting, uneasy feeling we get from the last paragraphs of the book; but there is no need really to labor the point. At times the voice that tells us about Faulkner's old planter families—about the Sartorises and the Compsons, the Benbows, the Sutpens, and the McCaslins—sounds as if it is afraid to stop talking, because to do so would be to lose what little chance it had of saying all there is to say about these strange, convoluted creatures. At others it tends to be more lavish and discursive, to drone on in the belief that by returning to the legends often enough it can work out every one of their puzzles. Always, though, whatever its specific tendencies, the impression this voice creates is of an infinitely receding series of perspectives: talking on and on so as to avoid the dangers inherent in any fixed attitude, it is forever creating new forms, new anatomies out of the old, old stories.

That they *are* old, old stories—the fact that, on the whole, yesterday is much more important to people like the Sartorises than today is— is something we ought never to forget, either. It is an obvious point, perhaps, but it helps remind us that, for all the fluidity and social mobility of Faulkner's imaginary world and the overall consistency of his techniques, there is a clear distinction to be made between his portraits of farm and plantation. His farm people may fall under the sway of the past, but they rarely succumb completely, and never for very long. Their lives are basically situated in the here and now; and, if there is one thing nearly all of them have in common, it is a firm commitment to activity, sustained purposeful movement. Lena Grove moving through Mississippi and Tennessee in search of her lover and Byron Bunch moving on in pursuit of her, the Bundrens moving steadily onward to Jefferson, where they are to bury Addie Bundren, and Flem Snopes moving steadily upward through the various levels of Yoknapatawpha society: these are just four examples of what I mean— people who show themselves to be supremely capable of seizing the day and pursuing an immediate goal in the face of every conceivable obstacle. By contrast Faulkner's plantation folk seem pretty goalless and stationary: fixed quite literally in the past like Bayard Sartoris I or fixated by the past like his great-grandnephew, they have about as few significant connections with the South of the interwar years as they possibly could have. One reason for this difference, I believe, is that Faulkner, like many writers involved in the Southern "renaissance," must have recognized just how anachronistic the strictly practical or programmatic side of the aristocratic ideal had become. He could still talk about the recovery of the Jeffersonian dream now and then, and even describe characters (such as the MacCallums) who had come close to realizing it during their lifetime. But he could not, he probably felt, or rather would not describe the myth of the old plantation in the same way. That had to be separated from the present before it could be used to any serious purpose at all; it had, in fact, to be located in a place that, like Tate's Pleasant Hill or Ransom's autumnal fields, was the special preserve of memory.

Anyway, for whatever reason or reasons the plantation dream *is* firmly associated with the past in Faulkner's novels; which of course raises real problems for those—like Bayard Sartoris III or his grandfather "Colonel" Bayard Sartoris II—who live in the present. Drawn back continually toward something that, like a half-remembered incident, at once obsesses them and eludes them, they can, as Sartre once put it in an essay on *The Sound and the Fury,*

> . . . be compared to . . . a man sitting in a convertible looking back.
> . . . The past here gains a surrealistic quality; its outline is hard, clear, and immutable. The indefinable and elusive present is helpless before it; it is full of holes through which past things, fixed, motionless, and silent, invade it.[38]

Such people find themselves dealing with a ghostly, confusing world, so close to them that it seems to control their thoughts and dominate their experience and yet so distant from them—because it *is* the past and they *are* cut off from their inheritance—that they cannot understand it, or objectify their feelings about it. Their lives become a sort of dialogue with specters, conducted in a language they hardly know. This, for example, is how old "Colonel" Bayard is introduced to us at the very beginning of *Sartoris,* as a man haunted.

> Freed as he was of time and flesh, . . . John Sartoris seemed to loom . . . above and about his son . . . so that as old Bayard sat with his crossed feet propped against the corner of the cold hearth, holding the pipe in his hand, it seemed to him that he could hear his father's breathing even, as though that other were so much more palpable than transiently articulated clay as to even penetrate into the uttermost citadel of silence in which his son lived.
>
> The bowl of the pipe was ornately carved, and . . . on the bit were the prints of his father's teeth, where he had left the very print of his ineradicable bones . . . like the creatures of that prehistoric day that were

too grandly conceived . . . either to exist very long or to vanish utterly when dead. . . .[39]

Colonel John, Bayard II's father (and a character based loosely on Faulkner's own great-grandfather), seems to be more alive than any of his descendants are, and yet he is a wraith—an insubstantial nothing whose nothingness nevertheless manages to dominate their being. Clearly he represents a force to be reckoned with, a memory his sons and their sons after them must come to terms with before they can ever hope to be free. But all Bayard Sartoris II can do, apparently, is try to lose himself in that memory, seal himself off from his surroundings behind his own personal smoke screen, while his grandson makes the equally desperate mistake of thinking that he can deny it, even though its influence is to be traced in almost every step he ever makes. To embrace a ghost or to flee from it, neither really constitutes an act of exorcism. Yet these are the only routes most members of the Sartoris family appear capable of following—and, for that matter, most of the Compsons and McCaslins as well.

This may not seem to be getting us anywhere in particular—in the sense that we still seem to be talking about the eccentricities of Faulkner's aristocratic characters, the things that give them a special, almost anthropological interest—but that, I think, is not really the case. Gradually we are coming to something quite central to Faulkner's work, which grows directly out of his preoccupation with the plantation myth and gives it a wider relevance and impact. I mean by this the interest he shares with so many other writers of the Southern "renaissance" in the *idea of history*, the precise nature of the relationship obtaining between past, present, and future. I am not trying to suggest that this interest is missing from the rest of his work—of course it is not and could not be, if only because Faulkner is a traditionalist writer, somebody who uses his inheritance as much as he can and recognizes how the past must impose itself upon everyone. But it is, I believe, his treatment of the planter families of Yoknapatawpha County that gives it a peculiar relevance and urgency. For people like Bayard Sartoris III and Quentin Compson the past is such a constant, nagging presence that the question of how to cope with it becomes their main preoccupation; so Faulkner can and, in a sense, must deal directly with the entire subject of the historical dimension whenever he describes them. The problems of time and identity are basic to their lives; and thanks to this they can be treated on one level rather like traditional hero figures, confronting dragons or meeting a challenge that (admittedly, in a much less obvious way) all of us must face. In one of his later novels, *Requiem for a Nun*, Faulkner even tries to define this challenge.

> There's no such thing as past. . . . The past is not dead, it's not even past . . .
> . . . you—everyone—must, or anyway may have to, pay for your past; . . . [the] past is something like a promissory note with a trick clause in it which, as long as nothing goes wrong, can be manumitted in an orderly manner, but which fate or luck or chance can foreclose on you without warning.[40]

But this, although helpful, is rather too much like a sermon in which the idea is abstracted from the experience and necessarily simplified in the process. For a more intimate and convincing exploration of what Faulkner is talking about here—that subject which is in turn *the* subject of so much Southern writing—we have to look elsewhere, I think; to what is perhaps the greatest of all his novels, *Absalom, Absalom!*, published forty years ago in 1936.

Like its author, *Absalom, Absalom!* is a bit of a puzzle. It is now generally regarded as one of the pinnacles of William Faulkner's achievement, and yet, when it first appeared, even its more intelligent reviewers were tempted to cite it as an exemplary piece of "bad writing."[41] It has been described, and by people whose word on Faulkner is respected, as the crucial work in the Yoknapatawpha series, despite the fact that the vast critical labors expended upon it, by those same people among others, have left it nothing less of an enigma. Unlike *The Sound and the Fury* or *Light in August, Absalom, Absalom!* has never been supplied with a satisfactory "key": something that, while not explaining all of its labyrinthine complexities, might at least offer the reader a convenient means of entry into them. The title of the novel is a case in point here. Most of the titles Faulkner gives to his books contain a clue to the larger meaning of the action, whatever personal associations they may contain besides, and to this rule *Absalom, Absalom!* forms no exception. Critics have admitted as much, but they seem unwilling to follow the admission with any close analysis; beyond saying that there is probably a reference intended to the Biblical account of King David, who, like Faulkner's central character Thomas Sutpen, broke the moral law and was punished through his children for doing so, they have either ignored the problem altogether, or more usually claimed that the scope of the reference is impossible to define. This, surely, is to mistake Faulkner's purpose. It *is* difficult to determine how far he would wish the reader to take the more detailed parallels between the stories of David and Sutpen: their common preoccupation with the crimes of incest and fratricide, for example, or the sense in which both describe an outsider rising to high station among men. But such difficulties hardly matter, I think, since

what is far more important is the feeling of historical recurrence—the
sense of the past repeating itself—which the broad rhythm of analogy
between the two situations is intended to evoke. For central to *Absalom, Absalom!* is its examination of both this recurrence and, more
generally, the tangled web of coinciding and conflicting forces that
we call history. The book is, as I have said, like *Sartoris* and nearly
all Faulkner's other ventures into the plantation tradition, a study of
the meaning of history; and that is why events and experiences in it
are so interrelated that each dimension of time seems to impinge physically on the other two, and each person appears transformed into "an
empty hall echoing with sonorous defeated names" that he must try
to understand if he ever wants to understand himself. The past, the
present, and the future are interwoven and every incident so rendered,
re-interpreted, and then rendered again as to seem designed to support an intuition attributed to Quentin Compson.

> *Maybe nothing ever happens once and is finished. Maybe happens is
> never once but like ripples maybe on water after the pebble sinks, the
> ripples moving on, spreading, the pool attached by a narrow umbilical
> water-cord to the next pool which the first pool feeds, has fed, did feed,
> let this second pool contain a different temperature of water, . . . reflect
> in a different tone the infinite unchanging sky, it doesn't matter: that
> pebble's watery echo whose fall it did not even see moves across its sur-
> face too at the original ripple-space, to the old ineradicable rhythm. . . .*[42]

History, Quentin seems to be saying here, is a continuum out of which
the individual person emerges and to which he eventually belongs. A
series of intricate and unbreakable "strings" bind him to all other
people before and after him, whom he influences and by whom in
turn he is influenced. In practical terms this means that any particular
experience, the moment when Thomas Sutpen knocks at a door, for
example, may be of enormous bearing subsequently, however trivial
it may appear at the time; and it means too that the past may so shape
the present or the present the past as to make the one a mirror image
of the other. As illustrations of this, there is the obvious tendency of
Quentin Compson to identify himself with Thomas Sutpen's son Henry, as well as the less obvious propensity of Quentin's father for seeing
the entire Sutpen story as emblematic of his own.

   This vision of history holds clear implications for the interpretation
of the human consciousness also, and of the relationship between that
consciousness and the things, commonly called reality, with which it is
engaged. Like Robert Penn Warren, Faulkner sees man as a kind of
spider entangled in the very web of historical circumstance he has
helped to create. He is involved, Faulkner argues, with many other
people in other times, and one result of this is that his life tends to

assume a certain, special sort of complexity which it is almost impossible for his conscious mind to encompass. The problem is articulated in another passage in the book, assigned to Thomas Sutpen's daughter Judith. I have quoted it once already, but it is well worth repeating.

> . . . you are born at the same time with a lot of other people, all mixed up with them, . . . all trying to make a rug on the same loom only each one wants to weave his own pattern into the rug; and it cant matter, you know that, or the Ones that set up the loom would have arranged things a little better, and yet it must matter because you keep on trying or having to keep on trying. . . .[43]

And clarification of the issue (provided by the structure of the book as a whole, its arrangement of speech and incident, as well as by this particular passage) leads in turn to the formulation of a standard of judgment. It is not just that the several narrators in the book, from whom we learn the story of Thomas Sutpen, offer perspectives that are in various ways biased and therefore inadequate. The point, as Faulkner makes it, is that any perspective must be so that does not take cognizance of this extraordinary interrelatedness, and consequent complicatedness, of men and events. The burden of *Absalom, Absalom!*, in other words, is not merely to tell us what history is, but to instruct us also in the way that we, the products and producers of history, should behave.

The importance of history, and its bearing on human behavior, are presented in their clearest and most consecutive form in the biography of Thomas Sutpen—insofar, that is, as there is any incontrovertible thread of facts in his case that can be said to emerge from the welter of countercommentary. According to General Compson, Quentin's grandfather, Sutpen's trouble is his "innocence," and this is one occasion on which the reader feels inclined to agree with the commentator. Sutpen does seem to be innocent in the sense that the tragic hero often is, in that he adopts a particular purpose or "design" and then tries to fulfill it without reference to circumstances and other people. He has little capacity for compromise and no especial interest in it, either. This becomes clear enough when the reasons for his adopting a "design" in the first place are rehearsed. He was, we learn, born in the highlands of the region later to be known as West Virginia, where he grew accustomed to primitive conditions and a pristine sense of equality and independence.

> . . . where he lived the land belonged to anybody and everybody and so the man who would go to the trouble and work to fence off a piece of it

and say "This is mine" was crazy; and as for objects . . . everybody had just what he was strong enough . . . to take and keep. . . .[44]

The birthplace of Thomas Sutpen is, in effect, presented as a kind of Eden, a more easygoing version of the place where the MacCallum family live. It is almost as if we have been returned to the world of Jeffersonian dream, or at least to a place where realization of that dream remains a possibility. But this lasts only for a moment: while Sutpen is still only a young boy he and his family travel down the mountains to the rich flatlands of Virginia, a region of great plantations where life seems to be a much more complex and puzzling affair. It is all the more puzzling for young Thomas, because, as he grows up, he senses the presence of certain artificial distinctions that make him, a poor boy, a less admirable creature than the planter. People, he suspects, have set up "words" between themselves and their fellows, to the detriment of human contact. However, this remains no more than a suspicion until one day Sutpen is sent by his father to deliver a message to a local planter. Without considering that he should do otherwise, the young boy knocks on the front door of the mansion— only to be told by the "balloon-face . . . nigger" who answers his knock that he should go around to the back. To describe this incident as traumatic hardly seems adequate. Quite suddenly, Sutpen is offered a glimpse of his family and himself as others, the privileged classes, see them—stripped of all individuality and reduced to a herd of "cattle, creatures heavy and without grace."[45] The boy's reaction to this humiliating experience is extreme but perhaps predictable. For instead of rejecting the vision, because it is no less biased than his own previous preconceptions about himself, he accepts it as fundamentally correct. His only recourse, as he sees it, is to become a member of the privileged classes too, and thereby assume an identity that might give him back his peace and sense of being in control of life.

The subsequent facts in the case of Thomas Sutpen are a record of his attempts to fulfill this "design," and form a pattern of rejections each of which reverses in some way the rejection previously suffered by Sutpen himself. He becomes as incapable of recognizing the individuality and shared humanity of another as the "balloon-face . . . nigger" ever was. This much becomes obvious when, by way of a first act in his new and self-ordained drama, he sails to Haiti and there marries Eulalia, the daughter of a local potentate. The match is made purely for his own aggrandizement, and when Sutpen discovers that his wife has some Negro blood running through her veins, a fact her father had concealed, he drops her as quickly as he took her. A mulatto wife would hardly be suitable as the consort of a plantation owner, and this he considers sufficient reason for claiming that his marriage "contract" is null and void. His moral blindness is such that he does not even see the obvious analogy between the humiliation Eulalia must necessarily feel when he deserts her and the humiliation he himself felt that time at the plantation house door; and he does not, therefore, consider the possibility that his abandoned wife might seek some kind of revenge. The details are difficult to locate in the paraphernalia of conflicting perspectives, but there is at least a chance that Thomas Sutpen's subsequent and fateful encounter with Charles Bon, his son by this first marriage, is a result of Eulalia's scheming; and of this Sutpen appears to have no suspicion.

Whatever the reason, Charles Bon does travel to Mississippi, after Sutpen has established himself there as a gentleman planter and thus fulfilled a part of his ambition. Sutpen has also remarried in the meantime and had two more children, one of whom, Henry, is actually responsible for bringing Charles to the Sutpen home. Charles soon begins to pay court to Judith Sutpen, although he knows her to be his half-sister, and eventually even proposes marriage to her. His motive is clear. Charles knows that Thomas Sutpen is his father and Sutpen, obviously, knows it too—but nobody else does. Sutpen will have to admit the fact of his paternity if he wishes to forbid the marriage, to acknowledge a relationship that cuts across the "decorous ordering" of his existence and that might even destroy it. This is the crucial test of Thomas Sutpen's commitment to his "design," the moment at which he might conceivably succumb to the demands of personal feeling. He does not, however. He rejects Charles just as he did Eulalia, and an incestuous match is only prevented when Henry learns the truth, too, and feels himself obliged to murder his stepbrother. Ironically, Sutpen discovers that he has ruined his "design" even while trying to preserve it. Henry is driven by his crime of fratricide into becoming an outcast from society, haunted by his own personal Furies; and once she has lost Charles, Judith Sutpen embraces spinsterhood as a way of retreating from life. Consequently, their father is left without an heir capable of assuming responsibility for the estate. Nobody remains to perpetuate the Sutpen image and plan, and the only inheritor to appear after the death of Thomas Sutpen is a half-caste and an idiot, a product at two generations' remove of the marriage to Eulalia Bon.

Not that Sutpen does not try to provide himself with a male heir in the years following his encounter with Charles. On the contrary, his subsequent relationships with women are dictated by this purpose, and so serve as further demonstrations of his willingness to subordinate everything to the furtherance of his "design." After his second wife dies, for example, he proposes marriage to her sister, Rosa Coldfield—

but only on condition that she first furnish him with a son. With his usual innocence, Sutpen regards his offer as an ordinary business arrangement in which Rosa has to prove her value before he makes his investment, and he seems genuinely surprised to be met with a refusal. The same breathtaking lack of consideration meets with fatal results when Sutpen actually fathers a child on the daughter of one of his tenants, Wash Jones. The child is female and so for Sutpen's special purposes quite worthless. He even tells Jones this with a frankness that is at once cruel and pathetic—cruel because Jones is clearly humiliated, and pathetic because Sutpen is just as clearly unaware that he is inflicting any humiliation. Like Charles Bon and Eulalia and the young Sutpen before him, Wash Jones experiences a deep sense of betrayal and responds to this with violence, hacking his master to death in an attempt to reassert his identity and power. The instrument of death is a scythe; and the reader is led by this to suspect that time itself, the kaleidoscopic flux effected by "each moment's experience," is having its revenge on Sutpen.

Even in making a summary such as this of the few comparatively unambiguous facts in the biography of Thomas Sutpen, it is difficult not to be false to the subject treated. And the reason for this, as well as for the problems experienced by most commentators when they discuss *Absalom, Absalom!*, is that (as so often in Faulkner's novels) it is almost impossible to separate the meaning of the story from its medium of communication, the various narrative and linguistic frames within which it is set. *What* is said in the history of Thomas Sutpen, in short, is more or less determined by *how* it is said; the different perspectives offered by the narrators furnish a means of definition and ultimately the standard of judgment also. Each perspective in turn clarifies the tragic error of Sutpen a little more, his tendency to see life in terms of some preconceived design; and it does so by offering a further example of that error. The historians are just as limited and limiting as was the man who provides the common subject of their histories. More than this, all those perspectives when taken together, as part of the composite effect of the novel, offer an approach to that sense of the complex simultaneity of every moment—and consequent interrelatedness of human beings—that Faulkner takes to be the prerequisite of the accomplished artist and the properly developed man. The historians may not know the truth as individuals, in other words, but their very contradictoriness pushes the reader toward some awareness of that truth, the multifaceted character of historical experience.

In many ways this is, of course, the same strategy as Faulkner employs in *As I Lay Dying*, using several, separate narrators to apprise us of "the truth intact." There are differences, though, and they stem from the fact that it is specifically *historical* experience, and by extension the idea of history, he is concerned with here. The focus of all this discussion for example, Thomas Sutpen, owes a certain, unique suggestiveness to his historical status. Other people like the Bundrens may belong to the South, but he seems to *be* it, to contain and epitomize a part of its past. He collapses into a lifespan the story of the Cotton Kingdom—its rise to power and eminence, its assumption of the prerogatives of an aristocracy, and its eventual fall precipitated by a complicated and ethically dubious relationship with the members of another race. The moments of decline are even coincident, as Faulkner has Henry Sutpen shoot his half-brother only three weeks áfter Lee has surrendered at Appomatox. What is even more important, perhaps, the nature of Faulkner's concerns gives an extra dimension, not just to Sutpen himself, but to the actual versions of his story we are presented with. For if we look closely at the two older narrators, Rosa Coldfield and Mr. Compson, then we find, I think, that they are doing more than merely expressing private opinions; their attitudes toward Sutpen are strongly colored by—are, in effect, personal equivalents of —the attitudes of Northerner (or abolitionist) and Southerner respectively toward the historical facts of the old plantation South and the Civil War. And if we look at the third narrator, Mr. Compson's son Quentin, we notice something just as interesting: that his verdict is of the kind that would probably be offered by anyone or any community that has lost all sense of a usuable past—and is, really, more aware of legends told about earlier events than of the events themselves. It would be pedestrian, not to say unhelpful, simply to describe Quentin as a representative of our own, modern society because of this, since Quentin is always first and last an individual. But nevertheless an inference of that kind is there, in his treatment of the Sutpen story, to be made. A movement toward a third generalization of the narrative perspective is there to be followed; and these three generalizations should lead in turn to the perception that the "designs" criticized in *Absalom, Absalom!*, and the historical truth explored there, have to do with the public level of experience as well as the private. They are evidence, ultimately, of Faulkner's sustained belief in the interdependence of the two levels and his consequent conviction that the distorted perspectives to which some men are prone, and the larger view achieved by others, are likely to be as much the product of communal mores, regional or national, as of personal idiosyncracies.

It is Rosa Coldfield who begins the story of Thomas Sutpen, and it requires little effort to realize that her version of him is dictated by hostility. In fact, she makes of her narrative an act of revenge for the humiliation its subject once visited upon her, by transforming him into a kind of bogey figure, a focus for all her bitterness and frustration. This is to be expected, perhaps, but what is less expected is her means of achieving and expressing this transformation. For Rosa has done nothing less than adopt the vision and rhetoric of her father, a rabid abolitionist, and then distort the man she remembers into a type of that entire race of planters whose "moral brigandage" ensured their damnation. Her version of the Sutpen story is, in effect, the personal equivalent of an antislavery tract—or, to put the matter in more general terms, a redaction of the Northern and abolitionist attack on the plantation system. The parallels are detailed and pretty difficult to ignore. For instance, John Greenleaf Whittier, the Quaker poet who became a leading spokesman for the abolitionist movement, liked to describe the Southern planter as a kind of Antichrist; and Rosa obviously thinks along the same lines, since her portrait of Sutpen turns him into a "fiend blackguard and devil," a "Moloch" carrying a "faint sulphur-reek still in clothes and beard." Again, Emerson (who although not as committed an abolitionist as Whittier nevertheless spoke out vigorously against slavery) referred to slaveowners as creatures of darkness—which is clearly what Rosa is doing in a more personal way when she describes her former suitor as a "light-blinded, bat-like being," "from abysmal and chaotic dark to eternal and abysmal dark completing his descending" into absolute degeneracy. Many more commonplace aspersions are resurrected as well. Some people, like the poet, critic, and abolitionist James Russell Lowell for example, tended to dismiss Southern gentlemen as "mad knights" blinded to the suffering of others by their own vainglory; and that too is something Rosa picks up and develops whenever (as she often does) she refers to Sutpen as a dangerous lunatic—someone who wanted to build a feudal stronghold for himself, to satisfy his "lust for vain magnificence,"[46] no matter how many lives were sacrificed as a result. All of this is not to say, of course, that either Rosa or her creator are necessarily indebted to these particular writers or are invoking any specific analogies. But it *is* to say that there is a common stock of assumptions and language on which every one of these hostile commentators, Emerson and Whittier, Lowell and Rosa, appear to draw; and that this helps forge a connection between Rosa's personal hostility and a larger, public cause.

Much the same can be said of the general atmosphere of Rosa's story. In its ethos and conventions it belongs to the Gothic mode—the mode, that is, on which numerous antislavery novelists drew when describing the plantation culture, and which the noted abolitionist Wendell Phillips was obviously invoking when he declared, "The South is the thirteenth and fourteenth centuries." The action is set in the familiar and grim castle, an "ogre-bourn" sealed off from the rest of

humanity. Its visible guardian, the reader is informed, is an old
Negro maid, Clytemnestra, who by virtue of being fathered by "fell
darkness" has become the "cold Cerberus" of this "private hell." But
a far more powerful protection is afforded by the "inexplicable, un-
seen" forces that dwell within it, and reserve it, apparently, for "some
desolation more profound than ruin." Their presence is witnessed by
the strange noises that haunt this "indomitable skeleton" and that seem
to Rosa, a woman of the same feverish type as Ann Radcliffe's heroines,
"louder than thunder, louder than laughing . . . with triumph." Thomas
Sutpen, too, the owner of this structure, is transformed into something
akin to the traditional villain of Gothic romance—the perpetrator of
horrible deeds upon innocent victims. His second marriage to Rosa's
sister Ellen, for example, is presented as an abduction. Ellen, it is
claimed, was carried off to an "ogre-djin"; and subsequently permitted,
by means of infrequent visits to church, "to return, through the dispensation of one day only, to the world she had quitted." The "two
half phantom children" born of this alliance are similarly condemned,
either to lifelong imprisonment in Sutpen's Hundred or to an early
death. Over this entire family there seems to hang a "doom" comparable to that which hovers above the Castle of Otranto and its occu-
pants: disaster follows upon disaster until the Sutpen "name and
lineage" are finally "effaced . . . from the earth."[47]

Of equal importance in evoking the strange world in which Rosa
Coldfield sets this family is the actual prose style of her account. True,
in some ways that style reminds us of the staple idiom of most of
Faulkner's major novels. Convoluted sentences and a cumulative syn-
tactical pattern create the effect of thought flow, of a consciousness
ranging free over the myriad possibilities latent in each moment's experience, while a disruptive use of parentheses and grammatical forms,
and the continual juxtaposition of contradictory images and sugges-
tions, prevent the reader from absorbing that experience into any
preconceived framework of value. Given this common element,
though, Rosa's style, like that of the other narrators in *Absalom, Absalom!*, does possess its own peculiarities or deviations from the norm;
and in her case, those deviations involve a carrying of things to the
extreme. The style used in passages of the novel attributed to Rosa
is characterized, that is, by rhythms and a syntax that are even more
claustrophobic and tortuous than usual, and by interjections even
longer and more bewildering than those to be found elsewhere. Sentences seem to have no end, possibilities no definite conclusion, and
the pervasive effect is one of hallucination or nightmare.

> *Or perhaps it is no lack of courage either: not cowardice which will not
> face the sickness somewhere at the prime foundation of this factual scheme*

from which the prisoner soul, miasmal—distillant, wroils ever upward sun-
ward, tugs its tenuous prisoner arteries and veins and prisoning in its own
turn that spark, that dream which, as the globy and complete instant of its
freedom mirrors and repeats (repeats? creates, reduces to a fragile evanes-
cent iridescent sphere) all of space and time and massy earth, relicts the
seething and anonymous miasmal mass which in all the years of time has
taught itself no boon of death but only how to re-create, renew. . . .[48]

This is a language that *creates* a sense of mystery. It encourages confusion and seems therefore eminently suited to a narrative in which
events are divested of logical explanation, in which people become
disembodied "faces," "voices," or "hands" and experience a numb "terror" at the mere suggestion that there is "something hidden" at the top
of a "nightmare flight of stairs." More important, such language is an
integral part of a larger plan in which the several narrative styles
counterpoint each other, serving to characterize the narratives as different variations on a common theme.

The second phase in this plan is supplied by Mr. Compson, whose
character is sketched in lightly but sufficiently for us to see him as just
as much of a failure as Rosa Coldfield. Like Rosa, too, Mr. Compson
seems to be seeking an explanation for his failure in the story of
Thomas Sutpen. The only difference is that in this case Sutpen emerges
not as the villain but the hero, of a decadent tragedy in which the
noblest possible "dream" is destroyed by the "illogical machinations of
fatality."[49] It would be too much to say that Sutpen is transformed
into a surrogate for the narrator as a result of this, but he does come
to possess a representative value, in that he provides Mr. Compson
with a reflection of his own misfortune, and of the pressures that
brought that misfortune about. And since the decline in both men's
circumstances is, as Mr. Compson sees it, in some way related to the
defeat and consequent collapse of the plantation South, it comes as no
surprise to find that this version of the Sutpen legend is in every way
the opposite of the one offered by Rosa Coldfield.

Mr. Compson's is in short a peculiarly Southern interpretation of the
facts at his disposal. Everything in his account is designed to make
Sutpen seem like a visionary, right down to the atmosphere of conscious artifice that percolates through every scene. Sutpen's "vision"
is, of course, a heroic one, a personal equivalent of that dream of a
new aristocracy I described in the first chapter. The gentleman is at
its center—William Byrd's gentleman, John Pendleton Kennedy's gentleman, the Agrarians' gentleman—a man courteous, noble, and accomplished who treats life as a "finely tragical" drama for which all
the moves have been prepared beforehand. From a Gothic monster the
protagonist of *Absalom, Absalom!* is suddenly transformed into a perfect

gentle knight, or at least into a person who tries more or less successfully
to *become* a perfect gentle knight—and who, in the course of doing
this, experiences the same sort of difficulties that, say, a boxer like
John L. Sullivan might be troubled with were he to try to teach himself the schottische. In order to turn life into dream Sutpen is ready
apparently to learn a new way of doing everything, to rehearse the
very language he must use over and over again; in fact, he is willing
to submit himself to a discipline so "painful and tedious" that it looks
sometimes as if he is pitting "his own fallible judgment against not
only human but natural forces."[50]

Whenever Mr. Compson takes over as narrator, and Sutpen is transformed in this way from a prince of darkness into a gentleman, certain
changes occur in the texture of Faulkner's prose as well. The long,
even serpentine sentences are still there, but they are arranged now in
an elaborate series of balanced phrases, graceful cadences, and accumulating rhythms. There is symmetry, a conscious attempt to shape
the material, implicit in almost everything that is said.

> That Sunday morning in June, with the bells ringing peaceful and per-
> emptory and a little cacophonous—the denominations in concord though
> not in tune—and the ladies and children, and house negroes to carry the
> parasols and flywhisks, and even a few men (the ladies moving in hoops
> among the miniature broadcloth of little boys and the pantalettes of little
> girls, in the skirts of the time when ladies did not walk but floated) when
> the other men sitting with their feet on the railing of the Holston House
> looked up, and there the stranger [Sutpen] was.[51]

The style here is restrained and unemotional, tending always toward
the formal. With its touches of delicate irony and self-consciously
felicitous description, it expresses something of Mr. Compson's own
state of mind, but it serves also, I think, to locate the character of
his protagonist—someone who attempts quite deliberately to live up
to an ideal version of himself.

Thanks to the way Mr. Compson describes them, the people grouped
around Sutpen also seem to be playing parts—and parts drawn, just
as much as his is, from the Southern version of its own past. Ellen
Coldfield, for example, is said "to rise to actual stardom in the role of
matriarch" with her "carriage . . . a little regal," her manner "gracious
and assured." The reference to the matriarchal role is intended, of course,
to evoke a whole series of associations with the good woman, keeper of
the mansion and mother to the plantation "family," who was and is
so crucial to the South's image of itself. And just as familiar to any
reader of *Swallow Barn* or any of its innumerable descendants is the
part played by Henry Sutpen here. "Given to instinctive and violent

action rather than thinking," Henry is now metamorphosed into a Southern Hotspur, an ideological descendant of Kennedy's Ned Meriwether, or the gay young Confederate officer of military lore.

> . . . his entire worldly experience consisted of sojourns at other plantations almost interchangeable with his own, where he followed the same routine which he did at home—the same hunting and cockfighting, the same amateur racing of horses. . . .[52]

As usual in stories of this kind, the figure of the young, bucolic squire is complemented by another: the plantation Hamlet, a character intended as a comment on the refinements of Southern society who is played here by Charles Bon. A more serious version of Kennedy's Singleton Oglethorpe Swansdown (or, if you prefer, a more temperate descendant of Poe's Roderick Usher), Bon is described by Mr. Compson as a "cerebral Don Juan," "handsome and elegant and . . . catlike." Given the fragile dilettantism of his nature—he seems, to borrow a phrase from John Crowe Ransom, to want to shape life into "a series of isolated perfections"—it is somehow appropriate that his final resting place should belong to the world of artifice; he is buried, we are told, in a spot that resembles a "garden scene by the Irish poet, Wilde," so redolent of the "hothouse" that people lose their ordinary personalities when visiting it and are translated into beings "Beardsley might have dressed."

The references to artists of the nineties suggest, I think, just how much Faulkner has learned to control his youthful enthusiasms by now; for we are not being asked to share in Mr. Compson's aestheticism, of course, but to see it as a clue to his feelings and reading of the past. This narrator (who at one point compares himself to a "stage manager") is clearly someone intent on giving the tragedy of Thomas Sutpen an emotionally pleasing and intellectually manageable form. Like the Southerners who retreated to what W. J. Cash called "Cloud Cuckoo Land" after the Civil War, he is concocting a highly fanciful myth—that distances the specters of guilt and defeat by exonerating the defeated and identifying "fateful mischance," rather than some moral law, as the force guiding the destinies of the world. The dominant tone is one of irony—an uncertain irony, perhaps, coupled with a rather desperate imitation of Wildean detachment—because, in fact, Mr. Compson is claiming that Sutpen did not deserve to fail at all. He rose to the momentary realization of a fine vision, and deserves full credit for having done so, and then fell prey to "destiny, retribution . . . irony—call him what you will."[53] He was a blameless and within the limits of human possibility even "heroic" victim of circumstance; which is an eminently comforting explanation of the affair for those, like Mr. Compson himself, who feel they have aspired and suffered in the same way.

The third interpretation of that affair, and of the events leading up to it, is offered by Mr. Compson's son Quentin, with his friend Shreve providing some help and accompanying comment. It is, as we have seen already, scarcely a definitive one. For Quentin simply adopts elements from both other versions of the story and then exaggerates them. At one moment Sutpen is seen as a Caesar, whose death, even, is symbolic of his triumph; at the next he is a demon, Faustus or Beelzebub, who meets an equally appropriate end under the rusty blade of a lunatic. The ambivalence is most noticeable perhaps in the diverse portraits that Quentin fashions out of the history of Henry Sutpen, whom he sees as a kind of alter ego. At first, the younger Compson's dependence on the stories told by his father is most obvious. Henry is presented as a young squire of "bucolic Mississippi" who has much to learn from his more stylish half-brother, Charles.

> . . . how to lounge about a bedroom in a gown and slippers such as women wore, in a faint though unmistakable effluvium of scent such as women used, smoking a cigar as a woman might . . . yet withal such an air of indolent and lethal assurance that only the most reckless man would have gratuitously drawn the comparison. . . .[54]

As Quentin continues with the description of Henry's "education" he even exaggerates the idealizing tendencies of his father, by showing the younger Sutpen completing a remarkable transition from squire to knight (from a Ned Meriwether, we could perhaps say, to somebody more like Kennedy's version of John Smith)—and crediting it entirely to the tutelage of Charles. The very growth of Henry's admiration for his mentor is taken as proof of the change since, as Quentin sees it, Henry's feelings become so selfless and reverential eventually that they are like nothing so much as the love a knight might feel toward his mistress. Henry ends, we are told, by attributing all possible graces of mind and body to Charles and then offering him "the humility which surrenders no pride—the entire proferring of the spirit." His devotion even makes him willing to condone incest between Charles and his sister Judith: in the traditional manner of the courtly lover, in fact, he is described citing various historical precedents for their liaison as a way of making "his conscience . . . come to terms" with his will. Only the additional fear of miscegenation recalls him in obedience to "conscience"—an "academic Hamlet waked from trancement" (as Quentin puts it), Henry then kills the man he loves most so that the honor they both hold dear may be vindicated. It is about now that Shreve comments, "Jesus, I would sure hate to have come from the South. Maybe I wouldn't come from the South anyway, even if I could stay there,"[55] and the mood in which this is said—at once incredulous, mocking and admiring—probably captures something of our own reaction to such an absurdly romantic yet strangely impressive tale.

The same combination of feelings—awe, bewilderment, and perhaps some amusement as well—is aroused, I think, by the way Quentin talks about Henry Sutpen later on in the novel, when he changes tack suddenly so as to turn the Sutpen story into a tale of terror rather like Rosa's. Faulkner leaves us in no doubt about the indebtedness to Rosa here, since he has this change of approach coincide with Quentin's description of a visit he once paid to Sutpen's Hundred—a visit, that is, which was made in Rosa's company the day after she had given him her account of its history. Recalling the occasion, Quentin now sees the Sutpen home as a typical Gothic mansion—as surreal as the House of Usher and more frightening even than the "grim ogrebourn" Rosa described.

> It loomed, bulked, square and enormous, with jagged half-toppled chimneys, its roofline sagging a little . . . beneath it, the dead furnace-breath of air . . . seemed to reek in slow and protracted violence with a smell of desolation and decay as if the wood of which it was built were flesh.[56]

Inside this strange dwelling Quentin and Rosa find three people, all of whom—as Quentin describes them now—seem as grim and macabre as their surroundings. They are Clytemnestra the housekeeper, a "tiny gnomelike creature" with a "worn coffee-colored face"; Jim Bond, a "saddle-colored and slack-mouthed idiot" who by virtue of two generations of bastardy has become "the scion, the heir-apparent" to the estate; and a third figure lying on a filthy bed in a "bare, stale room," whose "wasted yellow face with closed, almost transparent eyelids" and "wasted hands crossed on the breast" make him look "as if he were already a corpse." That last figure is the most important of the three: it is of course Henry Sutpen, just returned from his self-imposed exile and still oppressed apparently by the murder of his stepbrother. The gay young knight of Quentin's earlier imaginings has suddenly disappeared, been blotted out of the picture—and with him, for the moment, all memories of the chivalric dream.

Only for the moment, though: by the time the novel ends, the dream has resumed its place in Quentin's consciousness. There it remains, not to dominate his vision now, but to complicate it and to leave him finally in a state of ignorance as great as that of his father, and with a sense of uncertainty that the older man has rarely known. We are returned, in fact, to that moment of despair with which my discussion of Faulkner began.

"Now I want you to tell me just one thing more. Why do you hate
the South?" "I don't hate it," Quentin said, quickly, . . . *I don't hate it*,
he thought, panting in the cold air, the iron New England dark; *I don't.
I don't! I don't hate it! I don't hate it!*

The dilemma in which Quentin is left here is terrible but, given his
circumstances and state of mind, inevitable too. For, as we must realize
by now, he has not even begun to "know" the past; all he knows, all
he has been allowed to know really, are certain "decorous orderings"
or reinterpretations of that past bequeathed to him by his elders. It
remains an enigma to him—something in which he is deeply involved,
but the contrariness and complexity of which he can never understand.
And within the imaginative world of *Absalom, Absalom!*, where the
past is seen as an integral part of the human personality, this is a
desperate situation to find oneself in. Quentin is "tied," so Faulkner's
argument goes, to the various dimensions of history just as all men
are, and his failure to understand any one of those dimensions must
therefore result in a failure to understand himself. With the worst
possible consequences, "design" has got between him and living.

The same is true, I think, of every other character in the book,
from Thomas Sutpen down: nobody sees his fellows for what they
are, only in terms supplied to him by some abstract framework of
ideas. Everyone is, in a way, using everyone else, to enhance his sense
of himself and his own preconceived vision of experience. Eulalia Bon
(probably) uses her son to inflict vengeance on Sutpen. Charles Bon
uses Henry and Judith in the hope of gaining acknowledgment from
his father. Henry, even, "uses" Charles—to the extent that the murder
is prompted by his commitment to a set of abstract ideas about race
and serves to confirm them. The various narrators, too, are using the
facts at their disposal and the people to whom these facts apply to
support and substantiate their prejudices. And standing at the center
of the story they tell is the black-white racial dichotomy, itself the
supreme public example of this tendency to manipulate people rather
than approach and understand them. Not one character seems capable
of achieving any real knowledge of others, that sense of interdependence with men and women from the past, present, and the future,
which is the subject of Rosa Coldfield's meditations once when she
considers what she has missed.

> . . . *there is something in the touch of flesh with flesh which abrogates,
> cuts sharp and straight across the devious intricate channels of decorous
> ordering, which enemies as well as lovers know because it makes them
> both—touch and touch of that which is the citadel of the central I-Am's
> private own: not spirit, soul; the liquorish and ungirdled mind is anyone's
> to take in any darkened hallway of this earthly tenement. But let flesh*

touch with flesh, and watch the fall of all the eggshell shibboleth of caste and color too. . . .[57]

Rosa's description of the "flesh touch with flesh" is moving, certainly, but it is hardly enough in itself to counterbalance the series of tragic failures described in the narrative. Where, then, is the alternative, the dramatic rendering of possibility to set against this series? If Thomas Sutpen and his contemporaries did not achieve the kind of understanding defined here, and if Mr. Compson and Quentin and Rosa Coldfield cannot respond properly to the "umbilical water-cord" connecting them to people before and after them, what positive evidence is there of another way—a framework of value that will at least allow a chance of succeeding where all these characters fail? The answer to both these questions lies, of course, where it usually does in Faulkner's writing: in the texture of the work itself, in the total fictional "doing" rather than in any "words" uttered or any example offered by a single person. For within the "postage stamp" world of *Absalom, Absalom!*, as we have seen, the past *does* live in the present, reflecting it and being reflected by it, and time does therefore become a pattern of dependencies. The private and public levels of experience, also, *are* interrelated, affecting and to some extent even imitating one another. And experience itself within this psychic continuum *is* rendered in all its variability, its capacity for change and surprise: Faulkner's use of several, very different narrators and his kaleidoscopic prose style are alone enough to ensure that. The impetus created by the entire fictional technique in effect pushes the reader toward an awareness of the reality that the characters have evaded, and some consequent understanding of the function of history—which function, as the "sole owner and proprietor" of Yoknapatawpha County conceives of it, is to stimulate the growth of the consciousness by enlarging and complicating everything with which that consciousness must deal. History, it emerges even as we read *Absalom, Absalom!*, is an energy latent within us rather than a burden that, like Aeneas, we must carry on our backs.

Perhaps the amount of time I have devoted to *Absalom, Absalom!* reflects well enough my opinion of it: it represents, I believe, Faulkner's boldest excursion into the plantation mode and one of his seminal discussions of what it means to be a Southerner. History, its major concern, is what the Southern experience is really all about, the obsession with the historical dimension being the tie binding nearly all the writers of the "renaissance" together; which is why its characters— people like Quentin Compson, who reenact the past in the hope, partly, of understanding it—seem to offer us a paradigm of the regional case.

They are very different from their neighbors, maybe, as far as the particulars of their tragedy are concerned, but painfully like them when it comes down to the root causes of their problems and the ways in which they try to deal with them. Not only that: occasionally the Compsons, the Sutpens, and the Coldfields, all apparently so peculiar, must remind us or should remind us of ourselves as well. Standing at the extreme edge of a situation that includes us the readers, as people equally involved in the series of entangling alliances history creates, they describe what is in fact only an exacerbated form of a common human dilemma. So not for the first time the "unique" circumstances of the Southerner turn out to be not quite unique after all—or rather unique in degree only, not in kind.

But although *Absalom, Absalom!* may possibly be the nearest Faulkner ever got to a complete anatomy of the South in one narrative, it still has to leave a lot of things out—apart from those passages describing Sutpen's childhood, for example, not that much attention is paid to the poor white, the common farmer, and their histories— and to find completeness or something approaching it we have to turn elsewhere, I believe, to the Yoknapatawpha series as a whole. Starting with *Sartoris* and ending on an appropriately elegiac note with *The Reivers*, Faulkner wrote some fifteen novels and innumerable shorter pieces over the years, the aim of all of which, really, was the same: they were, for him, a way of getting to know his region. Faulkner wanted to embrace the contradictions latent in his background without forfeiting coherence, to describe the mansion and the country store and his own ambivalent feelings about them in one great variegated portrait; and his stories, or more accurately his gradual invention of Yoknapatawpha County *for* those stories, was his means of achieving this. By developing Yoknapatawpha as a medium he could see the South clearly and yet in extraordinary detail because Yoknapatawpha was, as he liked to put it, an apocryphal county. It was described in the novels and tales but somehow existed separate from them; it was a fiction located, as it were, behind the fictions Faulkner wrote and published—and as such it enabled him to investigate the different aspects of Southern life, to keep them at an aesthetic distance, *and* to metamorphose them into parts of a larger plan. This same process of strictly imaginative discovery and synthesis is, of course, to be found in William Carlos Williams's great poem of place, *Paterson,* and indeed Williams's Preface to his poem, where he outlines his aims, could equally well be used as a prologue to Faulkner's books.

> :a local pride; spring, summer, fall and the sea; a
> confession; a basket; a column . . .
> . . . by multiplication a reduction to one . . . an

> *identification and a plan for action to supplant*
> *a plan for action . . . a dispersal and a metamorphosis.*

> To make a start,
> out of particulars
> and make them general, rolling
> up the sum . . .

>   . . . rolling up out of chaos,
> a nine months' wonder, the city
> the man, an identity—it can't be
> otherwise—an
> interpenetration, both ways. Rolling
> up! obverse, reverse;
> the drunk, the sober: the illustrious
> the gross; one.[58]

Admittedly, Faulkner (again, like Williams) never defines his surroundings in any one way we can recognize as adequate: there is no simple verbal equivalent for the map of the county he drew as a frontispiece for his novels. But this is merely to say that Yoknapatawpha—like the region it recovers for us—is too full of alteration and possibility ever to be fixed by a single category, and in any case it still leaves its apocryphal status unimpaired. As a place eventually existing complete in the author's mind it stands behind almost everything he says—something greater than the sum of his perceptions, which is nevertheless *there* buttressing them, giving them a substance and congruence they would not otherwise possess.

All of which is by way of saying, of course, that if any Southerner comes near to fulfilling the demands made upon the writer by his historical context—the twin demands, that is, of coherence and inclusiveness—it is Faulkner. He comes as close as anybody does, and closer than most, to seeing his region steadily and seeing it whole. It was, as I have tried to show, Yoknapatawpha County that gave him the chance of doing this, of realizing the different possibilities running through his life, generalizing them, and giving them a unity (or, rather, a sense of relevant connection) that owes more to his strategies of imaginative reference and revision than it does to logic. And even with its help the achievement is not conclusive, by any means: there remains a feeling of open-endedness about the series, of ends left hanging loose and stories only partly told, which Faulkner himself acknowledged toward the end of his life when he referred to the writer's vocation as a "quest for failure"—and then formulated plans for adding whole new dimensions to his work. One plan, for instance, would have involved him in compiling what he called a "Doomsday" or "Golden Book" of all the people he had ever written about from

Jefferson and its environs, an "alphabetical, rambling genealogy . . . from father to son to son";[59] and another, represented in his creative work I think by a novel like *The Town*, required him to rehearse familiar incidents yet one more time in the hope, apparently, of rounding them off. He was still looking in these final years it seemed, or at least one part of him still was, for a way of writing "the end" to his saga—just as he had always been searching throughout his life for the right sentence in which to crystallize an experience. Even while he was doing this, though, there was another part of him—that part which finds expression in, say, the soliloquy of Addie Bundren—which recognized how futile this self-imposed task was; which saw, in fact, that he had done just about all he could do already. As far as he was able, it told him, he *had* written the "Golden Book" of his region. He *had* told practically all there was to tell about his own experience as a Southerner and, in doing so, arrived at the only kind of conclusion available to someone whose subject and condition is change. That perhaps is why, whenever Faulkner was tempted to confess that he had failed (and the temptation occurred to him the more frequently the older he grew), the confession tended to be made in a way that made it sound more like a boast, really, than anything else.

6. Aftermath: Southern Literature since World War II

~~~~~~

"Getting Out from Under Faulkner and the Magnolia Blossom": The Problems of the Post-"Renaissance" Writer

In 1967 a distinguished group of writers and commentators met at a small liberal arts college in Georgia to discuss one particular question: the state of Southern literature. What, they asked themselves and each other, had happened to the regional tradition since the great period of the "renaissance" between the wars? What would happen to it in the future? The excellence of Southern writing during this period was, as we have seen, partly the result of a specific historical occasion, a complex series of social and cultural pressures that had eased it into birth. Could this excellence survive its occasion; and could the qualities of imagination recognized as distinctively Southern still remain viable long after the circumstances that had given them prominence had passed away? To an extent these were practical questions that could be answered by a simple counting of heads. All that was necessary was to look around and see if there were any good new novelists, poets, or dramatists in the region and, if there were, how they compared with their predecessors. But they were questions that touched upon larger issues as well, since by implication they invoked all the difficulties faced by the artist in what used to be called a "silver age"—an age, that is to say, like our own era of post-industrialism when the great social changes seem completed and the major cultural statements made. As such, they reminded all interested parties that the very extremity of the Southern writer's condition, now as previously, has tended to make him acutely typical of his kind. He is a creature caught in the aftermath of an event, a man who perhaps feels that he has arrived too late; and this, in a broad, problem-solving sense, must draw him very close to many of his contemporaries, even though their problems may differ considerably in detail from his own.

I do not intend to summarize the conclusions of that meeting in Georgia here. They were, needless to say, many and contradictory; and, in any case, they are available for those who are interested in an edited record of the event published a short while afterward.[1] Rather, my purpose in mentioning it at all is simply to illustrate what is perhaps a fairly obvious point: that this, the problem of survival—by which I mean, of course, survival through the agency of genuine, creative development—is a major one for Southern literature now. For the writers born after the great generation that emerged in the twenties and thirties have been placed in a peculiarly disagreeable situation. They have been born too late, really, to benefit from the stimulus of crisis, and from the subtler advantages accompanying it that I tried to describe in the first chapter; but they have been born, equally, too early not to be oppressed by the example of those, the writers before them, who were able to enjoy what they have missed. They are without the large, new perspectives available to men writing at a moment of transition, and, what is perhaps worse, the perspectives they *do* enjoy have been overused, most of them, already. The scenes they witness have become a matter of common record, or assumed the dimensions of somebody else's myth. And the idiom they draw upon is fraught with danger, offering those easy temptations of rhetoric and cliché that are perhaps the special mark of a language too closely identified with a particular tradition of literature, an established means of collating and interpreting experience. Southern writing, to put it briefly, is in the same danger that any body of writing is after a period of immense achievement. It is in danger of going stale, and it does not necessarily help matters that (as that gathering in Georgia indicates) some South-ern writers are themselves aware of this.

What particular forms do these dangers assume? How does the dif-ficulty of "getting out from under Faulkner,"[2] as one critic has put it, betray itself in the details of a text? In a way, there are almost as many answers to that as there are people writing in the South. But one broad danger, one trap into which many tend to fall is illustrated well, I think, by two authors who enjoy perhaps the most colorful rep-utations in recent American letters. I mean by this the dramatist Ten-nessee Williams, who was born in the border state of Missouri, and Truman Capote, from Louisiana. The trap is, essentially, one of style: the writer takes the familiar characters, situations, and themes and then weaves them into a baroque conceit possessing neither original substance nor extrinsic value. The world so imagined hardly exists— or, at least, hardly deserves consideration—on any other level than the decorative: it offers us a group of charming grotesques, preserved in amber. What is Southern about it, really, is not a certain quality of perception, a sense of engagement between past and present, the pub-lic and the private, myth and history: but a turn of phrase or person-ality, a use of the bizarre and sensational for their own sake, which has the net effect of creating distance. For regionalism is substituted a form of local color, and a very precious and slightly decadent form at that, in which the gap between drama and audience seems delib-erately widened so that the latter can revel without compunction in a contemporary "Gothick" fantasy.

With Williams this reductive process is slightly more complicated

than it is with Capote, because the author himself, I think, remains
less than fully aware of it. Of course, Williams does have some suspicion of what he is doing, as his references to his own literary ex-
hibitionism indicate. But these references are scattered and nearly
always discreetly qualified. More to the point, they have never prevented him from reaching for some larger theme in his plays—and
reaching in such a way, unfortunately, as to emphasize his limitations
rather than go beyond them. Far from helping to charge his rich style
with a vision equal to it, all his occasional ventures into moral statement tend to do is to remind us how very much he depends on the
romantic commonplace; our attention is directed above all to the passing of time, the fragility of innocence, the loneliness of the sensitive
person in a brutal world. This can hardly provide the sort of framework he requires, within which each play's images could be satisfactorily accommodated; and without it the audience is left to experience
those images at random, to enjoy, in a fairly casual way, a series of
Gothic—and, as I have just suggested, largely *Southern* Gothic—
effects. Often, if we look closely at the different elements in the series,
we can even see from exactly where they came. Many of the characters, for example, seem when examined to trail the shadow of Yoknapatawpha behind them: Blanche Dubois, a major figure in *A Streetcar
Named Desire*, must remind us of Faulkner's predatory women; "Baby
Doll," of sensual girl-children such as Eula Varner in *The Mansion;*
and Sebastian Venable, the curious absent presence who dominates
Suddenly, Last Summer, of Quentin Compson, Horace Benbow, and
all those other depressed, world-weary young men who once haunted
the streets of Jefferson.[3] Needless to say, there is nothing intrinsically
strange or suspect about this kind of borrowing: Faulkner is so much
a part of the South by now that it would have been stranger, in a
sense, if Williams had tried to ignore him. But there is, surely, something suspect and even wrong about the *manner* of this borrowing.
For all Williams has been able to do with his adopted characters,
really, by way of making them new is to vulgarize and dilute. His
people (like his tropes, his settings) have been deprived of the functions and meanings assigned to them in their original context, and
they have assumed no satisfactory fresh ones to replace them. They
are there in the plays for the interest they inspire as exhibits, curios
of human nature, and that is just about all they are there for. Thus,
Williams's predatory women are not dangerous and frightening as
Faulkner's are, a subversive commentary on sexual and family relationships; they are just neurotics, and rather silly neurotics at that.
His girl-children are not mythic, Southern avatars of the Earth God-
dess, merely Gothic pinups. And, as for his aristocratic young men,

they are treated with the kind of approval, and taste for the pathetic
or bizarre detail, that recalls the literature of the *fin de siècle* more
than anything else. The funereal mansion, the intimations of incest,
violence, and miscegenation, the brooding over the past and the desperate attempt to recover some of its memories: many, if not all, of
the familiar elements of Southern writing reappear, but only, we must
suspect, for the local excitement they can produce—to punctuate the
narrative and, possibly, to intrigue. Yoked together as they are here,
the most that Williams is able to create out of them is an exotic, broken
world—a place that may provoke our lively curiosity at first but which,
precisely because it is so very much less than the sum of its constituent
parts, is likely to leave us feeling a little cheated.

Capote's, I have hinted, is a slightly different case, because he has
always understood only too clearly what he is doing. He began, as he
has explained on more than one occasion, as a prose purist, a stylist
par excellence. Every sentence he wrote was an elaborate concoction,
with the sort of purity of line and grace of cadence that is perhaps
the inevitable product of an aesthetic never seriously violated by life.
The inspiration was purely literary, an inbred one; and much of its
literariness stemmed from the fact that Capote seemed to know all of
the more important Southern writers intimately—know them so well,
in fact, that he could reproduce them with only the ornate, facile
beauty of his own phrasing added on. Reading his earlier fiction, consequently, is rather like reading a clever pastiche: the enjoyment lies
in the element of recognition involved as much as anything else, in
discovering the familiar and known beneath the altered surface. Here,
as an illustration of what I mean, is a passage from his first novel,
Other Voices, Other Rooms.

> Noon City is not much to look at. There is only one street, and on it are
> located . . . a combination barbershop-beautyparlor that is run by a one-
> armed man and his wife; and a curious, indefinable establishment known
> as R. V. Lacey's Princely Place . . . across the road . . . stand two . . .
> structures: a jail, and a tall queer tottering ginger-colored house. The jail has
> not housed a white criminal in over four years, . . . the Sheriff being a
> lazy no-good, prone to take his ease with a bottle. . . . As to the freakish
> old house, no one has lived there for God knows how long, and it is said
> that once three exquisite sisters were raped and murdered here . . . by a
> fiendish Yankee bandit who rode on a silver-grey horse . . . ; when told
> by antiquated ladies claiming . . . acquaintance with the beautiful victims,
> it is a tale of Gothic splendor. The windows of the house are cracked and
> shattered, hollow as eyeless sockets; . . . the . . . walls are ragged with
> torn, weather-faded posters that flutter in the wind.[4]

Most of the influences behind this passage are obvious enough, I think, and scarcely need to be mentioned here. It begins with a cunning imitation of Carson McCullers's prose, flat, dry, a little unnerving; moves on into the world of lazy backwoods whites that interested Caldwell so much; and then concludes with a series of macabre, Grand Guignol touches that recall in turn Eudora Welty, Poe, and Faulkner. What is perhaps less obvious on first reading, however, is how self-conscious, even narcissistic, Capote manages to remain throughout all this; he is acutely aware of the fact that he is parodying his masters—the people whose visions appear, appropriately diminished, in his sentences— and he seems to want us, his readers, to share in his awareness. So that, it may be, is one reason why he refers to "a tale of Gothic splendor" toward the end of the description. The phrase does, of course, have an immediate application—to the stories told by the old ladies about the "fiendish Yankee bandit." But coming when it does it seems to have a much wider relevance than that, to stretch out, in effect, and bring the entire portrait of Noon City within its scope. It, the city, is we feel being "placed' more than anything else is—identified with a context in which books can refer only to other books and for which, therefore, no forms of life are available except those already filtered through another imagination. And as if to confirm this impression, in the very next sentence following this one Capote uses two figures that could almost be described as emblems, or identifying signs, of the Southern Gothic mode: the windows staring out at the newcomer like eyeless sockets (compare the opening moments of *The Fall of the House of Usher*), and the posters fluttering like an abandoned banner in the wind (compare the closing pages of *Sartoris*). The magic circle is, as it were, closed by these further touches, the reduction of the landscape, to a twilight kingdom of remembered fictions, quite complete.

What has happened to Capote since the appearance of *Other Voices, Other Rooms* is, I think, just as interesting as this—and, in its own way, just as commonplace. He has tried a number of different genres and styles, some of them Southern, some not, and all without apparent conviction or originality: macabre fantasy in *The Tree of Night* has been followed by pastoral comedy in *The Grass Harp*, picaresque adventure in *Breakfast at Tiffany's* by straightforward reportage in *In Cold Blood*.[5] Every one of these, needless to say, is well enough done on the level of technical competence. But not one of them carries any sense of genuine engagement; more important, not one of them helps Capote to solve his major problem of achieving a synthesis between myth and event. *In Cold Blood* (his account of a mass murder committed in the Midwestern state of Kansas only a few years ago) is a perfect illustration of this since all it does, essentially, is reverse the terms of Capote's predicament. Pure fantasy, the legendary kingdom of *Other Voices, Other Rooms,* is replaced in this book by the cult of the fact; and the ornate style, by one of scrupulous meanness. As a result of these changes events are now seen through an eye that most resembles that of the camera, without values, beliefs, or allegiances. They are separated off from the human context, in which connections are made and meanings arrived at, and presented as if they possessed some significance of their own—*possessed* significance rather than *assumed* it from the ideas brought to, and the legends drawn from, them. History may have become Capote's subject here, perhaps, but it is history recorded as a series of arbitrary occasions, lacking the determining force of myth; and as such it is not likely to convince the reader that the book represents much of an advance on its predecessors. Certainly it will not encourage him to place it in the same category as those works—such as "Ode to the Confederate Dead," say, or *World Enough and Time*—for which fact and legend, event and interpretation, seem equally indispensable.

Although no other Southern writer of any distinction has followed precisely the same path as Capote—from a passive acceptance of legend to a passive acceptance of fact—this eclecticism of his and, even more, his lack of any real engagement is, as I have suggested, very common indeed. Moral neutrality, in particular, is a regular characteristic of Southern novels and poems now. Or perhaps it would be more accurate to call it moral laziness or apathy, since it is the sort of attitude that issues from dependence. Not only the images and idioms are received, in such cases, the judgments are as well; regional memories are elevated to the status of absolutes without the writer being very much bothered either to investigate or place them, let alone adapt them to changing circumstances. A case in point here is a writer who has been elevated to major status in perhaps the fastest time ever recorded even in American letters—the poet and, by virtue of his one piece of fiction, the novelist James Dickey. With Dickey we find ourselves in another branch of the Southern tradition altogether and one to which I have not given much attention as yet—the branch, I mean, that is primarily concerned with the wild woods and the hunter, beginning in the tall tales told about Daniel Boone and Davy Crockett and achieving its finest literary moment so far in Faulkner's famous novella, "The Bear." Hunting provides the framework for many, if not most, of Dickey's poems, as well as for his novel *Deliverance.* Its incidents are frequently his subject, its rituals supply him with a language, and its code, such as it is, seems to prescribe the nature and scope of his perceptions. It is, in effect, during and by means of the hunt that the majority of Dickey's heroes (the word seems exactly the

right one for describing the larger-than-life protagonists of pieces like
"On the Coosawattee" and "Listening to Foxhounds") achieve contact
with what their creator sees as the primeval bases of existence—go
down into the ground, as it were, to commune with the inhuman.
"Listening to Foxhounds," for example, one of the best poems in
Dickey's second collection, begins in this way:

> When in that gold
> Of fires, quietly sitting
> With the men whose brothers are hounds,
>
> You hear the first tone
> Of a dog on scent, you look from face
> To face, to see whose will light up.
>
> When that light comes
> Inside the dark light of the fire,
> You know which chosen man has heard
>
> A thing like his own dead
> Speak out in a marvelous, helpless voice
> That he has been straining to hear.[6]

This passage illustrates well, I think, both how accomplished
Dickey's verse can be and how limited, radically limited, it normally
is. Its excellence is really a matter of technical accomplishment, stemming from the finely nerved energy of its rhythms; from the accumulative, nervously expectant movement of the syntax; above all, from
the language—that fluidity of expression and sense of hidden melody
which show the Southern love of rhetoric at its best. Apart from this,
as far as what is normally termed its *content* or *attitude* is concerned,
the passage is derivative in the extreme and even, in some of its implications, morally suspect. Its subject is, after all, a more than familiar
one: the old story about the man who hunts and, in the process, discovers a certain, innate sympathy with the hunted. What is more to
the point, this subject, familiar as it is, is left largely unexamined and
unlocated. It is not, to adopt a useful comparison, absorbed into the
kind of analysis of history that characterizes "The Bear"; nor is it applied
to some more fully rendered and humanly relevant situation as it is,
say, in Thomas Wolfe's novel, *The Hills Beyond*. Neither in the lines
just quoted nor in the rest of the poem, in fact, is the myth of the hunt
ever properly related to the human dimension. It remains, as it begins,
a way of calling us to the wild. And left like this, to establish its own
priorities uncriticized, it must strike the reader as crude and simplistic
indeed—offering the sort of message that even a confirmed Darwinist
like Jack London would have tried to qualify, if only to make it jibe
more comfortably with the experience of our conscious, social lives.

The point, because it is an important one, is worth emphasizing. Dickey has restricted himself, in "Listening to Foxhounds" and elsewhere, to a notion of human experience that is at best extraordinarily reductive and at worst morally questionable. And this has occurred, essentially, because he has allowed his subject to dictate his attitudes to him. The myth of the hunt has been adopted as a moral reference: but it has been left in its own separate and private moral framework, uninvestigated as to its own premises and uncontaminated by any contact with the other areas of our existence. Quite simply, the hunting expedition, its activities and the priorities it establishes, has been presented as if it offered a straightforward microcosm of our lives. The result of this is, as it inevitably must be, to encourage atavism, just as the result of accepting the myth of the old plantation wholesale must be to prescribe nostalgia. It is, after all, the writer's *treatment* of such myths that fires them into life and meaning, that disposes the emphases properly, establishes the necessary connections with our own experience, personal and historical, and in sum develops the received material into a coherent statement of values. Without this treatment, only two courses are possible: aestheticism of the sort illustrated by the work of Tennessee Williams and the earlier Truman Capote, or a kind of moral distortion. In the one case, the legends are endowed with a purely contextual meaning. They are taken to refer to nothing but their own, variously charming or macabre, selves. In the other, they are permitted to transcend their contexts and assume a wider relevance, but this assumption is seriously hampered by the fact that they never seem to be altered or enriched in the process. The meanings, such as they are, are merely imposed. Both courses, as I have said, issue from the same inability to use the Southern tradition rather than be used by it; and it is not necessary, surely, to be of an apocalyptic turn of mind to draw a further conclusion from this. Which is, if people with the reputations of Williams, Capote, and Dickey cannot do anything really creative with their inheritance—then who can? Perhaps that inheritance has become so complex, and so thoroughly intimidating by this time, that the most that can possibly be done is what they have done: play with the baroque details, repeat the old, tired messages. Perhaps, to put it another way, the Southern writer is incapable of getting out from underneath Faulkner now, and all his other literary ancestors, for the simple reason that the ancestral shadow has begun to stretch too far.

This is, of course, to put the matter in the worst light possible, and to assume that because Williams, Capote, and Dickey are among the most publicized of contemporary Southern writers they are therefore necessarily the best. Neither this assumption, nor the rather pessimistic conclusions to be drawn from it, are, I feel, really correct. Admittedly, there has been something of a slackening off in recent years. There is no longer the sense, as there was often between the wars, that practically everybody below the Mason-Dixon line must be busy scribbling novels, poems, and plays; and, among those who *are* still writing, there is nobody to challenge comparison with Faulkner, or even Thomas Wolfe and Robert Penn Warren. That, however, does not argue for a complete absence of creativity. Nor should it be taken to imply that mannerism and imitation are all the South has to offer at present. Even a "silver age"—which is what, surely, the South is now in—can contribute in its own positive, if modest, way to a literary idiom. Even writers of a silver age can add to the systems of argument and configurations of imagery they have inherited—although, certainly, what they add may appear rather slight or tentative when compared with the achievement of their predecessors. Three writers, especially, seem to me to demonstrate this because they have contributed more than their share—and certainly more than Williams, Dickey, and Capote have so far—to the survival of the regional tradition. I mean by this Carson McCullers, Flannery O'Connor, and William Styron. Needless to say, there are others who have made their own special contribution and who, consequently, it would be well worth looking at if there were time: among them James Agee, the novelists Reynolds Price and Walker Percy, the short-story writer Peter Taylor, and the poet Randall Jarrell.[7] But the three writers I have just mentioned are, I believe, easily the most distinctive, exciting, and genuinely inventive to emerge in the South over the past twenty or thirty years; they, I think, have managed to "make it new" in a way and to an extent that none of their contemporaries have. Which is why I would like to look now, briefly, at each of them.

Moods and Absences: Carson McCullers

There is a peculiar quality of isolation about Carson McCullers's work, frequently remarked upon but never properly explained, that owes some of its intensity perhaps to her own status vis-à-vis the South. She does not belong to the great generation of the "renaissance," that is clear enough: indeed, she was only twelve years old when *The Sound and the Fury* was published, and her first novel, *The Heart is a Lonely Hunter,* did not appear until after the beginning of the Second World War. But she does not really belong to the new wave of Southern writers either, since apart from *Clock Without Hands*—a book dealing, among other things, with the issue of desegregation, which was not published until 1961—all of her more important fiction had been written by 1946; and was collected into a uniform edition some five years later. Her major period of creativity was very brief, consisting of about five years in all; and the last twenty or so years of her life were so marred by ill health that, in retrospect, it seems remarkable she was able to write the little, during the period, that she did. Certainly, illness offers a sufficient explanation for her gradual lapse into silence. Coming after the great fiction and poetry of the twenties and thirties, but before the more recent examples of Southern Gothic (before *Wise Blood* and *Lie Down in Darkness*, for example, before even *Other Voices, Other Rooms* and *A Streetcar Named Desire*) her novels and short stories occupy, consequently, a particular transitional moment of their own in the tradition. Theirs is a special, and especially separate, place in the history of Southern literature, which makes their author seem occasionally like one of her own characters—alone, cut off from all normal channels of communication, and strangely vulnerable.

Other factors, quite apart from her unusual literary situation, probably contributed to McCullers's interest in the dimensions of loneliness. Her childhood, for example, seems to have been a very quiet one. "Almost singularly lacking," as her biographer has put it, "in the excitement of external events,"[8] it reflected the particular milieu into which she was born; shabbily genteel, the McCullers family of Columbus, Georgia, were inordinately embarrassed by their fallen circumstances and actively discouraged contact or intercourse with anybody from outside the home. Then, when Carson did grow up and move away (to New York and, later, to Europe) her aloof and rather prickly personality tended to complete the process thus begun. Always afraid of a full commitment to others, searching for the possibility of betrayal and claiming to find it even when it was not there, she seemed to draw a magic circle around herself for much of the time, and live in an inner world that was compounded equally of memory and imagination. "I . . . have my own reality," she said once toward the end of her life, made out "of language and voices and foliage";[9] and it was this reality, I believe, her ghostly, private world, that she tried to reproduce in most of her fiction. She gave it many names, over the years, and placed it consistently in the South. Southern though its geographical location might be, however, it was like no South anybody had ever seen before. It was not the South of newspaper articles and political speeches, nor the South of country humor or magnolia-blossom romance; it was not even the South described so extensively in the Yoknapatawpha novels. In effect, it was another country altogether, created out of all that the author had found haunting, soft, and lonely in her childhood surroundings—a new place offering a new perspective on the experience from which it had been drawn.

Perhaps we can gain a better idea of this new place, the unique map that McCullers offered of her home, by looking at one of her characteristic attempts at depicting it. Her novella, "The Ballad of the Sad Café," for example, begins with this memorable description of a town without a name and, in doing so, establishes the climate, physical and emotional, in which all its characters are to move.

> The town itself is dreary; not much is there except the cotton-mill, the two-room houses where the workers live, a few peach trees, a church with two colored windows, and a miserable main street only a hundred yards long. On Saturdays the tenants from the near-by farms come in for a day of talk and trade. Otherwise the town is lonesome, sad, and like a place that is far off and estranged from all other places in the world. The nearest train stop is Society City, and the Greyhound and White Bus Lines use the Fork Falls Road which is three miles away. The winters here are short and raw, the summers white with glare and fiery hot.
>
> If you walk along the main street on an August afternoon there is nothing whatsoever to do. The largest building . . . is boarded up . . . and . . . looks completely deserted. Nevertheless, on the second floor there is one window which is not boarded; sometimes in the late afternoon . . . a hand will slowly open the shutter and a face will look down on the town . . . as likely as not there will not be another soul to be seen along the . . . street. These August afternoons—when your shift is finished there is absolutely nothing to do; you might as well walk down to the Fork Falls Road and listen to the chain gang.[10]

I have quoted a fairly long passage from the book because, it seems to me, the effect of McCullers's prose is accumulative. She does not work in a series of detached, glittering phrases as, say, Truman Capote does. Nor does she, imitating Faulkner, write sentences that coil up snakelike and then strike, suddenly, before the period. Her language is cool and lucid, almost classical in its precision, her descriptions clipped and occasionally cryptic. A nuance in one place, a repetition or a shading somewhere else: this is all she needs really because, like the painter Edward Hopper, she tends to rely on the resonance given to a detail by its total context—and to use concealment almost as a medium of communication. The inertia, the desolation, and the brooding violence of the small-town South are caught in images that are hermetic, despite their apparent candor, and in incidents brimming with undisclosed biography.

The act is performed so quietly that it may tend to go unnoticed: what McCullers has created here, in effect, is a world where emotion and vision can coalesce—in which, through the agency of her prose, her own particular sense of life can be externalized. The town is no dream kingdom, that is clear enough. It is anchored in this world, in a firm if understated way, by such details as the references to the bus and train services and by an implicit understanding of its economic function. But it is no ordinary place, either—the kind of town we might easily come across in Georgia, in the South, or anywhere else. Why? Because, quite apart from establishing this anchorage, the writer has used every means at her disposal to reorder, rearrange, and so metamorphose; in a way that must be familiar to us by now, she has created another country out of her own known home. In this respect, the anonymity of the prose ties in with the evasiveness of the narrator, the hermeticism of the imagery with the apparent emptiness of the scene. For together they direct our attention to precisely the same subject; a feeling of "lonesomeness" or loss seems to result from them all. This feeling, needless to say, is not imposed on the material: as other writers like Thomas Wolfe could testify, it is there in the Deep South already, waiting to be acknowledged.[11] McCullers has, however, emphasized it almost to the exclusion of everything else and, in doing so, cleverly established a nexus, a point of connection between the geometry of her self and the geography of her childhood surroundings. Gently, she has nudged the regional landscape into the expression of a fresh mood.

McCullers's aims are, of course, not just personal. Quite apart from externalizing her own state she is trying also, through the medium of the South, to anatomize human nature, to chart, in her plan of her region, the coordinates of all our lives. And in order to make this clear she will occasionally punctuate her narrative with little explanatory passages, like the following, which suggest that, remembering her own doubts about the possibility of proper contact between man and man—and, perhaps, experiencing some misgivings about her oblique methods elsewhere—the author is afraid the reader will otherwise miss the point.

> There are the lover and the beloved, but these two come from different countries. Often the beloved is only a stimulus for all the stored-up love which has lain quiet within the lover for a long time hitherto. And somehow every lover knows this. He feels in his soul that his love is a solitary thing. He comes to know a new, strange loneliness. . . . So there is only one thing for the lover to do. He must house his love within himself . . . ; he must create for himself a whole new inward world—a world intense and strange, complete in itself.[12]

The longing to communicate and the difficulty of ever properly communicating, the delusions attendant upon the human need to love: the themes could hardly be presented more explicitly than they are here (indeed, the existence of a triangular relationship between personal feeling, regional landscape, and moral reference is virtually insisted upon) and this does, naturally, tend to carry its own dangers with it. The "message" may, as a result, seem a little too pat to be convincing, too limited and limiting even for the purpose of fable. The writer may, in short, end up with didacticism of the crudest possible kind. McCullers is saved from such dangers most of the time, I think, though; and what saves her more than anything else is her constant awareness of the *human* situation—the specifically emotional and imaginative terms into which her ideas have to be translated. Her landscapes, for all their initial sparseness, *are* inhabited. More to the point, the figures inhabiting them possess a special kind of resonance, that sense of roots and a definite history which marks them out as the descendants of recognizable Southern types. They have the substance and immediate credibility of people long brooded over, and so well understood—and to this is added that freshness, the sense of surprise and valuable discovery, which can only come when someone as well known as this is seen from a radically altered standpoint. We may suspect, while we read a McCullers story, that we have seen characters like hers before; in fact, if we have read much earlier Southern fiction we are sure we have. But until now, she makes us feel, we have never been properly acquainted with them: there is something about them, some crucial side of them we have somehow managed to miss.

The major characters in "The Ballad of the Sad Café" offer a perfect illustration of this, the way in which the familiar is suddenly turned into the strange and new. And the nature of their *familiarity*, at least, is suggested by a bare summary of the "Ballad"'s plot, which is like something borrowed from the comic legends of the old Southwest. There is a kind of crazy, comic logic of frustration behind everything that happens: the beloved is always turning away from the lover to create a false idol of his or her own. So "Miss Amelia" Evans, the central character and the owner of the "terrible, dim" face which appears in the opening portrait of the town, refuses the love of her husband, Marvin Macey, and, having done so, falls in love with a newcomer to the district, the hunchback "Cousin" Lymon. Cousin Lymon, in turn, despises Miss Amelia and worships Marvin Macey—who despises *him*. Nobody gets what he wants in the story. Everybody is thwarted and, in the process, made to look utterly grotesque. This, for example, is how Miss Amelia is described before the charade has properly begun:

> She was a dark, tall woman with bones and muscles like a man. Her hair was cut short and brushed back from the forehead, and there was about her sunburned face a tense, haggard quality. She might have been a handsome woman if, even then, she was not slightly cross-eyed.[13]

By reducing her appearance to a series of conflicting angles, by emphasizing her physical defects and her masculinity (or, rather, her sexual ambivalence), McCullers effectively transforms Miss Amelia into a freak here—as much of a caricature in her own way as Sut Lovingood is, say, or any of the subhumans populating *Tobacco Road*. At least one of the strategies for presenting the character to us, in other words, seems to have been learned from Longstreet, Harris, and their imitators: we are distanced from Miss Amelia, made to inspect her and her country home with a clinical detachment, and then invited to consider her frustrations, such as they are—her utter failure to realize her ambitions in her given world—as at the very least potentially comic. As if to confirm McCullers's debt, there is even an epic fight at the end of the "Ballad," between Miss Amelia and Marvin Macey, which in its combination of the macabre and the grotesque (Macey greases himself, for instance, so that he can keep slipping through Miss Amelia's fingers) must remind us of those almost operatic trials of strength which enliven so many of the tales of the Southwestern school.

That is not the whole story, though. If it were, we could hardly talk about McCullers making her characters new. Miss Amelia is a grotesque, perhaps, but she is a grotesque for the same reason that most of McCullers's subjects are—because, as the author herself once put it, her "physical incapacity" is being used primarily as "a symbol of [her] spiritual incapacity . . . —[her] spiritual isolation." She is not just the comic loser, nor is she economically deprived in the way that Jeeter Lester and Ty Ty Walden are. She is, to use that word again, "lonesome," and her lonesomeness is intended eventually to figure our own. Like an image seen in a carnival mirror, she is meant to offer us an exaggerated, comically distorted, and yet somehow sadly accurate reflection of ourselves. Exactly what this means, in terms of the total effect she has upon us, will perhaps become clear if we look at the way she is described toward the end of the story, when both Marvin Macey and Cousin Lymon have deserted her.

> Miss Amelia let her hair grow ragged, and it was turning grey. Her face lengthened, and the great muscles of her body shrank until she was thin as old maids are thin when they go crazy. And those grey eyes—slowly day by day they were more crossed, . . . as though they sought each other out to exchange a little glance of grief and lonely recognition.[14]

This, surely, is to give the familiar caricature a fresh dimension. The details of Miss Amelia's appearance are just as grotesque as they ever were, but they appear to be placed now in a changed, and more sympathetic, context. We are drawn to the woman even while she still seems a little odd to us. The knowledge we have of her by this time has, of course, something to do with this development: we understand why she is odd and, understanding, we perhaps suspect that her odd-ity touches upon ours. And certain fragments of descriptive detail, which hint at pity as much as ridicule, are possibly relevant as well—the com-parison with "crazy" old maids, for example, or the partly funny, partly moving account that McCullers now gives us of Miss Amelia's crossed eyes. But of immeasurably more significance than either of these things, I think, is something almost indefinable—which, for want of a better phrase, we must call the sheer texture of her prose. It goes back, in fact, to what I was saying earlier about McCullers's style, that it manages to be lyrical and colloquial, lucid and enigmatic, at one and the same time. For it is as a direct consequence of this strange combination, really, that we find ourselves held back from Miss Amelia here—and brought close up into a special kind of intimacy with her as well. She is distanced from us by a certain lingering freakishness of expression, a mysterious image, it may be, or a quirky turn of phrase; and yet she is also brought into an immediate contact with us by our sense that this is, after all, a conventional idiom we are listen-ing to—that the language Miss Amelia inhabits, so to speak, belongs to normal, everyday conversation. This is an extraordinarily subtle rela-tionship to set up between character and reader—far subtler than anything we are likely to come across elsewhere, in the work of other writers who have experimented with the Southern comic mode. It has its origins, of course, in McCullers's belief that a paradox lurks at the heart of experience, naturally attaching itself to the idea of a *shared* isolation. As for its issue, that we find in the mood or *ambiance* to which our minds first return when recalling a McCullers novel—our memories of a quiet, but peculiarly inclusive, pathos.

Pathos: it is an unfashionable term partly because, through bad use, it has acquired an odor of sentimentality—become associated with what Ezra Pound once called that most inhumane of emotions, an in-discriminate sympathy. The unlucky man wallowing in his own bad luck, the account of poverty or suffering that begins and ends in moral posturing, without any reference being made to the possible agencies of change: these are the sort of things to which we tend to apply the word "pathetic" now. Nor are matters helped much, I sup-pose, by the memories most of us have of films that have been de-scribed as pathetic—where, more often than not, a patently contrived series of events is used as a pretext for self-indulgence. Pathos, in such cases, becomes the emotional equivalent of beating one's head against the wall—an exquisitely painful way of preparing for the mo-ment when the pain stops, and the release offered by the inevitable happy ending arrives. Still, there is no reason why misuse of a word should blind us to its proper uses; and I would like to suggest that McCullers's fiction, at its best (by which I mean "The Ballad of the Sad Café," *The Member of the Wedding*,[15] and parts of *The Heart is a Lonely Hunter*), can supply us with a valuable corrective to all this. For it shows, I think, how tough and really critical an emotion pathos can be. Her characters are pathetic, but they are pathetic in the finest sense—in the same way that, to continue an earlier analogy, a good Chaplin film is. That is to say, the melancholy we experience while contemplating Miss Amelia Evans or Frankie Addams in *The Member of the Wedding* stems principally from the shock of recognition, our feeling that part of our own lives has been accurately defined. It encourages us not to escape from problems, still less to accept them, but simply to become more aware—to understand, fully to understand, their general scope. In this way the pathetic is used as an agent of moral instruction more than anything else, a means of telling us, quietly and sadly, what we are and the most we can do and of advising us, by inference, as to how we should behave.

McCullers's is, then, the definitive use of a specific emotional effect —a pathos that at once lends a strange atmosphere to landscape and character, and helps establish an intimate, unusually searching relationship between tale and reader. This is an impressive achievement— showing the kind of subtlety and even deviousness of intent we are perhaps more inclined to associate with more "difficult" fiction—and its very impressiveness has, I believe, led one or two of McCullers's critics into overestimating her. For there is a tendency, noticeable especially among those with a bias toward the New Criticism, to assume that because her work represents a perfect adaptation of means to ends she is, therefore, more or less unsurpassed among writers of her own region. So Walter Allen, in his standard history of the modern English and American novel, places her second only to Faulkner; and Gore Vidal, going one characteristic step further than this, insists, "of all our Southern writers Carson McCullers is the one most likely to endure."[16] Such commentary, I think, is exaggerated and unhelpful: the very perfection of McCullers's work depends, after all, upon her own level-headed acceptance of her limitations. She knows that she can describe, quite subtly, one particular dilemma or area of life and she concentrates almost her entire resources on that. There is no place in her fiction, really, for the rich "over-plus" of experience—by which I mean any aspects of behavior that cannot be included under the heading of theme, or any dimensions of feeling that cannot be reconciled with the major effect of pathos. And recognizing this she demonstrates little interest in such matters as the historical and social context, and no commitment either to the idea of a developing consciousness. Her people walk around and around within the circle of their own personalities, their inner world of thought and desire hardly engaging with the outer world at all. They seldom change, except physically, they never reflect more than one aspect of our experience (admittedly, it is a significant one); and to inflate them, their world, or indeed their creator to a major status—to suppose, in fact, that McCullers's novels and short stories are any more important to the tradition than they genuinely are—is, I believe, to be guilty of what used to be called "overkill." It is, in other words, to smother a quiet but effective talent by heaping upon it unearned and patently unacceptable praise.

As for McCullers's actual achievement, though, setting aside all such exaggeration, that surely is certain and secure. She is not a major writer, despite anything that Allen, Vidal, or any other critic may say to the contrary. But she is a very good minor one—so good, indeed, that she seems to reap a definite advantage from her minor status and turn her limitations into virtues. The absence of the historical dimension is a useful illustration of this. With many other writers, and especially Southern ones, such an absence might prove fatal—indeed it *has* proved fatal, I think, in the case of Tennessee Williams and the earlier Capote. With McCullers, however, just the opposite is true; and this because in some strange way she manages to make history function as an *absent presence* in her work. It seems to be not so much omitted from her writing as concealed, made to disappear, and in such a way that the disappearance itself, like the disappearance of the religious perspective from later Victorian fiction, encourages our active comment. McCullers's characters, we infer, have not even this, the mere possibility of a tradition, to sustain them; they can only hang as Lowell's Czar Lepke does, "oas[es] in . . . [the] air/of lost connections"[17]—so disoriented as to have no point of reference really, no common denominator with which to chart their disorientation. They may suffer pangs of nostalgia; in fact most of them do, it is a natural consequence of their loneliness. But that nostalgia is for a condition they can hardly define. They may be adrift, homesick; but that homesickness is for a place that has never, personally, been theirs. Just as space seems to recede from them even while it is being described, to try to hide from them in a way, so time in its larger dimension appears somehow to mock them by remaining hidden; the vacuum its departure creates is, we sense, *there* as a positive force in the narrative contributing to their despair. One sometimes wonders if, in all this, McCullers is not trying to add her own idiosyncratic footnote to Nietzsche by suggesting that not only God, that traditional comforter of the loney and spiritually disfigured, is dead now—history, as a common secular resource and the modern substitute for God, is as well.

Comedy, Mystery, and the Bible Belt: Flannery O'Connor

We can perhaps only speculate about the apocalyptic meanings hidden in McCullers's work, and that precisely because they *are* hidden, operating merely as hints and guesses to be snatched up from below the surface of what is said. But with Flannery O'Connor—the novelist and short-story writer from Georgia who died in 1964 at the tragically early age of thirty-nine—to speculate in this way becomes unnecessary, really, because she was manifestly obsessed with the notion of apocalypse. A devout if highly unorthodox Roman Catholic, O'Connor interpreted experience according to her own reading of Christian eschatology—a reading that was, on her admission, tough, uncompromising, and quite without any of "the . . . hazy compassion" that "excuses all human weakness" on the ground that "human weakness is human." "For me," she declared, "the meaning of life is centered in our Redemption by Christ";[18] and to this she might well have added that she neither saw mankind as worthy of being redeemed, nor Redemption itself as anything other than a painful act of divorce from this world. If she is like any traditional theologian at all it is Saint John of the Cross, who said, "The Soul cannot be possessed of divine union, until it has divested itself of the love of created beings." For with rare exceptions the world she explores in her work is one of corrosion and decay, invested with evil, apparently forsaken by God and saved only in the last analysis by His incalculable grace. It is a netherworld, a place of nightmare comic because absurd, and (as in early Christian allegory) the one path by which its inhabitants can travel beyond it is that of renunciation, penance, and extreme suffering.

This, then, is what O'Connor brought to the old Southern images: not an entirely personal series of perceptions like McCullers, but her strict devotion to her Roman Catholic God and her fully developed sense of a universe that operates under the terms of His providence. "The two circumstances that have given character to my writing," she admitted, "have been those of being Southern and being Catholic"; and it was the mixture of these two, in the crucible of her own eccentric personality, that helped produce the strangely intoxicating atmosphere of her work—at once brutal and farcical, like somebody else's bad dream. I want, in a moment, to look at this atmosphere in a little more detail, and the interconnection of motives and forces responsible for it: but before doing that it is worth emphasizing, I think, that it *was* this—O'Connor's ability to relate her religious loyalties to her Southern experience—that saved her from many of the pitfalls of regionalism. She knew all about those pitfalls; in fact she has given us her own, characteristically down-to-earth and yet eccentric, description of them. For once when she was asked what her own main problems as a writer were, she replied,

> I think the writer is initially set going by literature more than life. When there are many writers all employing the same idiom, all looking on more or less the same social scene, the individual writer has to be more than ever careful that he isn't just doing badly what has already been done to completion. The presence alone of Faulkner . . . makes a great difference in what . . . [I] can and cannot . . . do. Nobody wants his mule and wagon stalled on the same track the Dixie Limited is roaring down.[19]

To put it rather less colorfully, O'Connor had, she knew, to discover her own sources of moral organization—a satisfactory way out of her Southern past that would help her to take what she needed from that past with her. She had to add and alter, rather than merely copy; and it is surely not to exaggerate to say that it was her faith, what she called her own "contact with mystery," that enabled her to do just that.

Suppose we look at the matter from a slightly different angle, though. Why should Flannery O'Connor, a Catholic novelist in a largely Protestant region, have been interested in the South in the first place? What possible reasons could she have had for devoting herself as a writer to people whose religious sympathies were so profoundly different from her own—and who have sometimes even tended to think of Catholics as aliens and subversives, a dangerous minority group like Jews and Negroes? The answers to this, I think, knit together articles of personal belief and purely literary considerations, and eventually take us to the heart of O'Connor's regionalism. Partly, it was a matter of necessity: "Southern writers," as O'Connor herself liked to put it, "are stuck with the South," if only because it is the place they know best. They therefore leave it, if they are able to leave it, at their peril. But beyond this it was also a matter of eagerly accepting the necessary, embracing it until it almost came to seem willed. "To know oneself," as O'Connor said on another occasion, "is to know one's region"; and we have only to reverse this formula to see that what she was perhaps required to do, because she was a Southerner, was something she felt she wanted to do as well. Like the good Christian she clearly wished to be, in fact, O'Connor could—in this one respect at least—discover in service a perfect freedom. That, anyway, is the feeling which comes across from her every time she talks (in her essays or letters) about her regional material: the South, she never stops claiming at such moments, is not just an acceptable location for the Catholic writer—it is a good, almost the perfect, one. Her reasons for making this claim are plausible enough, and expressed with the precision of somebody who appears to know what she is talking about.

Now the South is a good place for a Catholic literature in my sense for a number of reasons.

1) In the South belief can still be made believable and in relation to a large part of society. We're not the Bible Belt for nothing.

2) The Bible being generally known and revered in the section, gives the novelist that broad mythical base to refer to that he needs to extend his meaning in depth.

3) The South has a sacramental view of life.

4) The aspect of Protestantism that is most prominent . . . in the South is that of man dealing with God directly . . . and this is great for a Catholic novelist like myself who wants to get close to a character and watch him wrestle with the Lord.[20]

To this argument O'Connor would add occasionally that even in those particulars where the South seemed most inimical to Catholicism (in its indifference to ritual, for instance, or its strict construction of the Bible) it could usually act, by virtue of the very challenge it offered, as a valuable antidote or therapy. For by confronting her, as a Catholic writer, with a society to which her principles had only a partial application, it could force her, not to abandon her principles, but in applying them to fresh situations to come up with fresh reactions. Her Catholicism could perhaps be rejuvenated, during the engagement between natural occasion and personal motive, quite as much as her regionalism could.

This extremely sophisticated, self-conscious attitude toward both the implications of her faith and the uses of her region is, I think, equally noticeable in O'Connor's choice of fictional approach. Her South is in many ways the same one that Erskine Caldwell and Carson McCullers are interested in—a wasteland, savage and empty, full of decaying towns and villages, crisscrossed by endless tobacco roads—and like them she borrows from the techniques of the Southwestern humorists, showing a certain bizarre comic inventiveness in describing it. Her characters, for example, are not so much human beings as grotesque parodies of humanity; as O'Connor herself has suggested, they are "literal in the same sense that a child's drawing is literal"—people seen with an untamed and alien eye. Where O'Connor parts company with Caldwell and McCullers, though, and indeed with every other writer of the Southwestern school, is in what she intends by all this—and in the subtle changes wrought on her work by this difference of intention. This is how O'Connor explained what she was after, toward the end of her life.

The novelist with Christian concerns will find in modern life distortions which are repugnant to him, and his problem will be to make these appear as distortions to an audience which is used to seeing them as natural.

. . . When you can assume that your audience holds the same beliefs you do, you can relax a little and use more normal means of talking to it; when you have to assume that it does not, then you have to make your vision apparent by shock—to the hard of hearing you shout, and for the almost-blind you draw large and startling figures.[21]

O'Connor's characters are grotesques, in other words, because she wants us to see them as spiritual primitives. In order to describe to us a society that is unnatural by her own Christian standards—and to make us feel its unnaturalness—she creates a fictional world that is unnatural by almost any accepted standards at all. Caldwell's people are victims, twisted and misshapen by a world they never made, and beyond the surface of their lives lies their creator's belief in their unblemished innocence. But Flannery O'Connor's characters are active participants in their own corruption: their distortions are the product of their guilt, original sin, and they are no more innocent, no less to blame for their predicament, than all men as sons of Adam are.

This is only half the story, though. From close up O'Connor's characters may seem stubbornly foolish and perverse, ignorant witnesses to the power of evil. But ultimately, against their will, they reveal the workings of eternal redemption as well. They are the children of God, O'Connor believes, as well as the children of Adam; and through their lives shines dimly the possibility that they may, after all, be saved. So an extra twist of irony is added to everything that happens in O'Connor's stories. Absurd as her people are, their absurdity serves —as much as it does anything else—as a measure of God's mercy in caring for them. Corrupt and violent as their behavior may be, its very corruption can act as a proof, a way of suggesting the extraordinary scope of His forgiveness and love. Instead of broad satire, in fact (or even that delicate blend of the ridiculous and the pathetic that we find in Carson McCullers's fiction), O'Connor practices a comedy of savage paradox, in which every incident assumes a double edge because it reminds us, at one and the same time, that man is worthless and yet the favored of God—negligible but the instrument of Divine Will. The irremediable wickedness of humanity and the undeniable grace of God are opposites that meet head on in her writing, and it is in the humor, finally, that they find their issue, or appropriate point of release.

Wise Blood, Flannery O'Connor's first published volume and in many ways her most impressive, is I think an excellent illustration of this, and besides shows how she could invest a common, social and literary, pattern with unfamiliar meanings. Its central character, Haze Motes, the descendant of a long line of Fundamentalist preachers, has, when we first meet him, just left the army and returned to his home in the hills of Tennessee. When he gets there, however, he finds the house empty and collapsing, the land overgrown with weeds, and all his relatives either dead or dispersed to other parts of the state. So, after spending one night under the family roof, he leaves next day for the nearby industrial town of Taulkinham (a wild parody of Atlanta, Georgia), not because he has any particular desire to live there, but simply following his own stated advice that, once the stability of familiar surroundings has been lost, "You might as well go one place as another."[22] Haze becomes, in fact, a wanderer or—to borrow the title of one of O'Connor's short stories—a displaced person, without roots and without any perceptible direction to his life. Evidently there are certain historical reasons for this, immediate reasons at least, and they have to do with O'Connor's own feeling, expressed at length in her essays, that the South is changing too fast and for the worse—"every day . . . getting more and more like the rest of the country." Haze Motes, in other words, is that figure familiar in Southern literature since the time of the Agrarian symposium: the disinherited poor white who must drift to town because there is nowhere else for him to go. But although O'Connor shows sufficient tact, and caution, to imply these reasons, and so tentatively admit our world within the borders of her story, she does not in any way dwell upon them. They are intimated rather than explained because it is not this, the pattern of our lives in time, that she is really interested in. Where her interest does lie is in the religious dimension of experience; and it is to this Haze Motes directs our attention to the extent that his displacement is being used as a symbol—an emblem of alienation, moral and spiritual, rather than an example of a specific, historical problem. His estrangement from his traditional way of life and means of living figures, or so his creator intends, the plight of any man denied firm (which is to say, institutionalized) religious guidance, and this makes the usual, socially oriented meanings of his condition quite secondary.

Be that as it may, Haze moves to Taulkinham and there sets himself up as the founder of a new religion. "I preach the Church Without Christ," he declares,

> "I'm member and preacher to that church where the blind don't see and the lame don't walk and what's dead stays that way. . . . I'm going to preach there was no Fall because there was nothing to fall from and no Redemption because there was no Fall and no Judgment because there wasn't the first two. Nothing matters but that Jesus was a liar."[23]

Traveling around the town, preaching always from the top of an old Ford Essex car ("Nobody with a good car," says Haze in one of the novel's more glorious moments, "needs to be justified."), his conduct certainly seems pretty bizarre but it has its own unique explanation.

For in acting the way he does Haze is responding to the one thing that has always cut across his habitual aimlessness—which is his impulse—now become an obsessive need—to rebel against his Fundamentalist ancestors and obliterate "the ragged figure of Jesus" they have "planted at the back of his mind." By nature and training and, even more important, by metaphysical ordination, Haze is, we learn, a man of God, and he has chosen blasphemy as a way of resisting his vocation. What this leaves out of account, however, is something that Haze gradually comes to learn in the course of the story: that, as T. S. Eliot argued in a famous essay on Baudelaire, "Genuine blasphemy, genuine in spirit and not purely verbal, . . . is a way of affirming belief,"[24] because it depends on the presence of God to give it force and meaning. Without God it would be impossible to blaspheme, just as without His law it would be impossible to sin, and so, in turning his life into an act of iconoclasm, Haze perversely admits the power over him of the very faith he struggles to deny.

This, the fact that Haze is a Christian despite himself, is the central paradox of the story—and it generates many others. It would take too long, and in any case it would be redundant, I think, to discuss them all in detail, but perhaps one or two should be mentioned so as to illustrate the peculiar ironies that O'Connor manages to extract from what seem like familiar situations, and to suggest something of the strange, God-intoxicated atmosphere that hovers around her entire vision of the South. Some of the paradoxes she exploits are so ancient that they hardly require exegesis; they have been an integral part of the Christian idiom since the beginning, and form what is by now a traditional way of trying to express the inexpressible. The image of seeing, for example, has always provided one of the most fruitful of contradictions, issuing from the belief that spiritual insight has nothing at all to do with the ordinary instruments of perception: "The wise man's eyes are in his head, but the fool walketh in darkness" (Eccles. 2:14). And this O'Connor develops by allowing Haze only to see the truth—about himself and his relationship with God—after he has burned his eyes out with quicklime, as the first in a series of expiatory gestures. Before that, although he may protest, "Don't I have eyes in my head? Am I a blind man?" proper sight (what William Blake liked to call "double vision") remains unavailable to him; it is, we are told later, "something he . . . couldn't get without being blinded to everything else." Similarly, just as Haze stumbled when he saw so, it appears, he scarcely lived when he was alive, and only achieves real life, true being, when he is dead. Of course, O'Connor cannot either tell or show us *this*, since she will never permit herself to step beyond the barriers of this world. But she certainly implies it in the closing moments of the novel, when one of the other characters, in fact Haze's former landlady, Mrs. Flood, sits beside his corpse, trying somehow to possess its secret. A representative of the evil, fragmented world from which Haze himself has now escaped, Mrs. Flood seems to enjoy a momentary glimpse of the eternal as she watches and wonders.

> She had never observed his face more composed . . . the . . . sockets seemed to lead into the dark tunnel where he had disappeared. . . . She shut her eyes and saw the pin point of light but so far away that she could not hold it steady in her mind. . . . She sat staring with her eyes shut, into his eyes, and felt as if she had finally got to the beginning of something she couldn't begin, and she saw him moving farther and farther away, . . . into the darkness until he was the pin point of light.[25]

The "pin point of light" mentioned here has already been identified, earlier on in the story, with the star over Bethlehem, and this must confirm our growing suspicion that Haze has been enlightened and redeemed, lifted toward a new existence. His blasphemy, followed by his acts of self-immolation, have been stages in a gradual progress toward a grotesque kind of sainthood—which is perhaps the only kind possible in a world such as the one O'Connor describes, where God must be seen through a glass darkly.

More interesting perhaps than this, because far more unexpected, are the ironies and paradoxes of O'Connor's own invention, products of that special talent for word splitting and logic chopping that makes her seem sometimes like some medieval scholiast turned poet. The way, for instance, that she plays with the idea of "wise blood" is extraordinarily subtle and, as far as I know, originates with her work. On one level "wise blood" is synonymous with natural impulse, the needs Haze thinks he is satisfying by living with a woman when he first arrives in Taulkinham, and spending most of his days in blasphemy. But on quite another, a level that Haze is aware of and yet hardly acknowledges until just before his death, "wise blood" refers to the blood of his ancestors coursing through his veins, his inherited calling —and reminds us as well of the blood of Jesus Christ, shed in the act of Redemption. Haze believes he is following his "wise blood" in the first sense, but even at the beginning of the story this is not completely true. It is in the second sense that it exercises real power over him, and it is the conception of human nature flowing from this—the conception, that is to say, that emphasizes the *higher* nature of man—that he eventually obeys. So complete is the reversal by the end of the narrative that Haze can even defend his acts of penitence (his blinding of himself, for instance, or placing barbed wire under his shirt next to his skin) with the simple plea, "It's natural";[26] for by this time he has moved into a dimension where the ordinary definitions of the natural, and the human, no longer apply. From "the Church without Christ" he has flown to Christ, from the language of the commonplace world to the idiom of the Bible; and in a way the contradictions implicit in O'Connor's title are themselves enough to mark the trajectory of his flight.

I do not want to suggest that the sense of paradox in *Wise Blood* is a product of purely local effects, though, a matter of texture (to use John Crowe Ransom's term) and nothing else. On the contrary, the entire narrative structure contributes to it, I think, because this, like all O'Connor's books, resembles an elaborate piece of architecture or geometric plan—a system of cross-references, contrasts, and counterpointed images that holds everything that is said in a state of tension. By definition, this is not as easy to illustrate as local effects are, since to understand and appreciate it properly we have simply to read the story from start to finish several times, noting as we do so how every detail either latches into or opposes others. But we can at least gain some idea of how the strategy works by looking at a cornerstone of the edifice—in other words, at a seminal passage—and in this respect, because any novel is at least on one level a sequential work of art, one of the most seminal passages must be at the beginning, when Haze Motes is introduced to us, traveling by express train to Taulkinham.

> Hazel Motes sat at a forward angle on the green plush train seat, looking one minute at the window as if he might want to jump out of it, and the next down the aisle at the other end of the car. The train was racing through . . . plowed fields . . . and the few hogs nosing in the furrows looked like large spotted stones. Mrs. Wally Bee Hitchcock, who was facing Motes . . . said . . . "I guess you're going home." . . . He didn't look, to her, much over twenty, but he had a stiff black broad-brimmed hat on his lap, a hat that an elderly country preacher would wear. . . . He didn't answer her or move his eyes from whatever he was looking at . . . she found herself squinting . . . at his eyes. . . . They were the color of pecan shells and set in deep sockets. The outline of a skull under his skin was plain and insistent. . . . He had a nose like a shrike's bill and a long vertical crease on either side of his mouth . . . but his eyes were what held her attention longest. Their settings were so deep that they seemed . . . almost like passages leading somewhere. . . . What he was looking at was the porter. . . . "Going to the city," Haze said, "I . . . was raised in Eastrod." The porter didn't say anything. "Eastrod," Haze said, louder.[27]

In a sense, O'Connor's broad strategy is similar to Jane Austen's: a series of ironies, quiet jokes, is usually hidden in the opening paragraphs of her stories, like bombs planted to explode much later on. The verbal basis of this comedy is very different from Austen's, however, because unlike Austen she depends on subversive imagery and radical deviations from the common idiom for her effects: the vivid fragment, the unanticipated phrase, and the unusual figure are far more important to her than the use of epigram or antithesis is, or any of the other, more traditional devices of "wit." Here, for example, in this passage she brings together a number of apparently disconnected particulars so as to realize what one of her admirers, the novelist John Hawkes, has called "the truth of a fractured picture"—by which I take him to mean the harsh, broken, and opaque surfaces of our immediate world; then, building upon this, she tries to make her random particulars generate individual meanings, clues referring us chiefly to the idea that things may not after all be as bad as they seem. At first sight Haze Motes must strike us as a creature let loose from some absurdist version of hell: not so much a person, in fact, as a horribly diminished thing, strange, out of joint, and with his skull—a chilling memento mori—almost protruding through his skin. And the sense of death he carries with him is certainly compounded by the place in which he is set, where people appear to travel from nowhere in particular to nowhere else in particular and ignore each other along the way. We are reminded, perhaps, of the terminal condition Faulkner describes in *Sanctuary*, or some of the opening lines from Yeats's "The Second Coming":

> Things fall apart; the centre cannot hold;
> Mere anarchy is loosed upon the world;
> The blood-dimmed tide is loosed, and everywhere
> The ceremony of innocence is drowned . . .

Everything has fallen apart in Haze Motes's world as well, lacking a common axis, and it would be a vision as bleak as Yeats's that O'Connors offers us here, were it not that concealed in all this we can find traces of something else—hints of an alternative possibility, shining dimly through this landscape of nightmare. Of these hints the most important, I think, have to do with clothes and names, two ancient means of incarnating the life of the spirit. Like other characters in *Wise Blood*, Haze is placed for us partly by the things he wears, and the fact that his hat curiously resembles a preacher's is the first clue we are given about his secret vocation. It is a sort of talismanic sign, an emblem of that calling he will try to resist for much of the remainder of his life. And so also is the name of his hometown. For it requires very little ingenuity, surely, to see "Eastrod" as an anagram of "rood (or cross) of the East"—in other words, as a covert reference to the site of the Crucifixion and the source of Redemption. The name, which Haze offers with such insistence to the indifferent porter, is a further mark of his election. Really, it will require the rest of the book to decipher it for us, just as it will take until the final paragraph for us to learn exactly why Haze's eyes look "like passages leading somewhere" and exactly where those passages lead. But already, even before this happens, the mark is there, adding its own subtle comment to the situation, providing that sense of qualification, of one opinion being held in reserve while another is expressed, which characterizes the more positive forms of irony—and linking this scene, desolate though it appears to be, to the divine paradox at the heart of the novel.

This, the finely edged character of O'Connor's humor, which helps turn what would otherwise be a comedy of the absurd into the laughter of the saints, is the thing we need to remember above all about her work—partly because in remembering it we can also recall a whole battery of effects used in its service (the wit, the scrupulous use of figures, the detachment, and the tendency to give every incident a double meaning), and partly because it helps us, in any case, to define the scope and quality of her entire achievement. O'Connor has been accused often enough by her critics of "an excessive violence of conception," which presumably refers to such incidents as the one where Haze Motes burns his eyes out with quicklime or the whole business of his suffering and subsequent death. But it is the violence in her stories that is actually the heart of their imaginative power—as is, say, murder in Dostoievsky's novels or the brutality of war in Hemingway's. It is the violence of apocalyptic despair that she is concerned with, not sensationalism, the violence of the desolate and verbally inarticulate poor white Southerner and of souls no longer willing to be silent about their plight. Really, to accuse O'Connor in this way is to mistake the author for one of her characters, and to suppose that just because Haze Motes or Mrs. Flood are lost and brutal creatures then their creator must be somehow lost and brutal as well—somebody indulging, without forethought or explanation, in some "cult of the gratuitous Grotesque."[28] The carefully considered, elaborately "made" quality of her work should, I think, be enough to convince us just how wrong that is: like Jane Austen, O'Connor knows precisely what she is after and is utterly in control of any device she may adopt—including the device of violence—to fulfill her aims. She is taking people like Haze Motes along the path to God, and, while she takes them, revealing with sardonic wit the many miles they still have to go. Since this is a path that, by definition, she must have traveled already, her wit must also be a measure of the distance between her characters and herself—and so an index of her skill in accommodating the world she imagines to another, inherently critical and much more generous, frame.

Generous it may be, but it is not all encompassing; and if the terms I have been using in praise of O'Connor—skill, irony, wit, paradox—make her sound a little cold and distant, just a shade too detached, it is because she does after all have her limitations. The message of her fiction, although more inclusive than the surfaces of her prose would seem to indicate, is still a restricted one—inviting us as it does to a desperate acceptance of faith, and interpreting experience as a series of radical dualisms. Much of what she has to say in her fiction is of an extraordinarily private origin, and this privateness is indicated, I believe, by the repetitive, almost obsessional, nature of her material. The same character types are returned to again and again, the same situations and the same relationships are repeated from one story to the next, and her imaginative world, once established, never appears to grow. Even her irony, despite its excellence, seems rather exclusive in the end because (and here it is quite unlike Austen's) it depends upon a very special, almost hermetic, system of reference. It requires a considerable effort for us to understand it, then accept it for the duration of the story; and, when we have finished reading it, it seems almost too easy to raise objections. Our shadow world has been given shape and substance, yes, and our evil dreams objectified—but clearly much else has been left out. The picture is too stark, too unremitting, really, just as its frame—shaped out of a theology that few of O'Connor's readers will be willing to accept without qualification—appears too simple and too untested to invite complete imaginative belief. "In the greatest fiction," O'Connor once said,

> the writer's moral sense coincides with his dramatic sense, and I can see no way for it to do this unless his moral judgment is part of the very act of seeing, and he is free to use it.[29]

The beauty of O'Connor's fiction, in a way, is that, using her Southern inheritance, she normally manages to achieve the coincidence she is talking about here; the pity of it, that her "act of seeing" was (like Carson McCullers's) such a very eccentric one.

Victims of History and Agents of Revolution: William Styron

Carson McCullers and Flannery O'Connor are, as I have tried to suggest, both novelists who excel within limitations. What they do, they do incomparably well: but theirs remains an idiosyncratic vision that avoids most of the problems confronting men living in a public world—the problems, to use those portentous words, of history and society, tradition and modernity—and settles for the relative simplicity of the single, separate life. The third writer in our trio, however, William Styron, is built on a different scale altogether. Far from avoiding the big issues, he has always sought to grapple with them. Since the time he started writing, it seems to have been his conscious aim to perpetuate the great tradition in Southern literature, and to assume the throne left vacant by William Faulkner by producing something that, in terms of both its themes and its historical scope, could merit comparison with *The Sound and the Fury, Look Homeward, Angel,* and *All the King's Men.* Small wonder, then, that Norman Mailer, that supreme egotist and self-publicist, should see Styron as a kind of twin, and rival. Styron, it appears, wants to write the great novel of our time just as much as Mailer does; and this has necessarily led to a great deal of jealousy, and some back-biting, between the two of them. Small wonder, either, that Styron's first published book, *Lie Down in Darkness,* should have been treated with almost universal respect and had epithets like "brilliant," "major," and "tragic" showered upon it. *Lie Down in Darkness,* as befitted its author, had ambition written over its every page—it represented a deliberate stab at greatness—and the fact that Styron could back his ambitions up with an extraordinarily seductive style (by turns descriptive, lyrical, and elegiac) more or less guaranteed its initial success. It was almost too easy, thanks to the prodigious brilliance of its language and the intricacy of its narrative structure, to read more into the book than was actually there.

Not that *Lie Down in Darkness* is a poor or uninteresting novel—far from it. It is, I believe, a fascinating and to some extent a perceptive one because—whether Styron intended it or not—it presents us with such an honest account of the author's own predicament. It is, in a way, profoundly autobiographical; and since the area of autobiography it deals with bears upon Styron's problems as a *Southern* writer it is worth looking at briefly, I think, before we go on to examine the later and more successful work. *Lie Down in Darkness* concerns itself with one family, the Loftis family, living in Port Warwick, Virginia. In actual clock time it covers the events of one day, during which the body of the older daughter, Peyton Loftis, is brought back from New York for burial. But, in describing this particular day, the author reaches back continually into the past to investigate the circumstances leading to Peyton's death, which came at her own hands; and in the process the book becomes an intensive exploration of the family's almost effortless self-destruction. The father, Milton Loftis, is, we learn, a romantic who has never found a satisfactory object for his romantic longings in his wife, Helen, who wants simply to mother him. So his feelings, unrewarded there, have flowed into a latently incestuous relationship with Peyton, while Helen has turned for comfort to a second daughter, the helplessly crippled Maudie. "I think we've got a Freudian attachment,"[30] Peyton Loftis says of her father and herself—and it is this attachment, really, which precipitates the disaster. It is the immediate cause of rivalry between mother and daughter. More important, it leads eventually to the failure of Peyton's own marriage (which mirrors that of her parents), her neuroticism (which mirrors Helen's), her compulsive drinking (which mirrors Milton's), and her suicide (which, of course, mirrors the self-destructiveness of all the Loftises). Like the characters in Sartre's *No Exit,* the various members of the Loftis family constitute one another's Hell; their home life is a kind of prison house from which they are unable and, because of their mutual dependence, unwilling, even, to escape.

Put in this way, *Lie Down in Darkness* sounds rather like a Freudian closet drama, one of those psychological thrillers that were in fact quite popular during the period when the book was first published. What this leaves out of account, however, is how Styron's manner of telling the tale affects our reception of it. The overall framework of return he uses for the narrative, the complex layers of memory through which the characters speak to us, above all the powerful sense of re-enactment attaching itself to almost every thought and gesture—all this makes us feel that the dark backward and abysm of the old world lies just below the surface of landscape and consciousness, waiting for an appropriate moment to reappear. Further, it makes the Loftis family seem just as much imprisoned in *time* as they are by each other—or, to be more accurate, imprisoned in times passed. Theirs is "a land of the dying," Styron explains to us at one point in the novel, a Hades inhabited by half-remembered ghosts; and it requires no great stretch of the imagination, really, to see the Loftises themselves as ghost-haunted people, driven in some cases beyond endurance by voices from out of their past. Here, by way of illustration, is Milton Loftis in a typical mood, recalling the accents of his dead father:

> Heartsick, frightened, he . . . watched the water, listening. *I do not propose to convince,* his father had said (. . . thirty years ago, before the house was finally condemned, but not long before; when even the lightest foot-step on the stairs sent a plaintive wooden squeal through the joists and beams, reminder not only of the swiftly aging house but of the passing of a finer, more tranquil age), *I do not propose to convince you merely through paternal advice, . . . I only trust you will heed the warning of one . . . to whom . . . the temptations of the flesh have been potent . . . , and that you will . . . renounce a way of life which . . . can lead only to grief and . . . ruination. . . .* So his father had somehow realized that his youth would rise up eventually to betray him, even though he couldn't have foreseen the final calamity. . . . His father. No more than a shadow.

> A wave of self-pity swept over him. He felt tricked and defeated. . . .
> Not just that, Papa. Other things. Life tends toward a moment. Not just
> the flesh. Not a poet or a thief. I could never exercise free will.[31]

The movement of this passage is, I think, characteristic of the entire
novel. Milton is engulfed by memories, of an age now disappeared and
opportunities missed, without really being able to help himself: he is
summoned back into yesterday almost unawares. That in itself might
not be such a bad thing, of course. Other people, after all, have been
obsessed by the past and yet managed to use that obsession productively, to make it work for them. Milton's problem, however, is that
he clearly cannot do this. Tied as he is to times gone by he still does
not understand them because—and this is the clinching irony—he is
quite unable to establish a definite and objective relationship with
them. He does not know the dimensions of his prison and so he can
"never exercise free will" by escaping from it into the larger world
outside. In his own odd fashion—with his own mind, that is to say,
acting as the agent of persecution—he is a victim of history, and as
such a peculiarly subtle illustration of a saying attributed to Ben
Jonson, that those who cannot cope with the past are condemned to
repeat it all their lives.

To repeat the past can involve a number of things. It can mean allowing one's immediate ancestors to dictate one's actions and judgments—
this, as we have seen, is what Milton tends to do, and what Peyton
does as well, by trying to reenact both her own relationship with her
father and her mother's relationship with her father in her disastrous
marriage. It can also mean behaving like a character out of one of
Poe's tales, like a somnambulist driven by forces beyond one's personal
control, distilling within the blood the inherited obsessions of an entire race. And this too is a part of the Loftis makeup, as John Aldridge,
in a very interesting if brief discussion of the book, has suggested.

> Behind Milton's father-guilt and incest-guilt is the whole Southern blood-
> guilt. Behind Helen's jealousy and Puritanism is the timeless Southern
> gentlewoman madness, . . . that comes from too much inbreeding, too
> much Negro fear, too much sexual neglect. Behind Peyton's father-com-
> plex is a century of paternalism and man-hatred and sexual masochism.[32]

What I would like to emphasize, however, rather than either of these
possibilities, is a third form that imitation of the past can assume. This
is, not just to surrender to the preoccupations and special patterns of
yesterday, but to try to reproduce its life style, its code of morals and
manners—to essay being a man of the old world in an entirely new
one. This inevitably brings its own complications with it. For to divorce articles of belief from the context that has previously given

them meaning, to imitate them without the acknowledgment that times and people have changed, is really to set up a parodic relationship between imitator and imitated. It is to wear the right uniform at the wrong moment, to declare oneself an anachronism and so play the fool—and that is exactly what Milton, Helen, and Peyton Loftis are all doing. They are all fools, enacting a gross pastiche of their predecessors, and the tragic consequences of their behavior only serve to emphasize, I think, just how total—how blind and all-consuming— their commitment to their folly is.

Take Milton Loftis, for example. On the evidence of appearance alone, we could easily take him for a true Southern hero. He is the scion of an old if declining family, a graduate of the University of Virginia, an officer and subsequently a lawyer. All this, however, only goes to show us just how deceptive appearances can be. Milton is also a coward and a drunkard. He is emotionally dependent, first upon Helen and then on Peyton; worse still, for him, he is financially dependent too, since his law practice is almost worthless and the house in which he lives (that familiar emblem of authority in Southern culture) belongs to his wife. It seems appropriate, somehow, that one of the most glorious moments of his life should involve a wild parody of heroic action—when, drunker even than usual, he runs with the crowd across the football field after a college match carrying a Confederate flag. For Milton is nothing more than a parody himself, a comic travesty of the traditional Southern gentleman—just as, in another way, Helen Loftis is a parody of the Southern lady, her fragility and gentleness all dissolved into neuroticism, and Peyton a brutal parody of the Southern belle. He, and they, are shadows without substance, the products of what one of Styron's other characters calls "a *husk* of a culture";[33] and together their grotesque postures testify, not so much to the continuity of past and present as to a terrible entanglement—in which the present generation can neither reject the shibboleths of their ancestors nor give them any genuine meaning.

This brings us to the autobiographical nature of the book. For the question Styron seems to be asking in *Lie Down in Darkness* is briefly this: When the old institutions become irrelevant and the old myths obsolete, *and when our habits of thought and feeling continue nevertheless to be shaped by them*—how then do we change the situation? How can we create new institutions and new myths when our usual means of altering things—our minds and hearts, dictating the scope of our actions—are among the things to be altered? How do we will an act of defiance if our wills have been conditioned by the very forces we would defy? I have stated the problem oversimply, of course, in order to make it clear. Obviously Styron does not think that a *complete* break with the past is either necessary or possible. But a more active and detached relationship with it is necessary, Styron implies, if we are not to suffer the fate of Milton Loftis—and how is this to be achieved?

Styron never answers this question during the course of the book, nor is any satisfactory solution ever implied; and the reason for this, I think, is very simple. For all his perceptiveness in locating the problem, he, William Styron, the creator of the Loftis family, is as caught up in that problem as any of his creations are. He depends, to the point of parody, on the earlier *literary* tradition of the South just as Milton, Helen, and Peyton Loftis all depend on its broader cultural tradition. The most immediate and important debt Styron owes is (predictably enough, perhaps) to William Faulkner. In an interview published shortly after the first appearance of *Lie Down in Darkness*, Styron readily admitted that he had begun it following a thorough rereading of Faulkner's work; and we hardly need this admission, I believe, to see how close the similarities are. For the book amounts almost to an elegy, or imitative tribute, to the father figure of modern Southern literature. There, in the portrait of the Loftises, is the dissolving family familiar to us from *The Sound and the Fury*: the alcoholic father, the neurotic, selfish mother, the idiot child, and the older child who wanders around a strange Northern town for much of one day, clutching a timepiece, and then shortly afterward commits suicide. There, also, are the Negro characters performing the function of chorus, commenting on the Loftises just as they do on the Compson family, and coming together in a revival scene at the end of the action to round it off on an unexpectedly hopeful note. The narrative framework of Styron's book, involving a family's journey to inter a coffin, is modeled on *As I Lay Dying*; Peyton Loftis is modeled on Temple Drake in *Sanctuary*, another Southern belle turned nymphomaniac (she even crosses and uncrosses her legs nervously, just as Temple does!); Milton Loftis's father is modeled on the platitudinous Mr. Compson. And so on. "Son you don't have to be a campfollower of reaction," old Mr. Loftis tells Milton when he is still a young man, "but always remember where you came from";[34] and Styron's trouble really, like Milton's, is that he takes this advice to extremes. The result is a story that has an almost overpowering feeling of *déjà vu* about it, that is full of echoes and vague remembrances—the shadowy presence of all the characters and situations it imitates and, in a sense, memorializes. Is Styron himself aware of this dimension of the novel? It is difficult to say, although my guess, based on the available evidence, is that he probably is. Does he know what he could do to change it? That is an easier question to answer, because it is clear from the world he imagines that he does not. *Lie Down in Darkness* never escapes, for more than a moment, out from under the shade of William Faulkner and the magnolia blossom (to use that phrase again). It represents a cul-de-sac—a beautiful, spell-binding cul-de-sac admittedly, but a cul-de-sac nonetheless; and the gravity of its language, the brilliance of its structure—the impeccable nature, even, of its own self-reflexiveness—should never blind us to the fact that nearly everything in it is borrowed.

The two books that Styron wrote during the next nine years register no significant advance on *Lie Down in Darkness*, at least as far as this problem of liberation from the past is concerned. His novella *The Long March*, for example, published in 1956, merely describes the same predicament as his first novel does, only this time in simpler terms, using the army as the institutional frame that tends to fix the movement of life and inhibit choice. And his second full-length novel, *Set This House on Fire*, does not so much find a solution as impose one. Cass Kinsolving, its hero, suffers up until the last pages just as Milton Loftis does, then assures us in the last pages, and several years later, that through his suffering he finally found a way out.

> "Now . . . I wish I could tell you that I had found some belief, some rock, and that here on this rock anything might prevail—that here madness might become reason, and grief joy, and no yes. And even death itself death no longer, but a resurrection."
> "But to be truthful . . . I can only tell you this: that as for being and nothingness, the one thing I did know was that to choose between them was simply to choose being, not for the sake of being, or even the love of being, much less the desire to be forever—but in the hope of being what I could be for a time. This would be an ecstasy."[35]

This, despite the initial modest disclaimer, is pure bombast: Styron's attempt to make up in sheer verbal energy for what he clearly lacks in terms of substance, genuine conviction—and, if we take the rest of the novel into account, for his failure to realize the solution predicated in credible, human terms. Norman Mailer used this particular passage to buttress an attack on the entire book; and, after all due allowances have been made for the sense of rivalry between the two writers, he was, I think, quite right to do so. For at best what Styron says here exists as an expression of need—a cry for emancipation that, like Milton Loftis's, remains more or less trapped in the vocabulary and values of the very systems it wishes to defeat.

Which brings us to *The Confessions of Nat Turner*: Styron's fourth book and the one, I think, in which he has begun to find the answers he needs—both to his own problems as a Southern writer of the second, post-"renaissance" generation, and to the larger questions facing anyone who inherits, however unconsciously, a particular way of organizing and figuring experience. Its subject is that ultimate victim of the past, and the roles and mythologies the past bequeaths, the American Negro slave. Its method, as Styron puts it, is that of "a meditation on history";[36] since the story is based on an actual slave revolt that occurred in Virginia in 1831 and the supposed "confessions" made by its leader, Nat Turner, after his defeat and eventual capture. In this way, Styron places himself squarely at the center of the Southern tradition—and not, as in *Lie Down in Darkness*, merely to commemorate that tradition but so as to develop it, carry it a stage further. History —the relationship of past to present in the writer's own experience and in the lives of his characters—is as much the motivating force in this book as it is in Faulkner's work, say, in Ransom's or in Warren's. The only difference is that it is now what James Baldwin has called the "common history" of white and black that comes under scrutiny; and this change, far from being a superficial one, signals other changes of approach and interpretation that enable Styron to achieve a radically fresh understanding of familiar material. In a sense the *Confessions* represents the most significant attempt made over the last twenty years to fashion something new out of the creative inheritance of the region; and it is because of this that I would like, by way of a conclusion, to look at it in some detail—at the controversy it has aroused, the problems it investigates, and the meanings that it tentatively sketches out. This will also, I hope, serve the purpose of reminding us what that curious animal called "Southern literature" is and, by extension, what the writer's relationship to history can and should involve. For if Styron has succeeded at all in mapping out the territory ahead for Southern writing, as I believe he has, it is largely because he possesses such a clear understanding of the territory behind him. He knows how to cope with his inheritance, in other words, and even put it at full stretch; and in looking closely at how he does this we can, perhaps, recover that inheritance for a last time and recognize what is fundamental to it. We can see it, now as much as ever, as an area of growth rather than a finished argument—as a series of living, and still maneuverable, possibilities.

When *The Confessions of Nat Turner* was first published in 1967, it was greeted with almost unanimous critical acclaim—just as, once upon a time, *Lie Down in Darkness* had been. Reviewers might have varied in their choice of superlatives and the scope of their analyses, but few of them doubted that Styron had written one of the best American novels to appear since the Second World War. The consensus seemed just about complete, Southern historians like C. Vann Wood-

ward joining with black writers like James Baldwin to heap praises
on the book—and then suddenly, less than a year after publication,
opinion took a sharp and surprising turn. The immediate occasion and
in a way the symbol of this change was the appearance, early in
1968, of a collection of essays called *William Styron's "Nat Turner":
Ten Black Writers Respond.* Flatly contradicting most earlier commentators, the ten contributors to this book charged Styron with almost every literary crime under the sun. He had written an undramatic
and unexciting novel: that was one accusation. More to the point: in
the interests of his own condescending, and essentially hostile, attitude
toward Nat Turner, he had distorted history. Taking the 1831 text of
the *Confessions* (written by one Thomas Gray, and supposedly dictated by Turner while he was awaiting execution), Styron, the ten
black writers claimed, had omitted certain details and added others—
and all completely without justification. These were serious charges;
and they were made the more serious by the fact that, as Styron himself had suggested already, the theme of black revolt in the *Confessions* was and is of more than antiquarian interest. The shadow of Nat
Turner hovers so ominously behind the figures of Malcolm X, Stokely
Carmichael, and Eldridge Cleaver, as an example, warning, and inspiration, that to comment on him is in some sense to comment on
them, and on racial oppression and revolution in general. One of the
contributors, Charles V. Hamilton, made the point as dramatically as
possible. "Black people today," he said, "must not permit themselves
to be divested of their historical leaders"[37]—must not, in fact, allow
books like the *Confessions* to be accepted as the truth, either literal or
imaginative, because of the clear political dangers involved in doing
so.

Just as they intended, the ten black writers aroused a storm of controversy; and, I think, they went right to the heart of the book—what
Styron was really trying to do, and the problems this involved. Styron
had described the *Confessions* as "a meditation on history." Precisely,
his critics now replied—but in a meditation on history, how much
scope should be given to the "meditation" and how much to the "history"? At what point does historical interpretation topple over into
historical romance, myth into fantasy; and hadn't Styron passed that
point? Their questions had more than just an immediate application,
of course. For the approach Styron had chosen for the *Confessions*
was no different, in essentials, from the classic Southern strategy of
an imaginative reenactment of the past. In questioning it, consequently, they were by inference questioning the premises of such
novels as *Absalom, Absalom!* and *All the King's Men,* or poems like
"Antique Harvesters" and "Ode to the Confederate Dead." In calling

for a more precise definition of its aims and terms of reference they were, whether they were aware of it or not, calling for a more precise definition of the aims and terms of reference of Southern literature generally. On another level altogether, they were even asking how history—as a concept and as a series of events occurring in a specific society—could be used with justification in *any* literature. That is why their arguments merit serious appraisal—because even if we disagree with them they force us back, in the course of disagreeing, to a consideration of first principles.

A good example of this—of how, to put it another way, Hamilton and his colleagues tend to ask the right questions even if they do not always come up with the right answers—is offered by their criticism of the language Styron puts in the mouth of his slave characters, and, more particularly, in the mouth and mind of Nat Turner. Styron, as most of the contributors to *Ten Black Writers* point out, deploys two kinds of language in his portrait of Turner: the one a "Sambo" or "nigger" dialect that Turner shares with all the other slaves and uses in conversation, the other a mellifluous, incantatory rhetoric (reminiscent of certain passages in Faulkner's work, or Thomas Wolfe's) that is more or less unique to the protagonist and is supposed to describe the movement of his thoughts. Both, they argue, involve imposing a mask on the character. Turner is given an idiom (or, rather, idioms), and by inference an identity, that is not really his at all—which, if anything, must be seen as the product of certain, specifically "white" preconceptions.[38]

In a way this criticism is perfectly accurate—and useful, because it draws our attention to an aspect of the novel that most of its earlier reviewers preferred to ignore. Styron's Nat Turner does, for example, talk in a way that makes him sound very much like Twain's "Nigger Jim" or Joel Chandler Harris's Uncle Remus. What it fails to take account of, however, is Styron's motives for making his hero speak and think like this. The only explanation that people like Hamilton and Mike Thelwell (in another essay in *Ten Black Writers* called "Back With the Wind") can come up with is that Styron, like most Southern writers, must suffer from racial prejudice: which is plainly unsatisfactory since, once the peculiarities of Turner's language have been pointed out to us, we can, I believe, see that Styron has actually supplied explanations for them in the course of the narrative. Here, for instance, is Nat Turner himself giving one reason why he talks the way he does.

"I'se twenty, massah," I replied, "twenty-one come de first day October."
It is good for a Negro, when trying to ingratiate himself with a strange

white man, to convey an impression of earnest simplicity and this may often be achieved by adding to such a reply as mine some phrase like "Das de truth" or "Das right." I think that I must have tacked on then a sweet and open "Das de truth. . . . "[39]

The message is plain. It is, really, a moral necessity for Turner and his fellow-slaves to speak the way they do, because that is the only way they can defend themselves against the fear and suspicions, prompted by guilt, of their white oppressors. Language is something they use as a shield, a form of self-protection that gradually becomes second nature to the protected. Elsewhere Styron offers another explanation, that it is a matter of cultural necessity as well, since on a broader, historical level the Negro dialect can be seen as an example of those cruelly impoverished types of culture imposed by the white man upon the black—after his original African traditions had been taken away from him and only an embattled species of Christianity, and a hopelessly defensive kind of group identity, offered by way of a replacement. At once "a form of self-preservation" (as Styron puts it at one point in the book) and a proof of "the cultural barrenness of black life" in the South (as the Negro writer Richard Wright described it in his autobiography, *Black Boy*), "nigger talk" is consequently placed for us even while it is being used; it becomes part of the armory of Styron's criticism (of slavery and racial oppression in general) rather than something for which Styron himself should be criticized.

Turner's other idiom, the one Styron gives him whenever he is left alone to remember and meditate, is intended, really, to counter this: by offering a linguistic equivalent of a movement toward self-realization, in energetic denial of those processes of deculturization and depersonalization that helped create the "nigger" and his speech. The model here, I think, is what has often been called the "real language" of Negroes, something evolved out of African rhythms and phrasing and white vocabulary—and to be found nowadays, for example, in "jive talk," black spirituals, or the performance of a good black preacher. By definition, this is a difficult language to reproduce in print because it depends on what professional linguists call a "paralanguage" as much as anything else; it draws its energy, partly, from such things as gesture and physical expression, those resources of oral communication that can supplement or even give substance to the written word. Despite the difficulty, though, Styron had to find some way of reproducing it if another, more active and unusual side to Turner's life was to be suggested—which is what, surely, he is trying to do in passages like this:

Cloudless sunlight suggesting neither hour nor season glows down upon
me, wraps me with a cradle's warmth as I drift toward the river's estuary;
the little boat rocks gently in our benign descent together toward the
sea. On the unpeopled bank the woods are silent, silent as snowfall. . . .
Faintly now I hear the oceanic roar, mark the sweep of sunlit water far-
near, glinting with whitecaps, the ragged shoulder of a beach where sea
and river join in a tumultuous embrace of swirling waters. But nothing
disturbs me, I drowse in the arms of a steadfast and illimitable peace.
Salt stings my nostrils. The breakers roll to shore, the lordly tide swells
back beneath a cobalt sky arching eastward toward Africa.[40]

This is not, needless to say, a colloquial style. Nor, as Hamilton, Thelwell, and other contributors to *Ten Black Writers* argue, does it involve any attempt to impose the author's own, self-evidently "white"
rhetoric on his black characters, either. Styron's aim is, simply, to
create the sense of an emergent language. The opulent vocabulary,
the hypnotic repetitions and inversions, the lush sonorities of phrasing
and the pulsing, emphatic movement of the passage as a whole: everything points toward a voice intoning rather than just speaking. Every
resource at Styron's disposal is geared toward catching the buck, drive,
and lilt—the total effect—of "genuine" Negro speech, Of course, how
successful Styron is in achieving this is another matter entirely, although I for one believe that he comes as close as any novelist, or
person committed to purely written forms of communication, can.
Certainly, what he has done merits comparison, I think, with what
other, black writers have done along the same lines—with the nightmare episodes in *Native Son* and *Invisible Man,* for instance, or with
the "Threshing-Floor" section of *Go Tell It on the Mountain.*[41] And
to say that about any white novelist is, really, to say a great deal.

This criticism, in *Ten Black Writers*, of Styron's handling of Negro
idioms is carried over to his treatment of the Negro personality as well
—and naturally enough, since it is language after all that creates character in the novel. Again, Hamilton and his colleagues say something
that previous critics somehow managed to avoid saying: which is that
the black characters—even Nat Turner himself, to some extent—are
accorded a diminished and comparatively marginal status in the
Confessions. They act largely as a chorus, observing and commenting
on their white masters' behavior—and, even worse, as a chorus composed almost entirely of "Sambo" or nigger minstrel stereotypes.[42] But
again what is really a conscious device is read as unconscious hostility. Styron is attacked for his ignorance and even, by some of his
critics, for his instinctive hatred of an entire race: whereas it is clear,
I think, if we look at the novel closely, that the dehumanization of the
black man is one of Styron's subjects rather than his premise. He is

actively inviting us to consider how a system can eat away at character—pervert a man just as much as it can pervert his speech—which
is why something like, say, the peripheral status of the slave is explained for us in the course of the narrative, placed both by the action
and the occasional aside.

> It is impossible to exaggerate the extent to which white people dominate
> the conversation of Negroes . . . white people really see nothing of a Negro
> in his private activity, while a Negro . . . has often to suffer for . . . his ubi-
> quitous presence by being called a spy. . . .[43]

The point, as Styron makes it here and elsewhere in the story, is
that within the kind of social structure epitomized by the aristocracy
of the Old South the less privileged *are* dismissed to the periphery.
They form what was sometimes referred to, in the nineteenth century, as
the "mud sill" of the community, and as such their lives are considered
negligible except in so far as their labor acts as a support to, and their
voices supply a commentary on, the people above them. The *Confessions*
presents the reader, in fact, with a system the chief purpose of which
seems to be to deprive the underdog of any sense of separate identity
or intrinsic dignity. The message communicated to him by his situation is that he matters only to the extent that he makes possible the
life style of his oppressors; and the most pernicious aspect of this,
Styron argues, is that he is often inclined to believe the message himself, because there is nothing in his customary life to contradict it.
He becomes a "Sambo" stereotype, not because he is genetically limited in any way, still less because Styron thinks all Negroes must be
like this, but quite simply because he, like all men Styron believes, can
be no more than his society—the systems of language and value to
which he belongs—allows him to be.

This reading of slavery and the impact it has on the personalities
of the enslaved has wider implications which I will go into shortly—
although it will be fairly obvious at once, I suppose, that it helps
relate Nat Turner to Milton Loftis, Cass Kinsolving, and Styron's other
fictional victims. But what is worth pointing out before that, I think,
is that Styron owes the immediate stimulus for such a reading to a
professional historian—and to a book that he, Styron, had reviewed
for the *New York Review of Books* several years prior to the publication of the *Confessions*. The book, *Slavery: A Problem in American
Institutional and Intellectual Life* by Stanley Elkins, is one of the
most important treatments of the entire subject to appear in the past
few years. In it, Elkins argues that the "Sambo" character really did
exist, and he compares life on a slave plantation to life in a Nazi concentration camp in order to suggest the conditioning circumstances

that made such a character possible. Both the plantation and the concentration camp were, Elkins claims,

> . . . closed systems from which all standards based on prior connections had been effectively detached. A working adjustment to either system required a childlike conformity . . . all lines of authority descended from the master. . . . The individual, consequently, for his very psychic security, had to picture his master . . . as the "good father," even when . . . it made no sense at all.[44]

Only those slaves who lived "outside the full coercion of the plantation-system" escaped the full impact of this conditioning; and Elkins even cites Turner as one of the exceptions who proves the general rule. For Turner, he points out, developed an awareness of alternative sources of authority simply by learning to read and becoming apprenticed to a craft. This is a hint that Styron has taken up in drawing a distinction between his protagonist and most of the other slave characters: the kind of distinction implicit, for example, in the fact that Turner alone is given *two* idioms. It is not that, as many of his black critics suggest, Styron is attributing his own loathing of Negroes to his principal character. It is simply that he is describing somebody very similar to the kind of person Richard Wright describes himself as being in *Black Boy:* a man who, by one means or another, has become painfully aware of how rules are mapped out for his race—and whose very awareness of this fact has created a feeling of "eternal difference" between him and them. Of course, this is an arguable interpretation of slavery or racism and its psychological effects on the oppressed, but it is one drawn out of hostility to the slave system rather than any kind of sympathy with it. More to the point, perhaps, it depends upon as closely reasoned an idea of history—the involvement of the past with the present, and the public with the private life—as we are likely to find in any Southern book.

These, I think, are the two things we need to bear in mind about the *Confessions* in order to see it as a worthy exponent of the Southern tradition: that it is an attempt, not merely to record times passed, but to rediscover them in the light of contemporary concerns—and that it does this, not by a policy of deliberate distortion, but by reinterpreting the known and making calculated guesses about the unknown. For, when all is said and done, what *is* known about the actual revolt led by Nat Turner? Very little beyond the fact that there was a revolt, it failed, and Turner was executed. All the records by which the story has come down to us (and Styron) are suspect, from the 1831 text of the Confessions written by Gray, which was intended mainly as an awful warning to slaveholders; through the narratives provided by both abolitionists and apologists for the South later on in the nine-teenth century; to the more recent accounts of Southern historians, like Ulrich Phillips, and Marxist ones, such as Herbert Aptheker.[45] Every man has his own ax to grind. Every one has consequently tended to explain things in terms of his own reading of society and human nature—and, in those many areas where the truth is not known or the meaning ambiguous, has been tempted sometimes to invent. This accounts for many of the so-called "facts" that Styron is criticized for neglecting or altering: they are not facts at all, merely details from somebody else's myth. He has been attacked, for example, for omitting any mention of Turner's wife, and for claiming that the Nat Turner rebellion was "the only effective, sustained revolt in the annals of American Negro slavery."[46] But the attack itself is built on shaky ground, since the wife was an addition to the story made by later, Northern historians(motivated, needless to say, by feelings of gen-uine sympathy), and the belief that there were ever any serious revolts beside Turner's is based on evidence concocted by Herbert Aptheker—out of memories of strikes, plots scotched in the hatching, and rumors of rebellion. There is nothing to prove that Turner was married, any more than there is anything to prove that he was not. It is not certain that there are parallels for the Turner rebellion (in-deed, it has never been certain, since slaveholders tended to confuse fear of revolts with their existence) and, equally, it is not certain that there are not. In these respects, as in so many others, the story of Nat Turner is disputed territory where different voices have tried, and still do try, to establish their own versions of the truth. And Styron is simply following precedent in operating freely within the limits of discretion so allowed him—in recognizing, in fact, that his own medi-tation on history is quite as defensible as anyone else's as long as it sticks to the authenticated facts.

There are two occasions, though, when Styron definitely steps out-side these limits of discretion, two well authenticated facts he chooses to ignore. For it is a well established fact that Nat Turner attempted to escape North prior to the revolt and that, as Turner saw it at least, he owed a lot to the influence of his entire family; and both these things are omitted from the *Confessions*. The first omission can, I think, be fairly easily explained: Styron, we can guess, did not want to draw attention away from the subject of the revolt (for reasons, largely, of dramatic emphasis), and probably felt that he would be doing so by dwelling on earlier examples of defiance. But the second involves mo-tives that are at once more veiled and more interesting. Styron de-prives Turner of any sense of belonging to a coherent family group and allows him only one strong emotional attachment within the black community—to his mother. Why? Because, I believe, he wants Turner to assume a larger, representative status, and to illustrate the thesis—held, among others, by Stanley Elkins and the eminent Swedish authority on race relations, Gunnar Myrdal—that both slavery and racism, encouraging as they do a closed system of society, tend to be hostile to alternative centers of power such as the patriarchal family. In other words, Styron omits a specific truth so as to achieve that generality, the resonance of texture and meaning, which is usually the prerogative of the creative writer rather than the historian. There is, after all, this difference between Styron and previous interpreters of the Nat Turner story: that he is actually *aiming* at an imaginative interpretation of events rather than a factual account. The *Confessions* represents a deliberate attempt to explain history, and the status of man as a historical being, and Styron consequently feels justified (just as Robert Penn Warren does in *All the King's Men*) in changing or ignoring any details that might get in the way of this. Clearly, some tact is needed here if the result is not to look like special pleading; and this time, at least, it is perhaps fair to say that Styron could have been more tactful. However good his motives may have been, and however well established his approach, there is a certain tendentiousness about his treatment of the Turner family that suggests that, for once, his critics may possibly be justified in what they say.[47]

Along with the details Styron omits from the Nat Turner story, there are, as well, one or two things he chooses to add. These are less of a problem, really, because they are much more obviously the products of an attempt to discover the truth rather than evade it. Admittedly, Styron is guessing much of the time, but so must anybody be who tries to go beyond a plain statement of the known facts. What matters, in the end, is that his guesses should be founded on a coherent theory and that they should organize the facts into an intelligible, credible series; and even his most controversial additions to the story manage to do that. I am thinking, in particular, of the thing to which the black writers take more exception than anything else: the obsession with white women, and the dislike of most black women, that Styron attributes to his protagonist.[48] This is not, I believe (as people like Hamilton and Thelwell claim), an indication of Styron's racism—proof positive that he subscribes, like so many other white Southerners, to what W. J. Cash called "the rape complex." On the contrary, it is part of a radical, painstaking critique of racism that begins from the premise that physical and psychological oppression are inseparable. Nat Turner does lust after white women, and after one white woman—the appropriately named Margaret Whitehead—in particular. But this, far from turning him into a monster, is intended to show

how much he is a victim, a classic, bewildered victim, of history. He is not the fiend incarnate that some Southern historians prefer to remember. Nor is he, for that matter, the dispassionate tactician of revolt celebrated by many of the abolitionists. If anything, he is more like the Negro described by James Baldwin—somebody who, as Baldwin puts it, was "defeated long before he died because, at the bottom of his heart, he really believed what white people said about him."[49]

Styron's critics are right about one thing, though: the relationship between white woman and black man is, really, the crucial relationship in the *Confessions*—the key to its reading of history and consequent reappraisal of Southern conventions. And I would like to develop the point I am making about it now by suggesting another analogy, a comparison with a contemporary black writer other than Baldwin. For, in its analysis of the sexual implications of an oppressive and exploitative society, Styron's novel is, I think, very similar to a book to which it might otherwise seem to bear no relation at all: *Soul On Ice* by Eldridge Cleaver. I have two chapters of Cleaver's book in mind especially, "The Allegory of the Black Eunuch" and "The Primeval Mitosis," where Cleaver argues that a clear and definable connection exists between the given structure of any society and the personal lives and sexual drives of its members. Cleaver's theory is developed largely in terms of its negative implications, as manifested in what he calls a "Class Society."

> The Class Society projects a fragmented sexual image. Each class projects a sexual image coinciding with its class-function in society. And since its class-function will differ from that of other classes, its sexual image will differ also. . . . The source of the fragmentation of the Self in Class Society lies in the alienation between the function of man's Mind and the function of his Body.[50]

What is particularly relevant here is the special relationship that Cleaver claims is fostered in the American version of a "Class Society" between the oppressed black man and the privileged white woman. The black man, or "Supermasculine Menial" as Cleaver calls him, is reduced by the American system to the status of a workhouse donkey, a body without a mind; while the white woman, to whom Cleaver refers—in typically sardonic fashion—as "the Ultrafeminine" is placed on a pedestal, a frail mind or sensibility without a body. Each, Cleaver argues, perceives in the other what he or she lacks and what, within the terms of the social/sexual functions assigned to them, they must always lack. The "Supermasculine Menial," for example, soon senses that the "Ultrafeminine" is his opposite and necessary complement— and so, in a way, his "psychic bride."

> She is his 'dream girl'. She . . . exerts a magnetic attraction upon him. . . .
> Also, since standards . . . are set by the elite, the Ultrafeminine personifies
> the official standard of feminine beauty . . . imbued with this official stand-
> ard . . . the Supermasculine Menial develops an obsessive yearning . . .
> for sexual contact with the Ultrafeminine.[51]

Effectively, Cleaver is describing here a situation in which the
white woman is dangled in front of the black man as a kind of temp-
ting object, something that he cannot know and that consequently
serves to define both his incompleteness and his limitations. He longs
to possess her because to do so would, as he sees it, be to recover
wholeness and demonstrate his freedom. Cleaver puts the matter with
his usual feeling for the right, brutal and memorable, phrase: in this
context, he says, rape assumes a special, symbolic status. It comes to
seem like "an insurrectionary act."[52] Only *seem* like an insurrectionary
act, though; the black man, Cleaver goes on, may believe that he is
asserting his freedom in lusting after a white woman, but really all
he is doing is demonstrating his servitude. Despite anything he may
that he is still imprisoned within a fragmented sexual being, and still
think to the contrary, his longing for a white "dream girl" only proves
controlled by the standards of beauty and value his society engenders.
The "Supermasculine Menial," in fact, simply confirms that he is a
"Supermasculine Menial" by lusting after the "Ultrafeminine." Even
this paradoxical situation is not the whole truth, however. By a final
twist of logic Cleaver suggests that, while the black man is certainly
deluded in seeing the white woman as a means to freedom, he may
still discover his freedom in possessing her. And this is simply because in possessing her he may realize the emptiness of his dream,
and the scope and causes of his illusion. The point is not a difficult one
to grasp, although it adds to the complexity of the total situation. The
fulfillment of the desires of the "Supermasculine Menial," Cleaver is
saying, will inevitably be followed by disillusionment; and this in
turn may be followed by a moment of illumination, in which the limited and conditioned nature of his earlier ambitions is revealed to him.
Understanding the nature of his previous self, and the forces that
shaped and constricted it, the black man may finally enter into his
full manhood.

Returning to the *Confessions*, the main point can, I think, be made
at once. Nat Turner, as William Styron presents him, is clearly a close
relative of Cleaver's "Supermasculine Menial," somebody whose entire
being has been drastically reshaped by his society—and those institutions through which the past of his society perpetuates itself. The
language that structures his reality is, for much of the time, a white
language, so every attempt he makes to define new possibilities for

himself is hampered by the tools he is using. The life styles available to him are mainly those prescribed by his white masters, and require acceptance of the closed system into which he was born. His god is the white God; his instructors are white instructors; above all, his ambitions are focused in terms of the "dream girl" of the white community. Whether we take Turner in the way the ten black writers do, as a comment on a particular historical situation, or as illustrating a problem in which we all share, by being members of a society and inheritors of its past, the cruel paradox that haunts his life remains essentially the same: that he, like Cleaver's black man, can only dream dreams of freedom that tend to confirm his imprisonment.

Imprisonment is, in fact, Turner's condition for most of the novel; and it is an imprisonment that is double. He is caught within the confines of a closed system of society, and he is defined by the narrow possibilities of a repressed and fragmented self. He can neither objectify his feelings in terms of the world around him, nor achieve the more fundamental satisfaction of knowing what the full range of his feelings is and, consequently, what he himself might be. His life is really a series of withdrawals, from the outer world of action into the inner world of frustrated fantasy. In a way Turner recognizes this himself, but what he does not realize is that, initially at least, this inner world is as much of a prison for him as the outer one is—because the two are inseparable. The situation is a complex one, full of ironies that reach their climax, I think, at the actual moment of rebellion. For though Turner now seems to be acting in defiance of white society, really he is only betraying his continued allegiance to the dream it dictates. His definitive act during the revolt, the murder of Margaret Whitehead (the daughter of a local plantation owner, and the main object of Turner's erotic fantasies), involves not so much a rejection of white ideals as a positive attempt to embrace and realize them.

> Ah how I want her, I thought, and unsheathed my sword . . . she tripped forward, bare arms . . . outthrust as if to welcome someone beloved. . . . As she stumbled . . . I heard . . . her . . . ragged breathing, and it was with this sound in my ears that I plunged the sword into her side. . . .[53]

It takes very little stretch of the imagination, I think, to see that for Turner at this moment his violence is a means of fulfilling his earlier fantasies, more like a rape of his white "dream girl" than anything else. That the rape is itself internalized, and so quite literally a part of the dominant illusion, only adds a further dimension to the irony: Turner cannot, in effect, see his actions for what they are any more than, before this, he has been able to see Margaret Whitehead for what she is. Like Cleaver's "Supermasculine Menial" he remains trapped, an innocent victim, even while performing what is apparently an "insurrectionary act."

Nat Turner has very little time left for the further stage that Cleaver describes, leading from disillusionment to revelation. Still, the self-analysis that occupies his last days, and that accounts for the retrospective standpoint of the book, does offer him the possibility of a new direction. Turner manages a full look at the worst and this, in a fashion characteristic of tragedy, enables him to see that there may be a way to the better. Not only that, he begins to take that way. For how else are we to interpret the *language* of his meditations, which (as I mentioned earlier) owes less to his white masters and the culture they have imposed on him than it does to his own groping efforts toward self-realization? The very manner of Turner's remembrances suggests, I think, that he is beginning to find a trustworthy means of shaping his own experience, and so of defining his own being. And the suggestion is confirmed right at the end of the novel, with Nat Turner's death. At this moment, just as Turner is about to leave his prison cell for the gallows, an echo of an echo comes to his mind—the recollection of a phrase heard long ago in childhood, which seems to have acquired a new significance now, thanks to his experiences. It supplies the last line of the narrative proper:

Oh, how bright and fair the morning star . . .[54]

The immediate reference here is, of course, to the Bible and Turner's own religious upbringing—but it is surely not stretching a point too far to say that the phrase may also contain an echo of the last paragraph of Thoreau's *Walden*, an echo or association that is crucial to its meaning. For it reminds us, I think, just as the closing lines of *Walden* do, that the book we have been reading is about the "dark night" that precedes and the "new dawn" that announces the liberation of the self; it tells us, as clearly as any figurative expression can, that what we have witnessed is that stripping away of illusion, painful but inevitable, which must preface the discovery of a new identity. "Self-emancipation," asks Thoreau at one point in *Walden*, "even in the West Indies provinces of the fancy and imagination—what Wilberforce is there to bring that about?" The question, as Thoreau must have realized when he asked it, was a rhetorical one, which he was answering in his own life and writing. And for Styron, by the end of *Confessions*, it has become something of a rhetorical one as well, since his book, like Thoreau's (or, for that matter, Eldridge Cleaver's), actually describes the journey toward self-emancipation. Its hero is somebody who has come to understand the past, and with the past the full impact of the forces imprisoning him—and who, given the proper opportunity, could now use this understanding to begin life again.

Nat Turner dies, though, before he can actually embark on his new life: just as Thoreau disappears from view even before he has left Walden Pond, evading any questions we may ask about what happened to him when he returned to society. In practical terms, the process of self-emancipation described in the *Confessions*—like the one described in *Walden* and *Soul On Ice*—is left unfinished, equivocal; and the real, which is to say the only completed, liberation occurs not in the life of the protagonist but *in the consciousness, the mind and spirit, of the writer*. The freedom won in the book, and by the book in a sense, is an imaginative rather than an active, political one—a matter of private and, in fact, literary experience to which the writer's craft, his own act of writing bears witness. Perhaps it will be obvious enough already just how, in the *Confessions*, Styron achieves this freedom—by developing for the first time *beyond* his tradition, adding to the existing monuments, rearranging them and so endowing them with an original value. For the familiar ghosts of Southern literature—the great plantation, the gentleman farmer, the plantation lady, and the Southern belle—they are all there as usual. But they have all been made unfamiliar now, severed from their old connections. This time it is the underdog who presents them to us, the victim whose suffering has made their elegant games and playacting possible. We see them with altered vision, as if the past were being redeemed and revalued for us as we read, and the effect of this is, I think, rather like the experience Eliot describes in "The Dry Salvages."

> It seems, as one becomes older,
> That the past has another pattern . . .
> . . . .
> The moments of happiness—not the sense of well-being,
> Fruition, fulfilment, security or affection,
> Or even a very good dinner, but the sudden illumination—
> We had the experience but missed the meaning,
> And approach to the meaning restores the experience
> In a different form, beyond any meaning
> We can assign to happiness. . . .

As Eliot says, we have had the experience before but somehow missed its meaning—or, at least, one of its possible meanings. Many other novels and poems may have described the exotic setting of the *Confessions* for us, but Styron's novel places it in a new, and profoundly disturbing, light.

Of course, a simple change in narrative point of view, however significant it may be historically, does not go all the way to account for this metamorphosis. Even more important, in a sense, is the use Styron makes of the accepted structures of Southern writing. His general attempt to rewrite history—by engaging event with myth, yesterday with today, and by establishing what is essentially a symbiotic relationship between his characters and their environment—is familiar up to a point. We have, after all, seen other characters who have tried to reenact the past (among them Faulkner's Quentin Compson and Wolfe's Zachariah Joyner) and many other writers (Southern writers and historical writers generally) who have seen it as their main purpose to reconcile their ideas or beliefs with the received facts and legends of history. The difference in Styron's case, however, and it is a crucial one, is that these strategies are now being used not for nostalgia's sake nor even to demonstrate the virtues of precedent, ceremony, and ritual but so as to further the cause of a carefully formulated, highly sophisticated form of radicalism. Traditionalism in Styron's hands becomes, effectively, an agent of revolution, the kind of plea for immediate, drastic, and even violent change that one is more inclined to associate with political writers such as Cleaver, or visionaries such as Emerson and Thoreau, than with the likes of Robert Penn Warren, Thomas Wolfe, and William Faulkner. One way of charting the course Styron has taken, in fact, is to say that Faulkner and his generation could never have written something like the *Confessions*, if only because it is the sort of book that measures itself in terms of its distance from them and their work. It predicates a certain tradition, in other words, a particular orthodoxy from which it has developed and with which it can establish a definite, objective relationship; and that tradition is made up as much from the novels, plays, and poems of the "renaissance" as from the broader, social and cultural, patterns of the South. Without necessarily endorsing the aims of the *Confessions*, though, or sharing in the impulses that led Styron to write it, Faulkner and his contemporaries would, I believe, have understood the novel; they would have seen how it has grown out of their own work and, in growing, taken on a separate, distinct life of its own. The *Confessions* uses its given inheritance and then transcends it so as to present us with a broadly inclusive, yet cross-grained and self-evidently personal portrait of *all* our lives in history; and that, as Styron's predecessors would probably have recognized, is really the best that can be said about any Southern book.

Notes

~~~~~~

Chapter 1

1. *Absalom, Absalom!* (New York, 1936), p. 127.
2. The sources of information available on the social and economic conditions of the South since the First World War are enormous. For details of some of the more useful works on the period, see the bibliography.
3. Norfolk *Virginian-Pilot*, 29 December 1918, quoted in George B. Tindall, *The Emergence of the New South, 1813-1943*, vol. 10, Wendell H. Stephenson and E. Merton Coulter, eds., *A History of the South* (Baton Rouge, La., 1967).
4. John Faulkner, *Men Working* (New York, 1941) p. 63.
5. For further details of these difficulties and their consequences see, e.g., Thomas D. Clark and Henry W. Grady, *The South since Appomatox* (New York, 1967), pp. 106-7, 269 ff; J. S. Ezell, *The South since 1865* (New York, 1967), pp. 136 ff; Calvin B. Hoover and B. V. Ratchford, *Economic Resources and Policies of the South* (New York, 1951), pp. 115 ff; Joseph J. Spengler, "Demographic and Economic Change," in Allan P. Sindler, ed., *Change in the Contemporary South* (Durham, N.C., 1963).
6. *Sharecroppers All* (Chapel Hill, N.C., 1941), pp. 263-64.
7. Wilbur J. Cash, *The Mind of the South* (New York, 1941), p. 273.
8. See, e.g., Louis Morton, *Robert Carter of Nomini Hall: A Virginia Planter of the Eighteenth Century* (Williamsburg, Va., 1941); and Louis B. Wright, ed., *Letters of Robert Carter, 1720-1727* (San Marino, Calif., 1940), pp. 105-6.
9. Letter to Charles Boyle, Earl of Orrery, cited in Louis B. Wright and Marion Tinling, eds., *The London Diary and Other Writings*, (New York, 1958), p. 37.
10. See William R. Taylor, *Cavalier and Yankee: The Old South and the American National Character* (London, 1963).
11. The details of the Scopes trial are taken from Ray Ginger, *Six Days or Forever?: Tennessee v. John Thomas Scopes* (Boston, 1958).
12. "Emily Dickinson" in *Collected Essays* (Denver, Colo., 1932).
13. "The South and Tradition," in Edmund Wilson, ed., *The Collected Essays of John Peale Bishop*, (New York, 1948), p. 11.
14. The main sources for the following discussion of the colonial South are: Charles M. Andrews, *The Colonial Period of American History*, 4 vols. (New Haven, 1934–1938); Carl B. Bridenbaugh, *Myths and Realities: Societies of the Colonial South* (Baton Rouge, La., 1952); Philip A. Bruce, *Economic History of Virginia in the Seventeenth Century*, 2 vols. (New York, 1896), *Institutional History of Virginia in the Seventeenth Century*, 2 vols. (Richmond, Va., 1927); Richard B. Davis, *Literature and Society in Early Virginia, 1608–1840* (Baton Rouge, La., 1973); Thomas J. Wertenbaker, *The Old South: The Founding of American Civilization* (New York, 1942), *Patrician and Plebeian in Virginia* (Charlottesville, Va., 1910), and *The Planters of Colonial Virginia* (Princeton, 1922); Louis B. Wright, *The First Gentlemen of Virginia* (San Marino, Calif., 1940).
15. *An Anatomie of the World: The First Anniversary*, line 213.
16. Edward Williams, "Virginia, more especially the South Part thereof Richly and Truly Valued" (London, 1650), p. 19 in Peter Force, ed., *Tracts and Other Papers Relating Principally to the Origin, Settlement, and Progress of the Colonies in North America*, (New York, 1947 edition), vol. 3. See also William Strachey, *The Historie of Travaile into Virginia*, ed. Louis B. Wright and Virginia Freund, Hakluyt Soc. Reprint (London, 1953), pp. 30–31.
17. Williams, "Virginia . . . Richly and Truly Valued," p. 50. Other quotations in this paragraph are from: William Symonds, *Virginia: A Sermon Preached at Whitechapel* (London, 1609), pp. 19, 26; Robert Rich, *The New Life of Virginia*

(London, 1612) p. 17; John Rolfe, *A True Relation of the State of Virginia* (London, 1616), pp. 35, 39.

18. Richard Brathwaite, *The English Gentleman* (London, 1630), p. 332.

19. All subsequent quotations in this paragraph are from Richard B. Davis, ed., *William Fitzhugh: Letters and Other Documents* (Chapel Hill, N.C., 1963), pp. 17–18, 169–70, 171, 173, 244–46, 271. A comparable situation in the following century is illustrated in Jack P. Greene, ed., *The Diary of Colonel Landon Carter of Sabine Hall, 1752–1778*, 2 vols. (Charlottesville, Va., 1965).

20. See Wertenbaker, *Planters of Colonial Virginia*, pp. 159–60.

21. Robert Beverley II, *The History and Present State of Virginia* (London, 1722), p. 247. Compare this with more recent verdicts that come to the same conclusions: John R. Alden, *The South in Revolution*, vol. 3 (1957), of Stephenson and Coulter, eds., *A History of the South;* Wesley Frank Craven, *White, Red, and Black: The Seventeenth Century Virginian* (Charlottesville, Va., 1971); Richard Lee Morton, *Colonial Virginia* (Chapel Hill, N.C., 1963), 1: 144; Wertenbaker, *Old South*, pp. 19–30.

22. Hugh Jones, *The Present State of Virginia* (London, 1724), p. 43.

23. *Notes on the State of Virginia* (London, 1784), query 19. For a discussion of the intellectual background to the Revolution in the South, see Daniel J. Boorstin, *The Lost World of Thomas Jefferson* (New York, 1948); Richard B. Davis, *Intellectual Life in Jefferson's Virginia, 1790–1830* (Chapel Hill, N.C., 1964); Adrienne Koch, *The American Enlightenment* (New York, 1965).

24. The changes mentioned here are discussed in more detail in Thomas P. Abernethy, *The South in the New Nation, 1789–1819*, vol. 4 (1961), of Stephenson and Coulter, eds., *A History of the South;* and Charles S. Sydnor, *The Development of Southern Sectionalism, 1819–1848*, vol. 5 (1948), ibid.; Robert S. Cotterill, *The Old South* (Glendale, Calif., 1939), pp. 165 ff.; Clement Eaton, *A History of the Old South* (London, 1949), pp. 236 ff.; Francis B. Simkins, *A History of the South* (New York, 1953; Rev. ed., 1972), pp. 108 ff; Monroe Lee Billington, *The American South: A Brief History* (New York, 1971), pp. 96 ff.

25. *Sketches of the Life and Character of Patrick Henry* (Philadelphia, 1817), pp. 12, 34, 475.

26. Ibid., pp. 39, 44–49.

27. See, e.g., Charles Beard, *Economic Origins of Jeffersonian Democracy* (New York, 1927), pp. 322–52; E. T. Mudge, *The Social Philosophy of John Taylor of Caroline* (New York, 1939).

28. The principal texts in this respect are *Arator, Being a Series of Agricultural Essays, Practical and Political* (Baltimore, 1817); *An Inquiry into the Principles and Policy of the Government of the United States* (Fredericksburg, Va., 1814); *A Letter on the Necessity of Defending the Rights of Agriculture* (Petersburg, Va., 1821).

29. *Arator*, p. 178.

30. See *An Inquiry*, pp. 142, 298, 354, 357.

31. Ibid., pp. 87, 89, 226, 239, 259.

32. James Henry Hammond, "Hammond's Letters on Slavery," in *The Pro-Slavery Argument; as Maintained by the Most Distinguished Writers of the Southern States* (Charleston, S.C., 1852), pp. 162–63.

33. See Taylor, *An Inquiry*, pp. 85, 471–72, 530; *Pro-Slavery Argument*, pp. 110–11; George Fitzhugh, *Sociology for the South; or, the Failure of Free Society* (Richmond, Va., 1854), p. 90.

34. Sydnor, *Southern Sectionalism*, pp. 104 ff., 155, 180–81; Avery O. Craven, *The Growth of Southern Nationalism, 1846–1861*, vol. 6 (1953), of Stephenson and Coulter, eds., *A History of the South*, pp. 16 ff.; Allan Nevins, *Ordeal of the Union* (New York, 1942–1950), 2: 244; 4: 465; Cotterill, *Old South*, p. 193; Simkins, *History of the South*, pp. 167–78.

35. George Fitzhugh, *Cannibals All! or, Slaves Without Masters* (1857; Cambridge, Mass., reprint ed., 1960) p. 103.

36. In, e.g., "A Disquisition on Government" and "A Discourse on the Constitution and Government of the United States," in John C. Calhoun, *The Works of John C. Calhoun,* ed. Richard K. Cralle (New York, 1853), vol. 1. For two conflicting assessments of Calhoun, see Margaret L. Coit, *John C. Calhoun: American Portrait* (London, 1950); and Gerald M. Caspers, *John Calhoun, Opportunist: A Reappraisal* (Gainesville, Fla., 1960).

37. J. Franklin Jameson, ed., *Correspondence of John C. Calhoun, Annual Report of the American Historical Association, 1899* (Washington, D.C., 1900), 2: 671.

38. Speech on the Abolition Petitions, 6 February 1837, in *Works,* 2: 632.

39. Speech on the Oregon Bill, 27 June 1848, in *Works,* 4: 507-8.

40. Speech on the Bill Granting Pre-Emption Rights, 27 January 1838, in *Works,* 3: 135–37.

41. Remarks on the States' Rights Resolutions, in *Works,* 3: 180–81; *Correspondence,* 2: 179.

42. *Life of John C. Calhoun, 1811–1843* (New York, 1843), p. 74.

43. The following analysis of Kennedy's work owes a great deal to Taylor, *Cavalier and Yankee,* pp. 183 ff. The biographical details are from Charles Bohner, *John Pendleton Kennedy: Gentleman from Baltimore* (Baltimore, 1961).

44. "How to Read," in *Literary Essays of Ezra Pound* (London, 1954), pp. 27, 28.

45. See Kennedy's satirical novel, *Quodlibet: Containing Some Annals Thereof* (1840; uniform ed., New York, 1872), p. 217.

46. *Swallow Barn; or, A Sojourn in the Old Dominion* (1832). All references are to the New York, 1872, uniform edition.

47. For a comprehensive account of this tradition up until the present century, see Francis P. Gaines, *The Southern Plantation: A Study in the Development and Accuracy of a Tradition* (New York, 1924).

48. *Swallow Barn,* pp. 31, 39–40, 53, 86, 345.

49. Ibid., p. 51.

50. Ibid., p. 453.

51. Ibid., p. 123.

52. Ibid., pp. 25, 32–33.

53. Ibid., p. 71.

54. Ibid., pp. 214, 500.

55. "A Word in Advance to the Reader" (1852 and all subsequent editions).

56. "Baltimore Long Ago," in *At Home and Abroad: A Series of Essays* (New York, 1872), p. 167.

57. *Horse-Shoe Robinson: A Tale of the Tory Ascendancy* (1835; uniform ed., New York, 1872), p. 15.

58. Ibid., pp. 114, 140, 585.

59. Ibid., p. 41.

60. Ibid., p. 589.

61. "The People," in *At Home and Abroad,* p. 149.

62. See "Defence of the Whigs," in *Political and Official Papers* (New York, 1872), pp. 217-450, passim.

63. The developments mentioned here are discussed in detail in Clark and Grady, *South since Appomatox;* Ezell, *South since 1865;* Paul Gaston, *The New South Creed: A Study in Southern Mythmaking* (New York, 1970); C. Vann Woodward, *Origins of the New South 1877–1913,* vol. 9 (1951), of Stephenson and Coulter, eds., *A History of the South.*

64. Thomas Nelson Page, "Marse Chan: A Tale of Old Virginia," in *In Ole Virginia; or, Marse Chan, and Other Stories* (London, 1889), p. 10. Cf. Joel Chandler Harris, "A Story of the War" in *Uncle Remus; or, Mr Fox, Mr Rabbit, and Mr Terrapin* (London, 1883), p. 204. See also Rollin G. Osterweis, *The Myth of the Lost Cause, 1865–1900* (Hamden, Conn., 1973).

65. Sidney Lanier, "The New South," in *Retrospects and Prospects: Descriptive and Historical Essays* (New York, 1899), pp. 104–5.

66. Ibid., pp. 110–11. Some trenchant analyses of the situation as it really was are given in Alex M. Arnett, *The Populist Movement in Georgia* (New York, 1922); Solon J. Buck, *The Agrarian Crusade: A Chronicle of the Farmer in Politics* (New Haven, 1920); Frederick A. Shannon, *The Farmer's Last Frontier: Agriculture 1860–1897* (New York, 1945).

67. Little of great critical merit has been written on Glasgow despite her obvious importance. Useful for biographical information are H. Blair Rouse, *Ellen Glasgow* (New York, 1962); and E. Stanly Godbold, *Ellen Glasgow and the Woman Within* (Baton Rouge, La., 1972). The best critical account so far is probably Frederick P. McDowell, *Ellen Glasgow and the Ironic Art of Fiction* (New York, 1960). Also of interest are Sara Haardt, "Ellen Glasgow and the South," *Bookman* 69 (April 1929): 133–40; and Marion K. Richards, *Ellen Glasgow's Development as a Novelist* (The Hague, 1971).

68. *The Builders* (London, 1919), p. 112.

69. *Barren Ground* (London, 1925), p. 509; *Vein of Iron* (London, 1936), p. 126.

70. *Barren Ground*, p. 509. Cf. *The Deliverance* (New York, 1904), p. 125.

71. *The Romantic Comedians* (London, 1926), p. 319. Cf. *The Ancient Law* (London, 1908) pp. 95–103.

72. *The Voice of the People* (New York, 1900), p. 13. Cf. *The Miller of the Old Church* (London, 1911), p. 16; *One Man in his Time* (London, 1922), pp. 22, 92.

73. *Virginia* (London, 1913), p. 122.

74. *In This Our Life* (London, 1941), pp. 31, 32, 55, 122, 148, 218.

75. Ibid., p. 111.

76. Ibid., p. 13.

77. *The Woman Within* (London, 1955), p. 42. Ellen Glasgow had never explicitly denied the existence of the "cavalier" planter in ante-bellum times (indeed, in *The Battle-Ground* [London, 1902] she had gone far toward accepting it); only his relevance to post-bellum society.

78. William Faulkner in Malcolm Cowley, ed., *Writers at Work: The "Paris Review" Interviews* (London, 1958) p. 141.

79. Henry L. Mencken "The Sahara of the Bozart," in *Prejudices: Second Series* (New York, 1920). The couplet by one J. Gordon Coogler, "the last bard of Dixie," is quoted in this essay.

80. "Progress and Nostalgia: The Self Image of the Nineteen Twenties," in Malcolm Bradbury and David Palmer, eds., *The American Novel in the Nineteen Twenties* (London, 1971), pp. 38–39.

81. *To One in Paradise*, lines 11–13.

Chapter 2

1. *Guide to Kulchur* (New York, 1938), p. 58.

2. The following details are taken from longer accounts in John Malcolm Bradbury, *The Fugitives: A Critical Account* (Chapel Hill, N.C., 1958); Louise Cowan, *The Fugitive Group: A Literary History* (Baton Rouge, La., 1959); John Lincoln Stewart, *The Burden of Time: The Fugitives and Agrarians* (Princeton, 1965). Also of interest is Donald Davidson, "I'll Take My Stand. A History," *American Review* 5 (Summer 1935): 301–21.

3. "Forward," *The Fugitive* 1 (1922): 1.

4. Harriet Monroe, "The Old South," *Poetry* 22 (1923): 91; [Donald Davidson], "Merely Prose," *The Fugitive* 2 (June–July 1923): 66.

5. Louis D. Rubin, *The Faraway Country: Writers of the Modern South*

(Seattle, Wash., 1963). See also Rubin's *The Writer in the South: Studies in a Literary Community* (Baton Rouge, La., 1972).

6. Cited in Cowan, *Fugitive Group*, p. 244.

7. 1927, according to Cowan, *Fugitive Group*, p. 244; 1926, according to Virginia Rock, "The Making and Meaning of *I'll Take My Stand:* A Study of Utopian Conservatism, 1925–1939" (Ph.D. diss., University of Minnesota, 1961), pp. 222–23.

8. George B. Tindall, *The Emergence of the New South*, vol. 10, Wendell H. Stephenson and B. Merton Coulter, eds., *A History of the South* (Baton Rouge, La., 1967), p. 299.

9. All references are to the 1962 New York edition, edited by Louis D. Rubin.

10. [John Crowe Ransom], "Introduction: A Statement of Principles," in *I'll Take My Stand*, p. xix. All subsequent essays cited here are in *I'll Take My Stand*, unless otherwise stated.

11. In his introduction to the 1962 edition of *I'll Take My Stand*, Louis D. Rubin insists that the Agrarians merely use the Old South as a metaphor. So does Virginia Rock in "The Fugitive-Agrarians in Response to Social Change," *Southern Humanities Review* 1 (1967): 170–81. This claim seems to receive some support from the later use made by Agrarians of the idea of the Old South in their fiction and verse; and from some of the remarks made by various members of the group in "The Agrarians Today: A Symposium," *Shenandoah* 3, no. 2 (Summer 1952): 29, 30. But it conflicts with the almost entirely political and economic character of the essays contributed by Agrarians to Herbert Agar and Allen Tate, eds., *Who Owns America? A New Declaration of Independence*, and of the articles they wrote for the *American Review;* see, e.g., Frank Owsley, "The Pillars of Agrarianism," *American Review* (March 1935): 529–47. Other remarks made in the *Shenandoah* symposium seem to contradict Rubin's claim as well; see pp. 15, 19, 22.

12. Herman Nixon, "Whither Southern Economy?" pp. 195–96; John Crowe Ransom, "Reconstructed but Unregenerate," p. 10; Allen Tate, "Remarks on the Southern Religion," p. 159; Lyle H. Lanier, "A Critique of the Philosophy of Progress," p. 141; John Gould Fletcher, "Education Past and Present," p. 116.

13. [Ransom], "Introduction"; Tate, "Southern Religion," pp. 163, 172. For demonstrations of the specific arguments mentioned here, see Robert Penn Warren, "The Briar Patch," pp. 254, 260, 262; Andrew Nelson Lytle, "The Hind Tit," pp. 209–10; Fletcher, "Education, Past and Present," pp. 99–100; Tate, "Southern Religion," passim.

14. Fletcher, "Education, Past and Present," pp. 96, 111, 116; Nixon, "Whither Southern Economy?" p. 188; Henry Kline, "William Remington: A Study in Individualism," pp. 317, 325; Donald Davidson, "A Mirror for Artists," p. 34; [Ransom], "Introduction," p. xxiv; Lytle, "Hind Tit," p. 238; Tate, "Southern Religion," pp. 159, 163, 170.

15. Ransom, "Reconstructed but Unregenerate," p. 5; Lanier, "Philosophy of Progress," p. 123.

16. Lanier, "Philosophy of Progress," p. 125; Fletcher, "Education, Past and Present," p. 117.

17. Ransom, "Reconstructed but Unregenerate," pp. 4, 5; Nixon, "Whither Southern Economy?" p. 188; Lanier, "Philosophy of Progress," p. 123; Fletcher, "Education, Past and Present," p. 110.

18. Ransom, "Reconstructed but Unregenerate," p. 5. For illustrations of the techniques mentioned here, see Owsley, "Irrepressible Conflict," pp. 69, 71; Fletcher, "Education, Past and Present," pp. 101, 111; Tate, "Southern Religion," pp. 171, 182; Lytle, "Hind Tit," pp. 205, 207; Warren, "Briar Patch," p. 264; John Wade, "The Life and Death of Cousin Lucius," p. 282; Stark Young, "Not in Memoriam, but in Defense," p. 344.

19. Owsley, "Irrepressible Conflict," pp. 69, 72.

20. Lytle, "Hind Tit," pp. 219–20.

21. Lanier, "Philosophy of Progress," p. 150. For examples of the rhetorical devices mentioned here, see Ransom, "Reconstructed but Unregenerate," pp. 7, 10, 13, 14; Davidson, "Mirror for Artists," pp. 49, 58; Fletcher, "Education, Past and Present," pp. 11, 116; Lanier, "Philosophy of Progress," p. 123; Lytle, "Hind Tit,'" p. 203; Wade, "Cousin Lucius," p. 289; Kline, "William Remington," pp. 308, 324.

22. Wade, "Cousin Lucius," pp. 295, 299.

23. Owsley, "Irrepressible Conflict," p. 91; Fletcher, "Education, Past and Present," p. 118; Kline, "William Remington," p. 319.

24. Ransom, "Reconstructed but Unregenerate," p. 5.

25. Lanier, "Philosophy of Progress," p. 147; [Ransom], "Introduction," p. xxxi; Nixon, "Whither Southern Economy?" p. 199.

26. For examples of this association, see Ransom, "Reconstructed but Unregenerate," p. 25; Owsley, "Irrepressible Conflict," p. 72; Lanier "Philosophy of Progress," pp. 146–47; Lytle, "Hind Tit," pp. 217–18; Wade, "Cousin Lucius," pp. 279–80; Young, "Not in Memoriam," pp. 246–47.

27. Young, "Not in Memoriam," p. 334.

28. Davidson, "Mirror for Artists," p. 60.

29. Lytle, "Hind Tit," p. 245.

30. Ibid. Other quotations in the paragraph are from pp. 229, 234.

31. Ransom, "Reconstructed but Unregenerate," p. 12; Warren, "Briar Patch," p. 263.

32. Owsley, "Irrepressible Conflict," pp. 69–70, 71–72.

33. Essays from different periods that come to approximately the same conclusions include Robert Penn Warren, "John Crowe Ransom: A Study in Irony," *Virginia Quarterly Review* 11 (January 1935): 93–112; Harry M. Campbell, "John Crowe Ransom," *Southwest Review* 14 (1939): 476–89; most of the articles in "Homage to John Crowe Ransom: Essays on His Work as Poet and Critic," *Sewanee Review* 56 (Summer 1948): 365–476; Graham Hough, "John Crowe Ransom: The Poet and the Critic," *Southern Review* 1 (January 1965): 1–21; James E. Magner, *John Crowe Ransom: Critical Principles and Preoccupations* (The Hague, 1971).

34. "In Amicitia," *Sewanee Review* 67 (Autumn 1959): 582.

35. See "Poets without Laurels" in *The World's Body* (New York, 1938), p. 64; *God without Thunder: An Unorthodox Defense of Orthodoxy* (New York, 1930), p. 196. In "Poetry, the Final Cause," *Kenyon Review* 9 (Autumn 1947): 654, "reason" and "sensibility" are identified with, respectively, the Freudian "ego" and "id."

36. "Forms and Citizens," in *The World's Body*, p. 34. For the development of this argument see, e.g., *God without Thunder*, pp. 128, 195–96; "Poets without Laurels," pp. 64–71; "The Understanding of Fiction," *Kenyon Review* 12 (Spring 1950): 192.

37. "Introduction" to *I'll Take My Stand*, pp. xxiii, xxv; *God without Thunder*, pp. 196, 198–201; "Reconstructed but Unregenerate," p. 10; "The Aesthetic of Regionalism," *American Review* 1 (October 1933): 279; "The Content of the Novel: Notes Toward a Critique of Fiction," ibid., 7 (Summer 1936): 307; "Pragmatics of Art," *Kenyon Review* 2 (Winter 1940): 87.

38. "Forms and Citizens," p. 34; "Poets without Laurels," pp. 65–66.

39. *God without Thunder*, pp. 3, 5, 34, 128, 166.

40. "Eclogue," in *Selected Poems* (New York, 1963), p. 50, lines 83-84.

41. "A Poem Nearly Anonymous" in *The World's Body*, p. 28; "I.A. Richards: The Psychological Critic," in *The New Criticism* (Norfolk, Conn., 1941), p. 53.

42. *Selected Poems*, p. 5.

43. Ibid., pp. 70–71.

44. "Land! An Answer to the Unemployment Problem," *Harper's Magazine* 165 (July 1932): 217–18, 219, 222; "The State and the Land," *New Republic* 70 (17 February 1932): 9, 10; "Happy Farmers," *American Review* 1 (October

1933): 527–28; "What Does the South Want?" *Virginia Quarterly Review* 12 (January 1936): 190–91.

45. "The South Defends its Heritage," *Harper's Magazine* 58 (June 1929): 109, 112; "Forms and Citizens," p. 43; "Poets without Laurels," p. 64; "Aesthetic of Regionalism," pp. 293, 301.

46. *All the King's Men* (New York, 1946; London, 1948) p. 180; "T. S. Stribling: A Paragraph in the History of Critical Realism," *American Review* 2 (February 1934): 476; *Segregation: The Inner Conflict in the South* (New York, 1953), p. 26; "The Great Mirage: Conrad and 'Nostromo,'" in *Selected Essays* (London, 1958), p. 54; "A Note on Three Southern Poets," *Poetry* 40 (May 1932): 110; *Who Speaks for the Negro?* (New York, 1965), p. 413.

47. *World Enough and Time: A Romantic Novel,* (New York, 1950; London, 1951), p. 502; "William Faulkner," in *Selected Essays,* p. 69; *Night Rider* (London, 1939), pp. 225–26. *Band of Angels* was first published in 1955, and *At Heaven's Gate* in 1943.

48. *World Enough and Time,* p. 468.

49. *Night Rider,* pp. 19, 245; *World Enough and Time,* p. 44. *Wilderness* was first published in 1961, and *Flood* in 1964. Warren has developed the same preoccupations more recently in *Meet Me in the Green Glen* (New York, 1972).

50. *World Enough and Time,* pp. 6–7; "The Ballad of Billie Potts," in *Selected Poems: New and Old, 1923–1966* (New York, 1966), p. 238, lines 454–55, 458. *Brother to Dragons: A Tale in Verse and Voices* was first published in 1953. The metaphorical significance of the "clearing" is actually explained in "Knowledge and the Image of Man," *Sewanee Review* 63 (Spring 1955): 187.

51. See, e.g., Walter Allen, *Tradition and Dream: The English and American Novel from the Twenties to Our Time* (London, 1964), pp. 116–18; Victor Strandberg, *A Colder Fire: The Poetry of Robert Penn Warren* (Lexington, Ky., 1965).

52. Bradbury, *The Fugitives,* p. 209. For other examples of this approach to the novel, see N. R. Girault, "The Narrator's Mind as Symbol: An Analysis of *All the King's Men,*" *Accent* 7 (1947): 220–34; Charles R. Anderson, "Violence and Order in the Novels of Robert Penn Warren," *Hopkins Review* 6 (Winter 1953): 88–105; and the relevant pages in Charles H. Bohner, *Robert Penn Warren* (New York, 1964).

53. See, e.g., the essay by Hamilton Basso in Louis D. Rubin, ed., *All the King's Meanings* (Baton Rouge, La., 1957). Basso also wrote a novel, *The Sun in Capricorn,* which offers a very different picture of the Louisiana demagogue. See also the essays in *All the King's Men: A Symposium,* Carnegie Studies in English, no. 3 (1957); and John L. Longley, *Robert Penn Warren* (Austin, Tex., 1969).

54. *All the King's Men,* p. 448.

55. The following details are from T. Harry Williams, *Huey Long* (New York, 1969); Forrest Davis, *Huey Long, A Candid Biography* (New York, 1935); Hodding Carter, "Huey Long, American Dictator," in Isabel Leighton, ed., *The Aspirin Age, 1919–1941* (London, 1950); Allan P. Sindler, *Huey Long's Louisiana: State Politics, 1920–1952* (Baltimore, 1956); Reinhard H. Luthin, chap. 10 of *American Demogogues: Twentieth-Century* (Gloucester, Mass., 1959).

56. William A. Percy, *Lanterns on the Levee* (New York, 1941), p. 144.

57. See, e.g., Raymond Moley, *Twenty-Seven Masters of Politics* (New York, 1951), p. 221.

58. *All the King's Men,* p. 155.

59. Sindler, *Long's Louisiana,* p. 97.

60. See, e.g., Wilbur J. Cash, *The Mind of the South* (New York, 1941), pp. 86–89.

61. Ibid.

62. In a large number of instances where Warren changes the original story, the explanation is more straightforward than that: for obvious reasons of dramatic emphasis and brevity, he simply permits one characteristic person or event to

stand in the place of others, or he invents someone or something that epitomizes some broader aspect of Long/Stark's career. For example, the hospital and Stark's relationship with the Stantons serve to focus his idealistic impulses, just as Duffy, Sugar-Boy, and the impeachment episode suggest his partial commitment to the world of back-room deals and violence.

63. *All the King's Men,* p. 114.

64. Ibid., p. 200.

65. "Liberalism and Tradition," in *Reason in Madness* (New York, 1941), p. 207.

66. Ibid., pp. 210–11; see also pp. 208, 209; *Jefferson Davis: His Rise and Fall* (New York, 1929), p. 56; *Stonewall Jackson: The Good Soldier* (London, 1930), p. 39; "Southern Religion," p. 159.

67. "The Man of Letters in the Modern World," in *The Forlorn Demon: Didactic and Critical Essays* (London, 1953), p. 111; "Liberalism and Tradition," p. 208.

68. "Southern Religion," p. 166; "Hart Crane," in *Reactionary Essays on Poetry and Ideas* (London, 1930), p. 37.

69. "Ode to the Confederate Dead," in *Poems* (Denver, Colo., 1961), p. 21, lines 44–55; "Narcissus as Narcissus," in *Reason in Madness,* p. 140.

70. *The Fathers* (New York, 1938), p. 21.

71. Ibid., p. 125; see also p. 21.

72. Ibid., p. 23.

73. Ibid., p. 185; see also p. 44.

74. Ibid., p. 185.

75. Ibid., p. 54.

76. Ibid., pp. 57, 62; "Liberalism and Tradition," p. 210.

77. "The Symbolic Imagination," in *The Forlorn Demon,* p. 36; "The Present Function of Criticism," in *Reason in Madness,* p. 19.

78. "Ode," p. 21, lines 42–44; *The Fathers,* p. 3.

79. *The Fathers,* p. 32; "Ode," p. 23, line 87.

80. *The Fathers,* p. 179.

81. *Stonewall Jackson,* p. 12.

82. "The New Provincialism," in *Collected Essays* (Denver, Colo., 1959), p. 292. This discussion of Tate is indebted in particular to R. K. Meiners, *The Last Alternatives: A Study of the Works of Allen Tate* (Denver, Colo., 1963) and some of the essays in Radcliffe Squires, ed., *Allen Tate and His Work: Critical Evaluations* (Minneapolis, Minn., 1972).

83. *An Outland Piper* (Boston, 1924), pp. 35–36.

84. "Dryad," pp. 35-36, lines 2, 3, 5–8, 19–20; "Avalon," in *An Outland Piper,* p. 36, lines 19–20.

85. "Ecclesiasticus II," in *An Outland Piper,* p. 51, line 3; "The Wolf," in ibid., p. 51, line 4.

86. "The Tall Men," in *The Tall Men* (Boston, 1927), p. 5. The eight sections have separate titles, but it is generally accepted that they should be treated as a sequence; see, e.g., Richard C. Beatty, "Donald Davidson as Fugitive—Agrarian," in Louis D. Rubin and Robert D. Jacobs, eds., *Southern Renascence: The Literature of the Modern South* (Baltimore, 1953), pp. 402 ff; Bradbury, *The Fugitives,* pp. 71ff; and T. D. Young and M. T. Inge, eds., *Donald Davidson: An Essay and a Bibliography* (Nashville, Tenn., 1965).

87. "The Sod of Battle-Fields," in *The Tall Men,* p. 28. Review of *The American City, American Review* 1 (April 1930): 100.

88. "Fire on Belmont Street," in *The Tall Men,* pp. 114–15.

89. "The Long Street," in *The Tall Men,* pp. 1, 2; "The Tall Men," p. 5.

90. "Counter-attack 1930–1940: The South Against Leviathan," in *Southern Writers in the Modern World* (Athens, Ga., 1958), p. 45.

91. "Geography of the Brain," in *The Tall Men,* p. 31.

92. Ibid., p. 41.

93. "The Tall Men," pp. 9, 13; "Geography of the Brain," pp. 35, 43.

94. "A Sociologist in Eden," *American Review* 8 (November 1936): 178; review of *Backwoods America* in ibid., 4 (March 1935): 626; "Mr. Cash and the Proto-Dorian South," in *Still Rebels, Still Yankees, and Other Essays* (Baton Rouge, La., 1957), p. 195.

95. "Regionalism in the Arts," in *The Attack on Leviathan: Regionalism and Nationalism in the United States* (Chapel Hill, N.C., 1938), pp. 72, 74; "Gulliver with Hay Fever," *American Review* 9 (August 1937): 170.

96. "I'll Take My Stand. A History," p. 309.

97. Even John Crowe Ransom, that monument of tact where his friends are concerned, has remarked that Davidson's "enthusiasm" for the Old South "is rather more uncritical than my own." ("The South is a Bulwark," *Scribner's Magazine* 99 [May 1936]: 299).

98. The subsequent interest that many of the Agrarians took in aesthetics and critical theory, an interest that led them to develop and publicize what became known as the "New Criticism," is beyond the scope of the present study. Nevertheless, it is perhaps worth noting how directly and immediately the New Criticism grew out of certain aspects of Agrarianism. The same emphasis on tradition, a closed structure in which everything is to be found in the right place and which, ideally, refers back to other structures of the same kind—this same emphasis is to be found in both movements. More particularly, people like Ransom and Tate (and, less obviously, Warren) seem, as New Critics, to have regarded poetry as a final line of defense. Continuing to believe in the division of modern man, and less and less convinced that this division could be healed in a directly economic or political way—or even by an adept use of a common mythology—they began to see the poem (and sometimes the novel and drama) as a temporary, and last possible, means of recovering lost unity—a way of finding at least some provisional satisfaction for the "whole man" within an incomplete and therefore unsatisfactory order. For a full discussion of this development, see Alexander Karanikas, *Tillers of a Myth: Southern Agrarians as Social and Literary Critics* (Madison, Wis., 1966).

Chapter 3

1. There have been a number of quite useful discussions of Roberts in recent years (for which, see the bibliography), but in general the critical tendency has been to ignore her or merely to acknowledge her in passing.

2. *The Great Meadow* (New York, 1930), pp. 168, 207–9.

3. *The Time of Man* (New York, 1926), p. 248.

4. Ibid., pp. 348–49.

5. Ibid., p. 382.

6. Ibid., p. 374; see also p. 9. The inner focus of the narrative is discussed in F. Lamar Janney, "Elizabeth Madox Roberts," *Sewanee Review* 45 (Summer 1937): 388–410. For the quotation from Berkeley, see *The Great Meadow*, pp. 198–99; and, for a discussion of Roberts's own version of Idealism, see Henry M. Campbell and Ruel C. Foster, *Elizabeth Madox Roberts* (Norman, Okla., 1956), p. 80.

7. Published in New York, 1935 and 1938 respectively.

8. *A Buried Treasure* (New York, 1931), pp. 279–80.

9. *Tobacco Road* (New York, 1932), p. 23.

10. Ibid., p. 39.

11. "The Fight," in *Georgia Scenes*, pp. 50, 52–53. Caldwell's debt to the Southwestern humorists is mentioned in passing by Carl Van Doren, "Made in America, Erskine Caldwell," *Nation* 137 (18 October 1937): 444.

12. For different opinions of Longstreet's aims and achievement, see Con-

stance Rourke, *American Humor: A Study of the National Character* (New York, 1931); Walter Blair, *Horse Sense in American Humor: From Benjamin Franklin to Ogden Nash* (Chicago, 1942); Kenneth Lynn, *Mark Twain and Southwestern Humor* (Boston, 1960).

13. The complexity of Mark Twain's purposes in the book, and the various levels of interest on which it consequently operates, are brought out well in Walter Blair, *Mark Twain and Huck Finn* (Berkeley, Calif., 1960).

14. "Sut Lovingood's Sermon," in *Sut Lovingood: Yarns Spun by a "Natural Born Durn'd Fool"* (New York, 1867), p. 88; see also p. 172.

15. I am aware that this is an unorthodox interpretation of Harris, but I think it can be reconciled at least with the expressed opinions of Lynn and Tony Tanner, *The Reign of Wonder* (Cambridge, 1956), pp. 100–103. They argue that Harris is in sympathy with Sut Lovingood, and that this is one reason why he adopts Sut as narrator. I am essentially in agreement with this, but feel that the sympathy is as much for Sut's potential as for what he actually is. The kinds of values expressed by this potential, it need hardly be added, have nothing at all to do with the genteel culture that Sut criticizes.

16. "Trapping a Sheriff," in *Sut Lovingood's Yarns*, pp. 196–97.

17. See, e.g., the stories entitled "The Day we Rang the Bell for Preacher Hawshaw," "My Old Man and the Gypsy Queen," and "Handsome Brown's Day Off."

18. *God's Little Acre* (New York, 1933); *Tragic Ground* (Boston, 1944).

19. *God's Little Acre*, pp. 99–102. Cf. *Tragic Ground*, pp. 17, 236.

20. "Ty Ty is irascible and indestructible, but above all innocent." (R. Hazel, "Notes on Erskine Caldwell," in Louis D. Rubin and Robert D. Jacobs, eds., *South: Modern Southern Literature in its Cultural Setting* [New York, 1961], p. 325).

21. For the clearest and most succinct description of this entire process, see *You Have Seen Their Faces* (New York, 1937), pp. 32–33.

22. "Tenant Farmers," in *Some American People* (New York, 1935), p. 212.

23. See "The Fire and the Hearth," in *Go Down, Moses* (New York, 1942).

24. *Tobacco Road*, p. 28.

25. *God's Little Acre*, p. 108.

26. The theory of the "epic" theater was given its most elaborate and schematic expression in a statement written by Brecht in 1931, and cited by Ronald Gray, *Brecht* (Edinburgh, 1961), pp. 62–63.

27. Of course, this device would not be very different from the choric methods of more traditional drama, were it not that its purpose is specifically to detach the audience from the action (rather than to explicate an action in which they are otherwise involved) and to apprise it of the *social* nature of the problems being confronted.

28. *Tobacco Road*, pp. 82–83.

29. "Tenant Farmers," p. 259.

30. *A House in the Uplands* (New York, 1946), pp. 182–83.

31. Robert Reynolds, *Thomas Wolfe: Memoir of a Friendship* (Austin, Tex., 1965), p. 94.

32. For some fuller discussions of this period, see Hunter S. Thompson, *The Highlanders of the South* (New York, 1910), chaps. 1 and 2; Malcolm Ross, *Machine Age in the Hills* (New York, 1937), chap. 2; Jean Thomas, *Blue Ridge Country* (New York, 1942), chap. 1; or Isabella D. Harris, "The Southern Mountaineer in American Fiction, 1824–1910" (Ph.D. diss., Duke University, 1948), chap. 1.

33. John C. Campbell, *The Southern Highlander and his Homeland* (New York, 1921), pp. 72, 91; William G. Frost, "Our Contemporary Ancestors in the Southern Mountains," *Atlantic Monthly* 83 (March 1899): 311; John Fox, *The Trail of the Lonesome Pine* (New York, 1908), p. 97; Charles C. Givens, *The Devil Takes a Hill-Town* (New York, 1939), p. 30. For examples of the kind of idealization

that mountain novelists indulged in, see Louise C. Boger, *The Southern Mountaineer: A Bibliography* (Morgantown, W. Va., 1964), which also contains some useful plot summaries.

34. Thomas R. Ford, "The Passing of Provincialism," in Thomas R. Ford, ed., *The Southern Appalachian Region: A Survey* (Lexington, Ky., 1962), p. 34; Thomas Wolfe, *The Web and the Rock* (New York, 1939), p. 30.

35. Marion Pearsall, *Little Smoky Ridge: The Natural History of a Southern Appalachian Neighborhood* (Birmingham, Ala., 1959), p. 42.

36. Andrew Turnbull, *Thomas Wolfe* (New York, 1967), p. 78; Maxwell Geismar, *Writers in Crisis* (New York, 1942), p. 196; C. Hugh Holman, *Three Modes of Southern Fiction: Ellen Glasgow, William Faulkner, Thomas Wolfe* (Athens, Ga., 1966), p. 58; Wolfe, "The Story of a Novel. Pt. I," *Saturday Review of Literature* 13 (14 December 1935): 16; Elizabeth Nowell, ed., *The Letters of Thomas Wolfe* (New York, 1956), p. 111 (To Margaret Roberts, 19 July 1962). See also Elizabeth Nowell, ed., *The Notebooks of Thomas Wolfe* (Chapel Hill, N.C., 1970).

37. *The Web and the Rock*, p. 13; "The Story of a Novel. Pt. III," *Saturday Review of Literature* 13 (28 December 1935): 3; *Look Homeward, Angel: A Story of the Buried Life* (New York, 1929), p. 585.

38. *Of Time and the River: A Legend of Man's Hunger in his Youth* (New York, 1935) pp. 30–31.

39. Ibid., p. 35; *Letters*, p. 241 (To Maxwell Perkins, 17 July 1930).

40. *The Web and the Rock*, p. 14; see also p. 242; *Look Homeward, Angel*, p. 148; see also pp. 152, 154. For other observations Wolfe made about the Deep South, see C. Hugh Holman, "The Dark Ruined Helen of his Blood: Thomas Wolfe and the South," in Leslie A. Field, ed., *Thomas Wolfe: Three Decades of Criticism* (New York, 1968).

41. *The Web and the Rock*, p. 6; see also p. 17; "The Men of Old Catawba," in *From Death to Morning* (New York, 1935), p. 202. Compare the description of the highlander's common appearance in Horace Kephart, *Our Southern Highlanders* (New York, 1922), p. 288; and of his ethic in Earl Brewer and W. D. Weatherford, *Life and Religion in Southern Appalachia* (New York, 1962).

42. *The Web and the Rock*, p. 43; see also p. 15. Cf. Muriel E. Sheppard, *Cabins in the Laurel* (Chapel Hill, N.C., 1935), pp. 25ff., 112, 183.

43. "The Web of Earth," in *From Death to Morning*, p. 304; see also p. 303; *Letters*, p. 284 (To Maxwell Perkins, December 1930); *A Western Journal: A Daily Log of the Great Parks Trip, June 20–July 2, 1938* (Pittsburgh, 1951), p. 26. For a detailed discussion of superstitious practices in the Southern highlands, see Thomas, *Blue Ridge Country*, chap. 6.

44. "The Web of Earth," p. 303; see also p. 253. The stoicism of the highlander is something that seems to have made a deep impression on Margaret W. Morley, *The Carolina Mountains* (Boston, 1913), p. 161.

45. "The Web of Earth," p. 296; "The Men of Old Catawba," p. 195. Wolfe's remark about the speech of the hills is cited in Floyd C. Watkins, "Thomas Wolfe and the Southern Mountaineer," *South Atlantic Quarterly* (January 1951): 62. The best discussion of mountain eloquence is probably Maristan Chapman, "American Speech as Practised in the Southern Highlands," *Century Magazine* 12 (March 1929): 617–23.

46. *You Can't Go Home Again* (New York, 1940), p. 109; "The Return of Buck Gavin: The Tragedy of a Mountain Outlaw," in Frederick H. Koch, ed., *Carolina Folk-Plays: Second Series* (New York, 1924), p. 36; *Look Homeward, Angel*, p. 573. Mrs. Gant is very much a portrait, from life, of Wolfe's mother; see Hayden Norwood, *The Marble Man's Wife: Thomas Wolfe's Mother* (New York, 1943).

47. *The Web and the Rock*, pp. 57–58. For a description of Asheville during boom times see Floyd C. Watkins, *Thomas Wolfe's Characters: Portraits from Life* (Norman, Okla. 1957), pp. 117ff.

48. *The Hills Beyond* (New York, 1941), p. 238. Also *You Can't Go Home*

Again, p. 248; John S. Terry, ed., *Thomas Wolfe's Letters to his Mother, Julia Elizabeth Wolfe* (New York, 1943), p. 50 (May 1923).

49. See, e.g., Agatha B. Adams, *Thomas Wolfe* (Chapel Hill, N.C., 1950); C. Hugh Holman, *Thomas Wolfe* (Minneapolis, Minn., 1964); Richard S. Kennedy, *The Window of Memory: The Literary Career of Thomas Wolfe* (Chapel Hill, N.C., 1962), pp. 49–53; and some of the essays in Paschal Reeves, ed., *Thomas Wolfe and the Glass of Time* (Athens, Ga., 1971).

50. *Letters*, p. 230 (To Fred W. Wolfe, 2 June 1930). The one valuable discussion of the book that I have come across is Leslie Field, "*The Hills Beyond*: A Folk Novel of America," in *Wolfe: Three Decades of Criticism*. Field suggests the existence of certain parallels between the Joyners and folk heroes, a suggestion I have developed here.

51. *The Hills Beyond*, pp. 213–14.

52. Walter J. Blair and Franklin J. Meine, *Half Horse, Half Alligator* (Chicago, 1956), pp. 170–71. See Blair and Meine, *Mike Fink: King of the Mississippi Keelboatmen* (New York, 1933); and Richard M. Dorson, *Jonathan Draws a Long Bow* (Cambridge, Mass., 1946), for detailed discussions of these and other themes in Southern folk tales.

53. *The Hills Beyond*, p. 214; see also p. 222. Cf. Timothy Flint, *The First White Man of the West; or, The Life and Exploits of Colonel Dan'l Boone . . .* (Cincinnati, Ohio, 1856), p. 71; Constance M. Rourke, *Davy Crockett* (New York, 1934), p. 99, 113–14.

54. *The Hills Beyond*, pp. 217–18.

55. Ibid., p. 238; see also pp. 220–36.

56. Ibid., p. 223; see also pp. 224, 236, 248. For the trickster, see Rourke, *American Humor*.

57. *The Hills Beyond*, p. 208; see also pp. 212, 236.

58. *You Can't Go Home Again*, p. 393.

59. "A Note on the Hamlet of Thomas Wolfe," in *Wolfe: Three Decades of Criticism*, p. 216; *Hills Beyond*, pp. 212, 246.

Chapter 4

1. *Intruder in the Dust* (New York, 1948), p. 194.

2. *The Waning of the Middle Ages* (New York, 1954), pp. 39, 41.

3. *Penhally* (New York, 1931), p. 53. For further biographical details, see Frederick P. McDowell, *Caroline Gordon* (Minneapolis, Minn., 1966).

4. New York, 1934.

5. The following details are from *Aleck Maury*, pp. 36 ff.

6. *None Shall Look Back* (New York, 1937), p. 159.

7. Ibid., p. 30.

8. Ibid., p. 154; see also p. 340.

9. Danforth Ross, "Caroline Gordon's Golden Ball," in *Critique: Studies in Modern Fiction* 1 (Winter 1956): 70.

10. *The Women on the Porch* (New York, 1944), p. 185.

11. *The American Adam* (New York, 1955), p. 9.

12. "Green Centuries," poem 2 in "Experience in the West," in *Selected Poems* (New York, 1963), p. 68, lines 3–12.

13. *Act of Darkness* (1935; New York, reprint ed., 1967), pp. 17–18; William Styron, *The Confessions of Nat Turner* (New York, 1967), p. 55.

14. *Light in August* (New York, 1932), p. 270. This discussion of the Southern "sense of evil" owes a good deal to C. Vann Woodward's essay, "The Search for Southern Identity" in *The Burden of Southern History* (Baton Rouge, La., 1966). There is another possible reason for the black-evil association, apart from the ones I have mentioned here. This is that it has been a traditional part of the Southern argument since the beginning to defend the South's treatment of the

Negro in terms of the "un-ideal" nature of human experience generally. "To say that there is evil in any institution," as Chancellor Harper put it in "Harper on Slavery" (*The Pro-Slavery Argument; as Maintained by the Most Distinguished Writers of the Southern States* [Charleston, S.C., 1852], p. 9), "is only to say that it is human." The argument, clearly a rationalization in the first place, gradually became something even worse than that—a defense mechanism, a reflex conditioned to move at the first sign of outside disapproval. And it would take no more than a reversal of this reflex movement, really, for the equation blackness=evil to spring readily to mind. In such cases the abstract notions of guilt and human limitation would probably summon up the thought of the Negro and his place in the system, rather than vice versa; and a link would be forged for the writer (more or less consciously) to exploit.

15. New York, 1941.

16. *None Shall Look Back*, p. 93.

17. Ibid., p. 122; see also p. 120.

18. Ibid., pp. 127–28.

19. Ibid., pp. 134–35.

20. Other Southern writers, and other American writers too: see, e.g., Nancy M. Tischler, *Black Masks: Negro Characters in Modern Southern Fiction* (University Park, Pa., 1969) and Seymour L. Gross and John E. Hardy, eds., *Images of the Negro in American Literature* (Chicago, 1966).

21. See, e.g., *The Strange Children* (New York, 1951), and *The Malefactors* (New York, 1956).

22. "A Memory," in *A Curtain of Green, and Other Stories* (New York, 1941), p. 144; see also p. 143.

23. Ibid., pp. 147, 151.

24. "Place in Fiction," in *Three Papers on Fiction* (Northampton, Mass., 1962), p. 8.

25. *Delta Wedding* (New York, 1946), pp. 3–4.

26. Ibid., pp. 19, 60.

27. Ibid., p. 87.

28. "Song of Myself," sect. 4, lines 11–15; *Delta Wedding*, pp. 11, 12, 116–17, 217.

29. Ibid., p. 221.

30. Ibid., p. 8; see also p. 9. This aspect of the novel is emphasized by John E. Hardy, "*Delta Wedding* as Region and Symbol," *Sewanee Review* 60 (Summer 1952): 405, and Alfred Appel, Jr., *A Season of Dreams: The Fiction of Eudora Welty* (Baton Rouge, La., 1965), p. 203.

31. "Place in Fiction," p. 11.

32. "Pale Horse, Pale Rider," in *The Collected Stories of Katherine Anne Porter* (New York, 1965), p. 158.

33. Edward G. Schwartz, "The Fictions of Memory," *Southwest Review* 45 (Summer 1960): 204. See also Robert Penn Warren, "Katherine Anne Porter: Irony with a Center," in *Selected Essays* (London, 1958); Edmund Wilson, "Katherine Anne Porter," *New Yorker* 20 (30 September 1944): 72; M. M. Liberman, *Katherine Anne Porter's Fiction* (Detroit, 1971).

34. "The Circus," in *Collected Stories*, p. 346.

35. "The Grave," in *Collected Stories*, p. 366.

36. "The Journey," in *Collected Stories*, p. 326; "The Last Leaf," in ibid., p. 349.

37. "Old Mortality," in *Collected Stories*, p. 173. The autobiographical origins of these and other stories in the "Old Order" sequence are clear enough from "Portrait: Old South," in *The Days Before* (New York, 1952).

38. "Old Mortality," p. 174.

39. Ibid., p. 175.

40. Ibid., pp. 176, 178.

41. Ibid., pp. 197, 199.

42. Ibid., p. 203.
43. Ibid., pp. 206, 215, 216.
44. Ibid., p. 216.
45. Ibid., p. 219.
46. Preface to *Collected Poems* (New York, 1939). "The Downward Path to Wisdom" is the title of one of Porter's short stories.

Chapter 5

1. *Absalom, Absalom!* (New York, 1936), p. 378.
2. *The Sound and the Fury* (New York, 1929), p. 110.
3. *Absalom, Absalom!* p. 217.
4. "Of Modern Poetry," lines 15–18.
5. "Mississippi," in James B. Meriwether, ed., *Essays, Speeches, and Public Letters* (New York, 1965), p. 36. Other sources used here include Ward L. Miner, *The World of William Faulkner* (New York, 1952); and John Faulkner, *My Brother Bill* (New York, 1963). Joseph Blotner's monumental *Faulkner: A Biography* (New York, 1974) appeared, regrettably, after the typescript of this chapter had been completed.
6. "Mississippi," p. 14.
7. "L'Après Midi d'un Faune," in Carvel Collins, ed., *Early Prose and Poetry* (Boston, 1963), p. 39, lines 1–6.
8. Malcolm Cowley, ed., *Writers at Work: The "Paris Review" Interviews* (London, 1958), p. 141.
9. "Skirmish at Sartoris," in *The Unvanquished* (New York, 1938), p. 132. See also the next story, "An Odor of Verbena," where the ambivalence I am talking about gives a peculiar edge to Drusilla's relationship with Bayard Sartoris.
10. Robert A. Jelliffe, ed., *Faulkner at Nagano* (Tokyo, 1956), p. 81.
11. "Faulkner's Mythology," *Kenyon Review*, 1 (Summer 1939): 285. Delmore Schwartz simply asserts, "His [Faulkner's] values . . . are those of the idea of the Old South." "The Fiction of William Faulkner," *Southern Review*, 7 (Summer 1941): 156. The quotation that heads this discussion is taken from one of Faulkner's short stories, "Shall Not Perish."
12. Edmond L. Volpe, *A Reader's Guide to William Faulkner* (London, 1964), pp. 66–87; Cleanth Brooks, *William Faulkner: The Yoknapatawpha Country* (New Haven, 1963), chap. 2.
13. *The Hamlet* (New York, 1940), pp. 219–20.
14. *Sartoris* (1929; New York, reprint ed., 1964), p. 229.
15. *Georgia Scenes*, pp. 20–21. For folk versions of the "horse-swapping" theme, see Richard M. Dowson, *Jonathan Draws a Long Bow* (Cambridge, Mass., 1946), pp. 83 ff., and *American Folklore* (Chicago, 1954), pp. 71ff.
16. *The Hamlet*, pp. 37–38.
17. Ibid., pp. 306–7.
18. Ibid., p. 271.
19. Ibid., pp. 276–77.
20. *Light in August* (New York, 1932), pp. 440–41.
21. Frederick L. Gwynn and Joseph L. Blotner, eds., *Faulkner in the University: Class Conferences at the University of Virginia, 1957–1958* (Charlottesville, Va., 1959), p. 39.
22. See, e.g., Irving Howe, *William Faulkner: A Critical Study* (New York, 1952), pp. 127ff.; William Van O'Connor, *The Tangled Fire of William Faulkner* (Minneapolis, Minn., 1954); Robert Penn Warren, "William Faulkner," *New Republic*, 115 (17 August 1946): 177; Elmo Howell, "Faulkner's Jumblies," *Arizona Quarterly* 16 (Spring 1960): 70; André Bleikasten and Francois Pitavy, *William Faulkner's "As I Lay Dying" and "Light in August"* (Paris, 1970).
23. Gwynn and Blotner, eds., *Faulkner in the University*, p. 87.

24. *As I Lay Dying* (1930; New York, reprint ed., 1963), pp. 190–91.

25. Gwynn and Blotner, eds., *Faulkner in the University,* p. 273. Both Smollett and Eliot use the technique of multiple perspectives largely to criticize the partial, distorted visions of their narrator-characters, and behind this criticism lies the assumption that there is a clear, fairly easily definable "truth" that most *but not all* of them miss. Faulkner, however (as I try to explain here), sees his narrator-characters as all contributing in their own small way to a larger, much more complicated vision of "truth"—which *none* of them sees individually.

26. *As I Lay Dying,* p. 167.

27. Ibid., p. 192.

28. Ibid., p. 24.

29. Ibid., p. 93.

30. Ibid., p. 53.

31. Ibid., p. 161.

32. Ibid., pp. 136, 137–38. See Wallace Stevens, *Notes Toward a Supreme Fiction:* "It Must Give Pleasure," poem X, for the figure of the revolving crystal.

33. *Sartoris,* pp. 281–82. A very brief conversation, and a few more lines in the same vein, follow the passage quoted here.

34. Olga Vickery, *The Novels of William Faulkner* (Baton Rouge, La., 1964). p. 283.

35. Walter J. Slatoff, "The Edge of Order: The Pattern of Faulkner's Rhetoric," in Frederick J. Hoffman and Olga Vickery, eds., *William Faulkner: Three Decades of Criticism* (East Lansing, Mich., 1960), p. 174.

36. *Sartoris,* p .12.

37. Ibid., p. 7.

38. "Time in Faulkner: *The Sound and the Fury,*" in Hoffman and Vickery, eds., *Faulkner: Three Decades of Criticism,* p. 228.

39. *Sartoris,* p. 1.

40. *Requiem for a Nun* (New York, 1951), pp. 92, 162.

41. Clifton Fadiman, "Faulkner: Extra-Special, Double-Distilled," *New Yorker* (31 October 1936), p. 63. For some examples of more recent criticism, see Arnold Goldman, ed., *Twentieth Century Interpretations of "Absalom! Absalom!"* (Englewood Cliffs, N. J., 1970).

42. *Absalom, Absalom!,* pp. 261–62.

43. Ibid., p. 127. The comparison of history to a web, interestingly enough, is also to be found in R. G. Collingwood, *The Idea of History* (1946; New York, reprint ed., 1966), p. 242.

44. Ibid., p. 220. For the discussion of Sutpen's "innocence," see p. 127.

45. Ibid., p. 235.

46. Ibid., pp. 9, 15, 162, 171, 177, 260. Cf. Lorenzo Dow Turner, *Anti-Slavery Sentiment in American Literature Prior to 1865* (Washington, 1929), pp. 71, 196; Howard R. Floan, *The South in Northern Eyes, 1831–1861* (New York, 1958), pp. 24–25, 40, 57. That Faulkner knew more than most people about the Old South and the Civil War, and differing ways of interpreting them, is suggested among other things by his reading: of the twelve hundred volumes in his library, over a hundred are devoted to these two topics. See Joseph Blotner, ed., *William Faulkner's Library: A Catalogue* (Charlottesville, Va., 1964).

47. *Absalom, Absalom!,* pp. 11, 23, 27, 136, 138, 140, 167, 171. Cf. Francis P. Gaines, *The Southern Plantation: A Study in the Development and Accuracy of a Tradition* (New York, 1924), pp. 28ff.

48. *Absalom, Absalom!,* p. 143; see also, pp. 137, 139, 142, 149, 172.

49. Ibid., p. 102.

50. Ibid., pp. 33, 40, 46, 53, 72.

51. Ibid., p. 31.

52. Ibid., p. 109; see also pp. 31, 69, 95, 96, 97, 108, 109, 193.

53. Ibid., pp. 73, 74, 290. See Wilbur J. Cash, *The Mind of the South* (New York, 1941), pp. 88–89.

54. *Absalom, Absalom!*, p. 317. See also pp. 177, 178, 315.
55. Ibid., pp. 270, 304, 317, 342–43, 361.
56. Ibid., p. 366.
57. Ibid., p. 139.
58. Preface to *Paterson: Book One*, opening statement and lines 3–6, 21–28. See also *Book One*, sec. 1, lines 1–6. The parallels between Williams's poem and Faulkner's fictional "chronicle" are numerous and, I think, fascinating (although, of course, I am not trying to suggest that either writer in any way influenced the other); for example, like Faulkner, Williams tried to give the sense of an ending to his epic and yet also recognized that "there can be no end to such a story as I have envisioned" ("Author's Note" to the 1963 edition).
59. Malcolm Cowley, *The Faulkner-Cowley File* (New York, 1966), p. 25. On the importance of *The Town* (New York, 1957) as a particularly concentrated and intensive encapsulation of earlier work, see Steven Marcus, "Snopes Revisited," in Hoffman and Vickery, eds., *Faulkner: Three Decades of Criticism*. Faulkner was, as I mentioned earlier on in the chapter, continually reenacting and retelling familiar stories in the Yoknapatawpha series. As Marcus points out, though, and Arnold Goldman in "Faulkner and the Revision of Yoknapatawpha History," in Malcolm Bradbury and David Palmer, eds., *The American Novel in the Nineteen Twenties* (London, 1971), he carries this particular tendency very much further in the second volume of the Snopes trilogy; and his purpose seems to involve more than just another reenactment. I am particularly indebted to Goldman's essay, just mentioned, for the idea of the apocryphal status of Faulkner's Yoknapatawpha County. Goldman was, as far as I know, the first person to emphasize the importance of Faulkner's describing his own creation in this way.

Chapter 6

1. "The State of Southern Fiction," in George Core, ed., *Southern Fiction Today: Renaissance and Beyond* (Athens, Ga., 1969), pp. 51–87.
2. This phrase, which has since become something of a commonplace, originates, I think, with an essay by Louis D. Rubin in his *The Curious Death of the Novel: Essays in American Literature* (Baton Rouge, La., 1967).
3. *A Streetcar Named Desire* was first produced in 1947; *Suddenly Last Summer* in 1958; and *Baby Doll* was an original film-script written by Williams for Elia Kazan, and produced in 1956.
4. *Other Voices, Other Rooms* (New York, 1948), pp. 17–18. For Capote's description of himself as a stylist, see Malcolm Cowley, ed., *Writers at Work: The "Paris Review" Interviews* (London, 1958), p. 263.
5. Published respectively in 1949, 1951, 1958, and 1966.
6. "Listening to Foxhounds," in *Poems, 1957–1967* (London, 1968), p. 53, lines 10–12.
7. The following volumes in particular are, I think, very impressive: Agee, *A Death in the Family* (New York, 1957); Price, *A Long and Happy Life* (New York, 1962); Percy, *The Moviegoer* (New York, 1960); Taylor, *Happy Families Are All Alike* (New York, 1960); Jarrell, *Blood For A Stranger* (New York, 1942), *Losses* (New York, 1948), and *The Woman at Washington Zoo* (New York, 1960).
8. Oliver Evans, *Carson McCullers: Her Life and Work* (London, 1965), p. 10.
9. "The Flowering Dream: Notes on Writing," in Margarita C. Smith, ed., *The Mortgaged Heart: Carson McCullers* (London, 1972), p. 279.
10. Pp. 7–8. "The Ballad of the Sad Café" was first published in *Harper's Bazaar*, November, 1943 and in book form in 1951. All page numbers refer to the London, 1963 edition.
11. See Wolfe's description of South Carolina, quoted on p. 136.
12. "The Ballad of the Sad Café," p. 33.

13. Ibid., p. 8.
14. Ibid., pp. 82–83.
15. Published in 1946, six years after *The Heart is a Lonely Hunter.*
16. Cited in Evans, *McCullers,* p. 194. See also Lawrence Graves, *Carson McCullers* (Minneapolis, Minn., 1970).
17. Robert Lowell, "Memories of West Street and Lepke," lines 52–53.
18. "The Fiction Writer and His Country," in Sally and Robert Fitzgerald, eds., *Mystery and Manners* (London, 1972), p. 32; see also p. 43.
19. "The Grotesque in Southern Fiction," in Fitzgerald and Fitzgerald, eds., *Mystery and Manners,* p. 45. See also "The Catholic Novelist in the Protestant South," in ibid., p. 196.
20. Letter cited in Stanley Edgar Hyman, *Flannery O'Connor* (Minneapolis, Minn., 1966), pp. 40–41. See also "Fiction Writer and His Country," p. 35.
21. "Fiction Writer and His Country," pp. 33–34.
22. P. 11. *Wise Blood* was first published in 1949. All references are to the New York, 1962, collected edition, *Three by Flannery O'Connor,* which also includes *A Good Man Is Hard to Find* (first published in 1955) and *The Violent Bear It Away* (first published in 1960). See also "Fiction Writer and His Country," p. 29.
23. *Wise Blood,* p. 60. See also O'Connor's brief introduction to the 1962 edition.
24. "Baudelaire," in *Selected Essays* (London, 1932), p. 383.
25. *Wise Blood,* p. 126; see also pp. 34, 111.
26. Ibid., p. 122.
27. Ibid., pp. 9–10.
28. William Esty, cited in Hyman, *Flannery O'Connor,* p. 44. See also some of the criticisms mentioned in Josephine Hendin, *Flannery O'Connor* (Bloomington, Ind., 1970).
29. "Fiction Writer and His Country," p. 31.
30. *Lie Down In Darkness* (1951; New York, reprint ed., 1957), p. 235.
31. Ibid., pp. 14–15.
32. *In Search of Heresy* (New York, 1956), pp. 146–47.
33. *Lie Down in Darkness,* p. 363.
34. Ibid., p. 47. Many of these parallels with Faulkner are mentioned in Louis D. Rubin, *The Faraway Country: Writers of the Modern South* (Seattle, Wash., 1963), pp. 185–86. For a fuller discussion of Styron's early novels, see Marc L. Ratner, *William Styron* (New York, 1972).
35. Pp. 500–501. *Set This House on Fire* was first published in 1960.
36. "Author's Note" to *The Confessions of Nat Turner* (New York, 1967).
37. Charles V. Hamilton, "Our Nat Turner and William Styron's Creation," in John H. Clarke, ed., *William Styron's "Nat Turner": Ten Black Writers Respond* (Boston, 1968), p. 74. See also J. B. Duff and P. M. Mitchell, eds., *The Nat Turner Rebellion: The Historical Event and the Modern Controversy* (New York, 1971).
38. See, e.g., John O. Killens, "The Confessions of Willie Styron," in Clarke, ed., *Ten Black Writers,* p. 43; Mike Thelwell, "Back with the Wind: Mr. Styron and the Reverend Turner," in ibid., p. 81.
39. *The Confessions of Nat Turner,* p. 235; see also, p. 58; Wright, *Black Boy* (New York, 1945), chap. 2. See also Kenneth M. Stampp, *The Peculiar Institution: Slavery in the Ante-Bellum South* (New York, 1956), chap. 8; and Eugene D. Genovese, review of Elkins's *Slavery: A Problem in American Institutional and Intellectual Life,* in *Science and Society* (Winter 1961), for a discussion of how these personal and cultural factors necessarily complemented each other.
40. *The Confessions of Nat Turner,* p. 421. See also Thelwell, "Back with the Wind," pp. 80-81.
41. See Wright, *Black Boy,* chap. 1; Ralph Ellison, *Invisible Man* (New York, 1952), chap. 20; James Baldwin, *Go Tell It on the Mountain* (New York, 1953).

42. See, e.g., Clark, ed., *Ten Black Writers*, pp. 7–8, 16, 22, 56–58.

43. *The Confessions of Nat Turner*, pp. 54, 62.

44. *Slavery: A Problem in American Institutional and Intellectual Life* (Chicago, 1959), pp. 128–29. Styron's review appeared in the 26 September 1963, edition of the *New York Review of Books*. See also Wright, *Black Boy*, chap. 10.

45. The principal sources available to Styron were the accounts in the Richmond (Va.) *Enquirer* and *Whig* (written by Southern journalists and addressed to members of the slaveholding class); Thomas R. Gray, *The Confessions of Nat Turner: The Leader of the Late Rebellion in Southampton, Virginia* (Baltimore, 1831) (written with the intention of inciting fear, and encouraging vigilance, amongst the slaveholders); Thomas W. Higginson, "Nat Turner's Insurrection," in *The Atlantic Monthly* 8 (1862) (written by a committed abolitionist at the opening of the Civil War); William S. Drewry, *The Southampton Insurrection* (Washington, 1900) (written by a rather sentimental humanitarian who could understand some of the motives for the revolt but not its harsher realities and consequences); Herbert Aptheker, "Nat Turner's Revolt: The Environment, the Event, the Effects" (M.A. thesis, Columbia University, 1932) and *American Negro Slave Revolts* (New York, 1943) (written by a convinced Marxist with the avowed purpose of proving that Negro slaves in the South showed a continued and "heroic" resistance to their condition); Ulrich B. Phillips, *American Negro Slavery* (New York, 1918); and Joseph G. Carroll, *Slave Insurrections in the United States, 1800–1860* (Boston, 1939) (the two last serious historical assessments that are marred by their authors' clear bias toward the South).

46. Author's Note to *Confessions*. Compare the Introduction to Clark, ed., *Ten Black Writers*. Higginson was the first to suggest that Turner was married. Aptheker claims in his book to have found evidence for over 250 "revolts," but nearly all those he mentions can be considered as such only if the word is stretched so far as to be virtually deprived of meaning. For instance, of the three "revolts" which he takes to be of major significance—those of Gabriel Prosser, Denmark Vesey, and Nat Turner—two were no more than conspiracies, and of those in turn one—the Vesey plot—may have been a figment of the white imagination. See Richard C. Wade, "The Vesey Plot: A Reconsideration," *Journal of Southern History*, 30 (May 1964): 150.

47. Curiously, this one serious omission is not an unmixed blessing as far as Styron's own special purposes are concerned. It may lend some further support to his (and Elkins's) general thesis about slave life on the old plantation. But it leads him to neglect one of the special factors or "influences" that could have perhaps helped to explain Turner's "difference" from the other slaves.

48. See, e.g., Clark, ed., *Ten Black Writers*, pp. 6, 8, 11, 20–21. Also, Wilbur J. Cash, *The Mind of the South* (New York, 1941), p. 84. See also Gunnar Myrdal, *An American Dilemma: The Negro Problem and American Democracy* (New York, 1944), p. 591.

49. "My Dungeon Shook," in *The Fire Next Time* (New York, 1963). The desperate, and usually unsuccessful, attempt to deny the white image of the black man, and white-created values, is the crucial subject in what I take to be the major fictional works by black American writers in this century: Wright's *Native Son* (New York, 1940), Ellison's *Invisible Man,* and Baldwin's *Go Tell It on the Mountain.*

50. *Soul On Ice* (1968; London, reprint ed., 1970) p. 127.

51. Ibid., p. 136.

52. "On Becoming," in Cleaver, *Soul On Ice*, p. 25. Cf. Wright, *Native Son*, bk. 2; Ellison, *Invisible Man*, chap. 2; Baldwin, *Another Country* (New York, 1962), chap. 1.

53. *The Confessions of Nat Turner,* pp. 413–14; for the preceding dreams of rape, see pp. 232, 265, 347.

54. Ibid., p. 428. It should perhaps be emphasized, finally, that, although Elkins's thesis about slave life in the Old South dovetails neatly with Styron's

vision of human nature in general, that thesis remains a thoroughly arguable one. Compare Elkins's book with, e.g., Eugene Genovese, *The Political Economy of Slavery* (New York, 1965); John W. Blassingame, *The Slave Community: Plantation Life in the Ante-Bellum South* (New York, 1972); and Robert Fogel and Stanley Engerman, *Time on the Cross: The Economics of American Negro Slavery,* 2 vols. (Boston, 1974). Since Styron's novel was published, there have been a number of new books on Nat Turner. Of particular importance and/or interest are F. Roy Johnson, *The Nat Turner Story* (Murfreesboro, N.C., 1970); Henry I. Tragle, ed., *The Southampton Slave Revolt of 1831* (Amherst, Mass., 1971); Stephen B. Oates, *The Fires of Jubilee: Nat Turner's Fierce Rebellion* (New York, 1975).

Bibliography

This bibliography is by no means exhaustive. All I offer here is a list of some of the works that have proved most useful to me while learning about the literature and history of the American South. I hope they will provide a convenient starting point for those interested in taking their investigation of Southern literature or a particular Southern writer a little further. With one or two conspicuous exceptions (e.g., Donald Davidson's article and Virginia Rock's dissertation on the Agrarian movement), I have confined myself to published books. More detailed or specialized information can be obtained from the individual bibliographies included in the lists, or from the following:

Cantrell, Clyde H., and Patrick, Walton R. *Southern Literary Culture: A Bibliography of Masters' and Doctors' Theses*. University, Ala., 1955.

Gohdes, Clarence. *Literature and Theatre of the States and Regions of the U.S.A.* Durham, N.C., 1967.

————. *Bibliographical Guide to the Study of the Literature of the U.S.A.* Durham, N.C., 1970.

Leary, Lewis. *Articles on American Literature, 1900-1967*. 2 vols. Durham, N.C., 1970.

Nilon, Charles II, *Bibliography of Bibliographies in American Literature*. New York, 1970.

Rubin, Louis D., ed. *A Bibliographical Guide to the Study of Southern Literature*. Baton Rouge, La., 1969.

Spiller, Robert, et al., eds. *Literary History of the United States*. 2 vols. New York, 1963; supplement, 1970.

The bibliography is divided into five sections, as follows:

1. General Works
2. Virginia During the Colonial and Revolutionary Periods
3. The Ante-Bellum South
4. The Post-Bellum South
5. The Modern South and the Southern "Renaissance"

Section 1 is self-explanatory. Sections 2–4 are intended to give some preliminary idea of the wealth of material available on the earlier moments in the social and literary life of the South discussed in Chapter 1. And Section 5 covers roughly the period 1920 to the present. Each section is in turn divided into "Primary" and "Secondary Sources." I realize that this provides only the most rudimentary of divisions, but to have attempted anything else would, I think, have been to mislead. For example, to have divided the bibliography up in terms of particular topics or "themes" discussed would have been to ignore its essentially tentative, incomplete character, while to have made a categorical distinction between critical and historical works, or between (say) the writings of Thomas Jefferson and the writings of John Pendleton Kennedy, would have been false, really, to the whole nature of my approach. More specifically it would, I feel, have been to imply what I certainly do not wish to imply: that historical knowledge precedes rhetorical art and that the discussion of literature is somehow separable from the discussion of history.

General Works

PRIMARY SOURCES:

Alderman, Edwin A., et al., eds. *A Library of Southern Literature: Compiled under the Direct Supervision of Southern Men of Letters.* 17 vols. Atlanta, Ga., 1907–23.

Beatty, Richmond C., and Watkins, Floyd C., eds. *The Literature of the South.* Chicago, 1968.

Brooks, Cleanth, and Warren, Robert Penn, eds. *A Southern Harvest: Short Stories by Southern Writers.* Boston, 1937.

Paine, Gregory, ed. *Southern Prose Writers: Representative Selections, with Introduction, Bibliography and Notes.* New York, 1947.

Parks, Edd W., ed. *Segments of Southern Thought.* Athens, Ga., 1933.

———. *Southern Poets: Representative Selections, with Introduction, Bibliography and Notes.* New York, 1936.

Thorp, Willard, ed. *A Southern Reader.* New York, 1955.

Young, Thomas D., et al., eds. *The Literature of the South.* New York, 1952.

SECONDARY SOURCES:

Baskervill, William, et al. *Southern Writers: Biographical and Critical Studies.* 2 vols. Nashville, Tenn., 1897–1903.

Bertleson, David. *The Lazy South.* New York, 1967.

Billington, Monroe Lee. *The American South: A Brief History.* New York, 1971.

———. *The South: A Central Theme?* New York, 1969.

Bone, Robert A. *The Negro Novel in America.* New Haven, 1958.

Brown, William G. *The Lower South in American History.* New York, 1902.

Butcher, Margaret J. *The Negro in American Culture.* New York, 1956.

Cash, Wilbur J. *The Mind of the South.* New York, 1941.

Coles, Robert. *Farewell to the South.* Boston, 1972.

Couch, William T., ed. *Culture in the South.* Chapel Hill, N.C., 1934.

Courlander, Harold. *Negro Folk Music U.S.A.* New York, 1963.

Dabney, Virginius. *Liberalism in the South.* Chapel Hill, N.C., 1932.

Dodd, Donald B., and Dodd, Wynelle S. *Historical Statistics of the South, 1790–1870.* University, Ala., 1973.

Franklin, John Hope. *From Slavery to Freedom.* New York, 1956.

Gaines, Francis Pendleton. *The Southern Plantation: A Study in the Development and Accuracy of a Tradition.* New York, 1924.

Gerster, Patrick, and Cords, Nicholas, eds. *Myth and Southern History.* 2 vols. Chicago, 1974.

Gloster, Hugh M. *Negro Voices in American Fiction.* Chapel Hill, N.C., 1948.

Green, Fletcher M., ed. *Essays in Southern History.* Chapel Hill, N.C., 1949.

Hawk, E. O. *Economic History of the South.* New York, 1934.

Hesseltine, William B. *The South in American History.* New York, 1943.

Holliday, Carl. *A History of Southern Literature.* New York, 1906.

Holman, C. Hugh. *The Roots of Southern Writing.* Baton Rouge, La., 1972.

Hubbell, Jay B. *The South in American Literature.* Durham, N.C., 1954.

———. *Southern Life in Fiction.* Athens, Ga., 1960.

Jackson, George P. *White and Negro Spirituals.* New York, 1943.

Kendrick, Benjamin B., and Arnett, Alex M., eds. *The South Looks at Its Past.* Chapel Hill, N.C., 1935.

Killian, Lewis M. *White Southerners.* New York, 1970.

Lawless, Ray M. *Folksongs and Folksingers in America: A Handbook.* New York, 1965.

Link, Arthur S., and Patrick, R. W., eds. *Writing Southern History.* Baton Rouge, La., 1965.

Link, S. A. *Pioneers of Southern Literature.* 2 vols. Nashville, Tenn., 1899–1900.

Littlejohn, David. *Black on White: A Critical Survey of Writing by American Negroes.* New York, 1966.

McIlwaine, Shields. *The Southern Poor-White from Lubberland to Tobacco Road.* Norman, Okla., 1939.

Mitchell, Loften. *Black Drama.* New York, 1967.

Moses, Montrose J. *The Literature of the South.* New York, 1910.

Owsley, Frank L. *The South: Old and New Frontiers.* Athens, Ga., 1969.

Parkins, Almon Ernest. *The South: Its Economic and Geographic Development.* New York, 1938.

Redding, J. Saunders. *To Make a Poet Black.* Chapel Hill, N.C., 1939.

Rubin, Louis D., and Fitzpatrick, James J., eds. *The Lasting South.* Chicago, 1957.

Savage, Henry, Jr. *Seeds of Time: The Background of Southern Thinking.* New York, 1959.

Scott, Anne. *The Southern Lady: From Pedestal to Politics.* Chicago, 1970.

Sellers, Charles G., ed. *The Southerner as American.* Chapel Hill, N.C., 1960.

Simkins, Francis B. *A History of the South.* New York, Rev. ed., 1972.

———. *The Everlasting South.* Baton Rouge, La., 1963.

Simonini, Rinaldo C., ed. *Southern Writers: Appraisals in Our Time.* Charlottesville, Va., 1964.

Smith, C. Alphonso. *Southern Literary Studies.* Chapel Hill, N.C., 1927.

Stephenson, Wendell Holmes. *The South in History.* Baton Rouge, La., 1955.

Stephenson, Wendell Holmes and Coulter, E. M., eds. *A History of the South.* 10 vols. Baton Rouge, La., 1947–67.

Thompson, Edgar T. *Perspectives on the South: Agenda for Research.* Durham, N.C., 1967.

Trent, William P. *Southern Writers.* New York, 1905.

Vandiver, Frank E., ed. *The Idea of the South: Pursuit of a Central Theme.* Chicago, 1964.

Watters, Pat. *The South and the Nation.* New York, 1969.
Wilgus, D. K. *Anglo-American Folksong Scholarship.* New Brunswick, N.J., 1959.
Williams, Harold T. *Romance and Realism in Southern Politics.* Athens, Ga., 1963.
Woodward, C. Vann *The Burden of Southern History.* Baton Rouge, La., 1966.

Virginia During the Colonial and Revolutionary Periods

PRIMARY SOURCES:

Ashe, Thomas. *Travels in America Performed in 1806.* 3 vols. London, 1808.
Barbour, Philip L., ed. *The Jamestown Voyages Under the First Charter, 1606–1609.* 2 vols. Hakluyt Society Reprint. Cambridge, Mass., 1969.
Beverley, Robert, II. *An Essay upòn the Government of the English Plantations.* Edited by Louis Booker Wright. 1701. Reprint. San Marino, Calif., 1945.°
————. *The History and Present State of Virginia.* London, 1722.
Brissot de Warville, Jacques Pierre. *New Travels in the U.S.A. Performed in 1788.* New York, 1792.
Bullock, William. *Virginia Impartially Examined, and Lefte to Publick View, to be Considered by all Judicious and Honest Men.* London, 1649.
Byrd of Westover, William. *The London Diary and Other Writings.* Edited by Louis Booker Wright and Marion Tinling. New York, 1958.
————. *The Prose Works of William Byrd of Westover.* Edited by Louis Booker Wright. Cambridge, Mass., 1966.
————. *The Secret Diary of William Byrd of Westover, 1709–1712.* Edited by Louis Booker Wright and Marion Tinling. Richmond, Va., 1941.
————. *Another Secret Diary of William Byrd of Westover, 1739–1741, with Letters and Literary Exercises.* Edited by M. H. Woodfin and Marion Tinling. Richmond, Va., 1942.
————. *The Writings of Colonel William Byrd.* Edited by J. S. Bassett. New York, 1901.
Carter, Landon. *The Diary of Colonel Landon Carter of Sabine Hall, 1752–1788.* Edited by Jack P. Greene. 2 vols. Charlottesville, Va., 1965.
Carter, Robert. *Letters of Robert Carter, 1720–1727: The Commercial Interests of a Virginia Gentleman.* Edited by Louis Booker Wright. San Marino, Calif., 1940.
Chastellux, Marquis de. *Travels in North America in the Years 1780, 1781, and 1782.* Translated by "an English Gentleman." 2 vols. London, 1787.

°Here and throughout the bibliography, in those cases where a first edition is unusually difficult to obtain, I have (wherever possible) also cited a more accessible later edition.

————. *Declaration of the State of the Colonie and Affaires in Virginia, with the Names of the Adventurers.* London, 1620.

Drayton, John, ed. *Memoirs of a Monticello Slave, as Dictated to Charles Campbell in the 1840's by Isaac, one of Thomas Jefferson's Slaves.* Charlottesville, Va., 1951.

Fithian, Philip Vickers. *Journal and Letters of Philip Vickers Fithian: A Plantation Tutor of the Old Dominion.* Edited by Hunter Dickinson Farish. Williamsburg, Va., 1943.

Fitzhugh, William. *William Fitzhugh and His Chesapeake World, 1676–1701: The Fitzhugh Letters and Other Documents.* Edited by Richard Beale. Chapel Hill, N.C., 1963.

Force, Peter, ed. *Tracts and Other Papers Relating Principally to the Origin, Settlement, and Progress of the Colonies in North America, from the Discovery of the Country to the Year 1776.* 4 vols. New York, 1936–46.

Gilbert, Sir Humphrey. *The Voyages and Colonising Enterprises of Sir Humphrey Gilbert.* Edited by David Beers Quinn. 2 vols. Hakluyt Society Reprint. London, 1927.

Hakluyt, Richard. *The Original Writings and Correspondence of the Two Richard Hakluyts.* Edited by Eva Gonaver Remington Taylor. 2 vols. Hakluyt Society Reprint. London, 1935.

Hakluyt, Richard, ed. *Divers Voyages Touching the Discoverie of America.* London, 1582.

————. *The Principale Navigations, Traffiques, and Discoveries of the English Nation . . . within the Compass of these 1600 Years.* 8 vols. London, 1927–28.

Hall, Francis. *Travels in Canada and the United States.* London, 1818.

Hariot, Thomas. *A Briefe and True Report of the New Found Land of Virginia.* London, 1588.

Harrower, John. *The Journal of John Harrower: An Indentured Servant in the Colony of Virginia, 1773–1776.* Edited by Edward M. Riley. Williamsburg, Va., 1963.

Hartwell, Henry, et al. *The Present State of Virginia and the College.* London, 1727.

Jefferson, Thomas. *Correspondence of John Adams and Thomas Jefferson, 1812–1826.* Edited by Paul Wilstach. New York, 1925.

————. *The Correspondence of Jefferson and Du Pont de Nemours.* Edited by Gilbert Chinard. Baltimore, 1931.

————. *Correspondence of Thomas Jefferson and Francis Walker Gilmer 1814–1826.* Edited by Richard Beale Davis. Columbia, S.C., 1946.

————. *The Letters of Lafayette and Jefferson.* Edited by Gilbert Chinard. Baltimore, 1924.

————. *Notes on the State of Virginia.* London, 1784.

————. *The Papers of Thomas Jefferson.* Edited by Julian P. Boyd. Princeton, 1950–.

————. *Thomas Jefferson's Farm Book: With Commentary and Relevant*

Extracts from Other Writings. Edited by Edwin Morris Betts. Princeton, 1953.

―――――. *Thomas Jefferson's Garden Book: With Commentary and Relevant Extracts from the Writings.* Edited by Edwin Morris Betts. Philadelphia, 1944.

―――――. *The Writings of Thomas Jefferson.* Edited by H. A. Washington. 9 vols. New York., 1853–54.

Johnson, Robert. *Nova Britannia: Offering Most Excellent Fruits by Planting in Virginia.* London, 1609.

Jones, Hugh. *The Present State of Virginia; Giving a Short Account of . . . the Inhabitants of that Colony . . . from whence is Inferred a Short View of Maryland and North Carolina. . . .* London, 1724.

La Rochefoucald-Liancourt, Francois Alexandre Frederic de. *Voyage dans Les États-Unis d'Amerique.* 8 vols. Paris, 1799.

Lee, Richard Henry. *Memoir of the Life of Richard Henry Lee,* Edited by James Curtis Ballagh. 2 vols. New York, 1914.

―――――. *Memoir of the Life of Richard Henry Lee, and His Correspondence.* Edited by Richard R. Lee. 2 vols. Philadelphia, 1825.

Letters from Virginia, translated from the French. Baltimore, 1816.

Madison, James. *The Forging of American Federalism: Selected Writings of James Madison.* Edited by Saul K. Padover. New York, 1965.

Mason, George. *The Life of George Mason 1725–1792, Including His Speeches, Public Papers, and Correspondence.* Edited by Kate Mason Rowland. 2 vols. New York, 1892.

―――――. *The Papers of George Mason, 1725–1792.* 3 vols. Chapel Hill, N.C., 1970.

Munford, Robert. *The Candidates; or, The Humours of a Virginia Election.* Edited by Jay B. Hubbell and Douglas Adair. Williamsburg, Va., 1948.

Purchas, Samuel. *Hakluytus Posthumus; or, Purchas his Pilgrimes.* 20 vols. Glasgow, 1905–7.

Quinn, David Beers, ed. *The Roanoke Voyages, 1584–1590.* 2 vols. Hakluyt Society Reprint. London, 1956.

Randolph of Roanoke, John. *Letters of John Randolph to a Young Relative.* Philadelphia, 1884.

―――――. "Letters from the Virginia Loyalist John Randolph to Thomas Jefferson, Written in London in 1779," *Proceedings of the American Antiquarian Society, Worcester, Mass.* Worcester, Mass., 1921.

―――――. *A Memoir of the Life and Character of P. S. Physick.* Philadelphia, 1839.

Rolfe, John. *A True Relation of the State of Virginia, Lefte by Sir Thomas Dale Knight in May Last 1616.* London, 1617.

Rolfe, Robert. *The New Life of Virginia.* London, 1612.

Selden, John A., *The Westover Journal of John A. Selden.* Edited by J. S. Bassett. Northampton, 1931.

Smith, Captain John. *Travels and Works of Captain John Smith.* Edited by Edward Arber and Arthur G. Bradley. 2 vols. Edinburgh, 1910.

Stith, William. *The History of the First Discovery and Settlement of Virginia.* Williamsburg, Va., 1747.

Strachey, William. *The Historie of Travaile into Virginia.* Edited by Louis Booker Wright and Virginia Freund. Hakluyt Society Reprint. London, 1953.

Taylor of Caroline, John. *Arator: Being a Series of Agricultural Essays, Practical and Political.* 1813. Reprint. Baltimore, 1817.

————. *Construction Construed, and Constitutions Vindicated.* Richmond Va., 1820.

————. *An Inquiry into the Principles and Policy of the Government of the United States.* 1814. Reprint. New Haven, 1950.

————. *A Letter on the Necessity of Defending the Rights and Interests of Agriculture.* Petersburg, Va., 1821.

————. *New Views of the Constitution of the United States.* Washington, 1823.

————. *Tyranny Unmasked.* Washington, 1822.

The Three Charters of the Virginia Company of London, with Seven Related Documents. Jamestown 350th Anniversary Booklets, Richmond, Va., 1957.

Washington, George. *The Writings of George Washington from the Original Manuscript Sources, 1745–1799.* Edited by John C. Fitzpatrick. 39 vols. Washington, D.C., 1931–44.

Weld, Issac, Jr. *Travels through the States of North America . . . During the Years 1795, 1796, and 1797.* London, 1799.

Whitaker, Alexander. *Good Newes from Virginia.* London, 1617.

Williams, Edward. *Virginia, more especially the South Part thereof, Richly and Truly Valued.* London, 1650.

Wirt, William. *The Letters of the British Spy.* 1802. Reprint. Chapel Hill, N.C., 1970.

————. *Sketches of the Life and Character of Patrick Henry.* Philadelphia, 1817.

SECONDARY SOURCES:

Adams, Henry. *John Randolph.* Boston, 1897.

Adams, James Truslow. *The Living Jefferson.* New York, 1936.

Andrews, Charles, M. *The Colonial Period of American History.* 4 vols. New Haven, 1934–38.

Barbour, Philip. *The Three Worlds of Captain John Smith.* Boston, 1964.

Beard, Charles Austin. *Economic Origins of Jeffersonian Democracy.* New York, 1927.

Beatty, Richmond, C. *William Byrd of Westover.* Boston, 1932.

Boorstin, Daniel Joseph. *The Lost World of Thomas Jefferson.* New York, 1948.

Bowers, Claude Gernade. *Jefferson and Hamilton: The Struggle for Democracy in America.* London, 1925.

Brant, Irving. *James Madison.* 3 vols. New York, 1950–56.

Bridenbaugh, Carl. *Myths and Realities: Societies of the Colonial South.* Baton Rouge, La., 1952.

Brown, Alexander. *The Genesis of the United States . . . Set Forth with a Reissue of Rare Contemporaneous Tracts. . . .* 2 vols. London, 1890.

Brown, Robert E., and Brown, Katherine. *Virginia, 1705–1786: Democracy or Aristocracy?* East Lansing, Mich., 1964.

Bruce, Philip Alexander. *Economic History of Virginia in the Seventeenth Century: An Inquiry into the Material Condition of the People Based upon Original and Contemporaneous Records.* 2 vols. New York, 1896.

————. *Institutional History of Virginia in the Seventeenth Century: An Inquiry into the Religious, Moral, Educational, Legal, Military, and Political Condition of the People.* 2 vols. New York, 1910.

————. *Social Life in Virginia in the Seventeenth Century: An Inquiry into the Origins of the Higher Planting Class: Together with an Account of the Habits, Customs and Diversions of the People.* Richmond, Va., 1927.

————. *The Virginia Plutarch.* 2 vols. Chapel Hill, N.C., 1929.

Bruce, William Cabell. *John Randolph of Roanoke, 1773–1833: A Biography Based Largely on New Material.* 2 vols. New York, 1922.

Chatterton, E. Keble. *Captain John Smith.* New York, 1927.

Chinard, Gilbert. *Thomas Jefferson: The Apostle of Americanism.* Ann Arbor, Mich., 1957.

Crane, Verner W. *The Southern Frontier, 1676–1732.* Philadelphia, 1929.

Craven, Avery O. *Soil Exhaustion as a Factor in the Agricultural History of Virginia and Maryland.* Urbana, Ill., 1925.

Craven, Wesley Frank. *Dissolution of the Virginia Company: The Failure of a Colonial Experiment.* New York, 1924.

————. *The Virginia Company of London, 1606–1624.* Jamestown 350th Anniversary Historical Booklets. Richmond, Va., 1957.

————. *White, Red, and Black: The Seventeenth Century Virginian.* Charlottesville, Va., 1971.

Davis, Richard Beale. *Intellectual Life in Jefferson's Virginia, 1790–1830.* Chapel Hill, N.C., 1964.

————. *Literature and Society in Early Virginia, 1608–1840.* Baton Rouge, La., 1973.

Dowdey, Clifford. *The Virginia Dynasties.* Boston, 1969.

Eckenrode, Hamilton J. *The Revolution in Virginia.* New York, 1916.

Fiske, John. *Old Virginia and Her Neighbours.* 2 vols. Boston, 1900.

Freeman, Douglas S. *George Washington: A Biography.* 6 vols. New York, 1948–54.

Hill, Helen. *George Mason, Constitutionalist.* Cambridge, Mass., 1938.

Jones, Howard Mumford. *The Literature of Virginia in the Seventeenth Century.* Boston, 1946.

Jordan, Winthrop. *White Over Black: American Attitudes toward the Negro, 1580–1812.* Chapel Hill, N.C., 1968.

Kimball, Marie. *Jefferson: The Road to Glory, 1743–1776.* New York, 1943.

————. *Jefferson: War and Peace, 1776–1784.* New York, 1947.

————. *Jefferson: The Scene of Europe, 1764–1789.* New York, 1950.

Koch, Adrienne. *The American Enlightenment.* New York, 1965.

————. *The Philosophy of Thomas Jefferson.* New York, 1963.

Malone, Dumas. *Jefferson and His Times.* 3 vols. Boston, 1948–62.

Morton, Louis. *Robert Carter of Nomini Hall: A Virginia Tobacco Planter of the Eighteenth Century.* Williamsburg, Va., 1941.

Morton, Richard Lee. *Colonial Virginia.* 2 vols. Chapel Hill, N.C., 1963.

Mudge, E. T. *The Social Philosophy of John Taylor of Caroline.* New York, 1939.

The Papers of Randolph of Roanoke: A Preliminary Check-List. University of Virginia Bibliographical Series, no. 4. Charlottesville, Va., 1950.

Otis, William B. *American Verse, 1625–1807.* New York, 1909.

Parks, George P. *Richard Hakluyt and the English Voyages.* New York, 1928.

Paterson, Merrill D. *The Jeffersonian Image in the American Mind.* New York, 1960.

Simms, Henry. *Life of John Taylor: The Story of a Brilliant Leader in the Early Virginia States Rights School.* Richmond, Va., 1932.

Sydnor, Charles Sackett. *Gentlemen Freeholders: Political Practices in Washington's Virginia.* Chapel Hill, N.C., 1952.

Tyler, Lyon G. *Narratives of Early Virginia, 1606–1625.* New York, 1947.

Vail, Robert W. G. *The Voice of the Old Frontier.* Philadelphia, 1949.

Wegelin, Oscar. *Early American Poetry: A Bibliography.* New York, 1930.

Wertenbaker, Thomas. *Patrician and Plebeian in Virginia; or, The Origins and Development of the Social Classes of the Old Dominion.* Charlottesville, Va., 1910.

————. *The Planters of Colonial Virginia.* Princeton, 1922.

————. *Virginia under the Stuarts, 1607–1688.* Princeton, 1914.

Wright, Louis Booker. *The Cultural Life of the American Colonies, 1607–1763.* New York, 1957.

————. *The First Gentlemen of Virginia: Intellectual Qualities of the Early Colonial Ruling Class.* San Marino, Calif., 1940.

The Ante-Bellum South

PRIMARY SOURCES:

Allston, R. F. W. *The South Carolina Rice Plantation as Revealed in the Papers of R. F. W. Allston.* Edited by J. H. Easterby. Chicago, 1945.

The American Slave: A Composite Autobiography. Edited by George P. Rawick. Westport, Conn., 1972–.

Baldwin, Joseph Glover. *The Flush Times of Alabama and Mississippi: A Series of Sketches.* New York, 1853.

Barclay-Allardice, 'Capt. Robert. *Agricultural Tour in the United States and Upper Canada.* London, 1842.

Bledsoe, Albert. *An Essay on Slavery and Liberty.* Philadelphia, 1837.

Botkin, B. A., ed. *A Treasury of Mississippi Folklore.* New York, 1955.

————. *Lay My Burden Down: A Folk History of Slavery.* Chicago, 1945.

Bremer, Fredrika. *The Homes of the New World.* Translated by M. Howitt. 3 vols. London, 1853.

Buckingham, James Silk. *The Slave States of America.* 2 vols. London, 1842.

Burke, Thomas A., ed. *Polly Peasblossom's Wedding, and Other Tales.* Philadelphia, 1851.

Calhoun, John C. *Correspondence of John C. Calhoun.* Edited by J. Franklin Jameson. *Annual Report of the American Historical Association, 1899.* 2 vols. Washington, 1900.

[————.] *Life of John C. Calhoun, 1811–1843.* New York, 1843.

————. *The Papers of John C. Calhoun.* Edited by R. L. Merriwether and W. E. Hemphill. Columbia, S.C., 1959—.

————. *The Works of John C. Calhoun.* Edited by Richard K. Cralle. 6 vols. New York, 1853.

Carroll, B. R., ed. *Historical Collections of South Carolina.* 2 vols. New York, 1836.

Caruthers, William Alexander. *The Cavaliers of Virginia; or, The Recluse of Jamestown.* 2 vols. New York, 1834.

————. *The Knights of the Horse-Shoe: A Traditionary Tale of the Cocked Hat Gentry of the Old Dominion.* 1845. Reprint. Chapel Hill, N.C., 1970.

————. *The Kentuckian in New York; or, The Adventures of Three Southerners.* 2 vols. New York, 1834.

Chase, Richard, ed. *Davy Crockett: American Comic Legend.* New York, 1939.

Chesnut, Mary Boykin. *A Diary from Dixie.* Edited by B. A. Williams. New York, 1949.

Chivers, Thomas Holley. *The Lost Pleiad and Other Poems.* New York, 1845.

Cobb, Joseph B. *Mississippi Scenes; or, Sketches of Southern and Western Life and Adventure, Humorous, Satirical, and Descriptive.* Philadelphia. 1851.

Davis, Jefferson. *Jefferson Davis, Constitutionalist: His Letters, Papers, and Speeches.* Edited by Dunbar Rowland. 10 vols. New York, 1923.

————. *The Papers of Jefferson Davis* Baton Rouge, La., 1971—.

————. *The Rise and Fall of the Confederate Government.* 2 vols. 1881. Reprint. New York, 1958.

De Bow, James Dunwood Brownson. *The Industrial Resources of the Southern and Western States: Embracing a View of Their Commerce, Agriculture, Manufactures . . . Together with Historical and Statistical Sketches of the Different States and Cities of the Union.* 3 vols. New Orleans, 1852.

Douglass, Frederick. *Narrative of the Life of . . . an American Slave.* Boston, 1845.

Elliot, E. N., ed. *Cotton Is King, and Pro-Slavery Arguments.* Augusta, Ga., 1860.

Featherstonhaugh, George William. *Excursions through the Slave States:*

From Washington on the Potomac to the Frontier of Mexico, with Sketches of Popular Manners and Geological Notices. 2 vols. London, 1844.

Fisher, Miles Mark, ed. *Negro Slave Songs in the United States.* New York, 1963.

Fitzhugh, George. *Cannibals All! or, Slaves Without Masters.* 1857. Reprint. Cambridge, Mass., 1960.

————. *Sociology for the South; or, The Failure of Free Society.* Richmond Va., 1854.

Flint, Timothy. *The First White Man of the West; or, Life and Exploits of Colonel Dan'l Boone.* Cincinnati, 1856.

Furman, Richard. *Exposition of the Views of the Baptists Relative to the Coloured Population of the United States. . . .* Charleston, S.C., 1823.

Grayson, William J. *Hireling and Slave, Chicora, and Other Poems.* Charleston, S.C., 1854.

————. *Letters of Curtius. Charleston,* S.C., 1851.

Grund, Francis J. *Aristocracy in America.* Edited by G. Probst. New York, 1859.

Harris, George Washington. *Sut Lovingood: Yarns Spun by a "Nat'ral Born Durn'd Fool."* New York, 1867.

————. *Sut Lovingood's Yarns.* Edited by M. Thomas Inge. New Haven, 1966.

————. *High Times and Hard Times: Sketches and Tales by George Washington Harris.* Edited by M. Thomas Inge. Nashville, Tenn., 1967.

Helper, Hinton R. *The Impending Crisis of the South.* New York, 1857.

Hildreth, Richard. *The White Slave: A Story of Life in Virginia* London, 1852.

Hooper, Johnson Jones. *Some Adventures of Captain Simon Suggs, Late of the Tallapoosa Volunteers; Together with "Taking the Census" and Other Alabama Sketches.* 1845. Reprint. Philadelphia, 1857.

————. *The Widow Rugby's Husband, a Night at the Ugly Man's and Other Tales of Alabama.* Philadelphia, 1851.

Hudson, A. P., ed. *Humor of the Old Deep South.* New York, 1936.

Hughes, Henry. *A Treatise on Sociology, Theoretical and Practical.* Philadelphia, 1854.

Hundley, Daniel R. *Social Relations in Our Southern States.* New York, 1860.

Ingraham, Joseph Holt. *The South-West.* 2 vols. New York, 1835.

James, George Payne Rainsford. *The Old Dominion.* 3 vols. London, 1856.

Kemble, Frances Anne. *Journal of a Residence on a Georgian Plantation in 1838–1839.* 1863. Reprint. London, 1961.

Kennedy, John Pendleton. *At Home and Abroad: A Series of Essays.* New York, 1872.

————. *Horse-Shoe Robinson: A Tale of the Tory Ascendancy.* 1835. Reprint. New York, 1872.

————. *Memoirs of the Life of William Wirt, Attorney-General of the United States.* 1849. Reprint. New York, 1872.

————. *Occasional Addresses; and the Letters of Mr. Ambrose on the Rebellion.* New York, 1872.

————. *Political and Official Papers.* New York, 1872.

[————.] *Quodlibet: Containing Some Annals Thereof.* 1840. Reprint. New York, 1872.

————. *Rob of the Bowl: A Legend of St. Inigoe's.* 1838. Reprint. New York, 1872.

————. *Swallow Barn; or, A Sojourn in the Old Dominion.* 1832. Reprint. New York, 1872.

Kettell, Thomas Prentice. *Southern Wealth and Northern Profits, as Exhibited in Statistical Facts and Official Figures. . . .* New York, 1860.

Latrobe, Benjamin H. *The Journal of Latrobe; Being the Notes and Sketches of an Architect, Naturalist, and Traveller in the United States from 1796 to 1820.* New York, 1905.

[Lewis, Henry Clay.] *Odd Leaves from the Life of a Louisiana Swamp Doctor.* New York, 1850.

Longstreet, Augustus Baldwin. *Georgia Scenes: Characters, Incidents, etc., in the First Half-Century of the Republic.* 1835. Reprint. New York, 1848.

Mackay, Alexander. *My Diary North and South.* 2 vols. London, 1863.

Martineau, Harriet. *Society in America.* 3 vols. London, 1837.

Meine, Franklin J., ed. *Half Horse, Half Alligator: The Growth of the Mike Fink Legend.* Chicago, 1956.

————. *Tall Tales of South-West.* New York, 1930.

McKitrick, Eric L., ed. *Slavery Defended: The Views of the Old South.* Englewood Cliffs, N.J., 1963.

Moore, Francis. *A Voyage to Georgia.* London, 1744.

Murat, Achille. *A Moral and Political Sketch of the United States.* London, 1883.

Olmsted, Frederick Law. *A Journey in the Back Country in the Winter of 1853–1854.* 2 vols. New York, 1860.

————. *A Journey to the Seaboard Slave States: with Remarks on Their Economy.* 2 vols. London, 1856.

————. *A Journey through Texas.* New York, 1857.

————. *The Cotton Kingdom.* Edited by Arthur M. Schlesinger. New York, 1953.

Paulding, James Kirke. *Slavery in the United States.* New York, 1836.

————. *The Banks of the Ohio; or, Westward Ho!* 2 vols. 1832. London, 1833.

————. *The Lion of the West; retitled, The Kentuckian or, A Trip to New York.* Palo Alto, Calif., 1954.

Phillips, Ulrich Bonnell, ed. *Plantation and Frontier Documents, 1649–1853. Illustrative of Industrial History in the Colonial and Ante-Bellum South.* 2 vols. Cleveland, 1910.

Poe, Edgar Allan. *The Complete Works of Edgar Allan Poe.* Edited by James A. Harrison. 17 vols. 1902. Reprint. New York, 1965.

Porter, William Trotter, ed. *"The Big Bear of Arkansas," and Other Sketches*

Illustrative of Character and Incident in the South-West. Philadelphia, 1847.

———. *"A Quarter Race in Kentucky," Illustrative of Scenes, Characters and Incidents throughout the "Universal Yankee Nation."* Philadelphia, 1845.

Pringle, Edward J. *Slavery in the Southern States.* Cambridge, 1852.

The Pro-Slavery Argument; As Maintained by the Most Distinguished Writers of the Southern States, Containing the Several Essays on the Subject of Chancellor Harper, Governor Hammond, Dr. Simms, and Professor Dew. Charleston, S.C., 1852.

Ruffin, Edmund. *The Political Economy of Slavery; or, The Institution Considered in Regard to Its Influence on Public Health and General Welfare.* Richmond, Va., 1858.

———. *Slavery and Free Labour Described and Compared.* Washington, D.C. 1860.

Simms, William Gilmore. *Beauchampe; or, The Kentucky Tragedy.* New York, 1842.

———. *Eutaw; or, Sequel to the Forayers.* New York, 1836.

———. *The Forayers; or, The Raid of the Dog-Days.* New York, 1855.

———. *Guy Rivers, the Outlaw: A Tale of Georgia.* 3 vols. New York, 1834.

———. *Katharine Walton; or, The Rebel of Dorchester.* Philadelphia, 1855.

———. *The Kinsmen; or, The Black Riders of the Congaree.* 2 vols. Philadelphia, 1841.

———. *The Letters of William Gilmore Simms.* Edited by M. C. Simms Oliphant et al. 5 vols. Columbia, S.C., 1954–56.

———. *Mellichampe: A Legend of the Santee.* 2 vols. New York, 1836.

———. *The Partisan: A Tale of the Revolution.* 2 vols. New York, 1835.

———. *South Carolina in the Revolutionary War.* Charleston, S.C., 1853.

———. *The Sword and the Distaff; or, "Fair, Fat, and Forty."* Philadelphia, 1853.

———. *The Wigwam and the Cabin.* 2 vols. London, 1845.

———. *Views and Reviews in American Literature, History, and Fiction.* 1845. Reprint. Cambridge, Mass., 1962.

———. *The Yemassee: A Romance of Carolina.* 3 vols. London, 1835.

Stephens, Alexander H. *A Constitutional View of the Late War Between the States.* Philadelphia, 1868.

———. *The Correspondence of Robert Toombs, Alexander H. Stephens, and Howell Cobb.* Edited by Ulrich Bonnell Phillips. *Annual Report of the American Historical Association, 1912.* Washington, D.C., 1913.

Stirling, James. *Letters from the Slave States.* London, 1857.

Stowe, Harriet Beecher. *Dred: A Tale of the Great Dismal Swamp.* 2 vols. London, 1856.

———. *Uncle Tom's Cabin; or, Life Among the Lowly.* London, 1852.

Taliaferro, H. F. *Fisher's River (North Carolina) Scenes and Characters.* New York, 1859.

Thompson, William Tappan. *The Chronicles of Pineville; Embracing*

Sketches of Georgia Scenes, Incidents and Characters. Philadelphia, 1852.

[————.] *Major Jones's Courtship: Detailed with Humorous Scenes, Incidents, and Adventures.* 1843. Reprint. Philadelphia, 1844.

[————.] *Major Jones's Sketches of Travel, Comprising the Scenes, Incidents, and Adventures of His Tour from Georgia to Canada.* Philadelphia, 1848.

Timrod, Henry. *The Poems of Henry Timrod.* Edited by Paul H. Hayne. New York, 1873.

Trollope, Frances. *Domestic Manners of Americans.* 2 vols. London, 1832.

Tucker, George. *The Valley of Shenandoah.* New York, 1824.

Tucker, Nathaniel Beverley. *George Balcombe.* New York, 1836.

————. *The Partisan Leader: A Tale of the Future.* 1836. Reprint. Chapel Hill, N.C., 1970.

Tyron, Warren Stevenson, ed. *A Mirror for Americans: Life and Manners in the United States, 1790–1870, as Recorded by American Travellers.* 3 vols. Chicago, 1952.

Watterson, Henry, ed. *Oddities in Southern Life and Character.* Boston, 1882.

Whipple, Bishop. *Bishop Whipple's Southern Diary, 1843–1844.* Edited by L. B. Shippee. Minneapolis, Minn., 1937.

Wish, Harvey, ed. *Slavery in the South: First-Hand Accounts.* New York, 1964.

SECONDARY SOURCES:

Abernethy, Thomas P. *From Frontier to Plantation in Tennessee.* Chapel Hill, N.C., 1932.

Aptheker, Herbert. *American Negro Slave Revolts.* New York, 1943.

Barney, William. *The Road to Secession.* New York, 1972.

Blair, Walter. *Horse Sense in American Humor from Benjamin Franklin to Ogden Nash.* Chicago, 1942.

————. *Native American Humor, 1800–1900.* New York, 1937.

————. *Tall Tale America.* New York, 1944.

Blassingame, John W. *The Slave Community: Plantation Life in the Ante-Bellum South.* New York, 1972.

Bode, Carl. *Ante-Bellum Culture.* Carbondale, Ill., 1970.

Bohner, Charles H. *John Pendleton Kennedy: Gentleman from Baltimore.* Baltimore, 1961.

Braden, Waldo W. *Oratory in the Old South.* Baton Rouge, La., 1970.

Bradshaw, Sidney E. *On Southern Poetry Prior to 1860.* New York, 1900.

Campbell, Killis. *The Mind of Poe.* Cambridge, Mass., 1933.

Caspers, Gerald M. *John C. Calhoun, Opportunist: A Re-appraisal.* Gainesville, Fla., 1960.

Carpenter, Jesse T. *The South as a Conscious Minority, 1789–1861.* New York, 1931.

Catton, Bruce. *Two Roads to Sumter.* New York, 1963.

Clark, Thomas D. *Travels in the Old South: A Bibliography.* Norman, Okla. 1956.

Coit, Margaret L. *James C. Calhoun: American Portrait.* London, 1950.

Cotterill, Robert S. *The Old South: The Geographic, Economic, Political, and Cultural Expansion—Institutions and Nationalism of the Ante-Bellum South.* Glendale, Calif., 1939.

Craven, Avery O. *Civil War in the Making, 1850–1860.* Baton Rouge, La. 1961.

———. *The Coming of the Civil War,* Chicago, 1957.

———. *Edmund Ruffin, Southerner.* New York, 1932.

———. *The Repressible Conflict, 1830–1861.* Baton Rouge, La., 1939.

Davidson, Edward H. *Poe: A Critical Study.* Cambridge, Mass., 1957.

Davidson, James Wood. *The Living Writers of the South.* New York, 1869.

Davis, Curtis C. *Chronicler of the Cavaliers: A Life of William A. Caruthers.* Richmond, Va., 1953.

Degler, Carl. *Neither Black Nor White.* New York, 1971.

De Voto, Bernard. *Mark Twain's America.* New York, 1932.

Dodd, William Edward. *The Cotton Kingdom.* New Haven, 1919.

———. *Jefferson Davis: Statesman of the Old South.* Philadelphia, 1907.

———. *Statesmen of the Old South; or, From Radicalism to Conservative Revolt.* New York, 1939.

Dormon, James H. *Theatre in the Ante-Bellum South, 1815–1861.* Chapel Hill, N.C., 1967.

Dorson, Richard M. *American Folklore.* Chicago, 1959.

DuBose. John Witherspoon. *The Life and Times of William Lowndes Yancey: A History of Political Parties in the United States from 1834 to 1864, Especially as to the Origin of the Confederate States.* 2 vols. New York, 1864.

Eaton, Clement. *Freedom of Thought in the Old South.* Durham, N.C., 1940.

———. *The Freedom-of-Thought Struggle in the Old South.* New York, 1964.

———. *The Growth of Southern Civilization.* London, 1961.

———. *A History of the Old South.* London, 1949.

———. *The Mind of the Old South.* Baton Rouge, La., 1964.

Elkins, Stanley. *Slavery: A Problem in American Institutional and Intellectual Life.* Chicago, 1959.

Fogel, Robert F., and Engerman, Stanley L. *Time on the Cross: The Economics of American Negro Slavery.* 2 vols. Boston, 1974.

Gates, Paul W. *The Farmer's Age: Agriculture, 1815–1860.* New York, 1960.

Genovese, Eugene. *The Political Economy of Slavery.* New York, 1965.

———. *Roll, Jordan, Roll.* New York, 1974.

Genovese, Eugene, and Miller, Elinor, eds. *Plantation, Town and Country.* Urbana, Ill., 1974.

Gray, Lewis Cecil. *History of Agriculture in the Southern United States to 1860* 2 vols. Washington, D.C., 1933.

Hoole, W. S. *Alias Simon Suggs: The Life and Times of Johnson Jones Hooper*. Montgomery, Ala., 1952.

Jenkins, William Sumner. *Pro-Slavery Thought in the Old South*. Chapel Hill, N.C., 1939.

Johnson, James G., *Southern Fiction Prior to 1860: An Attempt at a First-Hand Bibliography* New York, 1909.

Lloyd, Arthur Y. *The Slavery Controversy*. Chapel Hill, N.C., 1939.

Lynn, Kenneth S. *Mark Twain and Southwestern Humor*. Boston, 1960.

Malone, Dumas. *The Public Life of Thomas Cooper, 1783–1839*. New Haven, 1937.

McElroy, Robert. *Jefferson Davis: The Unreal and the Real*. 2 vols. New York, 1937.

Nevins, Allan. *Ordeal of the Union*. 4 vols. New York, 1942–50.

Osterweis, Rollin J. *Romanticism and Nationalism in the Old South*. New Haven, 1949.

Owsley, Frank Lawrence. *Plain Folk of the Old South*. Baton Rouge, La., 1949.

Parks, Edd W. *Ante-Bellum Southern Literary Critics*. Athens, Ga., 1962.

Phillips, Ulrich Bonnell. *American Negro Slavery: A Survey of the Supply, Employment, and Control of Negro Labor by the Plantation Regime*. New York, 1918.

———. *The Course of the South to the Secession: An Interpretation*. Edited by E. Merton Coulter. New York, 1939.

———. *Life and Labor in the Old South*. Boston, 1945.

Potter, David. *The South and the Sectional Conflict*. Baton Rouge, La., 1968.

Quinn, Arthur H. *Edgar Allan Poe: A Critical Biography*. New York, 1942.

Rickels, Milton. *George Washington Harris*. New York, 1965.

Ridgely, J. V. *William Gilmore Simms*. New York, 1962.

Rourke, Constance. *American Humor: A Study of the National Character*. New York, 1931.

———. *Davy Crockett*. New York, 1934.

Stampp, Kenneth M. *And the War Came: The North and the Secession Crisis, 1836–1861*. Baton Rouge, La., 1950.

———. *The Peculiar Institution: Negro Slavery in the American South*. London, 1964.

Stanton, William R. *The Leopard's Spots: Scientific Attitudes Toward Race In America, 1815–1859*. Chicago, 1960.

Stephenson, Wendell Holmes. *Isaac Franklin: Slave-Trader and Planter of the Old South*. Baton Rouge, La., 1938.

Tandy, Jenette. *Crackerbox Philosophers*. New York, 1925.

Taylor, William R. *Cavalier and Yankee: The Old South and the American National Character*. London, 1963.

Thorpe, Earl E. *The Old South: A Psychohistory*. Durham, N.C., 1972.

Trent, William P. *William Gilmore Simms*. New York, 1892.

Turner, Lorenzo Dow. *Anti-Slavery Sentiment in American Literature Prior to 1865*. Washington, 1929.

Von Abele, Rudolph. *Alexander H. Stephens: A Biography*. New York, 1946.

Wade, John Donald. *Augustus Baldwin Longstreet: A Study of the Development of Culture in the South*. New York, 1924.

Wiltse, Charles M. *John C. Calhoun: Nationalist, 1782–1828*. New York, 1944.

———. *John C. Calhoun: Nullifier, 1829–1839*. New York, 1949.

———. *John C. Calhoun: Sectionalist, 1840–1850*. New York, 1951.

Wish, Harvey. *George Fitzhugh: Propagandist of the Old South*. Baton Rouge, La., 1943.

The Post-Bellum South

PRIMARY SOURCES:

Andrews, Eliza Frances. *The War-Time Journal of a Georgia Girl, 1864–1865*. New York, 1908.

Andrews, Sidney. *The South since the War: As Shown by Fourteen Weeks of Travel and Observation in Georgia and the Carolinas*. Boston, 1866.

Allen, James Lane. *The Blue-Grass Region of Kentucky*. New York, 1892.

———. *The Bride of the Mistletoe*. London, 1909.

———. *The Choir Invisible*. New York, 1897.

———. *Flute and Violin, and Other Kentucky Tales and Romances*. New York, 1891.

———. *A Kentucky Cardinal*. New York, 1895.

———. *Summer in Arcady: A Tale of Nature*. New York, 1896.

Bagby, George William. *The Old Virginia Gentleman, and Other Sketches*. New York, 1910.

Baylor, Frances Courtenay. *Claudia Hyde: A Novel*. London, 1894.

Boyle, Virginia Frazier. *Serena: A Novel*. New York, 1905.

[Brown, William Garrett.] *A Gentleman of the South: A Memory of the Black Belt from the Manuscript Memoirs of the Late Colonel Stanton Elmore*. New York, 1903.

Cabell, James Branch. *The Works of James Branch Cabell*. 18 vols. New York, 1927–30.

Cable, George Washington. *The Grandissimes*. New York, 1880.

———. *John March, Southerner*. New York, 1894.

———. *Old Creole Days*. New York, 1879.

———. *The Silent South*. New York, 1885.

Campbell, Sir George. *White and Black*. London, 1879.

Chamberlayne, John Hampden. *Address on the Character of General R. E. Lee: Delivered in Richmond, Jan. 19, 1876*. New York, 1878.

Chopin, Kate. *The Awakening*. New York, 1899.

———. *Bayou Folk*. New York, 1894.

Clemens, Samuel Langhorne [Mark Twain]. *The Mark Twain Papers*. Edited by Walter Blair, Hamlin Hill, et al. Berkeley, Calif., 1967–.

———. *The Writings of Mark Twain*. Edited by Albert B. Paine. 37 vols. New York, 1922–25.

Conway, Moncure Daniel. *Pine and Palm.* New York, 1889.

Cooke, John Esten. *Falifax; or, The Master of Greenaway Court.* New York, 1868.

————. *The Heir of Gaymount: A Novel.* New York, 1870.

————. *Hilt to Hilt; or, Days and Nights on the Banks of the Shenandoah in the Autumn of 1864.* New York, 1869.

————. *Justin Harley: A Romance of Old Virginia.* Philadelphia, 1875.

————. *A Life of General Robert E. Lee.* New York, 1871.

————. *Mohun; or, The Last Days of Lee and His Paladins: Final Memoirs of a Staff Officer Serving in Virginia.* New York, 1868.

————. *Stories of the Old Dominion.* New York, 1879.

————. *Stonewall Jackson: A Military Biography.* New York, 1866.

————. *Surry of Eagle's Nest; or, The Memoirs of a Staff Officer Serving in Virginia.* New York, 1866.

————. *The Virginia Bohemians.* New York, 1886.

————. *The Virginia Comedians; or, Old Days in the Old Dominion.* 2 vols. New York, 1854.

————. *Wearing of the Gray; Being Personal Portraits, Scenes, and Adventures.* New York, 1867.

Dabney, Robert Lewis. *A Defence of Virginia—and through Her of the South—in Recent and Pending Contests against the Sectional Party.* New York, 1867.

————. *Life of Lieutenant-General Thomas J. Jackson.* 2 vols. London, 1864–66.

Dinkins, James. *Personal Recollections and Experiences in the Confederate Army.* Cincinnati, 1897.

Dixon, Thomas. *The Clansman.* New York, 1905.

Douglas, Henry Kyd. *I Rode with Stonewall: Being Chiefly the War Experiences of the Youngest Member of Jackson's Staff from the John Brown Raid to the Hanging of Mr. Suratt.* Chapel Hill, N.C., 1940.

Eggleston, George Carey. *Dorothy South: A Love Story of Virginia just before the War.* New York, 1872.

————. *A Rebel's Recollections.* New York, 1878.

Falkner, William C. *The White Rose of Memphis.* New York, 1880.

Ford, Arthur Peronneau. *Life in the Confederate Army; Being Personal Experiences of a Private Soldier in the Confederate Army.* New York, 1905.

Fox, John B., Jr. *The Trail of the Lonesome Pine.* New York, 1898.

Gilmore, Harry. *Four Years in the Saddle.* London, 1866.

Glasgow, Ellen. *The Ancient Law.* London, 1908.

————. *Barren Ground.* London, 1925.

————. *The Battle-Ground.* London, 1902.

————. *Beyond Defeat.* Edited by Luther Gore. Charlottesville, Va., 1966.

————. *The Builders.* London, 1919.

————. *A Certain Measure.* London, 1943.

————. *The Collected Stories.* Edited by Ralph Meeker. Baton Rouge, La., 1963.

————. *The Deliverance*. London, 1904.

[————.] *The Descendant*. New York, 1897.

————. *In This Our Life*. London, 1941.

————. *Letters of Ellen Glasgow*. Edited by Blair Rouse. New York, 1958.

————. *Life and Gabriella: The Story of a Woman's Courage*. London, 1916.

————. *The Miller of Old Church*. London, 1911.

————. *One Man in His Time*. London, 1922.

————. *Phases of an Inferior Planet*. London, 1898.

————. *The Romance of a Plain Man*. London, 1909.

————. *The Romantic Comedians*. London, 1926.

————. *The Sheltered Life*. Garden City, 1932.

————. *They Stooped to Folly: A Comedy of Morals*. London, 1929.

————. *Vein of Iron*. London, 1935.

————. *Virginia: A Novel*. London, 1913.

————. *The Voice of the People*. New York, 1900.

————. *The Wheel of Life*. New York, 1906.

————. *The Woman Within*. London, 1955.

Gordon, John. *Reminiscences of the Civil War*. London, 1904.

Grady, Henry W. *The New South*. New York, 1890.

Harland, Marion. *His Great Self*. Philadelphia, 1892.

Harris, Joel Chandler. *Balaam and His Master, and Other Sketches and Stories*. London, 1891.

————. *The Chronicles of Aunt Minervy Ann*. London, 1899.

————. *Free Joe, and Other Georgian Sketches*. New York, 1887.

————. *Gabriel Tolliver: A Story of Reconstruction*. London, 1902.

————. *The Making of a Statesman, and Other Stories*. New York, 1902.

————. *Mingo, and Other Sketches in Black and White*. Boston, 1884.

————. *Nights with Uncle Remus: Myths and Legends of the Old Plantation*. Boston, 1883.

————. *On the Plantation*. New York, 1892.

————. *A Plantation Printer: The Adventures of a Georgia Boy During the War*. London, 1892.

————. *Sister Jane: Her Friends and Acquaintances*. London, 1896.

————. *Tales of the Home Folks in Peace and War*. Cambridge, Mass., 1898.

————. *The Tar-Baby, and Other Rhymes of Uncle Remus*. New York, 1904.

————. *Told by Uncle Remus: Stories of the Old Plantation*. London, 1905.

————. *Uncle Remus and Brer Rabbit*. New York, 1907.

————. *Uncle Remus and His Friends*. New York, 1892.

————. *Uncle Remus and the Little Boy*. New York, 1910.

————. *Uncle Remus; or, Mr. Fox, Mr. Rabbit and Mr. Terrapin*. London, 1891.

————. *Uncle Remus Returns*. New York, 1918.

Hayne, Paul Hamilton. *Poems*, Boston, 1882.

Hermann, Isaac. *Memoirs of a Veteran, Who Served as a Private in the*

60's in the War between the States: Personal Incidents, Experiences, and Observations. Atlanta, Ga., 1911.

Johnston, Joseph Eggleston. *Narrative of Military Operations Directed in the Late War between the States.* New York, 1874.

Johnston, Mary. *Lewis Rand.* Boston, 1908.

———. *Prisoners of Hope: A Tale of Colonial Virginia.* London, 1899.

[Johnston, Richard Malcolm.] *Dukesborough Tales.* 1871. Reprint. New York, 1883.

———. *Mr. Absalom Billingslea, and Other Georgia Folk.* New York, 1888.

———. *The Primes and Their Neighbors: Ten Tales of Middle Georgia.* New York, 1891.

Jones, John William. *Personal Reminiscences, Anecdotes and Letters of General R. E. Lee.* New York, 1875.

Kennaway, Sir John. *On Sherman's Tracks; or, The South after the War.* London, 1867.

King, Edward. *The Southern States of North America.* London, 1875.

King, Grace. *Monsieur Motte.* New York, 1888.

Lanier, Sidney. *The Centennial Edition of the Works of Sidney Lanier.* Edited by Charles R. Anderson. 10 vols. Baltimore, 1945.

Latham, Henry. *Black and White: A Journal of Three Months' Tour in the United States.* London, 1867.

Lee, Fitzhugh. *General Lee of the Confederate Army.* New York, 1892.

Lee, Capt. Robert F. *Recollections and Letters of General R. E. Lee.* London, 1904.

Long, Armistead Lindsay. *Memoirs of Robert E. Lee: His Military and Personal History.* London, 1886.

Longstreet, James. *From Manassas to Appomatox: Memoirs of the Civil War in America.* London, 1874.

McCabe, James D., Jr. *Life and Campaigns of General R. E. Lee.* Atlanta, Ga. 1886.

McCarthy, Carlton. *Detailed Minutiae of Soldier Life in the Army of Northern Virginia, 1861–1865.* Richmond, Va., 1882.

McDowell, Katherine Sherwood Bonner. *Like unto Like.* New York, 1879.

McKim, Randolph Harrison. *A Soldier's Recollections: Leaves from the Diary of a Young Confederate.* London, 1910.

Munson, John W. *Reminiscences of a Mosby Guerilla.* London, 1906.

Murfree, Mary Noailles. *In the Tennessee Mountains.* New York, 1884.

Nordhoff, Charles. *The Confederate States in the Spring and Summer of 1875.* New York, 1876.

Page, Thomas Nelson. *The Burial of the Guns.* London, 1894.

———. *In Ole Virginia; or, Marse Chan, and Other Stories.* New York. 1887.

———. *Meh Lady: A Story of the War.* London, 1893.

———. *The Old South.* New York, 1892.

———. *On Newfound River.* London, 1891.

———. *Red Rock.* London, 1898.

———. *Robert E. Lee: Man and Soldier.* New York, 1911.

Page, Walter Hines. *The Southerner, a Novel: Being the Autobiography of Nicholas Worth*. New York, 1909.

Polk, William. *Leonidas Polk: Bishop and General*. 2 vols. New York, 1915.

Pollard, Edward Albert. *The First Year of the War*. New York, 1863.

———. *Lee and His Lieutenants: Comprising the Early Life, Public Services, and Campaigns of R. E. Lee and His Companions in Arms, with a Record of Their Campaigns and Heroic Deeds*. New York, 1867.

———. *The Second Year of the War*. New York, 1864.

———. *The Third Year of the War*. New York, 1865.

———. *The War in America, 1863–1864*. New York, 1865.

Reid, Whitelaw. *A Southern Tour*. Cincinnati, 1866.

Rives, Amelie. *Virginia of Virginia*. New York, 1888.

Roman, Alfred. *The Military Operations of General Beauregard in the War between the States, 1861–1865*. 2 vols. New York, 1886.

Russell, Irwin. *Christmas-Night in the Quarters, and Other Poems*. Edited by Joel Chandler Harris. New York, 1917.

Simms, William Gilmore, ed. *War Poetry of the South*. New York, 1866.

Smedes, Susan Dabney. *A Southern Planter*. London, 1889.

Smith, Charles Henry. *Bill Arp, So Called: A Side Show of the Southern Side of the War*. New York, 1866.

Smith, Francis Hopkinson. *Colonel Carter of Cartersville*. London, 1891.

Somers, Robert. *The Southern States since the War, 1870–1871*. London, 1871.

Stevenson, William G. *Thirteen Months in the Rebel Army*. New York, 1862.

Stuart, Ruth, McEnery. *A Golden Wedding, and Other Tales*. New York, 1893.

Taylor, Richard. *Destruction and Reconstruction: Personal Experiences of the Late War in the United States*. London, 1879.

Taylor, William Herron. *Four Years with General Lee: Being a Summary of the More Important Events Touching the Career of General R. E. Lee in the War between the States*. New York, 1878.

Toney, Marcus B. *The Privations of a Private: The Campaign under General Stonewall Jackson*. Nashville, Tenn., 1905.

Trowbridge, John T. *The South: A Tour of Its Battle-Fields and Ruined Cities*. Hartford, Conn., 1866.

Washington, Booker T. *Up From Slavery*. New York, 1891.

Watkins, Samuel R. *"Co. Aytch," Maury Grays, First Tennessee Regiment; or, A Side-Show of the Big Show*. Nashville, Tenn., 1882.

Watson, Tom. *Bethany: A Story of the Old South*. New York, 1904.

Wyeth, James Allen. *With Sabre and Scalpel: The Autobiography of a Soldier and Surgeon*. New York, 1914.

Zincke, Foster Barham. *Last Winter in the United States*. London, 1868.

SECONDARY SOURCES:

Arnett, Alex Mathews. *The Populist Movement in Georgia*. New York, 1922.

Auchinloss, Louis. *Ellen Glasgow*. Minneapolis, Minn., 1964.

Baro, Gene. *After Appomatox: The Image of the South in Its Fiction, 1865–1900.* New York, 1963.

Beaty, John Owen. *John Esten Cooke, Virginian.* New York, 1922.

Blair, Walter. *Mark Twain and Huck Finn.* Berkeley, Calif., 1960.

Buck, Paul H. *The Road to Reunion, 1865–1900.* Boston, 1937.

Buck, Solon Justus. *The Agrarian Crusade: A Chronicle of the Farmer in Politics.* New Haven, 1920.

———. *The Granger Movement, 1870–1890.* Cambridge, Mass., 1913.

Cousins, Paul. *Joel Chandler Harris: A Biography.* Baton Rouge, La., 1969.

Eaton, Clement. *A History of the Southern Confederacy.* New York, 1954.

Field, Louise M. *Ellen Glasgow: Novelist of the Old and New South. An Appreciation.* Garden City, N.Y., 1923.

Fleming, Walter L. *The Sequel of Appomatox.* New Haven, 1919.

Foote, Shelby. *The Civil War: A Narrative.* 3 vols. New York, 1958–75.

Franklin, John Hope. *Reconstruction: After the Civil War.* Chicago, 1961.

Freeman, Douglas C. *Lee's Lieutenants.* 3 vols. New York, 1942–44.

———. *R. E. Lee: A Biography.* 4 vols. New York, 1934–35.

———. *The South to Posterity: An Introduction to the Writings of Confederate History.* New York, 1939.

Friedman, Lawrence J. *The White Savage: Racial Fantasies in the Post-Bellum South.* Englewood Cliffs, N.J., 1970.

Gaston, Paul M. *The New South Creed: A Study in Southern Mythmaking.* New York, 1970.

Godbold, E. Stanly. *Ellen Glasgow and the Woman Within.* Baton Rouge, La., 1972.

Gross, Theodore L. *Thomas Nelson Page.* New York, 1967.

Hammond, Mathew Brown. *The Cotton Industry: An Essay in American Economic History.* New York, 1897.

Harris, Julia C. *The Life and Letters of Joel Chandler Harris.* Boston, 1918.

Hicks, John Donald. *The Populist Revolt: A History of the Farmer's Alliance and the People's Party.* Minneapolis, Minn., 1931.

Kelley, William W. *Ellen Glasgow: A Bibliography.* Charlottesville, Va., 1965.

Knight, Grant C. *James Lane Allen and the Genteel Tradition.* Chapel Hill, N.C., 1935.

Lively, Robert C. *Fiction Fights the Civil War.* Chapel Hill, N.C., 1957.

Logan, Rayford W. *The Negro in American Life and Thought: The Nadir, 1877–1901.* New York, 1954.

McDowell, Frederick P. *Ellen Glasgow and the Ironic Art of Fiction.* New York, 1960.

Meier, August. *Negro Thought in America, 1880–1915.* Ann Arbor, Mich., 1963.

Osterweis, Rollin G. *The Myth of the Lost Cause, 1865–1900.* Hamden, Conn., 1973.

Pressley, Thomas J. *Americans Interpret Their Civil War.* New York, 1954.

Randall, James G. *The Civil War and Reconstruction.* New York, 1937.

Rankin, Daniel S. *Kate Chopin and Her Creole Stories.* Philadelphia, 1932.

Raper, J. R. *Without Shelter: The Early Career of Ellen Glasgow.* Baton Rouge, La., 1971.

Richards, Marion K. *Ellen Glasgow's Development as a Novelist.* The Hague, 1971.

Rouse, H. Blair. *Ellen Glasgow.* New York, 1962.

Rubin, Louis D. *No Place on Earth: Ellen Glasgow, James Branch Cabell, and Richmond-in-Virginia.* Austin, Texas, 1964.

Shannon, Frederick Albert. *The Farmer's Last Frontier: Agriculture 1860–1897.* New York, 1947.

Sheldon, William DuBose. *Populism in the Old Dominion: Virginia Farm Politics, 1885–1900.* Princeton, N.J., 1935.

Shugg, Roger W. *Origins of the Class Struggle in Louisiana.* Baton Rouge, La., 1939.

Simkins, Francis Butler. *Pitchfork Ben Tillman, South Carolinian.* Baton Rouge, La., 1944.

Smith, Henry Nash. *Mark Twain: The Development of a Writer.* Cambridge, Mass., 1962.

Stampp, Kenneth M. *The Era of Reconstruction.* London, 1965.

Starke, Aubrey H. *Sidney Lanier: A Biographical and Critical Study.* Chapel Hill, N.C., 1933.

Thompson, Henry T. *Henry Timrod: Laureate of the Confederacy.* Columbia, S.C., 1928.

Thompson, Holland. *The New South.* New Haven, 1919.

Turner, Arlin. *George W. Cable: A Biography.* Durham, N.C., 1956.

Wells, Arvin. *Jesting Moses: A Study in Cabellian Comedy.* Gainesville, Fla., 1962.

Wiley, Bell Irvin. *The Life of Johnny Reb: The Common Soldier of the Confederacy.* New York, 1943.

———. *The Plain People of the Confederacy.* Baton Rouge, La., 1943.

Wilson, Edmund. *Patriotic Gore: Studies in the Literature of the American Civil War.* London, 1962.

Woodward, C. Vann. *Tom Watson: Agrarian Rebel.* New York, 1963.

The Modern South and the Southern "Renaissance"

PRIMARY SOURCES:

Abaunza, Virginia. *Sundays from Two to Six.* New York, 1956.

Adams, Edward C. L. *Congaree Sketches.* New York, 1927.

Agee, James. *Collected Poems.* New York, 1968.

———. *Collected Prose.* New York, 1968.

———. *A Death in the Family.* New York, 1957.

———. *Letters of James Agee to Father Flye.* New York, 1962.

———. *Let Us Now Praise Famous Men.* New York, 1941.

———. *The Morning Watch.* Boston, 1951.

"The Agrarians Today: A Symposium." *Shenandoah* 3 (Summer 1952): 14–33.

Alexander, Lily M. *Candy.* New York, 1934.

American Review (1933–37).

Ammons, A. R. *Collected Poems.* New York, 1972.

Anderson, Barbara. *The Day Grows Cold.* New York, 1941.

Armfield, Eugene. *Where the Weak Grow Strong.* New York, 1936.

Armstrong, Anne W. *This Day and Time.* New York, 1954.

Arnow, Harriette L. S. *The Dollmaker.* New York, 1954.

———. *Hunter's Horn.* New York, 1949.

———. *Mountain Path.* New York, 1936.

Aswell, James. *Midsummer Fires.* New York, 1948.

Atlee, Philip. *The Inheritors.* New York, 1940.

Attaway, William. *Blood on the Forge.* New York, 1941.

Averitt, Barbara. *Hear the Cock Crow.* New York, 1949.

Baker, Charles. *Blood of the Lamb.* New York, 1946.

Ballard, James. *The Long Way Through.* New York, 1959.

Barnes, Carmen. *Time Lay Asleep.* New York, 1946.

Barry, Jane. *The Carolinians.* New York, 1959.

Barth, John. *The End of the Road.* New York, 1958.

———. *The Floating Opera.* New York, 1956.

———. *Giles Goat-Boy.* New York, 1966.

———. *Lost in the Funhouse.* New York, 1969.

———. *The Sot-Weed Factor.* New York, 1960.

Basso, Hamilton. *Cinnamon Seed.* New York, 1934.

———. *Courthouse Square.* New York, 1939.

———. *Days before Lent.* New York, 1939.

———. *In Their Own Image.* New York, 1935.

———. *A Quota of Seaweed.* New York, 1960.

———. *The Sun in Capricorn.* New York, 1942.

———. *The View from Pompey's Head.* New York, 1954.

Bell, Robert. *The Butterfly Tree.* New York, 1959.

Bell, Vereen. *Swamp Water.* Boston, 1941.

Bennet, Peggy. *The Varmints.* New York, 1947.

Berry, Wendell. *The Broken Ground.* New York, 1964.

———. *Findings.* New York, 1969.

———. *Nathan Coulter.* New York, 1960.

———. *Openings.* New York, 1969.

———. *A Place on Earth.* New York, 1968.

Bethea, Jack. *Cotton.* New York, 1928.

Bishop, John Peale, *Act of Darkness.* New York, 1935.

———. *The Collected Essays of John Peale Bishop.* Edited by Edmund Wilson, New York, 1948.

———. *The Collected Poems of John Peale Bishop.* Edited by Allen Tate. New York, 1948.

———. *Many Thousands Gone.* New York, 1931.

Bodenheim, Maxwell. *Selected Poems, 1914–1944*. New York, 1946.

Bontemps, Arna. *Black Thunder*. New York, 1936.

Boone, Jack. *Dossie Bell is Dead*. New York, 1939.

Bowers, Edgar. *The Astronomers*. New York, 1965.

Boyd, James. *Drums*. New York, 1925.

————. *Long Hunt*. New York, 1930.

————. *Marching On*. New York, 1927.

Bradford, Roark. *Ol' Man Adam an' His Chillun*. New York, 1938.

Bristow, Gwen. *Deep Summer*. New York, 1940.

————. *The Handsome Road*. New York, 1938.

————. *This Side of Glory*. New York, 1940.

Brown, Joe David. *Kings Go Forth*. New York, 1956.

Buck, Charles. *Flight to the Hills*. New York, 1926.

Buckner, Robert. *The Primrose Path*. New York, 1939.

Burton, Carl. *Satan's Rock*. New York, 1954.

Burman, Ben Lucien. *Blow for a Landing*. New York, 1938.

————. *Everywhere I Roam*. Garden City, 1949.

————. *The Four Lives of Mundy Tolliver*. New York, 1953.

————. *Rooster Crows for Day*. New York, 1955.

————. *Steamboat Round the Bend*. Boston, 1930.

Caldwell, Erskine. *The Bastard*. New York, 1929.

————. *Call It Experience*. New York, 1951.

————. *Certain Women*. New York, 1957.

————. *Close to Home*. New York, 1962.

————. *The Complete Stories*. New York, 1953.

————. *The Courting of Susie Brown*. New York, 1952.

————. *Episode in Palmetto*. New York, 1950.

————. *Georgia Boy*. New York, 1943.

————. *God's Little Acre*. New York, 1933.

————. *Gretta*. New York, 1955.

————. *Gulf Coast Stories*. New York, 1956.

————. *A House in the Uplands*. New York, 1946.

————. *In Search of Bisco*. New York, 1965.

————. *In the Shadow of the Steeple*. New York, 1966.

————. *Jackpot*. New York, 1940.

————. *Journeyman*. New York, 1935.

————. *Kneel to the Rising Sun*. New York, 1935.

————. *Love and Money*. New York, 1954.

————. *Men and Women*. New York, 1961.

————. *Miss Mama Aimée*. New York, 1967.

————. *Molly Cottontail*. New York, 1958.

————. *A Place Called Estherville*. New York, 1949.

————. *Poor Fool*. New York, 1930.

————. *Some American People*. New York, 1935.

————. *Southways*. New York, 1938.

————. *The Sure Hand of God*. New York, 1947.

——. *This Very Earth*. New York, 1948.

——. *Tobacco Road*. New York, 1932.

——. *Tragic Ground*. Boston, 1944.

——. *Trouble in July*. New York, 1940.

——. *The Weather Shelter*. New York, 1969.

——. *You Have Seen Their Faces*. New York, 1937.

Capote, Truman. *Breakfast at Tiffany's*. New York, 1958.

——. *The Grass Harp*. New York, 1951.

——. *In Cold Blood*. New York, 1966.

——. *Other Voices, Other Rooms*. New York, 1948.

Carter, Hodding. *A Tree of Night*. New York, 1949.

——. *Flood Crest*. New York, 1947.

——. *The Winds of Fear*. New York, 1944.

Caudill, Rebecca. *The Far-Off Land*. New York, 1964.

Chamberlain, W. W. *Leaf Gold*. New York, 1942.

Chapman, Maristan. *The Happy Mountain*, New York, 1928.

——. *Rogue's March*. New York, 1949.

——. *Tennessee Hazard*. New York, 1953.

——. *The Weather Tree*. New York, 1932.

Cheney, Brainard. *Lightwood*. New York, 1939.

——. *River Rogue*. New York, 1942.

Childers, James Saxon. *A Novel about a White Man and a Black Man in the Deep South*. New York, 1936.

Clark, Billy C. *A Long Row to Hoe*. New York, 1960.

Clayton, John Bell. *Wait, Son, October Is Near*. New York, 1953.

Clemons, Walter. *The Poison Tree*. New York, 1959.

Cochran, Edward. *Boss Man*. Caldwell, Idaho, 1939.

Coker, Elizabeth B. *Daughter of Strangers*. New York, 1950.

Coleman, Lonnie. *Escape the Thunder*. New York, 1944.

Coleman, Richard. *Don't You Weep—Don't You Moan*. New York, 1935.

Coleman, William L. *Adam's Way*. New York, 1953.

Colver, Alice B. *There Is a Season*. New York, 1957.

Corrington, J. W., and Williams, M., eds. *Southern Writing in the Sixties: Fiction*. Baton Rouge, La., 1966.

——. *Southern Writings in the Sixties: Poetry*. Baton Rouge, La., 1967.

Creekmore, Hubert. *The Fingers of the Night*. New York, 1946.

Cross, Ruth. *The Golden Cocoon*. London, 1924.

Crump, Louise E. *Helen Templeton's Daughter*. New York, 1952.

Cunningham, J. V. *Collected Poems and Epigrams*. New York, 1971.

Daingerfield, Foxhall. *Mrs. Haney*. New York, 1933.

Daniels, Lucy. *Caleb, My Son*. New York, 1956.

Dargan, Olive. *Highland Annals*. New York, 1925.

Davidson, Donald. *The Attack on Leviathan: Regionalism and Nationalism in the United States*. Chapel Hill, N.C., 1938.

——. "I'll Take My Stand. A History." *American Review* 5 (Summer, 1935): 301–21.

——. *Lee in the Mountains, and Other Poems*. Boston, 1938.

————. *The Long Street, and Other Poems.* Nashville, Tenn., 1961.
————. *An Outland Piper.* Boston, 1924.
————. *Poems, 1922–1961.* Minneapolis, Minn., 1966.
————. *Southern Writers in the Modern World.* Athens, Ga., 1958.
————. *The Spyglass.* New York, 1963.
————. *Still Rebels, Still Yankees, and Other Essays.* Baton Rouge, La., 1957.
————. *The Tall Men.* Cambridge, Mass., 1927.
————. *The Tennessee.* New York, 1948.
Davis, Burke. *The Ragged Ones.* New York, 1951.
Davis, Paxton. *Two Soldiers.* New York, 1956.
Davis, Wesley Ford. *The Time of the Panther.* New York, 1958.
Deal, Borden. *Dunbar's Cove.* New York, 1957.
————. *The Insolent Breed.* New York, 1959.
Demby, William. *Beetlecreek.* New York, 1950.
Dickey, James. *Babel to Byzantium.* New York, 1968.
————. *Deliverance.* New York, 1970.
————. *The Eyebeaters, Blood, Victory, Madness, Buckhead and Mercy.* New York, 1970.
————. *Poems 1957–1967.* New York, 1968.
Dillon, George. *The Flowering Stone.* New York, 1931.
Douglas, Ellen. *A Family's Affairs.* New York, 1962.
The Double-Dealer. 1921–26.
Dowdey, Clifford. *Bugles Blow No More.* Boston, 1937.
————. *Gamble's Hundred.* Boston, 1939.
————. *Tidewater.* Boston, 1943.
Downey, Harris. *Thunder in the Room.* New York, 1956.
Drewry, Carlton. *Proud Horns.* New York, 1933.
————. *The Writhen Wood.* New York, 1953.
Drury, Allen. *Advise and Consent.* New York, 1959.
Dykeman, Wilma. *The Far Family.* New York, 1966.
————. *The Tall Woman.* New York, 1962.
Ehle, John. *Kingstree Island.* New York, 1959.
Ethridge, W. S. *Mingled Yarn.* New York, 1938.
Faulkner, John. *Dollar Cotton.* New York, 1943.
————. *Men Working.* New York, 1941.
————. *My Brother Bill: An Affectionate Reminiscence.* New York, 1967.
Faulkner, William. *Absalom, Absalom!* New York, 1936.
————. *As I Lay Dying.* New York, 1930.
————. *Big Woods.* New York, 1955.
————. *Collected Short Stories.* 3 vols. London, 1958.
————. *Collected Stories.* New York, 1950.
————. *Doctor Martino, and Other Stories.* New York, 1934.
————. *Early Prose and Poetry.* Edited by Carvel Collins. Boston, 1962.
————. *Essays, Speeches, and Public Letters.* Edited by James P. Meriwether. New York, 1965.
————. *A Fable.* New York, 1954.

――――. *The Faulkner-Cowley File: Letters and Memories, 1944–1962.* Edited by Malcolm Cowley. New York, 1966.

――――. *Faulkner at Nagano.* Edited by R. A. Jelliffe. Tokyo, 1956.

――――. *Faulkner in the University: Class Conferences at the University of Virginia, 1957–1958.* Edited by F. L. Gwynn and J. L. Blotner. Charlottesville, Va., 1959.

――――. *Faulkner at West Point.* Edited by J. L. Fant and R. Ashley. New York, 1964.

――――. *Flags in the Dust.* Edited by Douglas Day. New York, 1973.

――――. *Lion in the Garden.* Edited by James B. Meriwether and Michael Millgate, New York, 1968.

――――. *Go Down, Moses.* New York, 1942.

――――. *A Green Bough.* New York, 1933.

――――. *The Hamlet.* New York, 1940.

――――. *Intruder in the Dust.* New York, 1948.

――――. *Knight's Gambit.* New York, 1949.

――――. *Light in August.* New York, 1932.

――――. *The Mansion.* New York, 1959.

――――. *The Marble Faun.* New York, 1924.

――――. *Mosquitoes.* New York, 1927.

――――. *New Orleans Sketches.* Edited by Carvel Collins. New Brunswick, N.J., 1958.

――――. *Notes on a Horsethief.* Greenville, Miss., 1951.

――――. *Pylon.* New York, 1935.

――――. *The Reivers.* New York, 1962.

――――. *Requiem for a Nun.* New York, 1951.

――――. *Salmagundi.* Edited by Paul Romaine. Milwaukee, 1931.

――――. *Sanctuary.* New York, 1931.

――――. *Sartoris.* New York, 1929.

――――. *Soldier's Pay.* New York, 1926.

――――. *The Sound and the Fury.* New York, 1929.

――――. *These Thirteen.* New York, 1931.

――――. *The Town.* New York, 1957.

――――. *The Unvanquished.* New York, 1938.

――――. *The Wild Palms.* New York, 1939.

――――. *The Wishing Tree.* New York, 1967.

Feibleman, Peter. *A Place without Twilight.* New York, 1958.

Fellows, Alice. *Laurel.* New York, 1950.

Flannagan, Roy. *Amber Satyr.* New York, 1932.

Fletcher, Inglis. *Men of Albemarle.* Indianapolis, 1942.

――――. *The Scotswoman.* New York, 1954.

Fletcher, John G. *Arkansas.* New York, 1947.

――――. *The Burning Mountain.* New York, 1946.

――――. *The Epic of Arkansas.* New York, 1936.

――――. *Irradiations: Sand and Spray.* London, 1915.

――――. *South Star.* New York, 1941.

Foote, Shelby. *Follow Me Down.* New York, 1950.

———. *Love in a Dry Season.* New York, 1951.

———. *Shiloh.* New York, 1952.

———. *Tournament.* New York, 1949.

Ford, Charles Henri. *The Garden of Disorder, and Other Poems.* Norfolk, Conn., 1938.

Ford, Jesse Hill. *The Liberation of Lord Byron Jones.* New York, 1965.

Fort, John. *God in a Straw Pen.* New York, 1931.

———. *Light in the Window.* New York, 1928.

The Fugitive (1922–25).

The Fugitive: An Anthology of Verse (New York, 1928).

Fox, Frances. *Ridgeways.* New York, 1934.

Furman, Lucy. *The Quare Women: A Story of the Kentucky Mountains.* Boston, 1923.

Gaither, Frances. *Follow the Drinking Gourd.* New York, 1940.

Garrett, George. *Do, Lord, Remember Me.* London, 1965.

———. *The Finished Man.* New York, 1959.

Garrett, Zena. *The House in the Mulberry Tree.* New York, 1959.

Garth, John. *Hill Man.* New York, 1954.

Gibbons, Robert. *The Patchwork Time.* New York, 1948.

Gibson, Jewel. *Joshua Beene and God.* New York, 1946.

Giles, Barbara. *The Gentle Bush.* New York, 1947.

Giles, Janice H. *Tara's Healing.* Philadelphia, 1951.

Givens, Charles G. *The Devil Takes a Hill-Town.* New York, 1939.

Glenn, Isa. *A Short History of Julia.* New York, 1930.

———. *Southern Charm.* New York, 1928.

Godchaux, Emily. *Stubborn Roots.* New York, 1936.

Gordon, Caroline. *Aleck Maury, Sportsman.* New York, 1934.

———. *The Forest of the South.* New York, 1945.

———. *The Garden of Adonis.* New York, 1937.

———. *The Glory of Hera.* New York, 1972.

———. *Green Centuries.* New York, 1941.

———. *The Malefactors.* New York, 1956.

———. *None Shall Look Back.* New York, 1937.

———. *Old Red, and Other Stories.* New York, 1963.

———. *Penhally.* New York, 1931.

———. *The Strange Children.* New York, 1951.

———. *The Women on the Porch.* New York, 1944.

Gowan, Emmett. *Old Hell.* New York, 1937.

Goyen, William. *The Faces of Blood Kindred.* New York, 1960.

———. *The Fair Sister.* New York, 1963.

———. *Ghost and Flesh.* New York, 1952.

———. *In a Farther Country.* New York, 1955.

———. *The House of Breath.* New York, 1959.

Graham, Alice Walworth. *Indigo Bend.* New York, 1954.

———. *Natchez Woman.* New York, 1940.

Granberry, Edwin. *Strangers and Lovers*. New York, 1928.

Grau, Shirley Ann. *The Black Prince*. New York, 1955.

————. *The Hard, Blue Sky*. New York, 1958.

————. *The House on Coliseum Street*. New York, 1961.

————. *The Keepers of the House*. New York, 1964.

Green, Paul. *The Field God*. New York, 1927.

————. *The Founders*. New York, 1957.

————. *The House of Connelly*. New York, 1931.

————. *In Abraham's Bosom*. New York, 1927.

————. *The Laughing Pioneer*. New York, 1932.

————. *This Body, the Earth*. London, 1936.

————. *Wide Fields*. New York, 1928.

Greene, Ward. *Death in the Deep South*. New York, 1936.

Griffith, Leon. *A Long Time since Morning*. New York, 1954.

Hamner, Earl, Jr. *Fifty Roads to Town*. New York, 1953.

————. *Spencer's Mountain*. New York, 1962.

Hannum, Alberta Pierson. *The Hills Step Lightly*. New York, 1941.

Hardwick, Elizabeth. *The Ghostly Lover*. New York, 1945.

Harris, Bernice Kelley. *Purslane*. New York, 1939.

Hassell, Harriet. *Rachel's Children*. London, 1938.

Hatcher, Harlan. *Patterns of Wolfpen*. New York, 1934.

Haun, Mildred. *The Hawk's Done Gone*. New York, 1940.

Heard, Annette. *Return Not Again*. London, 1938.

Hebson, Anne. *A Fine and Private Place*. New York, 1958.

Heddon, Worth Tuttle. *Love is a Wound*. New York, 1952.

Hellman, Lillian. *Another Part of the Forest*. New York, 1946.

————. *The Little Foxes*. New York, 1939.

————. *Toys in the Attic*. New York, 1960.

Henderson, George. *Ollie Miss*. New York, 1935.

Hervey, Harry. *Ethan Quest: His Saga*. New York, 1925.

Hewlett, John. *Cross on the Moon*. New York, 1946.

Heyward, DuBose. *Angel*. New York, 1926.

————. *Mamba's Daughters*. New York, 1929.

————. *Porgy*. New York, 1925.

Heyward, DuBose, with Allen, Hervey. *Carolina Chansons*. New York, 1922.

Hickey, Daniel. *Wild Heron*. New York, 1940.

Hill, Pati. *The Nine Mile Circle*. New York, 1957.

Hoffman, William. *Days in the Yellow Leaf*. New York, 1958.

————. *The Trumpet Unblown*. New York, 1955.

Hopkins, Stanley. *The Ladies*. New York, 1933.

Hornsby, Henry. *Lonesome Valley*. New York, 1949.

Hoskins, Katherine. *A Penitential Primer*. Cummington, Mass., 1945.

Hoss, May D. *The Pike*. New York, 1954.

Huddleston, Edwin. *The Claybrooks*. New York, 1951.

Humphrey, William. *Home from the Hill*. New York, 1958.

————. *The Ordways*. New York, 1965.

Hughes, Hatcher. *Hell-Bent for Heaven*. New York, 1924.

Hurston, Zora Neale. *Jonah's Gourd Vine*. New York, 1934.

Hyman, Mac. *No Time for Sergeants*. New York, 1954.

I'll Take My Stand: The South and the Agrarian Tradition by Twelve Southerners. New York, 1930.

Ingram, Bowen. *Light as the Morning*. New York, 1954.

Ivey, Caroline. *The Family*. New York, 1952.

Jarrell, Randall. *The Complete Poems*. New York, 1969.

————. *Pictures from an Institution*. New York, 1954.

Johnson, Gerald W. *By Reason of Strength*. New York, 1943.

Johnson, James W. *God's Trombones*. New York, 1927.

————. *Selected Poems*. New York, 1935.

Jones, Madison. *A Buried Land*. New York, 1963.

————. *A Cry of Absence*. New York, 1973.

————. *An Exile*. New York, 1967.

————. *Forest of the Night*. New York, 1960.

————. *The Innocent*. New York, 1957.

Joseph, Donald. *October's Child*. New York, 1929.

Justice, Donald. *A Local Storm*. New York, 1963.

————. *Night Light*. New York, 1967.

————. *The Summer Anniversaries*. New York, 1960.

Kane, Harnett. *Deep Delta Country*. New York, 1944.

Kelley, Edith Summers. *Weeds*. London, 1924.

Kelley, Welbourn. *Inchin' Along*. New York, 1932.

————. *So Fair a House*. New York, 1936.

Kennedy, R. Emmett. *Red Bean Row*. New York, 1929.

Kikes, Douglas. *The Southerner*. New York, 1957.

Killen, Joseph O. *Youngblood*. New York, 1954.

Kimbrough, Edward. *Night Fire*. New York, 1946.

————. *The Secret Pilgrim*. New York, 1949.

Kroll, Harry Harrison. *The Cabin in the Cotton*. London, 1932.

————. *Darker Grows the Valley*. New York, 1947.

————. *The Mountainy Singer*. New York, 1928.

————. *The Smouldering Fire*. New York, 1955.

————. *The Usurper*. New York, 1941.

Lamkin, Speed. *Tiger in the Garden*. New York, 1950.

Latham, Edythe. *Sounding Brass*. New York, 1953.

Leatherman, Leroy. *The Caged Birds*. New York, 1950.

————. *The Other Side of the Tree*. New York, 1954.

Lee, George. *River George*. New York, 1937.

Lee, Harper. *To Kill a Mockingbird*. New York, 1960.

Lee, Harry. *The Fox in the Cloak*. New York, 1938.

Linney, Romulus. *Heathen Valley*. New York, 1962.

Lloyd, Norris. *A Dream of Mansions,* New York, 1962.

Lochridge, Betsy. *Blue River*. New York, 1956.

Lowry, Walter. *Watch Night*. New York, 1953.

Lumpkin, Grace. *A Sign for Cain.* New York, 1935.

———. *To Make My Bread.* New York, 1932.

Lytle, Andrew Nelson. *At the Moon's Inn.* New York, 1941.

———. *Bedford Forrest and His Critter Comany.* London, 1939.

———. *The Hero with the Private Parts.* Baton Rouge, La., 1966.

———. *The Long Night.* New York, 1936.

———. *A Name for Evil.* New York, 1947.

———. *A Novel, a Novella, and Four Stories.* New York, 1958.

———. *The Velvet Horn.* New York, 1956.

———. *A Wake for the Living.* New York, 1975.

March, William. *The Bad Seed.* London, 1954.

———. *The Tallons.* New York, 1936.

Marshall, Robert K. *Julia Gwynn: An American Gothic Tale.* New York, 1952.

———. *Little Squire Jim.* New York, 1949.

Maund, Alfred. *The Big Box Car.* New York, 1957.

Maxwell, Gilbert. *The Sleeping Trees.* New York, 1949.

Mayfield, Julian. *The Hit.* New York, 1957.

———. *The Long Night.* New York, 1958.

McCullers, Carson. *The Ballad of the Sad Cafe.* New York, 1951.

———. *Clock without Hands.* New York, 1961.

———. *Collected Short Stories.* New York, 1973.

———. *The Heart Is a Lonely Hunter.* Boston, 1940.

———. *The Member of the Wedding.* New York, 1946.

———. *The Mortgaged Heart.* Edited by M. C. Smith. New York, 1972.

———. *Reflections in a Golden Eye.* New York, 1941.

———. *The Square Root of Wonderful.* New York, 1958.

McDonald, John P. *The End of the Night.* New York, 1960.

Meade, Julian. *The Back Door.* New York, 1938.

Millen, Gilmore. *Sweet Man.* New York, 1922.

Miller, Caroline. *Lamb in His Bosom.* New York, 1934.

Miller, Helen T. *Hawk in the Wind.* New York, 1938.

Miller, Vassar. *Onions and Roses.* Middletown, Conn., 1968.

Mills, Charles. *The Choice.* New York, 1943.

Mitchell, Margaret. *Gone with the Wind,* New York, 1939.

Molloy, Robert. *Pride's Way.* New York, 1945.

Montgomery, Marion. *Stones from Rubble.* Memphis, Tenn., 1965.

Moore, Merrill. *The Noise that Time Makes.* New York, 1929.

———. *One Thousand Autobiographical Sonnets.* New York, 1938.

———. *Case Record from a Sonnetarium.* New York, 1951.

Morehouse, Ward. *Gentlemen of the Press.* New York, 1938.

Morton, David. *Like a Man in Love.* Dublin, N.H., 1953.

Morton, Jane. *Blackbirds on the Lawn.* New York, 1944.

Munz, Charles C. *Land without Moses.* New York, 1938.

Newman, Frances. *The Hard-Boiled Virgin.* New York, 1926.

Norris, Helen. *Something More than Earth.* Boston, 1940.

O'Connor, Flannery. *The Complete Stories*. New York, 1971.

———. *Everything that Rises Must Converge*. New York, 1965.

———. *A Good Man Is Hard to Find*. New York, 1955.

———. *Mystery and Manners*. Edited by R. and S. Fitzgerald. New York, 1972.

———. *The Violent Bear It Away*. New York, 1960.

———. *Wise Blood*. New York, 1959.

O'Donnell, E. P. *Green Margins*. New York, 1936.

Odum, Howard Washington. *Cold Blue Moon*. Indianapolis, 1931.

Olmsted, Stanley. *At Top of Tobin*. New York, 1926.

Page, Myra. *Gathering Storm*. New York, 1932.

Peery, James Robert. *God Rides a Gale*. New York, 1940.

Percy, Walker. *The Last Gentleman*. New York, 1966.

———. *Love in the Ruins*. New York, 1971.

———. *The Moviegoer*. New York, 1961.

Percy, William Alexander. *Selected Poems*. New Haven, 1930.

Perry, George Sessions. *Hold Autumn in Your Hand*. New York, 1941.

Peterkin, Julia. *Black April*. New York, 1927.

———. *Scarlet Sister Mary*. New York, 1928.

Peyton, Green. *Rain on the Mountain*. New York, 1934.

Phillips, Thomas H. *The Bitterweed Path*. New York, 1950.

Pierce, Evelyn. *Hilltop*. New York, 1931.

Pierce, Ovid Williams. *On a Lonesome Porch*. New York, 1960.

———. *The Plantation*. New York, 1953.

Pinckney, Josephine. *Sea-Drinking Cities*. New York, 1927.

———. *Three O'Clock Dinner*. New York, 1945.

Pope, Edith Taylor. *Not Magnolias*. New York, 1928.

Porter, Katherine Anne. *Collected Essays and Occasional Writings*. New York, 1970.

———. *Collected Stories*. New York, 1965.

———. *The Days Before*. New York, 1952.

———. *Ship of Fools*. New York, 1962.

Price, Reynolds. *A Generous Man*. New York, 1966.

———. *A Long and Happy Life*. New York, 1962.

———. *Love and Work*. New York, 1968.

———. *The Names and Faces of Heroes*. New York, 1963.

———. *Permanent Errors*. New York, 1970.

Putnam, Clay. *The Ruined City*. New York, 1959.

Ramsey, Robert. *Fire in Summer*. New York, 1942.

Ransom, John Crowe. *Beating the Bushes: Selected Essays, 1941–70*. San Francisco, 1972.

———. *Chills and Fever*. New York, 1924.

———. *God without Thunder: An Unorthodox Defence of Orthodoxy*. New York, 1930.

———. *Grace after Meat*. London, 1924.

———. *The New Criticism*. Norfolk, Conn., 1941.

————. *Poems about God.* New York, 1919.

————. *Poems and Essays.* New York, 1962.

————. *Selected Poems.* New York, 1963.

————. *Two Gentlemen in Bonds.* New York, 1927.

————. *The World's Body.* New York, 1938.

Rawlings, Marjorie Kinnan. *Cross Creek.* New York, 1942.

————. *Golden Apples.* New York, 1935.

————. *Jacob's Ladder.* New York, 1931.

————. *The Sojourner.* New York, 1953.

————. *South Moon Under.* New York, 1933.

————. *When the Whipperwill.* New York, 1940.

————. *The Yearling.* New York, 1938.

Reece, Byron Herbert. *Better a Dinner of Herbs.* New York, 1950.

————. *The Hawk and the Sun.* New York, 1955.

————. *The Season of Flesh.* New York, 1955.

Rehder, Jessie. *Remembrance Way.* New York, 1956.

Renard, Frances. *Ridgeways.* New York, 1934.

Rich, Adrienne. *Poems: Selected and New, 1950–74.* New York, 1975.

Roberts, Elizabeth Madox. *Black is My Truelove's Hair.* New York, 1938.

————. *A Buried Treasure.* New York, 1931.

————. *The Great Meadow.* New York, 1930.

————. *He Sent Forth a Raven.* New York, 1935.

————. *Jingling in the Wind.* New York, 1928.

————. *My Heart and My Flesh.* New York, 1927.

————. *Not by Strange Gods.* New York, 1941.

————. *The Time of Man.* New York, 1926.

————. *Under the Tree.* New York, 1922.

Rogers, Lettie. *Birthright.* New York, 1957.

Root, E. Merrill. *Lost Eden, and Other Poems.* New York, 1927.

Ross, Fred. *Jackson Mahaffey.* Boston, 1951.

Rubin, Louis D. *The Golden Weather.* New York, 1961.

Russell, William. *A Wind Is Rising.* New York, 1946.

Rylee, Robert. *Deep Dark River.* New York, 1935.

Sachs, Emanie. *Talk.* New York, 1924.

Salamanca, J. R. *The Lost Country.* New York, 1958.

Sancton, Thomas. *By Starlight.* New York, 1960.

Sass, Herbert. *Look Back to Glory.* Indianapolis, 1933.

Saxon, Lyle. *Father Mississippi.* New York, 1927.

Scarborough, Dorothy. *Can't Get a Redbird.* New York, 1929.

————. *In the Land of Cotton.* New York, 1923.

Scarborough, George. *The Course is Upward.* New York, 1951.

Scott, Evelyn. *The Wave.* New York, 1929.

Scott, Glen. *A Sound of Voices Dying.* New York, 1954.

Shapiro, Karl. *Poems 1940–1953.* New York, 1953.

Shelby, Gertrude M., and Stoney, G. *Po' Buckra.* New York, 1930.

Simon, Charlie May. *The Sharecropper.* New York, 1932.

Skidmore, Hubert. *I Will Lift Up Mine Eyes.* Garden City, N.Y., 1936.

Smith, Lillian. *Strange Fruit*. New York, 1944.

Smith, William Jay. *Poems 1947–1957*. Boston, 1957.

Spencer, Elizabeth. *Fire in the Morning*. New York, 1948.

———. *The Light in the Piazza*. New York, 1960.

———. *No Place for an Angel*. New York, 1967.

———. *This Crooked Way*. New York, 1952.

———. *The Voice at the Back-Door*. New York, 1956.

Stallings, Lawrence. *Plumes*. New York, 1924.

Steele, Max. *Debby*. New York, 1950.

Stewart, John Craig. *Through the First Gate*. New York, 1950.

Stephens, Nan Bagby. *Glory*. New York, 1932.

Still, James. *River of Earth*. New York, 1940.

Stone, Alma. *The Harvard Tree*. New York, 1934.

Stone, Philip. *No Place to Run*. New York, 1959.

Street, James. *In My Father's House*. New York, 1941.

Stribling, Thomas. *Birthright*. New York, 1922.

———. *Bright Metal*. New York, 1928.

———. *The Forge*. London, 1931.

———. *The Store*. London, 1932.

———. *Teeftallow*. New York, 1926.

———. *Unfinished Cathedral*. London, 1934.

Stuart, Jesse. *The Good Spirit of Laurel Ridge*. New York, 1953.

———. *Man with a Bull-Tongue Plow*. New York, 1932.

———. *Taps for Private Tussie*. New York, 1943.

Styron, William. *The Confessions of Nat Turner*. New York, 1967.

———. *Lie Down in Darkness*. New York, 1951.

———. *The Long March*. New York, 1956.

———. *Set This House on Fire*. New York, 1960.

Sullivan, Walter. *The Long, Long Love*. New York, 1959.

———. *Sojourn of a Stranger*. New York, 1957.

Summers, Hollis. *The Walk Near Athens*. New York, 1959.

Sumner, Cid R. *Quality*. New York, 1946.

Tallant, Robert. *A State in Mimosa*. New York, 1950.

Tarleton, Fiswoode. *Bloody Ground: A Cycle of the Southern Hills*. New York, 1929.

———. *Some Trust in Chariots*. New York, 1930.

Tate, Allen. *Collected Essays*. New York, 1959.

———. *Essays of Four Decades*. New York, 1969.

———. *The Fathers*. New York, 1938.

———. *The Forlorn Demon*. Chicago, 1953.

——— "The Fugitives, 1922–1925." *Princeton University Library Chronicle* 3 (April 1942): 75–84.

———. *The Golden Mean and Other Poems*. Nashville, Tenn., 1923.

———. *The Hovering Fly*. Cummington, Mass., 1949.

———. *Jefferson Davis: His Rise and Fall*. New York, 1929.

———. *The Mediterranean and Other Poems*. New York, 1936.

———. *On the Limits of Poetry*. New York, 1948.

————. *Poems.* New York, 1960.

————. *Poems: 1928–1931.* New York, 1932.

————. *Poems: 1922–1947.* New York, 1947.

————. *Mr. Pope and Other Poems.* New York, 1928.

————. *Reactionary Essays on Poetry and Ideas.* New York, 1936.

————. *Reason in Madness.* New York, 1941.

————. *Selected Poems.* New York, 1937.

————. *Stonewall Jackson: The Good Soldier.* New York, 1928.

————. *The Swimmers, and Other Selected Poems.* New York, 1970.

————. *The Vigil of Venus.* Cummington, Mass., 1943.

————. *The Winter Sea.* Cummington, Mass., 1944.

Taylor, Peter. *Collected Stories.* New York, 1969.

————. *The Death of a Kinsman.* New York, 1949.

————. *Tennessee Day in St. Louis.* New York, 1957.

————. *A Woman of Means.* New York, 1950.

Tillery, Carlyle. *Red Bone Woman.* New York, 1950.

Toomer, Jean. *Cane.* New York, 1923.

Tucker, Lael. *Lament for Four Virgins.* New York, 1952.

Uhler, John E. *Cane Juice.* New York, 1931.

Upshaw, Helen. *Day of Harvest.* New York, 1953.

Vines, Howell. *A River Goes With Heaven.* New York, 1930.

Vollmer, Lula. *Sun-Up.* New York, 1923.

Walker, Margaret. *For My People.* New York, 1942.

Walter, Eugene. *Untidy Pilgrim.* New York, 1954.

Warren, Lella. *Foundation Stone.* New York, 1940.

————. *Whetstone Walls.* New York, 1952.

Warren, Robert Penn. *All the King's Men.* New York, 1946.

————. *At Heaven's Gate.* New York, 1943.

————. *Audobon: A Vision.* New York, 1969.

————. *Band of Angels.* New York, 1953.

————. *Blackberry Winter.* Cummington, Mass., 1946.

————. *Brother to Dragons: A Tale in Verse and Voices.* New York, 1953.

————. *The Cave.* New York, 1959.

————. *The Circus in the Attic, and Other Stories.* New York, 1947.

————. *Democracy and Poetry.* Cambridge, Mass., 1975.

————. *Eleven Poems on the Same Theme.* Norfolk, Conn., 1942.

————. *Flood.* New York, 1964.

————. *Homage to Theodore Dreiser: On the Centennial of His Birth.* New York, 1971.

————. *Incarnations: 1966–1968.* New York, 1968.

————. *John Brown: The Making of a Martyr.* New York, 1929.

————. *The Legacy of the Civil War.* New York, 1961.

————. *Meet Me in the Green Glen.* New York, 1972.

————. *Night Rider.* London, 1939.

————. *Promises: Poems, 1954–1956.* New York, 1957.

————. *Segregation: The Inner Conflict in the South.* New York, 1953.

————. *Selected Essays.* New York, 1958.

————. *Selected Poems, 1923–1943*. New York, 1944.

————. *Selected Poems, New and Old: 1923–1966*. New York, 1966.

————. *Thirty-Six Poems*. New York, 1935.

————. *Who Speaks for the Negro?* New York, 1965.

————. *Wilderness*. New York, 1961.

————. *World Enough and Time: A Romantic Novel*. New York, 1950.

————. *You, Emperors, and Others: Poems 1957–1960*. New York, 1960.

Weaver, John D. *Wind Before Rain*. New York, 1942.

Welty, Eudora. *The Bride of Innisfallen, and Other Stories*. New York, 1955.

————. *A Curtain of Green, and Other Stories*. New York, 1941.

————. *Delta Wedding*. New York, 1946.

————. *The Golden Apples*. New York, 1949.

————. *Losing Battles*. New York, 1970.

————. *One Time, One Place*. New York, 1971.

————. *The Optimist's Daughter*. New York, 1973.

————. *The Ponder Heart*. New York, 1954.

————. *The Robber Bridegroom*. New York, 1942.

————. *Three Papers on Fiction*. Northampton, Mass., 1962.

————. *The Wide Net, and Other Stories*. New York, 1943.

Westheimer, David. *The Magic Fallacy*. New York, 1950.

White, Walter. *The Fire in the Flint*. New York, 1924.

Wicker, Tom. *The Kingpin*. New York, 1953.

Wilder, Robert. *Flamingo Road*. New York, 1942.

Williams, Jonathan. *An Ear in Bartram's Tree: Selected Poems 1957–1967*. New York, 1969.

Williams, Tennessee. *Baby Doll*. New York, 1956.

————. *Camino Real*. New York, 1953.

————. *Cat on a Hot Tin Roof*. New York, 1955.

————. *The Glass Menagerie*. New York, 1945.

————. *Hard Candy*. New York, 1954.

————. *In the Winter of Cities*. Norfolk, Conn., 1956.

————. *The Milk Train Doesn't Stop Here Anymore*. New York, 1964.

————. *The Night of the Iguana*. New York, 1962.

————. *One Arm*. New York, 1948.

————. *Orpheus Descending*. New York, 1958.

————. *Period of Adjustment*. New York, 1960.

————. *The Roman Spring of Mrs. Stone*. New York, 1950.

————. *The Rose Tattoo*. New York, 1951.

————. *A Streetcar Named Desire*. New York, 1947.

————. *Suddenly Last Summer*. New York, 1958.

————. *Summer and Smoke*. New York, 1948.

————. *Sweet Bird of Youth*. New York, 1959.

————. *Twenty-Seven Wagons Full of Cotton, and Other One-Act Plays*. New York, 1966.

Williams, Vinnie. *Walk Egypt*. New York, 1960.

Willingham, Calder. *End as a Man*. New York, 1947.

————. *Eternal Fire.* New York, 1963.

————. *Natural Child.* New York, 1952.

Wills, Ridley. *Harvey Landrum.* New York, 1924.

Wilson, John W. *High John the Conqueror.* New York, 1948.

Winslow, Anne Goodwin. *It Was Like This.* New York, 1949.

————. *The Springs.* New York, 1949.

Wolfe, Thomas. *From Death to Morning.* New York, 1935.

————. *Gentlemen of the Press: A Play.* New York, 1941.

————. *The Letters of Thomas Wolfe.* Edited by Elizabeth Nowell. New York, 1956.

————. *Letters to His Mother, Julia Elizabeth Wolfe.* Edited by John S. Terry. New York, 1943.

————. *Look Homeward, Angel: A Story of the Buried Life.* New York, 1929.

————. *Mannerhouse: A Play in a Prologue and Three Acts.* New York, 1948.

————. *The Mountains.* Edited by Pat M. Ryan. Chapel Hill, N.C., 1970.

————. *The Notebooks of Thomas Wolfe.* Edited by R. Kennedy and Paschal Reeves. Chapel Hill, N.C., 1970.

————. *Of Time and the River: A Legend of Man's Hunger in His Youth.* New York, 1935.

————. *The Return of Buck Gavin: The Tragedy of a Mountain Outlaw,* in *Carolina Folk-Plays: Second Series,* Edited by F. H. Koch. New York, 1924.

————. *The Story of a Novel.* New York, 1936.

————. *The Web and the Rock.* New York, 1939.

————. *A Western Journal: A Daily Log of the Great Parks Trip.* Pittsburgh, 1951.

————. *You Can't Go Home Again.* New York, 1940.

Wood, Charles. *First, the Fields.* Chapel Hill, N.C., 1941.

Wood, Clement. *Nigger.* New York, 1922.

Wright, Richard. *Black Boy: A Record of Childhood and Youth.* New York, 1945.

————. *Eight Men.* New York, 1961.

————. *The Long Dream.* New York, 1958.

————. *Native Son.* New York, 1940.

————. *The Outsider.* New York, 1953.

————. *Twelve Million Black Voices.* New York, 1941.

————. *Uncle Tom's Children: Five Long Stories.* New York, 1940.

Yentzen, Vurrell. *A Feast for the Forgiven.* New York, 1954.

Young, Jefferson. *A Good Man.* New York, 1952.

Young, Stark. *The Colonnade.* New York, 1924.

————. *Feliciana.* New York, 1935.

————. *Heaven Trees.* New York, 1926.

————. *The Pavilion: Of People and Times Remembered, of Stories and Places.* New York, 1951.

————. *River House.* New York, 1929.

————. *So Red the Rose.* New York, 1935.

————. *Stark Young: A Life in the Arts, Letters 1900–62.* Edited by John Pilkington. Baton Rouge, La., 1975.

————. *The Torches Flare.* New York, 1928.

————. *The Twilight Saint.* New York, 1925.

Zugsmith, Leane. *The Summer Soldier.* New York, 1938.

SECONDARY SOURCES:

Adams, J. Donald. *Elizabeth Madox Roberts: An Appraisal.* New York, 1938.

"Agrarianism as a Theme in Southern Literature: A Symposium." *Georgia Review.* (Summer 1957).

Allen, Charles, Hoffman, Frederick J., and Ulrich, Carolyn. *Little Magazines: A History and a Bibliography.* Princeton, 1946.

Appel, Alfred, Jr. *A Season of Dreams: The Fiction of Eudora Welty.* Baton Rouge, La., 1965.

Arnold, Willard B. *The Social Ideas of Allen Tate.* Boston, 1955.

Bailey, Kenneth K. *Southern White Protestantism in the Twentieth Century.* New York, 1964.

Barth, J. Robert, ed. *Religious Perspectives in Faulkner's Fiction.* Notre Dame, Ind., 1972.

Bassett, John. *William Faulkner: An Annotated Checklist of Criticism.* New York, 1972.

Bassett, John, ed. *William Faulkner: The Critical Heritage.* London, 1975.

Beebe, Maurice. "Criticism of William Faulkner: A Selected Checklist with an Index to Studies of Separate Works." *Modern Fiction Studies,* 2 (1962): 150–64.

Beebe, Maurice, ed. *"All the King's Men": A Critical Handbook.* Belmont, Calif., 1966.

Beck, Warren. *Man in Motion: Faulkner's Trilogy.* Madison, Wis., 1961.

Bishop, Ferman. *Allen Tate.* New York, 1967.

Bleikasten, André, and Pitavy, Francois. *William Faulkner's "As I Lay Dying" and "Light in August"* Paris, 1970.

Blotner, Joseph. *William Faulkner: A Biography.* New York, 1974.

————. *William Faulkner's Library: A Catalogue.* Charlottesville, Va., 1964.

Boger, Lorise C. *The Southern Mountaineer in Literature: A Bibliography* Morgantown, West Va., 1964.

Bohner, Charles H. *Robert Penn Warren.* New York, 1964.

Bradbury, John Malcolm. *The Fugitives: A Critical Account.* Chapel Hill, N.C., 1958.

————. *Renaissance in the South: A Critical History of the Literature, 1920–1960.* Chapel Hill, N.C., 1963.

Brittain, Joan. "Flannery O'Connor: A Bibliography." *Bulletin of Bibliography,* 25 (1967): 98–100, 123–24.

Brooks, Cleanth. *William Faulkner: The Yoknapatawpha Country.* New Haven, 1963.

Bryant, James A., Jr. *Eudora Welty.* Minneapolis, Minn., 1968.

Buffington, Robert. *The Equilibrists: John Crowe Ransom's Poems, 1916–1963.* Nashville, Tenn., 1967.

Cambell, Harry M., and Foster, Ruel E. *Elizabeth Madox Roberts: American Novelist.* Norman, Okla., 1956.

——. *William Faulkner: A Critical Appraisal.* Norman, Okla., 1951.

Campbell, John Charles. *The Southern Highlander and His Homeland.* New York, 1921.

Carr, John. *Kite-Flying and Other Irrational Acts: Conversations with Twelve Southern Writers.* Baton Rouge, La., 1972.

Carter, Hodding. *Southern Legacy.* Baton Rouge, La., 1949.

Casper, Leonard. *The Dark and Bloody Ground.* Seattle, Wash., 1960.

Clark, John H., ed. *William Styron's "Nat Turner": Ten Black Writers Respond.* New York, 1968.

Clark, Thomas D. *The Emerging South.* New York, 1961.

Clark, Thomas D., ed. *Travels in the New South: A Bibliography.* 2 vols. Norman, Okla., 1962.

Clark, Thomas D., and Grady, Henry W. *The South since Appomatox.* New York, 1967.

Coles, Robert. *Children of Crisis.* 3 vols. New York, 1967–71.

Conrad, David E. *The Forgotten Farmer: The Story of Sharecroppers in the New Deal.* Urbana, Ill., 1965.

Coughlan, Robert. *The Private World of William Faulkner.* New York, 1954.

Cowan, Louise. *The Fugitive Group: A Literary History.* Baton Rouge, La., 1959.

Dabney, Virginius. *Below the Potomac: A Book about the New South.* New York, 1942.

Daniels, Jonathan. *A Southerner Discovers the South.* New York, 1938.

Davenport, F. Garvin. *The Myth of Southern History.* Nashville, Tenn., 1971.

Davidson, Donald. *"I'll Take My Stand.* A History." *American Review* 5 (Summer 1935): 301–21.

David, Allison, et al. *Deep South: A Social Anthropological Study of Class and Caste.* Chicago, 1941.

Dollard, John. *Caste and Class in a Southern Town.* New Haven, 1937.

Drake, Robert. *Flannery O'Connor.* New York, 1966.

Duff, John B., and Mitchell, Peter M., eds. *The Nat Turner Rebellion: The Historical Event and the Modern Controversy.* New York, 1971.

Edmonds, Dale. *Carson McCullers.* Austin, Tex., 1969.

Embree, Edwin R., and Johnson, Charles S. *The Collapse of Cotton Tenancy.* Chapel Hill, N.C., 1935.

Evans, Oliver. *Carson McCullers: Her Life and Work.* New York, 1965.

Ezell, J. S. *The South since 1865.* New York, 1963.

Falkner, Murry. *The Falkners of Mississippi.* Baton Rouge, La., 1967.

Feeley, Kathleen. *Flannery O'Connor: Voice of the Peacock.* New Brunswick, N.J., 1972.

Ferguson, Suzanne. *The Poetry of Randall Jarrell.* Baton Rouge, La., 1971.

Field, Leslie A., ed. *Thomas Wolfe: Three Decades of Criticism.* New York, 1968.

Ford, Thomas R., ed. *The Southern Appalachian Region: A Survey.* Lexington, Ky., 1962.

Foster, Ruel C. *Elizabeth Madox Roberts.* Norman, Okla., 1956.

————. *Jesse Stuart.* New York, 1968.

Friedman, Melvin J., and Lawson, Lewis A., eds. *The Added Dimension: The Art and Mind of Flannery O'Connor.* New York, 1966.

Friedman, Melvin J., and Malin, Irving, eds. *William Styron's "The Confessions of Nat Turner": A Critical Handbook.* Belmont, Calif., 1970.

Gatewood, William B. *Preachers, Pedagogues, and Politicians: The Evolution Controversy in North Carolina.* Chapel Hill, N.C., 1970.

Goldman, Arnold, ed. *Twentieth-Century Interpretations of "Absalom, Absalom!"* Englewood Cliffs, N.J., 1970.

Gossett, Louise Y. *Violence in Recent Southern Fiction.* Durham, N.C., 1965.

Graham, Hugh D., and Bartley, Numan V. *Southern Politics and the Second Reconstruction.* Baltimore, 1975.

Crantham, Dewey D., ed. *The South and the Sectional Image.* New York, 1967.

Graves, Lawrence. *Carson McCullers.* Minneapolis, Minn., 1970.

Griscom, Joan. "A Bibliography of Caroline Gordon." *Critique* 1 (Winter 1956): 74-78.

Gross, Seymour L. "Eudora Welty: A Bibliography of Criticism and Comment." *Sec.'s News Sheet,* Bibliographical Society, University of Virginia, 45 (April 1960): 1–32.

Gross, Seymour L. and Hardy, John E., eds. *Images of the Negro in American Literature.* Chicago, 1966.

Hemphill, George. *Allen Tate.* Minneapolis, Minn., 1963.

Hendin, Josephine. *The World of Flannery O'Connor.* Bloomington, Ind., 1970.

Hendrick, George. *Katherine Anne Porter.* New York, 1965.

Hoffman, Frederick J. *The Art of Southern Fiction.* Carbondale, Ill., 1967.

————. *William Faulkner.* New York, 1961.

Hoffman, Frederick J., and Vickery, Olga, eds. *William Faulkner: Three Decades of Criticism.* East Lansing, Mich., 1951.

Holman, C. Hugh. *Thomas Wolfe.* Minneapolis, Minn., 1960.

————. *Three Modes of Southern Fiction: Ellen Glasgow, William Faulkner, Thomas Wolfe.* Athens, Ga., 1966.

"Homage to Allen Tate: Essays, Notes, and Verses in Honor of His Sixtieth Birthday." *Sewanee Review* 67 (Summer 1959): 528–631.

"Homage to John Crowe Ransom: Essays on His Work as Poet and Critic, Prepared and Here Collected in Honor of His Sixtieth Birthday." *Sewanee Review* 56 (Summer 1948): 365–476.

Hoover, Calvin B., and Ratchford, B. V. *Economic Resources and Policies of the South.* New York, 1951.

Howe, Irving. *William Faulkner: A Critical Study.* New York, 1952.

Hyman, Stanley. *Flannery O'Connor.* Minneapolis, Minn., 1966.

Irwin, John T. *Doubling and Incest/Repetition and Revenge: A Speculative Reading of Faulkner.* Baltimore, 1975.

Isaacs, Neil D. *Eudora Welty.* Austin, Tex., 1969.

Karanikas, Alexander. *Tillers of a Myth: Southern Agrarians as Social and Literary Critics.* Madison, Wis., 1966.

Kennedy, Richard S. *The Window of Memory: The Literary Career of Thomas Wolfe.* Chapel Hill, N.C., 1966.

Key, V. O., Jr. *Southern Politics in State and Nation.* New York, 1969.

Knight, Karl F. *The Poetry of John Crowe Ransom.* The Hague, 1964.

Landess, Thomas, ed. *The Short Fiction of Caroline Gordon: A Critical Symposium.* Dallas, Tex., 1972.

Leiserson, Avery O., ed. *The South in the 1960's.* New York, 1964.

Liberman, M. M. *Katherine Anne Porter's Fiction.* Detroit, 1971.

Dodwick, Hartley and Core, George, eds. *Katherine Anne Porter: A Critical Symposium.* Athens, Ga., 1969.

Longley, John L. *Robert Penn Warren.* Austin, Tex., 1969.

―――. *The Tragic Mask: A Study of Faulkner's Heroes.* Chapel Hill, N.C., 1963.

Longley, John L., ed. *Robert Penn Warren: A Collection of Critical Essays.* New York, 1967.

Mackin, Cooper R. *William Styron.* Austin, Tex., 1969.

Magner, James E. *John Crowe Ransom: Critical Principles and Preoccupations.* The Hague, 1971.

Maguire, Merrill. *The Folk of Southern Fiction.* Athens, Ga., 1972.

Malin, Irving. *William Faulkner: An Interpretation.* Palo Alto, Calif., 1951.

McDowell, Frederick P. *Caroline Gordon.* Minneapolis, Minn., 1966.

―――. *Elizabeth Madox Roberts.* New York, 1963.

McGill, Ralph. *The South and the Southerner.* Boston, 1963.

McKinney, John H., ed. *The South in Continuity and Change.* Durham, N.C., 1965.

Meiners, R. K. *The Last Alternatives: A Study of the Works of Allen Tate.* Denver, Colo., 1963.

Meriwether, James B. *The Literary Career of William Faulkner.* Princeton, N. J., 1961.

―――. *The Short Fiction of William Faulkner: A Bibliography.* Columbia, S.C., 1971.

―――. *William Faulkner: A Checklist.* Princeton, 1957.

Millgate, Michael. *The Achievement of William Faulkner.* London, 1967.

Miner, Ward L. *The World of William Faulkner.* Durham, N.C., 1952.

Mooney, Harry J., Jr. *The Fiction and Criticism of Katherine Anne Porter.* Pittsburgh, 1957.

Moore, L. Hugh, Jr. *Robert Penn Warren and History.* The Hague, 1970.

Mowry, George E. *Another Look at the Twentieth Century South.* Baton Rouge, La., 1973.

Muller, Herbert J. *Thomas Wolfe.* Norfolk, Conn., 1947.

Nance, William B. *Katherine Anne Porter and the Art of Rejection.* Chapel Hill, N.C., 1964.

————. *The Worlds of Truman Capote.* New York, 1970.

Nelson, Benjamin. *Tennessee Williams: The Man and His Work.* New York, 1961.

Nicholls, William H. *The Southern Tradition and Regional Progress.* Chapel Hill, N.C., 1960.

Nilon, Charles H. *Faulkner and the Negro.* New York, 1965.

Nixon, Herman C. *Forty Acres and Steel Mules.* Chapel Hill, N.C., 1938.

Norwood, Hayden. *The Marble Man's Wife: Thomas Wolfe's Mother.* New York, 1943.

O'Connor, William Van. *The Tangled Fire of William Faulkner.* Minneapolis, Minn., 1954.

Odum, Howard Washington. *Southern Regions of the United States.* Chapel Hill, N.C., 1936.

Ohlin, Peter H. *Agee.* New York, 1966.

Parsons, Thornton H. *John Crowe Ransom.* New York, 1969.

Pearce, Richard. *William Styron.* Minneapolis, Minn., 1971.

Percy, William Alexander. *Lanterns on the Levee.* New York, 1941.

Peirce, Neal R. *The Deep South States of America.* New York, 1974.

Perlo, Victor. *The Negro in Southern Agriculture.* New York, 1953.

Phillips, Robert S. "Carson McCullers, 1956–1964: A Checklist." *Bulletin of Bibliography* 24 (1964): 113–16.

Powdermaker, Hortense. *After Freedom: A Cultural Study in the Deep South.* New York, 1939.

Preston, George R., Jr. *Thomas Wolfe: A Bibliography.* New York, 1943.

Randolph, Vance. *The Ozarks: An American Survival of a Primitive Society.* New York, 1931.

Ratner, Marc L., *William Styron.* New York, 1972.

Reed, John S. *The Enduring South: Subcultural Persistence in a Mass Society.* Lexington, Va,. 1972.

Reeves, Paschal, ed. *Thomas Wolfe and the Glass of Time.* Athens, Ga., 1971.

Reynolds, Robert. *Thomas Wolfe: Memoir of a Friendship.* Austin, Tex., 1965.

Raper, Arthur F. *Preface to Peasantry: A Tale of Two Black Counties.* Chapel Hill, N.C., 1936.

————. *Tenants of the Almighty.* New York, 1943.

Raper, Arthur F. and Reid, Isa De Augustine. *Sharecroppers All.* Chapel Hill, N.C., 1941.

"Recent Southern Fiction: A Panel Discussion." *Bulletin of Wesleyan College* (Macon, Ga.) 41 (January 1961).

"Rhetoric in Southern Writing: A Symposium." *Georgia Review* (Spring 1968):74–86.

Rhylich, Frank. *Dixie Demagogues.* New York, 1947.

Rock, Virginia. "The Making and Meaning of *I'll Take My Stand:* A Study in Utopian-Conservatism, 1925–1939." Ph.D. diss., University of Minnesota, 1961.

Rovit, Earl H. *Herald to Chaos: The Novels of Elizabeth Madox Roberts.* Lexington, Ky., 1960.

Rubin, Louis D. *The Faraway Country: Writers of the Modern South.* Seattle, Wash., 1963.

————. *Thomas Wolfe: The Weather of His Youth.* Baton Rouge, La., 1955.

————. *William Elliott Shoots a Bear: Essays on the Southern Literary Imagination.* Baton Rouge, La., 1975.

————. *The Writer in the South: Studies in a Literary Community.* Baton Rouge, La., 1972.

Rubin, Louis D. and Jacobs, Robert D., eds. *Southern Renascence: The Literature of the Modern South.* Baltimore, 1953.

————. *South: Modern Southern Literature in Its Cultural Setting.* New York, 1961.

Sherrill, Robert. *Gothic Politics in the Deep South.* New York, 1968.

Sindler, Allan P., ed. *Change in the Contemporary South.* Durham, N.C., 1963.

Slatoff, Walter J. *Quest for Failure: A Study of William Faulkner.* Ithaca, N.Y., 1960.

Squires, Radcliffe. *Allen Tate: A Literary Biography.* New York, 1971.

Squires, Radcliffe, ed. *Allen Tate and His Work: Critical Evaluations.* Minneapolis, Minn., 1972.

Stallman, Robert W. "John Crowe Ransom: A Checklist of his Critical Writings." *Sewanee Review.* 56 (Summer 1948): 442–76.

————. "Robert Penn Warren: A Checklist of his Critical Writings." *University of Kansas City Review* 14 (1947): 78–83.

Stephens, Edna B. *John Gould Fletcher.* New York, 1967.

Stewart, John L. *The Burden of Time: The Fugitives and Agrarians.* Princeton, N.J., 1965.

————. *John Crowe Ransom.* Minneapolis, Minn., 1962.

Stewart, Stanley. "Carson McCullers, 1940–1956: A Checklist." *Bulletin of Bibliography* 22 (1959): 182–85.

Strandberg, Victor H. *A Colder Fire: The Poetry of Robert Penn Warren.* Lexington, Ky., 1965.

Stuckey, W. J. *Caroline Gordon.* New York, 1972.

Sullivan, Walter. *Death by Melancholy: Essays on Recent Southern Fiction.* Baton Rouge, La., 1972.

Swiggart, Peter. *The Art of Faulkner's Novels.* Austin, Tex., 1962.

Tate, Allen. "The Fugitives, 1922–1925." *Princeton University Library Chronicle* 3 (April 1942): 75–84.

Taylor, Peter, et al., eds. *Randall Jarrell, 1914–1965.* New York, 1967.

Thompson, Lawrance. *William Faulkner: An Introduction and Interpretation.* New York, 1963.

Thorp, Willard. "Allen Tate: A Checklist." *Princeton University Library Chronicle* 3 (Spring 1942): 85–98.

Tindall, George B. *The Disruption of the Solid South*. Athens, Ga., 1972.

Tischler, Nancy M. *Black Masks: Negro Characters in Modern Southern Fiction*. University Park, Pa., 1969.

Tuck, Dorothy. *A Handbook of Faulkner*. New York, 1965.

Turnbull, Andrew. *Thomas Wolfe*. New York, 1967.

Vance, Rupert B. *All These People: The Nation's Human Resources in the South*. Chapel Hill, N.C., 1945.

———. *Human Factors in Cotton Culture: A Study in the Social Geography of the American South*. Chapel Hill, N.C., 1929.

Vance, Rupert B., and Demerath, Nicholas J., eds. *The Urban South*. Chapel Hill, N.C., 1954.

VandeKieft, Ruth M. *Eudora Welty*. New York, 1962.

Vickery, Olga. *The Novels of William Faulkner*. Baton Rouge, La., 1959.

Volpe, Edmond. *A Reader's Guide to William Faulkner*. New York, 1964.

Waggoner, Hyatt H. *William Faulkner: From Jefferson to the World*. Lexington, Ky., 1959.

Wagner, Linda W., ed. *William Faulkner: Four Decades of Criticism*. East Lansing, Mich., 1973.

Waldrip, Louise, and Bauer, Shirley Ann. *A Bibliography of the Works of Katherine Anne Porter*. Metuchen, N.J., 1969.

———. *A Bibliography of Criticism of the Works of Katherine Anne Porter*. Metuchen, N.J., 1969.

Watkins, Floyd C. *The Death of Art: Black and White in the Recent Southern Novel*. Athens, Ga., 1970.

———. *Thomas Wolfe's Characters: Portraits from Life*. Norman, Okla., 1957.

Watkins, Floyd C., and Cullen, John B. *Old Times in the Faulkner Country*. Chapel Hill, N.C., 1961.

Webb, Constance. *Richard Wright*. New York, 1968.

Wells, Henry W. *Poet and Psychiatrist: Merrill Moore*. New York, 1955.

West, Paul. *Robert Penn Warren*. Minneapolis, Minn., 1964.

West, Raymond B. *Katherine Anne Porter*. Minneapolis, Minn., 1963.

White, Robert L. *John Peale Bishop*. New York, 1966.

Williams, Miller. *The Poetry of John Crowe Ransom*. New Brunswick, N.J., 1972.

Williams, T. Harry. *Huey Long*. New York, 1969.

Woodward, C. Vann. *The Strange Career of Jim Crow*. New York, 1955.

Woofter, T. J., and Fisher, A. E. *The Plantation South Today*. Washington, D.C., 1940.

Young, T. D., ed. *John Crowe Ransom: Critical Essays and a Bibliography*. Baton Rouge, La., 1968.

Young, T. D., and Inge, M. Thomas. *Donald Davidson*. New York, 1971.

———. *Donald Davidson: An Essay and a Bibliography*. Nashville, Tenn., 1965.

Index

Library of Congress Cataloging in Publication Data

Gray, Richard J.
    The literature of memory.

    Bibliography: p. 325.
    Includes index.

    1. American literature—Southern States—History
and criticism. 2. American literature—20th century
—History and criticism. I. Title.
PS261.G68   810'.9'0052   76–18941
ISBN 0–8018–1803–6

DATE DUE

MAY 3 73			
GAYLORD			PRINTED IN U.S.A.